D1303220

A CHRONOLOGY
OF PRINTING

A CHRONOLOGY
OF PRINTING

Colin Clair

FREDERICK A. PRAEGER, *Publishers*
New York · Washington

BOOKS THAT MATTER

PUBLISHED IN THE UNITED STATES OF AMERICA IN 1969
BY FREDERICK A. PRAEGER, INC., PUBLISHERS
111 FOURTH AVENUE, NEW YORK, N.Y. 10003

© Colin Clair 1969

Library of Congress Catalog Card Number: 75–83974

PRINTED IN GREAT BRITAIN

PREFACE

As the title of this work implies, it is designed as a compendium of information on matters connected with printing, its first introduction into Europe and its spread throughout the world; being an attempt to set in their chronological order those matters judged most important in the history of the printed book, its manufacture, design and dissemination. Such information is set out in the form of short and factual entries, in an endeavour to provide the widest range of information rather than to study any one factor in depth. Under each year the entries are grouped on a national basis, the national entries being placed in order of precedence based on the date of first printing in that particular country. Thus entries relating to German printing will always come first in any one year.

The information given in this chronology has been drawn from a wide variety of sources, both standard works and articles in specialist journals. Many of these standard works were compiled in the last century and contain errors of detail only exposed by modern research. Where such a conflict of authorities occurs, the information given here is based upon the most recent findings, although the nature of the work forbids the insertion of a footnote to indicate the source.

The key to this mass of information is provided by a comprehensive index of over 10,000 entries compiled by Mr. J. W. Gurnett. In it references are to the year under which the particular entry appears. In view of the fact that, for example, the title of a book may be mentioned under a date important in the life of its author or printer, the date given in the index should never be assumed as the date of publication, and reference for information of this sort should always be made to the body of the text.

The illustration at the opening of the text is a copy (reduced) of the device of the Parisian bookseller, Michel de Roigny (1544–91), the grandson of Josse Bade; and is taken from *Le tiers volume de Froissart*, Paris [Pierre l'Huillier?], 1574.

105

Reputed invention of paper in China by Ts'ai Lun. In that year, he officially reported the invention to the Emperor, but whether he was the actual inventor, or merely the official patron of it, is not known. The materials used were tree-bark, hemp, rags and fish nets. It is unlikely, however, that the invention of paper was the work of any one man, and the probability is that Ts'ai Lun or another merely perfected a rough and ready pre-existing form of paper. (*See* 1931.)

114

The generally accepted date for the incising of the inscription at the base of Trajan's Column, Rome, possibly the finest extant example of Roman lettering, and one which has proved a constant source of inspiration to letter-cutters and type designers. In the words of the type designer Frederic W. Goudy: 'The great merit of Roman capitals is simplicity; every useless and meaningless line has been eliminated. The letters vary in shape and proportion; to bring out their full beauty requires a nice discrimination in the spacing and combining of their irregular forms.'

868

The earliest printed book extant is the *Diamond Sutra* (Prajnâ Pâramitâ) of A.D. 868, which bears the statement 'printed on 11 May, 868, by Wang Chieh'. Found in 1907 by the explorer Sir Aurel Stein, it is in the form of a roll, sixteen feet long by a foot wide, made up of seven sheets pasted together, and was printed from wooden blocks. From the excellence of the craftsmanship, it would appear that this method of printing had already reached an advanced stage of technique, but so far no Chinese printing in book form earlier than this has been discovered.

1040

In China, between the years 1040 and 1048, printing from movable type was invented by Pi Sheng, of the Northern Sung dynasty, who made the first set of types from clay, baked hard. No development took place along these lines owing to the particular characteristics of the Chinese language. The process might have had important results for the history of printing if Chinese had been alphabetic instead of ideographic.

1361

A Korean book, a xylographic work dated 1361, was on view at the Paris Exposition Universelle of 1900.

1399

The exact date of Gutenberg's birth is unknown. According to the investigations of Severin Corsten ('Wann wurde Gutenberg geboren?' in the *Gutenberg Jahrbuch*: 1966), it probably lies between 1399 and 1406.

1403

Printing from movable type made of metal was practised in Korea in the fifteenth century, and a set of 100,000 copper types was cast in 1403 by command of the king and used for the printing of many books until the year 1544.

1423

The earliest dated European wood-block print is of this year, and shows Saint Christopher bearing the infant Christ. It is now in the John Rylands Library at Manchester. At Brussels, in the Royal Library, is a woodcut print of the Madonna with four Virgin Saints, dated 1418, but there is the probability that it is only a copy, made about 1450, of an earlier print now lost, on which the artist retained the date of the original.

1436

Johann Gensfleisch zur Laden, known from the house in which his family lived at Mainz as Johann Gutenberg, was busily occupied at Strassburg with his experiments in the art of printing. He had left his native town of Mainz in 1428 and settled at Strassburg.

1438

At Strassburg, Gutenberg made a contract with Hans Riffe, Andreas Dritzehn and Andreas Heilmann concerning the practice of a certain secret art. He possessed a press built by the joiner, Konrad Saspach, had need of lead for his experiments, and manufactured 'forms' which could be melted down.

1439

Andreas Dritzehn having died around Christmas 1438, his brothers Georg and Claus asked to be taken into partnership in his place. When Gutenberg refused, they took him to court, which decided in Gutenberg's favour. Although the depositions in this case reveal little as to what work Gutenberg was actually engaged in, they show that his expenses were heavy and that he had borrowed considerable sums of money to finance his experiments. The most significant statement was that made by the witness Hans Dünne, a goldsmith, who told the court that, as early as 1436, he had received 100 guilders from Gutenberg 'allein das zu dem trucken gehöret' (just for that which appertains to printing).

1444

Foundation of the Bibliotheca Medicea Laurenziana, Florence, the first public library, by Cosimo de' Medici.

A goldsmith named Procopius Waldvoghel, a native of Prague who had settled in Avignon, drew up in this year and at later dates contracts for partnerships and loans with various inhabitants of the town, under the terms of which he contracted to teach, to some the trade of a silversmith (*artem argenterie*), to others a certain method of writing artificially (*artem scribendi artificialiter*). To one such associate, Manaud Vital, he promised on 4 July, 1444, to deliver, 'duo abecedaria calibis, et duas formas ferreas, unum instrumentum calibis vocatum vitis, quadraginta octo formas stangni, necnon diversas alias formas ad artem scribendi pertinentes.' (Two steel alphabets, and two iron forms, one steel instrument called a *Vitis* [vice, or press ?], forty-eight tin forms, and also various other forms appertaining to the art of writing.) Whether or not the word 'form' (*forma*) here means type, as it later did, the tools mentioned in the Avignon contracts seem to embrace almost everything needed for printing. But there is no evidence to show that Waldvoghel ever developed or used his invention in actual printing.

1445

The Abbot of Saint Aubert, Cambrai, noted in his diary that he had acquired at Bruges a *Doctrinal* 'jetté en molle'. It is just possible that he may have been alluding to a printed book.

1448

Arnold Gelthuss zum Echtzeler, a relative of Gutenberg, borrowed for the latter's use at Mainz, but on his own security, the sum of 150 guilders from Reinhard Brumser and Henchin Rodenstein and heirs, at an annual interest rate of 5 per cent.

1454

In this year came the earliest and first dated documents printed from movable type. A 30-line Indulgence granted by Pope Nicolaus V to those who donated money for the struggle against the Turks (who had captured Constantinople in 1433) was printed towards the end of 1454 in two issues, the first dated 1454 and known only in a single state, the second dated 1455 for the purpose of sale in the following year, and known in five variants. This edition is attributed to the press of Gutenberg, Fust and Schöffer, as the headings are printed in the type of the 42-line Bible. Another edition in 31 lines, with headings in the earliest form of the type of the 36-line Bible, was printed about the same time in 1454, again in two issues, one dated 1454 (known in four variants) and the other (in three variants) dated 1455.

An early state of the 36-line Bible was next used in the *Türkenkalender*, a propaganda calendar for the year 1455 directed against the Turks, which presumably appeared at the end of 1454. Progressive modifications of the type are found in various works, including other calendars and numerous editions of the popular Latin grammar of Donatus. The so-called *Astronomical Calendar* of 1448, which was previously thought to have been printed in 1447, has been shown by Dr. Carl Wehmer (*Mainzer Probedrucke in der*

Type des sogennanten Astronomischen Kalenders für 1448: Leibniz Verlag, Munich, 1948) to fall typographically late in this series, and must have been printed not earlier than 1457, immediately before the commencement of the 36-line Bible.

The identity of the anonymous printer, who produced the above works in earlier states of the 36-line Bible type at Mainz in the period 1454–58, and then moved to Bamberg to produce the 36-line Bible, remains unestablished. It is not impossible that this printer was Gutenberg himself, working on his own account both before and after his lawsuit with Fust and Schöffer in November, 1455.

Around 1454 or 1455, an unidentified printer at Mainz issued an edition of *De octo partibus orationis*, an elementary Latin grammar by Aelius Donatus in what appears to be an earlier state of the 36-line Bible type. Parchment fragments of three different editions are known, two of which were found in the binding of a book printed at Strassburg in 1488.

In 1892, a fragment of the *Sibyllenbuch*, sometimes called the *Fragment of the Last Judgment* because the surviving section of the book deals with this subject, was discovered in an old binding at Mainz. Part of a single leaf is in type similar to that used in the 36-line Bible, and it is estimated that the complete book was of 37 leaves with 28 lines to the page. Its date of printing has been variously conjectured as from 1442 onwards, but most authorities are now of the opinion that it was printed around 1454.

1455

The 42-line Bible, in Latin, and often called the 'Gutenberg' Bible was printed at Mainz, probably by Gutenberg, Fust and Schöffer. It is not dated, but was probably begun about 1453 and completed in 1455. It was certainly finished before 15 August, 1456, which is the rubricator's date in the Paris copy, known as the Mazarine Bible from having formed part of Cardinal Mazarin's library. It is printed in the textura type already used for headings in the 30-line Indulgence of 1454. The privately printed *Die Gutenberg—Ein Census* (1951), by Edward Lazare, lists 46 known copies, 12 on vellum and 34 on paper; the number of complete copies is 4 vellum and 17 paper copies.

On 6 November, Johann Fust brought a lawsuit against Gutenberg to recover sums of money he had advanced to the latter since about 1450, together with the accrued interest. The total claim of 2,026 gulden was made up of two separate loans each of 800 gulden, made in 1450 and 1452, together with interest. Gutenberg was ordered to reimburse Fust and, though nothing has come to light regarding the ultimate outcome of the lawsuit, it is unlikely that Gutenberg was able to comply with his obligations. This seems apparent from the fact that the press and its equipment passed into the hands of Fust, since they had been pledged as security for the loans. Yet may Gutenberg not have saved something from the wreck? A man who had worked so arduously at an invention of prime importance might be expected to resume his activities as best he could, and we know that at the time of his death, which is thought to have taken place in February, 1468, he still had some printing equipment, consisting of 'sundry forms, letters, instruments, tools, and other things pertaining to the work of printing', which a certain Dr. Conrad Humery had placed at his disposal.

Les Neuf Preux, the only block-book printed in France, is generally thought to have been printed at Paris around 1455.

1456

First edition of the Bull against the Turks of Pope Calixtus III (Alonso Borgia). This Bull was issued at Rome 29 June, 1456, and was presumably printed shortly afterwards at Mainz by the unidentified printer of the 36-line Bible. This edition, of which only one copy is known, is in Latin; another edition, in German, of which likewise only one copy has survived, bears the rubricator's date 1456.

The first known medical work to be printed was the calendar commonly referred to as the 'Bloodletting Calendar' for 1457, probably printed in 1456. This form of calendar, popular during the Middle Ages, gave the lucky and unlucky days on which to indulge in blood-letting or purging. The type used is similar to that used in the astrological tables printed about 1457. (*See* 1454.)

1457

Completion, on 14 August, of the *Psalterium latinum*, printed at Mainz by Johann Fust and Peter Schöffer. This was the first printed book to give both the name of the printers and the date of printing. This famous book, the first to bear the names of Fust and Schöffer, was the most beautiful volume to come from their press, with magnificent lombardic initial letters in red, light purple and blue. Ten copies of the book are at present known, all printed on vellum, half of them having 143 leaves and the remainder 175 leaves. The two-colour initials were produced from metal plates in two separate parts which fitted together. Each part was inked separately, the plates were reassembled, and printed together at one pull of the press. The colophon refers to the invention of printing as having been brought to completion by Johann Fust and Peter Schöffer.

1458

The type and initials used in the *Psalter* of 1457 were employed again in the *Canon missae* printed by Fust and Schöffer about 1458 (after August 1457). Only two complete copies of this work (12 sheets printed on vellum) are known, of which one is in the Bodleian Library at Oxford and the other at the National Library, Vienna.

About 1458, Johann Mentelin set up his first press at Strassburg. Originally a scribe and illuminator, Mentelin, a native of Schelestadt, turned to printing for his living. Most of his books are undated, but P. de Lignamine in his *Chronicle* states that he was working in Strassburg by 1458. Mentelin died in 1478. (*See also* 1460.)

Between 1458 and 1460 was completed the 36-line Latin Bible, probably published at Bamberg by an unidentified printer who had previously worked at Mainz, where he printed the *Türkenkalender* in 1455 (*see* 1454). The actual date of the printing of this 36-line Bible, for long attributed to Gutenberg, is unknown, but the copy in the Bibliothèque Nationale at Paris is rubricated 1461. D. A. Randall writes: 'Current opinion [1962] tends to credit Bamberg as the place of origin and perhaps Albrecht Pfister as the printer, or the unknown Mainz printer of the *Turkenkalender*.'

Charles VII sent Nicolas Jenson to Mainz to learn about 'messire Jehan Guthemberg's' new invention.

1459

On 29 August, Johann Fust and Peter Schöffer completed the second edition of the *Psalterium latinum* (*see* 1457). This 23-line edition, a folio of 136 leaves, was arranged for monastic use, being printed, says the *B.M.C.*, 'in accordance with the reformed Monastic Breviary of the Union of Bursfeld, known also as the Observantia per Germaniam.' The same type and initials were used in both editions. Of the thirteen known copies, all are printed on vellum.

A little more than a month after the publication of the Psalter, Fust and Schöffer brought out the *Rationale Divinorum Officiorum* of Durandus, a popular work dealing with the origin and meaning of ecclesiastical services. This was a large folio volume of 160 leaves, and to make it easier to read, Schöffer, a gifted calligrapher, designed a small book face, now known as the 'Durandus' type—a 'Fere-humanistica' or 'Gotico-antiqua'.

1460

At Mainz, the first large non-religious book was printed. This was the *Catholicon*, an encyclopaedic work by Johannes Balbus (Giovanni Balbi of Genoa), a Dominican who wrote the work in the thirteenth century. It is a large volume of 373 leaves printed in double column in an undistinguished type which Zedler states was in existence earlier than the 91 of Fust and Schöffer used in 1459. The book has a colophon which reads (translated) 'This book was produced not with a reed, stylus, or quill, but by the admirable design, proportion, and adjustment of punches and matrices'. Dr. Zedler, in *Das Mainzer Catholicon*, confidently attributes the book to Gutenberg, but conclusive evidence as to the printer is still lacking. Remainder copies appeared in Peter Schöffer's book-list in 1470.

Matthias de Cracovia, *Tractatus rationis et conscientiae*, was printed by the printer of *Catholicon* at Mainz about 1460.

The first volume of Canon Law to be printed was completed on 25 June, by Johannes Fust and Peter Schöffer: it was the first edition of the *Constitutiones* of Pope Clement V. This folio volume was set in Schöffer's new Bible type, smaller and more legible than the large gothic of the 42-line Bible of *c.* 1455, but larger and more harmonious in form than the Durandus type, in which the commentary surrounding the text columns is set.

The first known printer at Bamberg, Albrecht Pfister, issued what was presumably his first work, the undated *Der Ackermann aus Böhmen* by Johannes von Saaz, thought to have been printed in 1460. He was the first printer to use woodcuts and although the only known copy of the first edition, at Wolfenbüttel, has no woodcuts, A. M. Hind considers that it probably had the five woodcuts found in the second edition, about 1463.

The first printer at Strassburg, Johann Mentelin, issued his first known work, a *Biblia Latina*, printed probably in 1460. There is a copy of this 49-line Bible at Freiburg, the first volume of which has been dated 1460 by the rubricator, while the second volume is dated 1461.

1461

The first dated book with woodcut illustrations is a book of fables, *Der Edelstein*, by Ulrich Bonner, a Dominican monk of Berne. It is also the earliest dated book in the German language. It was printed by Albrecht Pfister, prototypographer of Bamberg, and has 101 woodcuts. The colophon states that 'this little book is completed at Bamberg in the year of our Lord Jesus Christ one thousand four hundred and sixty-one, on Saint Valentine's day.' An undated edition, probably about 1464, has 103 cuts.

The oldest specimen of printing in Italy is a fragment of a Passion of Christ in Italian, described by Konrad Haebler in *Beiträge zur Forschung, Neue Folge 1*, Munich, 1927. It is thought to have been printed about 1461.

1462

On 27 October, 1462, the sack of the city of Mainz by contending and rival Archbishops, Adolph von Nassau and Diether von Isenburg, halted printing there for the next couple of years, and contributed to the spread of printing. Writes Updike: 'It wiped out commerce there, and the consequent lack of money led printers, who were established in a kind of industrial group, to scatter widely. This accounts for the German names we find among the earliest printers in other countries throughout Europe.'

The first dated Bible, *Biblia Latina*, came from the printing house of Fust and Schöffer at Mainz, and bears the date 14 August, 1462. It is set in two tall columns of 48 lines, in a beautiful book face, extremely legible and thereafter frequently imitated.

The first printer's mark ever used in a printed book is that of Fust and Schöffer. It was first cut for the 1462 Bible printed at Mainz. It is known in a copy at Vienna of the 1457 Psalter, but is thought to have been added to this book at a later date. The device of two shields hanging from a bough, represents the partnership of Fust and Schöffer, and the shields bear their respective housemarks.

1463

Peter Schöffer became the first printer to use a regular printed title-page in Pope Pius II's Bull against the Turks—*Bulla Cruciatae contra Turcos*, or *Bul zu deutsch*. The title-page was thus composed:

> Bulla cruciata sanctissimi do—
> mini nostri Pape cõtra turchos.

However, the title-page did not become widespread for a number of years to come.

1465

The first Greek printing in Germany seen in the Cicero, *De Officiis et Paradoxa*, printed by Peter Schöffer and Johannes Fust at Mainz.

The first extant book printed in Italy—Cicero, *De oratore*. Subiaco: Conrad Sweynheym and Arnold Pannartz. It was finished at the end of 1464 or beginning of 1465. A *Donatus pro puerulis*, of which no copy is now known, probably preceded it by a month or two. Sweynheym and Pannartz printed four books at Subiaco and 48 known works at Rome. The Cicero was the first book produced in roman type.

First Greek printing in Italy occurs in the Lactantius, *Opera*, completed by Sweynheym and Pannartz at Subiaco on 30 October, 1465.

The earliest edition of the block-book *Biblia pauperum*, a copy of which is in the Print Room at the British Museum, and of Netherlands origin, is assigned by Dr. Allan Stevenson to the year 1465 on the basis of watermarks. This is also the approximate date for the first issue of the *Speculum humanae salvationis*, printed in Holland by an unidentified press. 'Each edition of the *Speculum*,' says Dr. Stevenson, 'was printed first on a type press and then on blocks by rubbing, and thus their make-up is that of complex folios, in the manner of type-books.'

1466

Editio princeps of the printed Bible in German and in any modern language. Strassburg: Johann Mentelin.

In or before 1466 printing was started at Cologne by Ulrich Zell (d. 1501), a native of Hanau. His first book, Cicero, *De Officiis*, was undated. His first signed and dated work, 1466, was St. Chrysostom, *Super psalmum Miserere*.

The earliest copy of the block-book *Canticum canticorum*, in the Bayerische Staatsbibliothek at Munich, is dated 1466, or possibly late 1465, by Dr. Allan Stevenson. The same authority considers that the early block-book *Ars Moriendi* in

Lambeth Palace Library was also made around 1466.

Johann Fust died in Paris, probably of the plague, during a business trip to that city. His widow married in 1468 the bookseller Konrad Henckis.

1467

The first book printed by Peter Schöffer after the death of Johannes Fust, St. Thomas Aquinas, *Summa theologiae, secunda secundae*. Dated 6 March, 1467.

Before 20 July, 1467, appeared *De sermonum proprietate, seu de universo*, by Hrabanus Maurus, or Rabanus, Archbishop of Mainz (*c*. 776–856), a pupil of Alcuin. Written about A.D. 820, it has been termed the first printed medical book, but it is rather an encyclopaedia, only one chapter being devoted to medicine. Strassburg: Adolph Rusch.

Editio princeps of St. Augustine, *De Civitate Dei*. Subiaco: Sweynheym and Pannartz. A folio of 269 leaves in double column. This is the third extant book printed in Italy. The type used served as a model for the 'Subiaco' type employed by St. John Hornby at his Ashendene Press (*see* 1894).

The first dated book with illustrations cut in wood to appear in Italy is Cardinal Turrecremata, *Meditationes* printed by Ulrich Han of Ingolstadt who thus introduced printing into Rome. There are 31 cuts, Germanic in style though of Italian derivation. The second edition (1473) has 33 cuts.

Conrad Sweynheym and Arnold Pannartz set up their second press at Rome. They issued one book in 1467—Cicero, *Epistolae ad familiares*.

1468

On 3 February, died Johann Gutenberg. He was buried in the church of the Mainz Franciscans.

Augsburg's first printer, Günther Zainer of Reutlingen, who came to Augsburg from Strassburg, completed his first dated book, Bonaventura, *Meditationes Vitae Christi*, on 12 March, 1468. He worked at Augsburg until 1477.

Publication of the first volume of the two-volume edition of St. Jerome, *Epistolae*—the first complete edition of the Letters. Rome: Sweynheym and Pannartz. The editor, Johannes Andreae, mentions, in the dedication, the invention of printing in Germany. This edition contains also, included in error, the diatribe of Valerius to the philosopher Rufinus against the dangers of matrimony, taken from *De nugis curialium* by Walter Map (or Mapes), a wit who flourished around 1200, and who thus became the first English author to appear in print. Map is best known as the reputed author of the drinking song beginning, 'Meum est propositum in taberna mori', though it is now generally included in the work of the anonymous 'Archipoeta' (*c*. 1163).

Printing was probably introduced into Basel by Berthold Ruppel, although this supposition is not established by definite evidence. (*See* 'The beginnings of printing at Basel' by Victor Scholderer in *The Library*, 5 Ser., Vol. 3, No. 1, 1948.) Only one of Berthold Ruppel's books is signed (with the Christian name only), and none is dated, except Conradus de Mure, *Repertorium vocabulorum*, 1477. The *Biblia Latina*, undated, might be not later than 1468, but there is no conclusive evidence for this. There exists a copy of the Basel-printed Gregorius I, *Moralia in librum Job*, which bears the MS. note: 'Hunc solvi anno MCCCCLXVIII', but this inscription is now considered a forgery. Ruppel was admitted to citizenship of Basel on 14 February, 1477. He printed *inter alia*, Nicholas de Lyra, *Postilla super Evangelia*, a book which greatly influenced Martin Luther.

The first book known to have been printed in Bohemia, and the first printed book in the Czech language was the *Trojanská Kronika*, printed probably at Pilsen by an unknown printer. (*See also* 1476.)

Pasquier Bonhomme, the famous Paris bookseller, is first mentioned in a document of 6 October, 1468, in which he is described as 'one of the four principal booksellers of the University of Paris', although he was not officially appointed *libraire-juré*, or official bookseller, of the university until 1475. He specialised at first in the sale of manuscripts and later installed a printing press in his house, although he did not himself print.

1469

There are two contenders for the honour of having printed the *editio princeps* of Virgil. Sweynheym and Pannartz at Rome, and Johann Mentelin at Strassburg, each brought out an edition of his works in 1469 and it is not known which is the earlier.

Johannes de Spira (Hans von Speier), a native of Speier on the Rhine, introduced printing into

Venice, as we are told in the colophon of his first book, the earlier of two editions of Cicero, *Epistolae ad Familiares*, both printed in 1469. The first edition consisted of 100 copies; the second of 300. In this year he also printed the first edition of Pliny, *Historia Naturalis*. Johannes de Spira died in the following year and the business was carried on by his brother, Vindelinus (Wendelin).

In this year an unidentified printer was working at Utrecht. The beginning of printing in this city is bound up with the so far unsolved riddle of the undated Dutch Donatuses. The first recorded printers at Utrecht were Nicolaus Ketelaer and Gerardus de Leempt, who worked there from 1473. (*See* 1473.)

1470

Early this year, or late in 1469, Peter Schöffer issued his first book-list enumerating twenty-one titles, including the *Canon Missae* of 1458, the *Catholicon* of 1460, and the 42-line Bible of 1462. Only one copy has survived, in the Munich State Library. In the same year, on 7 September he completed one of his most beautiful books, the *Epistolae* of St. Jerome in two volumes, large folio. About a dozen copies on vellum are known.

The first printed edition of the *Confessiones* of St. Augustine, Bishop of Hippo. Strassburg: Johann Mentelin. Undated; not later than 1470.

Probably in 1470 Heinrich Eggestein of Strassburg issued the second Bible in German. In 1470, he issued the first printer's advertisement.

An edition of the block-book *Biblia Pauperum* with text in German inscribed at the end 'Friderich Walthern Mauler zu Nördlingen und Hans Hurning habent dis buch mitt einander gemacht 1470.' 40 leaves comprising a series of composite illustrations. The central compartment of each shows a scene from the New Testament flanked by scenes from the Old Testament.

The first book issued with printed foliation— Adrianus Carthusiensis, *De remediis utriusque fortunae*. Cologne: A. Ter Hoernen.

First edition of the Aggregator (*Aggregatio medicamentorum*) of Jacobus de Dondis, thought to have been printed at the monastery of the Brethren of the Common Life at Weidenbach, near Cologne. This was the first printed medical dictionary worthy of the name.

Johann Sensenschmidt, the first printer at Nuremberg, began work there in or before 1470, in which year he printed Franciscus de Retza,

Comestorium vitiorum, in which he may have been assisted by Heinrich Kefer.

First dated edition of the celebrated work of Josephus, *De antiquitate Judaica*, and the first book printed by Johann Schüssler at Augsburg. Dated 28 June, 1470.

At Beromünster a press was set up by the prebendary Helyas Helyae, whose edition of *Mammotrectus*; 10 November, 1470, is the first dated book printed in Switzerland.

Nicolas Jenson (*see* 1458), a native of Sommevoire in France, and at one time Master of the Mint at Tours, set up as printer-publisher in Venice. His first book was the *editio princeps* of Eusebius of Caesarea, *De preparatione Evangelica*, translated from the Greek by Georgius Trapezuntius. Jenson's roman types, based on the Neo-Caroline hand of the period, became famous for their beauty. Bruce Rogers declared that, 'The roman letter was done once, perfectly, and for all time, when Nicolas Jenson cut the type that appears perhaps in its greatest perfection in his *Eusebius* of 1470.'

The first printer's mark used in Italy, and the second in chronological order, was that used by Ulrich Han at Rome in Paulus II, *Regulae cancellariae apostolicae* (after 20 September, 1470). His device copied that used by Fust and Schöffer.

The first printer to make use of a *registrum*, or index, was the Roman printer of the *Epistolae Hieronymi* (Sixtus Riessinger?), published not later than 1470. It was not called a *registrum* in this work but under the title *Inchoationes quinternorum* the printer gave a list of the first words of each of the eighty or more gatherings. Ulrich Han was the first to employ a more normal register in his Turrecremata, *Expositio Psalterii* completed 4 October, 1470, giving not only the catchwords of the gatherings but also those of the double sheets.

First edition of the celebrated Lives of the Caesars—Caius Tranquillus Suetonius, *De Duodecim Caesarum Vitis*. Rome: Joannes Philippus de Lignamine.

Sixtus Riessinger of Strassburg introduced printing into Naples. His first dated book is Bartolus de Saxoferrato, *Lectura super prima et secunda parte Codicis* (Anno M.CCCC.LXXI) but an undated poem by Giorgio Fieschi on the capture of Chalcis by the Turks (July 1470) may have preceded it, and the *Bulla anni iubilei* of Paul II must be before 19 April, 1470.

Johann Neumeister of Mainz worked the first

press at Foligno, established by the Papal Mint-master, Emiliano Orfini, in his own house. The first known work from this press was Leonardo Aretino, *De bello Italico adversus Gothos*, 1470.

Johannes Reinhardi (Reynhard) became the first printer at Trevi, beginning in 1470 with a small pamphlet *Quomodo Beatus Franciscus . . .* dealing with the 'Perdono d'Assisi'. In the same year he began a large folio edition of Bartholus de Saxo-ferrato, *Lectura super prima parte Infortiati*.

In this year the first printing press was set up in France, when Jean Heynlin, called Jean de la Pierre, and Guillaume Fichet, both professors at the Sorbonne, brought from the Rhineland three printers who established their workshop within the precincts of the Sorbonne at Paris. They were Michel Friburger of Colmar, a former student at the University of Basel, and two workmen, Ulrich Gering from Constance and Martin Krantz of Stein. In the summer of 1470, they finished the first book printed in France—*Gasparini Perga-mensis Epistolarum Opus*. Between 1470 and 1473 they printed twenty-three books, all of them Latin texts for the students at the Sorbonne.

1471

The first printer's mark in Germany following that of Fust and Schöffer was used by Arnold Ter Hoernen at Cologne, and appeared in Adrianus Carthusiensis, *De remediis utriusque fortunae* (8 February, 1471). The device is a shield with his housemark and the initials *a. h.*

The astronomer Johannes Müller of Königs-berg (Regiomontanus) with the help of Bernhard Wetter set up a press at Nuremberg for the pro-duction of scientific works.

The earliest dated book printed at Speier—*Postilla scholastica super Apocalypsin*—was the product of an anonymous press.

The first Bible in the Italian language was pub-lished at Venice by Vindelinus de Spira. The translation was made by a Venetian Benedictine named Niccolò Malermi (*c.* 1422–81). At least ten editions of Malermi's translation appeared before the end of the fifteenth century, and it was often reprinted down to 1567 (Venice: Girolamo Scotto).

Decor puellarum (sometimes attributed to Saint John of God), an early courtesy book, was printed at Venice by Nicolas Jenson with the erroneous date 1461.

Editio princeps of Boccaccio, *Il Decamerone*. Venice: Christopher Valdarfer.

Clement of Padua (Clemens Patavinus) began to print in Venice. Self-taught at the craft, he was the first priest, and also the first native Italian, to become a printer. He is known by one book only, Joannes Mesue, *Opera*, probably completed in May 1471, though this may not have been his earliest work.

Publication of Eutropius Flavius, *De historiis italice provincie ac Romanorum*, the first edition of the history of Rome and apparently the first book in which a printer made use of semi-circular parenthesis brackets. Rome: Georgius Lauer.

A Frenchman, Andreas Belfortis (André Beau-fort, or Belfort), became the first printer at Ferrara. The first known book from his press is Augustino Dati, *Elegantiae minores*, dated 12 March, 1471. In the same year, on 2 July, he completed an edition of Martial's *Epigrams*.

Printing was introduced into Padua by L. Canozius (Laurenzo Canozio da Lendinara) who printed there a Mesue, *Opera*, dated 9 June, 1471, hitherto wrongly assigned to Florence. (*See* R. Ridolfi, *La Stampa in Firenze*, 1958.)

The first duly authenticated Milanese printing was the Sextus Pompeius Festus, *De verborum significatione*, dated 3 August, 1471, which came from the press owned by Pamfilo Castaldi. The actual printers are thought to have been the brothers De Zarotis of Parma.

Printing introduced into Florence by a native of that city, Bernardo Cennini, assisted by his son Dominico. They are known by one book only, the Commentary of Servius on Virgil, the three parts of which are dated respectively 7 November, 1471; 9 January, 1471/2; and 7 October, 1472.

The first printer at Treviso was a Fleming from Harlebeke, Gerardus de Lisa (Gerard van der Leye). He produced at least four tracts by the end of 1471, the earliest fully dated one being Leo Baptista Alberti, *Ipolito e Lionora*, a booklet of 16 leaves dated 8 November, 1471. He printed about twenty books at Treviso between 1471 and 1476, and printed also at Venice, Cividale and Udine.

The first press at Bologna was set up by Balthasar Azoguidus (Baldassare degli Azzoguidi). His first dated book was the *editio princeps* of works of Ovid, though an undated Phalaris, *Epistolae*, may have preceded it. With Baldassare degli Azzoguidi were associated Francesco dal Pozzo of Parma and Annibale Malpiglio of Padua. Hannibal supervised the printing, but Baldassare seems to have provided the capital and premises for the press.

The first printers at Genoa—Antoine Mathias from Antwerp and Lambert Laurenszoon of Delft. None of their books has survived.

Printing introduced into Perugia by two Germans, Petrus Petri of Cologne and Johannes Nicolai of Bamberg. Their first book, undated, was probably Baldus de Ubaldis, *Circa materiam statutorum*.

Caxton went to Cologne, where he learned the craft of printing so that eventually he could set up his own press.

1472

Johann Kölhoff, celebrated printer of Cologne, began work in that city. He was the first to introduce printed signatures at the foot of the page in Johannes Nider, *Praeceptorium divinae legis*. This innovation was soon adopted by other printers. Kölhoff, who had been a pupil of Vindelinus de Spira at Venice, began his career in Cologne with the printing of twelve tracts by Thomas Aquinas.

Conrad Fyner set up the first press at Esslingen. His first production was part of the *Summa* of Thomas Aquinas.

Probably in 1472 was issued the first printed edition of Bartholomaeus Anglicus, *De proprietatibus rerum*. Cologne: Printer of the *Flores Sancti Augustini*. It was on this book that Caxton is stated by Wynkyn de Worde to have worked while in Cologne.

The first dated book from the press of Anton Koberger, who began printing at Nuremberg in or before 1471, is Alcinous, *Disciplinarum Platonis Epitome*, 24 November, 1472.

Printed catchwords occur for the first time in Antoninus, *Medicina dell' anima*. Bologna: Baldassare degli Azzoguidi. Häbler, in his *Study of Incunabula*, states that catchwords are first found in the undated *Tacitus*, printed at Venice by Vindelinus de Spira, which he assigns to a date not after 1471. Bibliographical research has since given 1473 as the date of the *Tacitus*, thus giving priority to the work of Antoninus.

Editio princeps of Dante Alighieri, *La Divina Commedia*, completed at Foligno on 11 April, 1472, by Johann Neumeister, who came from Mainz. It was followed in the same year by two further editions, one at Mantua and the other at Venice.

Appearance of the first illustrated book on a technical subject—Roberto Valturio, *De re militari*. [Verona]: Joannes Nicolai de Verona. The book is famous for the woodcuts of engines

of war, the design of which has been attributed to Matteo de' Pasti, without, however, any documentary support. After the publication of this work, six years passed before printing was resumed at Verona. The edition of Georgius Summaripa's Italian translation of the *Batrachomyomachia* subscribed 'Verone die xv Januarii M CCCC LXX' was printed at Venice, either by Jenson or by a printer making use of his type. The Valturio was the second book printed at Verona and the second illustrated book printed in Italy. (*See* 1467.)

The first edition of Aristotle, *De anima*. Padua: L. Canozius.

The second press in Milan was established by Philippus de Lavagnia. His name is last found in 1490.

The first printer at Parma was Andreas Portilia, whose first book was an edition of Plutarch, *De liberis educandis*, etc., dated 23 September, 1472.

The first book to appear at Mondoví was an edition of Antoninus, *Summa confessionum* signed by Antoine Mathias from Genoa, and dated 24 October, 1472.

The first press at Mantua was established by Petrus Adam de Michaelibus, a native of that town and a doctor of law. The first two signed books from his press were Angelus de Aretio, *Tractatus maleficiorum*, and Boccaccio, *Il Decamerone*. He seems to have abandoned printing in 1473.

1472 is the earliest date that can be connected definitely with the press of Michael Wenssler at Basel. In partnership with Friedrich Biel he issued Gasparinus Barzizius, *Epistolae*, not later than 1 December in that year.

1473

The first Psalter in German issued as a separate book came from the Strassburg press of Heinrich Eggestein, undated, but probably 1473.

Editio princeps of Thomas à Kempis, *De Imitatione Christi*. Augsburg: Günther Zainer. First written in 1418, more than 2,000 printed editions have been published, and it has been translated into over fifty languages. The author was a monk in the Augustinian convent of St. Agnes at Zwolle.

On 4 December, 1473 an edition of Vincent de Beauvais, *Speculum historiale* was issued by Johann Mentelin at Strassburg. This immense encyclopaedia is one of the few books signed and dated by Mentelin.

Jean Gerson, *Collectorium super Magnificat* (Esslingen: Conrad Fyner) contains the earliest known effort to print music by means of five descending square notes representing sol, fa, mi, re, ut.

Printing was started at Ulm in Swabia by Johann Zainer, whose first dated book (11 January, 1473) was Heinrich Steinhöwel, *Ordnung wider die Pestilenz*, the first plague treatise to appear in print.

In the same year he also printed Boccaccio, *De claris mulieribus*, in a Latin and also a German edition. The eighty woodcut illustrations were copied in subsequent editions published at Augsburg (1479), Louvain (1487), Strassburg (1488) and Saragossa (with Spanish text, 1494). The French edition (Paris, Vérard, 1493) has different illustrations. This was the most frequently repeated of Boccaccio's works during the Renaissance, and of the Ulm Boccaccio, one of the earliest of picture books, Goldschmidt says that it 'was practically the first to show the German wood engraver as a fully competent artist, not merely as a clumsy craftsman'.

Editio princeps of Richard de Bury (Ricardus d'Aungerville), *Philobiblon*. Cologne: [Printer of *Augustinus de Fide* (Goiswin Gops?)]. For the first English edition *see* 1599.

Lucas Brandis, from Delitzsch near Leipzig, was the first printer at Merseburg, whence he issued St. Augustine, *De quaestionibus Orosii*, dated 3 August, and Aristotle, *Lapidarius* (20 October). In the following year he went to Lübeck. (*See* 1475.)

The partnership between Sweynheym and Pannartz was dissolved some time in 1473. In 1474 Pannartz resumed publication on his own account.

The Frenchman, Jacques Le Rouge (Jacobus Rubeus), set up his press in Venice. He was an intimate friend of his compatriot, Nicolas Jenson. The first book printed by Le Rouge at Venice was the *editio princeps* of Omnibonus Leonicenus, *De octo partibus orationis*. Of the thirty-one books definitely known to have been printed by Le Rouge, no fewer than ten, and probably eleven, are first editions of the text.

First edition of *Mirabilia Urbis Romae* appeared at Rome about 1473. The earliest 'Baedeker', it was intended as a guide for pilgrims and gave descriptions of the various churches in the Holy City, including their art treasures.

Etienne Corallus published Statius, *Achilleis*, at Parma. He states that the book was printed quicker than one can cook asparagus (*citius quam asparagi coquantur*) in order to beat some envious competitors.

First printed edition of Aristotle, *Metaphysica* and *De Coelo et Mundo*. Padua: L. Canozius.

Dionigi da Paravicino and Stefano dei Merlini, in partnership, produced the first dated book at Cremona—Angelus de Ubaldis, *Lectura super primam partem Digesti novi*, which is dated 26 January, 1472–73. It may have been preceded by other works now lost.

The first exactly dated book printed at Brescia —a *Virgil*, finished on 21 April, 1473. The printer is unnamed, but the type suggests Georgius de Butzbach, who had already printed at Mantua.

The first book printed at Pavia—Angelus de Aretio, *Lectura super Institutionum*, dated 30 October, 1473, was the work of Joannes de Sidriano, a printer formerly employed at Milan by Philippus de Lavagnia.

Around 1473 (some say 1478) Heinrich Alding from Cologne introduced printing at Messina with the rare *La Vita e Transito e li Miracoli del Beatissimo Hieronimo*.

In this year was printed the anonymous and controversial *Missale speciale Constantiense*, a folio of 192 leaves, printed throughout with a single fount of type in an earlier state of the smaller of the two types used for the text of the 1457 Psalter printed by Fust and Schöffer. The German designer and engraver, Otto Hupp, arrived at the conclusion that it was the earliest production of Gutenberg himself, and antedated the 42-line Bible. But later evidence in the way of notes of provenance, bindings and watermarks, pointed to the now generally accepted conclusion that it was produced at Basel, or in the neighbourhood of that city, by a craftsman who had been employed at Mainz in the office of Gutenberg, or Fust and Schöffer, and had acquired matrices of the Psalter type, or perhaps some of the type itself. For many years controversy raged concerning the probable date of printing, until Dr. Allan Stevenson settled the matter once and for all by proving, from a minute examination of the watermarks, that the Missal was actually printed in the first half of the year 1473; considerably later than had been generally assumed. (*See* his *The Problem of the Missale speciale*. The Bibliographical Society, London, 1967.)

Only four copies of the Missal are known: in the Zentralbibliothek, Zürich; the Bayerische Staatsbibliothek, Munich; the Morgan Library,

New York; and the Staats- und Stadtbibliothek, Augsburg. The Augsburg and Zürich copies are both virtually perfect.

Attributed to the year 1473 is the publication of the earliest known book of music printed from type. It is known as the Constance Gradual since it is printed with the text type used in the Constance Breviary, itself dated 'not after 1473'.

On 5 June was completed the first book printed in Hungary—the *Chronica Hungarorum*. Buda: Andreas Hess.

The first dated and signed book to appear in Holland was an edition of Petrus Comestor, *Historia Scholastica*. Utrecht: Nicolaus Ketelaer and Gerardis de Leempt. There may have been an earlier printer at Utrecht, referred to in *B.M.C.* as 'the Printer of the Text of the *Speculum*'. (*See* 1465 and 1469.)

On July 30, Jan Veldener matriculated at Louvain University. He became the city's first printer. (*See* 1474.)

The printing press was first introduced into Belgium at Alost, where in 1473 were printed two unsigned Latin tracts, Aeneas Sylvius, *De duobus amantibus*, and Dionysius Carthusiensis, *Speculum conversionis peccatorum*. The third book printed at Alost, in the same type, the *Textus summularum* of Petrus Hispanus, bears the names of Johannes de Westfalia and his associate, Thierry Martens of Alost.

The first printed book from Lyons to bear a date is Lotharius (Innocent III), *Compendium breve*, dated 17 September, 1473. It was printed by Guillaume Le Roy, a native of Liège, and published by a wealthy merchant of Lyons, Barthélemy Buyer.

Heinrich Botel, Georg von Holtz, and Johann Planck, Germans, introduced printing into Spain at Barcelona with their production of Aristotle, *Ethica, Oeconomica et Politica*. On 5 January, 1473 Botel entered into an agreement by which he was to teach the other two the art of printing, in return for which they were to provide capital for the enterprise. (*See* George D. Painter: 'The first press at Barcelona' in *Gutenberg Jahrbuch*, 1962.)

Lambert Palmart set up the first press at Valencia, and his undated edition (after March, 1474) of Fenollar, *Les obres e trobes . . . de la Sacratissima Verge Maria*, was until recently thought to be the first book printed in Spain; it was, however, preceded by Palmart's edition of

Aristotle, *Ethica, Oeconomica et Politica* printed towards the end of 1473.

A Calendar for 1474 was printed at Cracow at the end of 1473 by a printer thought to have been Kasper Straube. (*See* also 1475.)

1474

The first Biblical Concordance, the *Concordantiae Bibliorum* of Conradus de Alemannia, was printed at Strassburg by Johann Mentelin, in, or about, 1474.

The earliest book of historical importance illustrated with woodcuts to be printed at Cologne was Werner Rolewinck, *Fasciculus Temporum*. The earliest dated editions were those printed separately in 1474 by Nicolaus Gotz and Arnold Ter Hoernen. This book was the first and one of the most popular of printed epitomes of history as conceived by the Middle Ages. The Gotz edition (undated) is thought to have preceded that of Ter Hoernen.

Günther Zainer, Augsburg's first printer, printed an advertisement of his edition of the *Pantheologia* of Rainerius de Pisis and fourteen other books.

Printing introduced into Marienthal by the Brothers of the Common Life, whose first dated book (12 March) was the *Pars aestivalis* of a *Breviarium Moguntinense*. This was probably preceded by the undated Jean Gerson, *Opusculum tripartitum*.

The earliest printed Greek classic seems to have been the *Batrachomyomachia*, undated, but probably 1474, and attributed to the press of Tomaso Ferrando at Brescia. The Greek text is accompanied by an interlinear Latin prose translation on the recto of each leaf and a metrical Latin version on the verso.

The first extant book printed at Genoa was the *Supplementum* to Nicolaus de Auximo, *Summa Pisanella*. It was printed by Mathias Moravus and Michael de Monacho whilst the former was staying at Genoa on his way from Olmütz to Naples. (*See* 1472.) The work is dated 22 June, 1474. Moravus printed at Naples in 1475, but nothing more is known of Michael de Monacho.

The first book printed at Como—Sancto Georgio, *Tractatus appellationum*. Dated 9 August, 1474, it bears the names of Ambrosius de Orchi and Diogini da Paravicino (Dionysius Paravisinus).

Printing introduced into Vicenza by Leonardus de Basilea, who had previously worked at Padua

(1472–73) and Sant' Orso (1474). His first book at Vicenza, dated November 1474, was Fazio degli Uberti, *Dittamondo*.

From a press installed in the monastery of Savona, near Genoa, came an unsigned and undated edition of Alexander de Villa Dei, *Doctrinale*, probably issued in 1474.

Johannes Fabri (Jean Fabre), a native of Langres in Burgundy, was the first printer in Turin. His name occurs for the first time in the colophon of a *Breviarium Romanum*, dated 1474, printed by him at Turin in conjunction with another Frenchman, Johanninus de Petro, of whom nothing more is known. The press was set up at the expense of Pantaleone de Confienza, physician to Ludovico, Duke of Savoy.

The first book printed in English by William Caxton (at Bruges) was completed towards the end of 1473 or the beginning of 1474. It was the *Recuyell of the Histories of Troy* translated by Caxton from the French of Raoul Le Fèvre. None of the six books printed by Caxton at Bruges is dated.

The first book printed at Bruges by Colard Mansion, a mystical treatise called *Le Jardin de dévotion*, a small undated folio, was probably printed either at the end of 1474 or beginning of 1475.

Jan Veldener introduced printing into Louvain, his first book (after 7 August) being Jacobus de Theramo, *Belial*. He worked in Louvain until 1477 or 1478, in which latter year he printed in Utrecht *Epistelen en Evangelien*. Veldener is thought to have been the printer who instructed Caxton in his art, for he is considered, on typographical grounds, to have been the printer at Cologne of the *Flores S. Augustini* (c. 1472) on which Caxton worked, according to Wynkyn de Worde.

On 9 December, Johannes de Westfalia (John of Paderborn) printed his first book at Louvain—Petrus de Crescentiis, *Liber ruralium commodorum* (the second edition of the first printed book on agriculture). He had previously worked with Thierry Martens at Alost for about a year before setting up his own press at Louvain, where he printed nearly 200 books.

The first edition of the New Testament in French appeared in, or about, 1474. It begins *Cy commence la table du nouveau testament*. Lyons: Barthélémy Buyer. Two editions appeared, neither dated, within a short space of time. The edition without signatures is the earlier.

In February, Louis XI of France granted letters of naturalisation to Ulrich Gering, Martin Krantz and Michel Friburger, who were the first printers in France. (*See* 1470.)

1475

The first dated book of Lucas Brandis at Lübeck is *Rudimentum Novitiorum*, 5 August, 1475, but an undated Josephus and a Low German *Psalter* preceded it. Brandis was printing at Lübeck as late as 1499. (*See* 1473.)

The first dated book printed at Breslau was *Statuta Synodalia Vratislaviensia*, completed 9 October, 1475 by Caspar Elyan, the only printer who worked at Breslau during the fifteenth century. After 1482 Breslau was without a printer, until the arrival of Conrad Baumgarten in 1503.

The first dated book printed in Hebrew was printed at Reggio di Calabria by Abraham ben Garton. It was a *Commentary on the Pentateuch* by the Rabbi Salomon Rashi.

First printed edition of Ptolemy's *Cosmographia*, translated into Latin by Jacobus Angelus. Vicenza: Hermann Liechtenstein (Levilapis). This edition had no maps; the first with maps was probably that of Bologna, erroneously dated 1462, but in fact printed in 1477.

Printing introduced into Modena by Johannes Vurster, who arrived there from Bologna in July 1474. His first recorded book at Modena is an edition of Virgil, bearing the date 23 January. He worked at Modena until 1479.

At Cagli, near Urbino, Robertus de Fano and Bernardinus de Bergomo set up the first press and completed, on 29 June, a small book of 6 leaves only—Maphaeus Vegius, *De morte Astyanactis*.

Joannes Petrus de Ferratis established the first press at Piacenza and printed, as his first work, a Latin Bible. Unlike most Bibles of the early period of printing it was a quarto in format.

Johann Amerbach (1444–1513) set up his press at Basel. He had been a pupil of Johann Heynlin at the Sorbonne, and was a scholar who edited his texts with scrupulous care. His eleven-volume edition of St. Augustine (1506) was one of the highlights of Basel printing.

The first appearance of the portrait of a printer (and first printer's mark used in Belgium) occurs in *Justiniani Institutiones* printed at Louvain (21 November) by Johannes de Westfalia. In the form of a small medallion with a head of the printer, it was used as a printer's mark in seven books printed by him between 1475 and 1484.

Earliest dated book attributable to the press of the Brothers of the Common Life at Brussels, the first printers in that city, was Gerson, *Opuscula*, dated 3 March, 1475.

The first use of Greek type in Spain occurred in Nicolaus Perottus, *Rudimenta Grammaticae*, completed at Barcelona on 12 December, 1475 by Johannes de Salsburga and Paulus Hurus de Constantia. (*See* D. E. Rhodes: 'The First use of Greek type in Spain', in *Gutenberg Jahrbuch*, 1960.)

The third printing office in Spain was set up at Saragossa. On 15 October, 1475, Mateo Flandro (Matthew of Flanders) completed a *Manipulus curatorum*, which is the first book produced in Spain to have a complete imprint.

The first book printed at Cracow, Franciseus de Platea, *Tractatus restitutionum*. The printer was Kasper Straube, connected with the local Franciscans.

1476

Johann Zainer, the first printer at Ulm, issued an Aesop in Latin and German, *Vita et Fabulae* (*Das Buch und Leben des hochberühmten Fabeldichters Aesop*), which was published about 1476–77, to which the *Historia Sigismundae* formed a supplement. The German version was the work of Heinrich Steinhöwel, and the 205 woodcuts were later used at Augsburg by Günther Zainer about 1477–78, and by Anton Sorg soon after 1480. The illustrations were so popular that they were used in some twenty German editions of the Fables before the end of the fifteenth century. Those of *Sigismunda* were used by Johann Bämler in 1482.

The first dated printing at Rostock, where the Brothers of the Common Life completed, on 9 April, Lactantius, *Opera*.

Michael Greyff brought printing to Reutlingen with Eberhard of Württemberg, *Brief an Herzog Sigmund* (not before 18 October 1476).

The first separate displayed title-page occurs in the *Kalendario* of Johannes Müller (Regiomontanus) printed at Venice by Erhard Ratdolt and his associates, Bernhard Maler and Peter Löslein. For the first time the title occurred on a separate page at the beginning of the volume, accompanied by the imprint giving place, date, and name of printer. It took several years before the practice of having a separate title-page became general. This book and the Latin version, also 1476, were the first books dated with Arabic numerals.

The South Slavonic printer Andrija Paltašić (Andreas de Paltasichis Cattarensis) began his career as a printer in Venice, having in all probability acquired the material of Jacob de Fivizzano. His first book was completed 31 January, 1477 (1476 old style), an edition of Diodorus Siculus and the *Germania* of Tacitus. Between that date and 1492, he printed and published more than thirty works—in 1478 in association with his countryman Dobrić Dobrićević (Boninus de Boninis), and in 1483 with Johann Leodio. Paltašić was himself the publisher of all his works except the Marchesinus *Mammotrectus* of 1482, which was published by the famous Venetian publisher Octaviano Scoto.

The first book with music to be printed in Italy was the *Missale Romanum*, printed at Rome by Ulrich Han. It has music before and in the Canon in two columns, printed from type throughout in roman notation and C clef only. For the first time the five-line staff and music notes were printed with the letterpress.

The first book printed wholly in Greek—the Greek grammar of Constantine Lascaris. Milan: Diogini da Paravicino (Dionysius Paravisinus). (30 January.) The fount is thought to have been designed by the Cretan, Demetrius Damilas.

Editio princeps of Petrarch, *De viris illustribus*; the only book printed in the village of Pojano, or Pogliano, just north of Verona. The printers were Felix Antiquarius (*Feliciano*) and Innocens Ziletus in partnership.

First printing at Trent, where Albrecht Kunne brought out a German version of *Historia de passione pueri Simonis*.

First edition of the *Fioretti* of St. Francis of Assisi (d. 1226). Vicenza: Giovanni Leonardo Longo.

At Vicenza, Liechtenstein printed the first Italian version of Virgil's *Aeneid* (*Fatezze de Eneio*).

The establishment at Florence of a press run by the convent of Dominican nuns 'apud Sanctum Jacobum de Ripoli'. In 1476 this conventual press, at which the nuns are said to have worked as compositors, issued an Italian *Donatus*.

The first to print at Faenza, were two otherwise unknown printers, Kilian Fer and Heinrich Kandler who produced there an edition of *Doctrinale Alexandri*, of which only one imperfect copy has survived. No other work of theirs is known.

In Switzerland, the first printer's mark was used by Michael Wenssler at Basel in Clement V, *Constitutiones* dated 2 May, 1476. It shows two shields hung from two horns; the one on the left has an incomplete cross—that on the right a brook with two stars, arms of the Wenzel family of Sternbach.

At Pilsen, an unidentified printer issued what is the oldest certain printing in this town—*Statuta provincialia Arnesti*. It is not known for certain whether the *Kronika trojanska*, 1468, was actually printed at Pilsen. (*See* 1468.)

First printed edition of Aristotle, *Ethica*. Louvain: Conrad Braem.

At Bruges, Colard Mansion printed Boccaccio, *Livre de la Ruigne des Nobles Hommes et Femmes*, translated by Pierre Favre, and illustrated with copper-plate engravings stuck on at the beginning of each of the nine chapters of the volume after the printing had been completed.

The first Latin Bible appeared in France, printed at Paris by Ulrich Gering, Martin Krantz and Michel Friburger. An undated folio, printed in double column in a handsome gothic type, it is usually assigned to the year 1476.

The first dated book printed in the French language in France was *La Légende Dorée*, a French translation by Jean de Vignay of Jacobus de Voragine, *Legenda Aurea*. Lyons: Guillaume Le Roy and Barthélemy Buyer.

The first dated book known to have been printed at Toulouse was Andreas Barbatia, *Repetitio solemnis rubrice de fide instrumentorum* dated 20 June, 1476 [Henricus Turner]. After Paris and Lyons, Toulouse is the third oldest centre of printing in France.

The first dated French book printed at Paris was begun in 1476 and completed at the beginning of 1477—*Chroniques de France* (Chronicle of Saint Denis). Paris: Pasquier Bonhomme.

Not later than 1476 (date of rubricated copy) a printer at Cracow, probably Casper Hochfeder, issued Joannes de Turrecremata, *Explanatio in Psalterium*.

At Michaelmas, 29 September, Caxton's name was entered on the Account Roll of John Esteney, Sacrist of Westminster Abbey, as paying a year's tenancy in advance for the premises in which he set up his press.

The first known piece of printing done in England, a Letter of Indulgence by John Sant, Abbot of Abingdon, with the date of purchase 13 December, 1476, printed at Westminster by William Caxton. Its existence was unknown until February 1928, when it was discovered at the Public Record Office.

1477

First printed edition of *Parsifal*, the famous legend of Wolfram von Eschenbach. Strassburg: Johann Mentelin. The same author's *Titurel* was also issued by Mentelin in this year.

First edition of Marco Polo, *Das puch des edelñ Ritters uñ landtfarers Marcho polo*. Nuremberg: Fricz Creüszner (Friedrich Creussner). Although first written down in French (1298–99), the original French text was not published until 1824. The above German version was the first printed edition of Marco Polo's *Travels*. On the verso of the first leaf is a woodcut full-length portrait of Marco Polo. The German edition was reprinted by Sorg at Augsburg in 1481; a Latin translation was printed at Antwerp by Gerard Leeu, probably in 1485; an Italian edition followed in 1496, a Spanish version in 1503, a French edition in 1556, while the first edition in English was J. Frampton's translation from the Castilian version of R. Fernandez, published in London by R. Newbery, 1579.

First illustrated edition of Ptolemy, *Cosmographia*, with 26 copper-plate maps was printed at Bologna, 1477, by Dominicus de Lapis. The maps were the work of Taddeo Crivelli. (For the *editio princeps* of this work (without maps) *see* 1475.)

At Naples, Arnaldus de Bruxella issued the first printed edition of Odo of Meung, *Macer Floridus de Virtutibus Herbarum*. This work, compiled around 1080, was based on Pliny, Dioscorides, and other ancient writers. The name 'Macer Floridus' under which the work is designated, was that of an ancient botanist mentioned by Pliny, whose works are now lost. Many 'Macers' were printed until superseded by the much better herbals of Brunfels and Fuchs.

The earliest copper-plate engravings to be printed as an integral part of the book appeared in the first Florentine illustrated book—Antonio Bettini, Bishop of Siena, *Monte Santo de Dio*, printed by Nicolaus Laurentii, Alemannus, of Breslau. The designs were supplied by Baccio Baldini.

The first press at Lucca was established by Bartholomaeus de Cividale, who issued, on 17 May, the first book of the *Trionfi* of Francesco Petrarch.

At Delft a Dutch Bible (*Biblia Neerlandica*) was completed 10 January, 1477 by Jacob Jacobszoon van der Meer and Mauritz Yemantszoon van Middelborch. This was the first time the Old Testament had been printed in Dutch. Although styled a Bible, it includes neither the Psalter nor the New Testament.

Gerard Leeu became the first printer at Gouda. The earliest known work from his press is the unsigned *Epistelen en Evangelien*, dated 24 May. He printed at Gouda until the middle of 1484, when he moved to Antwerp. (*See* 1484.)

Printing introduced into Deventer by a German from Cologne, named Richard Pafraet. Two books came from his press in 1477: the *Cypriani Epistolae* (sine nota) and the signed *Reductorium Morale* of Petrus Bertorius.

Johann Parix of Heidelberg became the second printer in Toulouse, where he remained until 1502. He printed several legal works, as well as books in Spanish.

The first dated book to appear at Albi was Angelus de Aretio, *Tractatus maleficiorum*, which the colophon states to have been completed on 15 April, 1477. Only four books with the Albi imprint are known from the earliest press at Albi, and none bears the printer's name, though from the type and general appearance of these books the printer probably came from Rome. The earliest book (1475?) was Aeneas Sylvius, *Epistola de amoris remedio*.

At Vienne, France, the first press was set up by Johannes Solidi, whose first book was Bartolus de Saxoferrato, *Litigatio Satanae contra genus humanum*. He had previously worked at Basel under the German form of his name Hans Schilling.

Jean de la Tour established the first press at Angers in association with Jean Morel. The first book from this press was an edition of Cicero, *Rhetorica nova*, dated 5 February, 1476/7.

First to introduce printing into Seville, and the first Spaniards to print in their native land, were Alfonso del Puerto, Antón Martinez and Bartolomé Segura. Their first book was Alfonso Diaz de Montalvo, *Repertorium*.

William Caxton printed at Westminster *The Dictes or Sayengis of the Philosophres*, the first dated book printed in England. It was completed on 18 November, 1477. This book was translated from the French by Caxton's friend and patron, Earl Rivers.

About 1477 Caxton produced the only known example of a printer's advertisement in England in the fifteenth century. It reads: 'If it plese ony man spirituel or temporel to bye ony pyes of two and thre commemoraciõs of salisburi use, enpryntid after the forme of this presēt lettre whiche ben wel and truly correct, late hym come to westmonester in to the almonesrye at the reed pale and he shal have them good chepe.' Underneath was the appeal in Latin, *Supplico stet cedula* (Please do not remove this notice). Two copies survive, in the Bodleian Library, Oxford, and the John Rylands Library, Manchester. The poster was to advertise Caxton's edition of an *Ordinale* for Sarum use, printed about 1477.

1478

Between 1478 and 1480 (the exact date is still undecided) Heinrich Quentell of Cologne published the first Low German Bible, illustrated with handsome page-width woodcuts. Two editions were printed within a short space of time—the first in Low Saxon dialect and the second in the dialect of Holland and the Lower Rhine. The first of these has 113 woodcuts; the second the same 113 plus ten others. The blocks were later used by Koberger in his Nuremberg Bible of 1483.

The earliest printed book on arithmetic, the *Arte del Abaco*, was printed at Treviso by Michele Manzolo, the second printer in that town. He began work at Treviso in April 1476, at the time when Gerardus de Lisa was about to leave for Venice.

What is thought to be the first known example of the use of printers' flowers occurs in [Capranica], *Arte de ben morire*, on the colophon page. Verona: Giovanni Alberto Alvise. This is an Italian version of the *Ars Moriendi* and is one of several recensions not mentioning Capranica as the author. It is dated 28 April, 1478.

The only known incunabulum printed at Viterbo—a book containing two grammatical treatises by Servius Maurus Honoratus, *De ultimis syllabis; Centimetrum*—is dated 12 January, 1488, but this is considered to have been a misdating and that the book was probably printed in 1478. The printer remains unidentified.

At Colle di Valdelsa, one of the Italian towns where paper was first made, the first printer was Johannes de Medemblick, known only from a single book, dated July 1478, which is the first printed edition of the Latin translation of Dioscorides, *De Materia Medica*, edited by Petrus de Abano.

An Italian edition of Johannes Climacus, *Scala Paradisi*, signed and dated by Giovanni Leonardo Longo, 19 September, 1478, is the first book known to have been printed at Torrebelvicino.

A press was set up at Palermo by Andreas Vyel, a native of Worms. Only one book from his press is known—*Consuetudines urbis Panormi*, dated 1478.

Printing introduced into Cosenza by Octavianus Salamonius, who printed four books there, two of which are dated 1478.

Printing was introduced into Geneva by Adam Steinschaber, of Schweinfurt, who completed Francisco Jiménez, *Le Livre des saints anges* on 24 March, 1478. The first known book to bear his name is Pierre d'Arras, *Histoire de la belle Mélusine*, completed August of that year.

The *Statuum utraquistorum articuli*, considered the earliest printing at Prague (Hain 1879), cannot now be traced. (*See* 1487.)

The first illustrated book published in France was *Le Mirouer de la Rédemption de l'umain lignaige*. Lyons: Martin Huss. This was a French version of the *Speculum Humanae Salvationis*. Dated 26 August, 1478, it has 256 illustrations reprinted from the original blocks from Bernard Richel's edition, Basel, 1476. It was reissued by Martin Huss in 1479 and 1482, and later by Matthaeus Huss.

First printed edition of Guy de Chauliac, *Le livre appelé guidon de la pratique en cyrurgie*. Lyons: Barthélemy Buyer. This treatise on surgery, written around 1363, was one of the most important works on the subject during the Middle Ages.

Pierre Le Rouge, a relative of Jacques Le Rouge, made his début as a printer at Chablis, into which town he introduced the art of printing with *Le livre de bonnes moeurs* by the Augustinian Jacques Legrant. He later went to Paris, where he worked from 1484 onwards. In 1488 he became King's Printer.

In Robert Gaguin, *Ars versificatoria* (Paris:

Ulrich Gering) an epigram by the author, *In laudem artis impressorie*, refers to the invention of printing in Germany.

Nicolaus Spindeler of Zwickau and Pierre Brun of Geneva, printed at Barcelona the commentaries of St. Thomas Aquinas on the *Ethics* and *Politics* of Aristotle, after which they separated.

First printed edition of Chaucer, *The Canterbury Tales*. Westminster: William Caxton. Undated, it was probably completed in 1478.

The first book printed at Oxford—Rufinus, Bishop of Aquileia, *Exposicio Sancti Ieronimi in Simbolum apostolorum*. It bore no printer's name and the date was erroneously printed MCCCCLXVIII. The printer was perhaps Theodoric Rood, a native of Cologne, whose name first occurs in the colophon of Alexander Hales's commentary on Aristotle, *De Anima*, completed by Rood on 11 October, 1481. But the identity of the press with Rood's remains unestablished.

1479

The first dated book to come from the press of Heinrich Quentell at Cologne was Astesanus de Ast, *Summa de casibus conscientiae*, dated 31 August, 1479. Quentell's first press closed down in 1482, when he was wrongfully imprisoned.

It was probably in 1479 that Johann Otmar began to print at Reutlingen. He produced five dated books in 1482, but three others are inferentially dated between 1479–80. Otmar printed at Reutlingen until 1495, and in 1498 had a press at Tübingen. (*See* 1476.)

Printing began at Würzburg, where Georg Reyser issued a *Breviarium Herbipolense*.

The earliest book to contain the portrait of the author is Paulus Florentinus (Paolo Attavanti), *Quadragesimale de reditu peccatoris ad Deum*. Milan: Uldericus Scinzenzeler and Leonardus Pachel. The book bears the date 10 September, 1479.

The first book to have printed catchwords on each page was Eusebius Pamphilius Caesariensis, *Historia ecclesiastica*, printed at Mantua by the physician-printer Johann Schall. It was the first book printed at his second press. He only printed four books at Mantua.

The first known work to bear the name of the printer Andrea Torresano (b. Asola, Lombardy, 4 March, 1451), who later entered into partnership with Aldo Manuzio, is a Breviary dated 12

October, 1479. He himself stated that he had been a pupil of Nicolas Jenson and an active printer since 1475. His daughter married Aldo Manuzio. (*See* 1505.)

At Pinerolo in Savoy, Jacobus Rubeus set up the first press from which he issued in 1479 two books—a Boethius, *De consolatione philosophiae,* and the *Satires* of Juvenal.

Printing introduced into Toscolano by Gabriele de Pietro, whose first book in that town was Guarinus, *Regulae grammaticales.*

Although undated, the first book printed in Zürich was probably issued in 1479. It was Albertus de Albolapide, *De indulgentiis ecclesiarum Thuricensium,* printed by Sigmund Rot.

The first book issued by the unidentified schoolmaster-printer of St. Albans was an edition of Augustinus Datus, *Super Eleganciis Tullianis,* undated, but probably printed in 1479 or 1480.

1480

Conrad Kachelofen may have begun to print at Leipzig in the latter part of 1480, in which case he, and not Marcus Brandis (*see* 1481), may claim the honour of being the city's prototypographer. He acquired citizenship in 1476. Two broadside manifestos by the Town Council of Erfurt in December 1480, are said by Dr. Adolf Schmidt to be printed with Kachelofen's type 80; but the first conclusive evidence of his printing activity is the Latin Psalter of 1485 in Leipzig University Library.

The first printer at Magdeburg was Bartholomaeus Ghotan who issued there a *Missale Magdeburgense,* printed with the assistance and type of Lucas Brandis.

Death of the printer Nicolas Jenson. He bequeathed his punches to Peter Ugelheimer (Ugelleymer), a Venetian born at Frankfurt. As far as is known he was a bookseller and probably a type-founder, but he does not appear to have been a printer. The material then passed into the hands of Torresano, father-in-law of Aldo Manuzio, who after Ugelheimer's death acquired the punches.

The first printed secular music appeared in the *Grammatica* of Francis Niger. Venice: Theodor of Würzburg (Theodorus Francus). The musical notes are in lozenge form, without staves, printed from metal blocks, or perhaps type, the lines being added by hand.

At Naples, Francesco di Dino printed *Theoricum Opus Musice* by Franchinus Gafurius (1451–1522), the earliest printed book dealing entirely with music. The writings of Gafurius covered the whole field of musical theory. The above work was also the first book published in Naples to contain woodcuts.

The first printing at Reggio Emilia was an edition of N. Perottus, *Rudimenta grammaticae,* dated 29 July, 1480, and printed by the brothers Bartholomaeus and Laurentius de Bruschis.

At Cividale, printing was introduced by Gerardus de Lisa from Treviso, who printed and signed an edition of Platina, *De honesta voluptate,* completed 24 October.

Printing begun at Passau by Benedict Mayr, whose first publication was a protest by the Chapter of the Cathedral against the election of Georg von Hasler to the see of Passau. (*See* 1481.)

Gerard Leeu, a woodcutter of Gouda, began his career as a printer of illustrated books with the *Dialogus Creaturarum,* dated 3 June, 1480. The work is enlivened with 121 woodcuts, and Leeu printed six editions of it between 1480 and 1482.

Printing introduced into Hasselt, Overijssel, by Peregrinus Bermentlo, who printed there the *Epistelen ende Evangelien.*

The first edition in French of the *Itinerarius* of Sir John Mandeville was printed at Lyons by Guillaume Le Roy. At Milan, in the same year, the first Italian version was printed by Petrus de Corneno.

At Caen two printers, Jacques Durand and Gilles Quijoue, of whom nothing further is known, printed not only the first book at Caen, but also the first edition in France of the *Epistolae* of Horace.

The first known printing at Salamanca—*Leyes hechas en las cortes de Toledo* (c. 1480). The printer has not been identified. Early Salamanca printing is the product mainly of anonymous presses, which issued more than a hundred incunabula as against a dozen by named printers.

John Lettou established the first printing press in the City of London. The name suggests a Lithuanian origin. His first work in London was to print John Kendale's *Indulgence* asking for aid against the Turks, an edition of which had recently been printed by Caxton. The type used by Lettou for his first books is, apart from the capitals, similar to that used by the printer Johannes Bremer, alias Bulle, who printed at Rome.

1481

Printing was introduced into Leipzig (*but see* 1480), the first dated book being Joannes Annius, *De futuris Christianorum triumphis*. It is unsigned but almost certainly from the press of Marcus Brandis, completed 28 September, 1481. The first book signed by Brandis was *De regimine hominis* by Archbishop Albicus, finished on 26 August, 1484.

First printing at (Treves) was von Schilditz, *Speculum sacerdotum*, unsigned, but probably by J. Colini and G. de Nova Cicitate (Gérard de Villeneuve).

The earliest dated liturgical book with printed music in gothic notation was the Würzburg Missal printed in that town by Georg Reyser.

An edition of Dante Alighieri, *La Divina Commedia*, illustrated with metal cuts, was published at Florence by Nicolaus Laurentii Alemannus, dated 30 August. It includes a series of engravings by Baldini from drawings by Botticelli, made from a manuscript of this work said to have been commissioned by Lorenzo de' Medici.

The earliest book of the Bible to be printed in Greek—a liturgical Psalter in the Septuagint version, with a Latin translation, edited by Johannes Chrestonus. Printed at Milan and dated 20 September, 1481. The printer remains unidentified.

The first German edition of the *Itinerarius* of Sir John Mandeville [Basel: Bernhard Richel]. The woodcuts are reproduced in Schramm, *Der Bilderschmuck der Frühdrucke*, Vol. XXI.

Vincent de Beauvais, *Liber gratiae*, etc. (Basel: Johann Amerbach), is the first signed work of Amerbach; but he was at work as early as 1478, when he printed Johann Reuchlin, *Vocabularius breviloques*.

The first and only incunabulum printed at Rougemont, in Switzerland—Werner Rolewinck, *Fasciculus temporum*, printed by Heinrich Wirtzburg.

The first printer at Antwerp, Mathias van der Goes, completed on 8 June, the *Boexken van der officien ofte dienst der Missen* by Simon van Venloo.

Benedict Mayr is presumed to have printed at Passau with Conrad Stahel the Passau Breviary completed 6 August, 1481.

The first dated book to bear the name of Jean Du Pré, the famous Paris printer-publisher, was a Paris Missal printed by him in association with Didier Huym, completed 22 September, 1481. It contains two full-page cuts which are the first native wood engravings, owing nothing to outside influence, to appear in France. Two months later, on 26 November, new and better executed illustrations appeared in the Verdun Missal. (Du Pré's real surname was Larcher.)

Geoffroy de Marnef set up shop as a licensed bookseller in Paris, at the sign of the Pelican. He also had a branch at Bourges. His brothers Enguilbert and Jean, and his son Hiérosme, were all booksellers.

The first dated book printed at Salamanca: the original edition of the Latin grammar of Antonio de Nebrija, a work which remained in favour for three centuries.

The first known printing at Valladolid—*Bula de indulgencias en favor de la iglesia de S. Salvador de Avila*. Printed in the monastery of Nuestra Señora del Prado, not after 1481.

Caxton printed his first edition of *The Mirrour of the World*, the first illustrated book produced in England. This has two sets of cuts, 34 in all, one set showing masters and pupils, the other consisting of diagrams so badly executed that the printer put several of them in the wrong position. A second edition was printed in 1490.

Caxton printed the first edition in English of the famous German classic *Reineke Fuchs* under the title of *Reynart the Foxe*. It was translated by Caxton himself, as a comparative reading shows, from the Dutch edition printed at Gouda by Gerard Leeu in 1479.

1482

At Ulm, on 16 July, Lienhart Holle produced his first dated book, one of the finest produced in Germany during the fifteenth century. This was Ptolemy, *Cosmographia*, translated by Jacobus Angelus and edited by Nicolaus Germanus. The large type in which it is printed is said to have been copied from the handwriting of Germanus, and it was upon this roman type that the 'Ptolemy' type used by the Ashendene Press (*see* 1894) was based.

Printing began at Munich with a German

edition of *Mirabilia Urbis Romae*, from the press of Hans Schauer.

The first printed edition of Euclid, *Praeclarissimus liber elementorum Euclidis in artem geometriae.* Venice: Erhard Ratdolt. Dated 25 May, 1482. The only known fifteenth-century example of printing in gold ink is seen in the Dedication (to the Doge). It is also the first printed book with mathematical figures. Possibly only the British Museum copy has the gold printing. A close reprint of Ratdolt's edition was printed at Vicenza in 1491.

The first press started at Pisa, when a solitary book—Franciscus de Accoltis, *Consilia,* was produced by an unidentified printer.

At Aquila a press was set up by Adam de Rottweil, who had previously worked at Venice. His first book at Aquila was a selection of Plutarch's *Lives,* in an Italian translation by Battista Jaconello.

Printing began in Vienna with the production of *Vocabolista Italico-Tedesco* by an unnamed printer thought to have been Stephan Koblinger, who had printed at Vicenza, 1479–80. He can probably be identified with the 'Steffan Koglinger' who acquired citizenship of Vienna in 1481.

Jean Du Pré introduced printing into Chartres, where he printed a Missal and a Breviary for the canon, Pierre Plumé.

At Chambéry an unidentified printer produced the first printing in that town, a Breviary commissioned by the Bishop of Sion. (*See* 1484.)

The first press at Metz was established by Jean Colini and Gérard de Villeneuve, who printed the first part of the *Imitatio Jesu Christi.*

William Caxton printed and published Ranulf Higden, *Polycronicon,* one of the standard world histories of the time, translated by John Trevisa into English and brought down to the year 1460 by Caxton himself.

William de Machlinia printed at London a book treating of the plague. This has the first known title-page in an English printed book; it runs, 'A passing gode lityll boke necessarye & behouefull agenst the Pestilence.' The book is a translation of Johannes Jacobi, *Regimen contra epidemiam sive pestem.*

The first book printed in Denmark (and the first in any part of Scandinavia)—Gulielmi Caorsini, *De obsidione et bello Rhodiano,* an account of the Turkish siege of Rhodes. Odense: Johann Snell. Snell, who also worked in Lübeck and Stockholm (*see* 1483), printed in that same year a *Breviarium Ottoniense.*

1483

The first proper title-page used in Germany occurs in Gruner, *Officii sacrique canonis expositio.* Reutlingen: Johann Otmar. A Psalter with a title-page was printed in Zwolle by Pieter van Os around 1480, but the actual date has not been ascertained with certainty. (*See also* 1476.)

A *Breviarium Misnense* dated 16 July was the first work printed at Meissen, possibly by Simone Koch.

The first armorial of any kind was printed at Augsburg by Anton Sorg. It was Ulric von Reichenthal, *Das Concilium buch geschehen zu Costencz.* It has 44 illustrations and 1,156 coats of arms of all countries of the known world (including many mythical ones). The author was a canon of Constance.

A reference to Gutenberg as the inventor of printing in 1440 is contained in Pamphilus Eusebius, *Chronicon a S. Hieronymo . . .* Venice: Erhard Ratdolt.

Editio princeps of the *Herbarium* of Apuleius Barbarus. [Rome: Joannes Philippus de Lignamine.] The woodcuts were based on illustrations in a ninth century manuscript in the Abbey of Monte Cassino.

Printing introduced into Kuilenburg, in the northern Netherlands, by Jan Veldener, who completed there on 6 March, *Geschiedenis van het heilige Kruis.* Veldener (*see* 1473) also worked at Louvain and Utrecht.

Arend de Keysere, after printing at Audenarde (1480), introduced the art into Ghent. His first book there, completed on 8 April, was *Traité de paix et de mariage* [The Treaty of Arras, 1482].

Printing introduced into Leyden by Heynricus Heynrici. His first dated book was the *Cronike van Hollant,* 9 July, 1483; but three unsigned books of that year are also attributed to his press.

Jacob Bellaert set up a press at Haarlem, probably as a branch of the business of Gerard Leeu at Gouda, and later Antwerp. The first work attributed to this printer is a Dutch *Passion* with woodcuts similar to those used by Leeu in a Gouda edition of the same work which he had printed in 1482.

The first printer's mark to appear in France was

that of Nicolaus Philippi at Lyons. It consists of an orb and cross together with a monogram which can be read as either NM or MN, the exact significance of which is not known. It can be seen in his *Vitae sanctorum patrum*.

Jean Le Rouge, who worked with Pierre Le Rouge at Chablis, was called to Troyes, where he printed the first book in that town, a Breviary for local use, which he completed 25 September, 1483.

The *Golden Legend*, compiled by Jacobus de Voragine, Archbishop of Genoa, was printed for the first time in English by William Caxton at Westminster. Caxton himself made the translation from the French version by Jean de Vignay.

The unique Caxton *Psalterium* in the British Museum (Duff 354, Blades 38) has been dated by Dr. Allan Stevenson as 1483 or 1484.

A travelling German printer, Johann Snell, was the first to print in Stockholm, to which city he had been called from Lübeck in order to print a Missal for the diocese of Uppsala. He also printed there a few other books including a collection of fables called *Dialogus Creaturarum*. But the first properly established press in Sweden was that set up at Uppsala in 1510.

A Glagolitic Missal was published without mention of place or printer. It has recently been conjectured that it was printed at Kosinj, or at Modrŭs in Croatia. If so, the date of the first printing in Jugoslavia would have to be advanced by a decade, since the Makarije *Oktoich* of 1494 (*q.v.*) has hitherto been considered as such. (*See* Josip Badalić, *Jugoslavica Usque Ad Annum MDC*, Baden-Baden, 1966.)

1484

The first dated book from Heïnrich Quentell's second press at Cologne (*see* 1479) is Petrus Lombardus, *Sententiarum libri quattuor*, 13 August, 1484. Quentell died between 8 January and 27 October, 1501, and was succeeded by his sons and heirs. In 1518 the press was run by his son Peter alone.

Marcus Brandis, who may have been the first printer at Leipzig (*see* Kachelofen, 1480), produced his first signed and dated book, Albicus, Archbishop of Prague, *De regimine hominis*, on 26 August, 1484. But Joannes Annius, *Glosa super Apocalypsim*, dated 28 September, 1481, is thought to have come from his press.

The *Sachsenspiegel* of Eike von Repgow was

printed at the first press owned and worked by a woman. Augsburg: Anna Rügerin. Dated 22 June, 1484. It is probable that Johann Schönsperger who had been associated with Thomas Rüger assisted the latter's widow.

Printing at Eichstätt was *Statuta Synodalia Eystettensia* from the press of Michael Reyser, with types of Georg Reyser.

The first arithmetical treatise was printed at Venice by Ratdolt—the *Arithmetica* of Pietro Borgo.

Printing introduced into Udine by Gerardus de Lisa. His first book was *Constituzioni della patria di Friuli*.

The first book printed at Siena was Paulus de Castro, *Lectura super vi Codicis*. The printer was Henricus de Colonia.

At Bruges, Colard Mansion printed the first edition in French of Ovid, *Metamorphoses*, one of the finest early woodcut books printed in the Netherlands.

Gerard Leeu (*see* 1477) signed at Antwerp: on 15 April, 1484 the first part of *Exercitium puerorum grammaticale* which he may have begun at Gouda. His first book entirely printed at Antwerp was *Gemmula Vocabulorum*, dated 18 September, 1484.

Gerard Leempt became the first printer at s'Hertogenbosch (Bois le Duc) when he issued *Tondalus visioen*.

The first illustrated book in French published in Paris—Boccaccio, *Des cas et ruynes des nobles hommes et femmes infortunés*. Paris: Jean Du Pré.

The first printer's mark used in Paris was that of Louis Martineau in John Bacon, *Liber primus Sententiarum*, dated 20 February, 1484.

The first known printer at Chambéry was Antoine Neyret, who printed there *Le Doctrinal de sapience*, dated 5 May.

The German printer Johann Higman settled in Paris, where he went into partnership with a compatriot, Wolfgang Hopyl (*see* 1489), who succeeded him in 1498.

Printing introduced into Toledo by Juan Vasquez, who printed there a *Bula de indulgencias de la Santa Cruzada*.

An Act of Richard III regulated the conditions under which aliens might carry on their trade in England, but exempted from restrictions the printing and bookselling industries. The free trade in books came to an end in the reign of Henry VIII.

1485

In this year, Friedrich Creussner of Nuremberg made use of a type which, says A. F. Johnson, 'became the most popular German type for books in the vernacular and received the name of Schwabacher'. Writing in 1959, the same authority stated, 'German printers of today have revived Schwabacher, and it is now being used to a greater extent than at any time since the sixteenth century'. Why this variety of German Bastarda should be given the name of Schwabacher is still something of a puzzle, since it certainly did not originate in the town of Schwabach, which had no printing or type-founding industry in the early days.

First appearance of the *Herbarius zu deutsch: Gart der Gesundheyt*. Mainz: Peter Schöffer. This was the first printed herbal in German. By the end of the century no fewer than thirteen editions had been printed.

Printing begun at Münster, where Johann Limburg completed on 31 October J. Kerckmeister, *Comoedia Codri*.

At Heidelberg a press was working, established probably by Heinrich Knoblochtzer from Strassburg. The first book was Hugo de Prato Florido, *Sermones*, dated 21 January.

One of the most celebrated of the early woodcut books is Aesop, *Vita et Fabulae,* with the Italian paraphrase of Francesco del Tuppo. Naples: Francesco del Tuppo. There are 87 large cuts framed in richly decorated 'passe-partout' borders.

A valuable document on Renaissance architecture—*De re aedificatoria* by the great architect Leo Baptista Alberti (1404–84). Florence: Nicolaus Laurentii Alemannus. Alberti was the architect *inter alia* of the Pitti Palace in Florence and the church of San Francesco at Rimini.

First printed edition of the works of Plato in the Latin translation of Marsilio Ficino. Florence: Laurentius Venetus. It was completed before April 1485 and contains a dedication by Ficino to Lorenzo de' Medici.

First complete printed edition of the *Summa Theologica* of Thomas Aquinas (*c.* 1227–74). Basel: Michael Wenssler.

Antoine Vérard, among the most famous of early French booksellers and publishers, set up shop on the Pont Nôtre Dame at Paris. Calligrapher and miniaturist, he was one of the first to popularise the illustrated book. The earliest book in which his name appears is the *Horae B.V.M.* with the date 2 September, 1485. This is the first known *Horae* printed in France. Soon afterwards appeared Boccaccio, *Les Cent Nouvelles* (a translation of the *Decameron* by Laurent du Premier-Fait) dated 22 November, 1485, and probably printed by Jean Du Pré.

At Grenoble, Guy Marchant published Part I of *La danse macabre*, the first of a series of editions of the 'danse des Morts'. It is a book of 20 pages with 17 cuts, finished on 28 September, 1485. It was reprinted by Marchant at Paris in the following June as *Miroir salutaire pour toutes gens,* and in 1491 Marchant brought out the *Danse Macabre des Femmes.* Other editions were printed elsewhere. The only copy known of the 1485 edition is in the Bibliothèque de Grenoble.

The first publisher's device in a French book is that of the Angers bookseller Jean Alexandre in *Coutumes de Bretagne,* printed for him at Rouen by Martin Morin, 26 March 1484–85. It consists of a tree with three shields surrounded by a border bearing the motto *Laus Honor Virtus et Gloria.*

Guillaume Le Talleur introduced printing into Rouen. He is thought to have been the printer of the undated and unsigned *Prologue de l'entrée du Roi* [Charles VIII] probably printed in April 1485. (*See also* 1487.) He printed a number of books for the English market.

Printing introduced into Rennes by Pierre Bellescullée, whose first known book, completed 26 March, 1485, was the *Coutumes de Bretagne.* In 1486 he removed to Poitiers.

Printing introduced into Burgos by Friedrich Biel, who had previously been in partnership with Michael Wenssler at Basel. Biel became one of the finest printers in Spain.

The first printing from movable type in the island of Majorca was the *Tratados* of Jean Gerson, printed by Nicolai Calafau (Nicolas Calafat) at the cost of Rev. Bartolomé Caldenten. The book is dated 20 June, 1485. (The xylographic printing of a Bull is recorded as having been carried out in Majorca in 1480.)

The first printer's mark used in a book printed in England was that of the anonymous schoolmaster printer of St. Albans, and is found in the *Chronicle of England*, undated, but probably printed in 1485. The device consists of a double cross and orb with the arms of St. Albans.

First printed edition of Thomas Malory, *Le morte d'Arthur*. Westminster: William Caxton. The only perfect copy known is in the Pierpont Morgan Library, dated 31 July, 1485.

Peter Actors, a stationer and native of Savoy, was appointed Stationer to the King by Henry VII. Actors was succeeded in the post by William Faques who, since he was a printer, was given the official title of King's Printer.

1486

Editio princeps of Bernhard von Breydenbach, *Peregrinationes in Terram Sanctam*. Mainz: Erhard Reuwich. Folio. Breydenbach, a canon of Mainz cathedral, made a pilgrimage to the Holy Land (1483–84) and wrote his account of the journey with the help of the Dominican Martin Roth. Breydenbach had taken with him the Utrecht painter, Erhard Reuwich, and it was from the artist's sketches that the wood engravings which illustrate the book were made. Reuwich is named as the actual printer of the book, though the types used in it apparently belonged to Peter Schöffer. The most remarkable feature of this book are the seven large panoramas of Venice, Parenzo, Corfu, Modon, Crete, Rhodes and Jerusalem—in most cases the earliest printed views of these places. The book was highly successful, a German translation was issued in 1488 and various other editions and translations followed.

Erhardt Ratdolt, a native of Augsburg, returned there from Venice and set up his office first in the St. Katherinen-Viertel, and from 1507 in the Frauengraben. On 1 April, 1486, Ratdolt issued the earliest known type-specimen, which Updike believes to have been printed at Venice shortly before the printer left for Augsburg. The unique copy is in the Bavarian State Library at Munich. Ratdolt died in 1527 or 1528 at the age of 81.

At Ulm, Conrad Dinkmuth printed the *Eunuchus* of Terence with 14 striking woodcuts. In the same year he issued Thomas Lirer, *Schwäbischer Chronik*.

The first press at Stuttgart issued (after 16 February) *Erwählung Maximilians zu einem römischen Könige*. Unsigned, but printed with the material of Conrad Fyner.

The Archbishop of Mainz issued a mandate forbidding the translation into the vulgar tongue of Greek, Latin, and other books without the previous approbation of the university.

The first book wholly in Greek to be printed at Venice was a *Batrachomyomachia* printed by Laonicus Cretensis. It is remarkable for the enormous number of different sorts employed (at least 1,223) and is the only known book by this printer.

The earliest known example of a printed miniature book—the Latin *Horae* printed at Naples by Mathias Moravus. The text page measures $1\frac{3}{4}$ by $1\frac{1}{8}$ inches.

Joannes Rubeus Vercellensis, who began printing at Treviso (1480–85), and had printed one book at Venice in 1482, finally settled in the latter town in 1486. His name occurs for the last time in 1519.

Pierre Gérard, who introduced printing into Abbeville in 1486 with the *Somme Rurale* of Boutillier, began in the same year, in partnership with Jean Du Pré, St. Augustine, *La Cité De Dieu*, in two folio volumes. The beautiful plates were executed in Paris and were based on an illuminated manuscript belonging to the Bâtard de Bourgogne. The third and only other example of the work of this Abbeville press is *Le Livre des neufs preux*, also 1486, which contains a striking portrait of Bertrand du Guesclin, the first example of a woodcut portrait to appear in France.

The series of treatises on hawking, hunting and coat armour, known collectively as the *Book of St. Albans*, was printed by the unidentified printer of that town. The treatise on coat armour has the distinction of containing the first colour work in English printing.

The press of Theodoric Rood at Oxford closed down and there was no further printing in that city until 1517 at the earliest.

Stephen Arndes, a native of Hamburg, who had worked with Johann Neumeister at Foligno, 1470–81, went to Slesvig in 1486, where he printed in that year a *Missale Slesvicense*, one of the handsomest books printed in Denmark.

1487

In this year Pope Innocent VIII issued the first Papal Bull concerned with printers, and entitled *Bulla S.D.N. Innocentii contra Impressores Librorum Reprobatorum*.

The earliest known book with music printed extensively by wood block—Nicolaus Burtius,

Opusculum musices. Bologna: Ugo Rugerius for Benedictus Hectoris.

The first press at Prague was established by Jonata z Vysokého Mýta (Jonathan von Hohenmauth), who printed in that year a Psalter and a *Historia Trojanska.*

The New Testament was printed at Pilsen by an unknown press.

Jean du Pré (de Prato), after a brief collaboration with Nicolas Müller, alias Philippi, set up as a printer on his own account at Lyons. His first book, Guillermus, *Postilla,* was completed 30 November, 1487. His best work was an edition of the *Mer des hystoires* in 1491. (Not to be confused with the Paris printer of the same name.)

Guillaume Maynial of Paris printed a Sarum Missal for Caxton in which the latter's well-known printer's mark was used for the first time.

The first dated work printed at Rouen—the *Chroniques de Normandie* produced by Guillaume Le Talleur, a native of Rouen.

Printing first introduced into Murcia by Lope de la Roca in partnership with Gabriel Luis de Arinyo. The first book was an *Oracional* by Fernán Pérez de Guzmán.

The first book printed in Portugal of whose existence there is conclusive proof was a Pentateuch in Hebrew completed at Faro on the press of Don Samuel Porteira, 30 June, 1487. The press was financed by Don Samuel Gacon. Only one copy of this work is known to exist, the vellum copy in the British Museum. Haebler was in error when he mentioned a copy in the Bodleian Library.

1488

At Heidelberg, Heinrich Knoblochtzer printed what is probably the first edition of the *Totentanz.* It portrays thirty-eight persons of different stations in life overcome by Death. In each scene Death holds a different musical instrument.

Joshua Solomon Soncino produced the first printed Hebrew Bible. The family of German Jews surnamed Soncino from the town where they first printed, were the most distinguished of the early Jewish printers. They issued some 130 books in Hebrew founts.

Editio princeps of the Czech Bible. Prague: [Jan Kamp].

The first known use of Greek type in Holland is in Alexander de Villa Dei. *Doctrinale,* Pars I, printed at Deventer by Richard Pafraet and dated 9 August, 1488.

By letters patent, Charles VIII of France granted to printers the privileges enjoyed by members of the University of Paris.

The first book printed in France with copperplate illustrations, the French translation of Breydenbach's *Peregrinationes in Terram Sanctam* (*see* 1486), printed at Lyons by Michel Topié and Jacques Heremberck. The illustrations were copied from the Mainz edition, but instead of being cut on wood were engraved (same size) on metal. It was the fifth edition of this popular work, but the first in French.

Pierre Le Rouge, who printed first at Chablis, produced at Paris the first illustrated edition of *La Mer des Hystoires* in two folio volumes which he printed for Vincent Commin (July 1488 and February 1489). The book is translated from an epitome of legend and history called *Rudimentum Novitiorum* first printed at Lübeck in 1475. It is one of the most beautiful of French incunabula, embellished with hundreds of fine woodcuts, freely adapted from the Lübeck edition together with a variety of new material. The Le Rouges of Chablis were a family of scribes and illuminators who became printers.

The first verifiable date in connection with the French press of Philippe Pigouchet is that of the *Heures* (use of Rome) completed for Simon Vostre 16 September, 1488. The book was described by Brunet, but has since disappeared. The first extant book is Guido de Monte Rocherii, *Manipulus curatorum,* 22 September, 1489.

1489

At Hagenau, a printing office was established by Heinrich Gran, who printed some 250 books, mainly for the publisher, Johann Rymann.

First printed edition of the *Iliad* and *Odyssey* in Greek. Homer, *Opera.* Florence: Demetrius Damilas for Bernardus Nerlius. One of the handsomest editions of Homer ever printed.

Printing introduced into Capua by Christannus Preller, who later printed at Naples. His first work was a *Breviarum Capuanum* dated 10 March 1489.

A corrected reprint of the first Czech Bible (*see* 1488) was issued at Kuttenberg by Martin z Tišňova. This, and an undated *Aesop* were the first books printed in this town, about 40 miles from Prague.

First edition of François Villon, *Le Grant Testament et le Petit* . . . Paris: Pierre Levet. Only three copies are known.

The printer and bookseller, Wolfgang Hopyl, began business in Paris in the rue St. Jacques. He printed a number of books for the foreign market, including England. He died 1521.

The Rabbi Eliezer Toledano set up the first press in Lisbon, where he printed books in Hebrew characters until 1497. His first Lisbon book (and the second known book printed in Portugal) was Moses ben Nahman's *Commentary on the Pentateuch* (Perusch ha-Tora), issued in July, 1489.

1490

At Venice, Giovanni Ragazzo printed for Lucantonio di Giunta his remarkable edition of the *Biblia Vulgar Istoriata* in the Italian translation of Niccoló Malermi (*see* 1471), illustrated with no fewer than 386 woodcuts—210 in the Old Testament and 176 in the New. An edition with different illustrations was printed in 1493 by Guilelmus Anima Mia.

Running heads appear for the first time in the edition of Albertus Magnus, *Philosophia pauperum*, published at Brescia by Baptista Farfengus.

Stephanus Foreti (Etienne Foret) printed the first book at Grenoble—*Decisiones Parlamenti Dalphinalis per Guidonem Papae compilatae*, dated 29 April.

The first printer's mark used in Spain was probably that of Paulus (Pablo) Hurus of Zaragoza, in Diaz de Montalvo, *Ordenanzes Reales* (3 June, 1490), though it may possibly have been preceded by that of the Compañeros Alemanes (*see below*) at Seville, in Alfonso de Palencia, *Vocabulario universal*, which was printed sometime in 1490. The device of Hurus consists of two triangles, each with a letter *h* inside (for the brothers and partners Pablo and Juan) separated by a cross. That of the Compañeros consists of the initials P. I. M. T. (for the four partners) in a circle, together with their housemark.

Queen Isabella of Spain commissioned the printing of a Spanish dictionary, the first of a line of officially sponsored national dictionaries. This *Vocabulario universal en latin y en romance*, the work of A. de Palencia, was printed at Seville by 'Paulo de Colonia y socios'. This handsome book

was, in fact, the first production of a group of German printers who settled in Seville at the invitation of Ferdinand and Isabella, and called themselves the 'Cuatro Compañeros Alemanes'. They were Pablo de Colonia (whose name always comes first and was the director of the association), Johann Pegnizer of Nuremberg, Magno Herbst and Tomas Glockner. Their antecedents are unknown, but, from typographical evidence, Haebler concluded that they had worked previously in Venice. The last known book printed by them was Diego de San Pedro, *Carzel de Amor*, dated 3 March, 1492. In that year they also produced the first book with music printed in Spain, the *Lux Bella* of Domingo Marcos Durän.

At Pamplona, Arñao Guillén de Brocar issued his first known work—a Manual for Pamplona use, dated 15 December, 1490. The printed date, 'M.CCCC.XC xviij kal. ianuarij' is ambiguous, and Vindel takes it to mean 15 December, 1489. However, the *B.M.C.* remarks: 'In accordance with Proctor's assumption in such cases (Index, Pt. 1, p. 16) the date 15 December, 1490 is here taken to be intended.' The book is not recorded in Haebler.

An entry in the Churchwardens' Account of St. Margaret's, Westminster, runs:

Item, atte buryeing of Maude Caxton
    for torches & taperes   *iijs. iid.*

It is very probable that this was William Caxton's wife.

The first book printed in Copenhagen is said to have been a *Donatus*, now lost, printed by Govaert van Ghemen and issued in March 1490.

1491

Editio princeps of the Latin *Hortus Sanitatis*, the first book printed by Jacob Meydenbach at Mainz. A book of prime importance in the history of natural science, and illustrated with more than a thousand woodcuts of plants, animals, birds, fishes, and precious stones. It was, in fact, an enlarged edition in Latin of Schöffer's *Gart der Gesundheyt* (1485).

At Nuremberg, Anton Koberger issued *Schatzbehalter der wahren Reichtümer des Heils*, a religious treatise very popular in the Middle Ages. It contains many full-page woodcuts by Michael Wohlgemuth.

Printing introduced into Hamburg by Johann Borchard, in association with his brother Thomas.

Johann Froben (1460–1527) opened his printing office at Basel and issued the first octavo Latin Bible. It was Froben's first dated book and probably his first production.

The first Greek printing in Belgium occurred in Alexander de Villa Dei, *Doctrinale Pars II*, printed by Thierry Martens at his Alost press and dated 6 September, 1491. (*See* G. D. Painter: 'The first Greek printing in Belgium' in the *Gutenberg Jahrbuch*, 1960.)

Printing introduced into Dijon by Pierre Metlinger, who had already printed at Besançon (1487–88) and at Dôle (1490). The first book he printed at Dijon was *Collectio privilegiorum ordinis Cisterciensis*.

First known book printed at Angoulême (Charente) was *Auctores octo* edited by Foucaud Monier and printed by Petrus Alanus and Andreas Calvinus.

The history of east Slav printing begins in principle at Cracow, with the year 1491, when the Augsburg bookseller Johann Haller paid for the printing of several books which he hoped to sell to the clergy of the Orthodox Church in Poland and Russia. He engaged as printer Swietopek Fiol (Sweybold Veyl, Szwaipolt Fieol, etc.), who came from a German family long established in Poland. He printed five works in Cyrillic characters, the punches for which were cut by a Brunswick engraver, Rudolf Borsdorf. The books in question were the eight-part Choral book (*Oktoich*), a Psalter, the *Triod' Postnaja*, the *Triod' Cvetnaja*, and the *Horologion*. The venture was not a success, for, in January 1492, the Catholic clergy forbade the printing of books in Cyrillic destined for a rival Church.

The first Westminster title-page appears in one of Wynkyn de Worde's earliest and undated books—the *Chastysing of goddes Chyldern*, printed probably towards the end of 1491. It takes the form of a descriptive title printed in three lines in the middle of the first recto.

About this year, though undated, appeared the octavo volume of prayers printed by Caxton and called the *Fifteen O's*, from the fifteen prayers each beginning with 'O'. It is the only book known of Caxton's that is ornamented with woodcut borders.

In this year, though the exact date is unknown, died William Caxton. His burial is recorded in the parish accounts of St. Margaret's, Westminster:

Item. atte Buryeing of William Caxton for iiij torches	*vijs. viijd.*
Item for the belle atte same bureying	*vid.*

1492

The first known printing with Greek type in France occurs in a Virgil, *Opera*, finished at Lyons by Antoine Lambillion on 5 November, 1492. It was used almost simultaneously in the same town in Jodocus Badius, *Silvae morales*, finished on 14 November by Johann Trechsel.

Jean Petit (Parvus, Pusillus) set up in Paris as bookseller-publisher in the rue St. Jacques. For some thirty-five years he was one of the most important Paris publishers and had many printers working for him. He was the founder of a family of publishers which continued for almost a century.

Henry VII appointed Quintin Poulet of Lille as the first recorded Keeper of the Royal Library.

At Leiria, Portugal, a Hebrew press was set up under the direction of Samuel de Ortas and his son Abraham, and continued until 1496. The Hebrew types used are thought to have been the work of Abraham de Ortas. Only four works from this press seem to have survived. (*See* 1496.)

1493

Publication of the *Liber Chronicarum* of Hartmann Schedel, commonly known as the 'Nuremberg Chronicle', Nuremberg: Anton Koberger. This compendium of history, geography and natural wonders is a large folio of just over 300 leaves with 65–66 lines to the page, and contains 1,809 illustrations from 645 woodcuts, some of which do multiple duty. Most of the cuts were by Michel Wohlgemuth and Wilhelm Pleydenwurff. German translation by Georg Alt issued in the same year.

The first printing at Urbino was Tancredus de Corneto, *Summa quaestionum compendiosa*, signed and dated 15 May, 1493, and printed by Henricus de Colonia.

The first edition of the Gospels in the Croatian tongue was printed in the Latin alphabet at Venice and signed by Damianus Gorgonzola of Milan. The actual originator of this work was the Croat Bernadin Splićanin (Bernard of Spoleto), while the real editor and publisher is thought to have been the Croat prebendary Blaž Baromić of Senj, who later set up a press in that town.

First printing at Cagliari, and first in Sardinia.

On October 1, Salvador de Bologna completed there a book in Catalan, the *Speculum ecclesiae* of Hugo de S. Caro.

First edition of *Der Ritter vom Turn*. Basel: Johann Bergmann von Olpe. This German translation of the original by the Chevalier de Latour de Landry, was illustrated by an unknown artist who has been identified by some with the young Dürer.

The first book printed at Lausanne—*Missale ad usum Lausannensem*, printed by Jean Bellot.

The Dutch printer Gerard Leeu was killed at Antwerp by one of his workmen during the course of a quarrel. He had printed more than 200 incunabula since he began printing in 1477 in Gouda. His last book was an edition of the *Chronicles of England*.

At Lyons Johann Trechsel printed the *Comoediae* of Terence. This was the first illustrated Terence, as well as being the first printed book to contain illustrations of a theatrical performance. Arthur M. Hind calls this work, 'the high-water mark of book illustration at Lyons in the XVth century'.

The letter of Christopher Columbus to Gabriel Sanchez announcing the discovery of America (or the Indies as Columbus thought), was printed in the original Spanish at Barcelona before the middle of April 1493, without date or place but in the type of Pedro Posa. This 2-leaf folio was followed by a quarto edition of 4 leaves printed probably at Naples before the end of April. A Latin translation was printed four times in the same year.

The first press in Montenegro was set up in the castle of Obod by Prince George Tsernoievitj (another version says in the monastery at Cetinje). It was directed by the monk Makarije (Hieromonachos Makarios), who printed an *Octoechus*, completed in 1494, in Glagolitic characters.

1494

Stephan Arndes of Hamburg, who settled at Lübeck in 1488, printed a Low Saxon Bible with cuts which show some improvement upon those in previous German Bibles.

Editio princeps of Sebastian Brant, *Das Narrenschiff* (Ship of Fools). Basel: Johann Bergmann von Olpe. This work, illustrated with 114 woodcuts, gained instantaneous popularity, and imitations of the Basel edition were printed and circulated all over Germany. In 1497, Bergmann published a Latin edition by Jacob Locher, and three French and two English versions had appeared before 1509. The engravers of the cuts are not known.

Johann Amerbach published at Basel the *Liber de scriptoribus ecclesiasticis* by Johann Tritheim (1462–1516), Abbot of Spanheim. This book, which lists about a thousand theological writers and their works, was the first specialised bibliography.

The first confirmable date for printing at Tours. In this year Simon Pourcelet printed a Breviary for local use.

The first edition in Spanish of Bartolomaeus Anglicus, *El libro de proprietatibus*, translated by Vicente de Burgos, was printed at Toulouse by the itinerant German printer Heinrich Mayer and dated 18 September, 1494.

1495

The only known product of the press of the Cistercian monastery at Zinna, near Magdeburg, dates from about 1495. It was the *Novum Psalterium* of Hermann Nitzschewitz, printed at the expense of the Emperor Frederick III and his son Maximilian (afterwards Emperor) whose kneeling figure can be seen in every border. It was printed after 19 August, 1493 (date of Frederick's death), and before 1496, the date recorded by the rubricator of the Bodleian copy. There are 2 full-page cuts and 166 smaller ones. The type was previously used by Conrad Kachelofen at Leipzig.

Death of Hans Bämler, the third Augsburg printer.

Thomas Anshelm of Baden-Baden introduced printing into Pforzheim with an Almanac for 1496. He worked there until March, 1511.

In February, Aldo Manuzio (Aldus Manutius) (1450–1515), obtained from the Venetian government a monopoly privilege for his Greek type. In March, appeared his first Greek book, the Lascaris *Erotemata*, or Greek grammar, followed in the same year by first editions in Greek of Musaeus, *Hero and Leander*, and Theodorus Prodromus, *Galeomyomachia*. In the same year he brought out Pietro Bembo, *De Ætna*, in one of the most satisfactory roman founts ever made, which stood model for the Monotype 'Bembo'. It was cut by Francesco Griffo of Bologna, who also designed Aldo's 'Polifilo' type and the italics which won fame in the popular series of classical authors in pocket size. From this time onwards punchcutters establish themselves as independent tradesmen.

An astrological book, Antonio Manilio, *Pronosticon dialogale*, was the one and only book printed at Cesena, Italy, in the fifteenth century. The printers, Paulus Guarinus and Joannes Jacobus de Benedictis, who completed this book on 26 March, 1495, left shortly afterwards for Forlí, where they printed Nicolaus Ferettus, *Commentariola isagogica de ordine et junctura compositionis ornatae*. This was so poorly executed that a second and much better edition was issued a few weeks later, on 25 May, 1495, by an otherwise unknown printer called Hieronymus Medesanus. Thus two presses were set up at Forlí in that year.

Giustiniano de Rubiera set up his press in Bologna, where he worked until at least 1532.

The Canons Regular of the monastery of St. Michael in Den Hem near Schoonhoven started printing with an edition of a *Breviarium Trajectense*.

The earliest Greek printing in Paris is contained in the Gregorius *Moralia in Job*. It occurs merely as two type-set words in Gering and Rembolt's device. The first occurrence of Greek printing in Paris in the text of a book is in Perottus, *Cornucopiae*, printed by Gering and Rembolt in 1496. The 1494 edition of this work mentioned by Brunet is not known to be extant and is probably a 'ghost'.

First appearance in print of Erasmus, with a letter prefaced to Robert Gaguin, *Compendium de origine et gestis Francorum*. Paris: Pierre le Dru.

In 1495, or early in 1496, Wynkyn de Worde printed Bartholomaeus Anglicus, *De proprietatibus rerum*, in the English translation of John of Trevisa. The colophon of this book divulges the fact that Caxton had worked on the undated Cologne edition of this book, and also tells us that the paper was made by John Tate the Younger, who had the Sele mill in Hertfordshire.

The first printed book in the Danish language was a rhymed chronicle, *Danske Rimkrønike* printed at Copenhagen by Govaert van Ghemen, a Dutchman from Gouda.

The first book in Swedish, the *Bok af Djäfvulsens frästilse* (Temptation of the Devil), by Jean Gerson, was printed by Johannes Fabri at

CCP

Stockholm. Fabri had been assistant to Bartholomaeus Gothan and succeeded to his business. This is not, however, the first printing in Swedish, for he had printed an indulgence in that language in 1490.

The first incunable in the Portuguese language: Ludolphus de Saxonia, *De Vita Christi*, translated by Fr. Bernardo de Alcobaza and Fr. Nicolau Vieira. Lisbon: Valentim Fernandez (Valentinus de Moravia) e Nicolau de Saxonia. Four volumes. Ludolphus de Saxonia (*c.* 1300–*c.* 1370) was Prior of the Carthusian monastery at Strassburg. Deslandes, in his *Documentos para a Historia de Typographia Portugueza nos seculos XVI e XVII* (1888), calls it 'one of the typographical marvels of the fifteenth century'.

1496

The first known book to contain printing from movable type to indicate measured music was *Lart et Instruction de bien dancer*. [Paris] Michel de Toulouze. A facsimile edition, edited by Victor Scholderer, was printed for the Royal College of Physicians, London, in 1936. The college possesses a unique copy of the original edition, under the colophon of which is written the date 1488. According to Dr. Scholderer, however, the actual date of printing is more likely to have been around 1496.

Printing was started at Granada by Meinard Ungut and Johann Pegnitzer with Francisco Jiménez, *Vita Christi*.

The first known book printed by Julian Notary was an edition of the *Questiones Alberti de modis significandi*, published in London 'at St. Thomas the Apostle's' in association with the Rouen stationer Jean Huvin and John Barbour of Coventry.

Publication of the *Almanach Perpetuum* of Abraham ben Samuel Zacuto. Leiria: Samuel de Ortas. This is the only Portuguese incunabulum printed in Gothic letters to be issued from a Hebrew press. It is said to have been the book that Columbus used to predict the eclipse of the moon to the terrified natives of Jamaica.

1497

First edition of Hieronymus Brunschwig, *Das Buch der Cirurgia*. Strassburg: Johann Grüninger. This was the earliest important work on surgery in German. It has 48 woodcuts.

The *Terence* printed at Venice by Simon de Luere for L. Soardis, with cuts in a classic style based on those of Trechsel's edition of 1493, is remarkable for the two full-page frontispieces, Terence and his Commentators in a Classic Hall, and the Performance in a Theatre. The designs were recut for the editions of Girolamo Scotto (Venice, 1545) and Roigny (Paris, 1552).

At Paris Johann Higman and Wolfgang Hopyl printed a Missal for Utrecht use—one of the relatively small number of French music incunabula.

Pierre Rohault, a Lyons printer, and probably a former pressman of Jean Du Pré introduced printing into Avignon in partnership with Michel Riczeau and Ricard le Gentilhomme. His first dated but unsigned book is a collection of Latin texts for schools known as *Luciani Palinurus*, dated 15 October, 1497. The book was financed by the Avignon merchant Nicolas Tepe, and the promoter of the enterprise and compiler and editor of the texts was a pedagogue named Gellio Bernardino Marmita, of Parma.

1498

At Tübingen, the first press was set up by Johann Otmar, who had printed at Reutlingen from 1482 to 1495. The first book from Otmar's Tübingen press was Paulus Scriptor, *Lectura in Johannem Duns Scotum super libro primo Sententiarum*, dated 24 March, 1498.

The Aldine Press at Venice issued the first catalogue of its publications: *Haec sunt graecorum voluminum nomina quae in Thermis Aldi Romani Venetiis impressa sunt ad usque diem s. primum Octobris M.IID.*

The Carmelite, F. Battista Mantovano (1448–1516), published his *Bucolica seu adolescentia in decem eglogas divisa* (Mantua: Vincentius Bertochus), of which more than 300 editions were published during the century following the *editio princeps*. This was the 'good old Mantuan' mentioned by Shakespeare.

Ottaviano Petrucci of Fossombrone (who had arrived in Venice c. 1491) was granted a patent by the Signoria of Venice granting him the exclusive right of printing music for voices, organ and lute. He worked in Venice until 1511, when he returned to Fossombrone. He was the first to design a music type for mensural notation which fitted together sufficiently well to allow of perfect registration of the notes on the stave. (*See also* 1501.)

First edition of the complete works of Cicero printed at Milan by the brothers Le Signerre in four volumes folio. 1498–99.

Printing began in Schiedam with Johannes Brugman, *Vita S. Lidwinae* by an unknown printer, possibly Otgier Nachtegael.

The first printer at Pilsen whose name we know was Mikuláš Bakalar, or Nicholas the Bachelor. A Roman Catholic printer, he maintained his press there until 1513. (*See also* 1476.)

The first dated edition bearing the name of Thielman Kerver as printer is Diomedes, *De arte grammatica*, printed by him for Jean Petit and completed at Paris 26 May, 1498.

At Paris, Antoine Vérard published (undated but probably 1498) the first edition of his successful *Bible Historiée*, translated from the Latin of Pierre le Mangeur (Peter Comestor) by Guyart Des Moulins.

Nicolas Wolf, born at Lutter in the Duchy of Brunswick, set up his printing office at Lyons, where he is first recorded in 1493 as type-founder. He was one of the earliest recorded type-founders and before setting up his own business as a printer applied himself exclusively to type-founding. Among his clients were Neumeister, Balsarin, Klein, Trechsel, De Vingle and Du Pré.

Julian Notary moved his printing office to King Street, Westminster, where he printed a Sarum Missal, the first edition printed in England, for Wynkyn de Worde.

1499

At Cologne, Johann Kölhoff the younger printed the *Cronica van der hilliger stat van Coellen*. It contains a reference to Gutenberg in the account of the origins of the art of printing said to have been told to the author by Ulrich Zell, Cologne's first printer, who calls Gutenberg, 'der eyrste vynder der druckerye' (fol. cccxii, line 18). This Cologne *Chronicle* contains 371 woodcut illustrations, but the book was confiscated and banned by the authorities. Kölhoff was exiled, and died in 1502.

Printing was introduced into Danzig by Conrad Baumgarten, who completed there a Donatus, *Ars minor*, before 10 June.

Editio princeps of Francesco Colonna, *Hypnerotomachia Poliphili*. Venice: Aldo Manuzio. This curious dream-allegory is remarkable for its delightful illustrations in the Venetian classical style, but strangely enough the artist has never been identified. It was the only book of Aldo issued with numerous illustrations, and was printed in Francesco Griffo's third roman fount. (A magnificent collotype facsimile of this work was issued in 1963 by the Eugrammia Press, with an introduction by George D. Painter.)

At Venice, the press of the Cretan Zacharias Callierges produced for the wealthy bookseller Nicolaus Blastus, during the years 1499 and 1500, four Greek books set in a cursive type which differed from the Aldine Greeks in having accents cast in one piece with the letters. The first of these books was the *Etymologicum* completed 8 July, 1499. Callierges ceased to print at Venice in 1500, possibly owing to the death of his patron. His name does not appear again until 1509.

The printer Josse Bade (1462–1535), a native of Asch, near Brussels, established himself in Paris, where he worked as printer, publisher, engraver and founder. One of his daughters married Robert Estienne.

In *La grāt danse macabre* printed at Lyons by Mathias Huss occurs the earliest known illustration of a printing press.

At Toledo, Pedro Hagembach printed a *Missale Mixtum* (a Mozarabic Missal). This Missal was first printed at Venice in 1488, but the errors in it were so numerous that it never received Papal approval, and the copy eventually printed by Hagembach was corrected by order of Cardinal Ximenez de Cisneros. Hagembach's edition is a superb example of sumptuous liturgical printing.

At Burgos, Fadrique de Basilea printed the *editio princeps* of Fernando de Rojas, *Celestina*.

1500

At Leipzig, Wolfgang Stöckel, who printed in that city from 1495 to 1526, printed the first book with a complete title-page, giving subject title, name of publisher, name of printer, and date and place of printing.

The first use of italic type occurs in *Epistole Devotissime da Sancta Catharina da Siena*. Venice: Aldus. St. Catharine is shown in the only woodcut holding an open book bearing a short text set in italic. The woodcut is in the style of those illustrating the *Hypnerotomachia* (1499).

The earliest and probably the only work printed at Sursee, in the canton of Lucerne, is a rhyming chronicle of the Swabian wars by Nikolaus Schradin. This war decided the separation of the

Swiss Confederacy from the Holy Roman Empire. The printer is unknown.

The *Adagia* of Erasmus first published at Paris by Johann Philipp.

Printing was introduced into Perpignan by Joannes Rosenbach, the Barcelona printer, with a Breviary, the colophon of which states that it was printed by him 'in nobilissimo opido celtiberie perpiniani'.

The splendid Sarum Missal printed by Richard Pynson at the cost of Cardinal John Morton was finished on 10 January. This 'Morton Missal' remains one of the finest specimens of early printing in England. It was also the earliest book with music printed in England, printed from type in Roman notation by double impression.

At London, Julian Notary printed one of the earliest miniature books, a 64mo *Horae ad usum Sarum*, of which only 16 pages exist in the form of a half-sheet (i–k) now in the Public Library at Victoria, Australia. The printed page measures 1 by $1\frac{3}{8}$ inches. The colophon, which survives, gives the date as 2 April, 1500.

After having printed at least a hundred books at Westminster, Wynkyn de Worde moved from Caxton's old printing-house and settled in Fleet Street, at the sign of the Sun.

1501

First printed edition of the works of Hrosvita, nun of the Benedictine Abbey of Gandersheim, and the first German woman playwright. Among the artists who illustrated the book are Wolf Traut and probably Dürer. Nuremberg: Printer for the Sodalitas Celtica [F. Peypus ?].

Beginning of the famous series of octavo classics printed by Aldo Manuzio in the italic type designed by Francesco (Griffo) da Bologna, who later founded a press of his own in his native city. The first book in which the Aldine italic was used at length was the 8vo *Virgil* of April 1501. (*For first use, see* 1500.) Despite the fact that this new type had been granted an exclusive privilege both from the Venetian Senate and the Vatican, it was soon pirated, both in France and Italy, and at Lyons not only was the Virgil counterfeited, but the Aldine device also.

Petrucci printed his famous work *Harmonicae Musices Odhecaton* at Venice. It was printed by triple impression—first the staves, secondly the text, and thirdly the notes. Petrucci, born 1466 at Fossombrone, printed at least forty-three musical works, the last of them in 1520, when he took over a paper-mill near his native town. (*See* 1511.)

1502

Martin Tretter established the first press at Frankfurt an der Oder. He printed two books there before going to Danzig, where he worked from 1505 until about 1520.

After printing at Brescia and at Barco (1491–97), the Jewish scholar-printer Gershom Soncino settled at Fano in 1501 and began printing there in 1502. (*See also* 1507.)
Aldo Manuzio edited and printed at Venice the *editio princeps* in Greek of the *Historiae* of the father of history, Herodotus.

Jacob Cromberger founded one of the most celebrated presses in Seville.

First edition of Marco Polo's Travels in Portuguese—*Marco paulo. no livro de Nycolao veneto.* Lisbon: Valentim Fernandes.

1503

Editio princeps of the *Margarita philosophica* of Gregorius Reisch, Prior of the Carthusian monastery at Freiburg, printed in that city by Johann Schott. It was an attempt to summarise in one volume the whole then university course.
Nikolaus Marschalk, who had earlier printed at Erfurt, set up the first press at Wittenberg.

Peter Schöffer died at Mainz after 20 December, 1502, but before 8 April, 1503.

The first book which can be definitely attributed to the press of Filippo di Giunta at Florence is an edition of the works of Catullus, Propertius, and Tibullus dated 5 August, 1503. Previously two Greek books had been printed for him in 1497 and 1500 respectively, probably by Benedictus Ricardinus.

First edition in Spanish of Marco Polo's travels, *Libro de Marco Polo veneciano*, printed at Seville by Jacob Cromberger and Ladislaus Polono.

About this year, the Jew David Nachmias and his son Samuel left Spain and went to Constantinople, where they set up a press, and there in 1505 they printed an edition of the Pentateuch. They were soon followed by other Jewish printers, including the wandering printer Rabbi Gershom-Soncino (d. 1530).

1504

Amerigo Vespucci, *Mundus Novus*. Augsburg: Johann Otmar. The first and only dated edition of Vespucci's report to Lorenzo de' Medici on his second and third voyages to the New World in 1499 and 1501–02.

Henri I Estienne printed the *Ethics* of Aristotle in the Latin version of Aretinus. This was the first book issued by Estienne bearing his sole imprint (he had previously been associated with Wolfgang Hopyl), and so becomes the earliest publication of a dynasty of printers whose activity continued for a century and a half.

In England, William Faques, a native of Normandy, was appointed King's Printer the first to hold this position, as we learn from his *Statutes of An. XIX Hen. VII* printed in this year. He was then working at St. Helen's, near Bishopsgate Street, but later moved to Abchurch Lane. He died about 1508, in which year Richard Pynson was appointed to the post.

1505

First German translation of the works of Livy was printed at Mainz by Johann Schöffer, son of Peter Schöffer, Fust's partner. He took over the business after Peter's death in 1503. The colophon of the book states how the art of printing was invented in the year 1450, after which it was, 'improved and perfected by the perseverance, expense and labour of Johann Fust and Peter Schöffer'. The book, which has 214 woodcuts, was reprinted seven times before the firm closed down in 1559.
Printing introduced into Braunschweig (Brunswick) by Hans Dorn who worked there until around 1525.

Aldo Manuzio, having been freed by the Pope from his vow to become a priest, married Maria Torresano, the daughter of the printer Andrea Torresano of Asola, who entered into partnership with his son-in-law in 1508. The wedding took place probably in February or early March. A letter from Alberto Carpi to Aldo dated 11 March, 1505, regrets he was unable to come to the wedding 'at this carnival time'. (*See* Mario Ferrigni: *Aldo Manuzio*, 1925.)

At Vienna the brothers Leonhard and Lukas Alantse founded a publishing firm which soon became widely known.

At Toul, in France, printing was introduced by Pierre Jacobi.

The German Johann Haller from Rothenburg set up the first permanent press in Poland at Cracow.

1506

Raffaello Maffei of Volterra (1451–1522) published his *Commentarii Urbani*. This encyclopaedia, which was printed eight times up to 1603, is remarkable for the importance it gives to geography, and also to biography, a subject not included in previous encyclopaediae. Rome: Joannes Besicken.

Johann Schäffler became the first printer at Constance, where he worked until 1527.

The first dated book printed at Amsterdam, *Een wandelinghe der kersten menschen mit Jhesu*. It bears the date of completion 18 December, though the year is given in error 'M.CCCCCC ende vi'. (1606 instead of 1506). The type is that of the punch-cutter Hendrick Lettersnijder of Rotterdam.

For the first edition of the *Kalender of Shepherdes* issued in England, Richard Pynson borrowed most of the blocks used by Vérard in 1503. Editions of this work were printed in England by Wynkyn de Worde (1508) and Julian Notary (c. 1518).

1507

At Augsburg, the Benedictine calligrapher Leonhard Wagner began work on his *Proba centum scripturarum*. This book was dedicated to the Emperor Maximilian and includes the written model for the new Fraktur which was seen in print for the first time in 1513 in the *Liber Horarum ad Usum Ordinis Sancti Georgii (q.v.)*.

At Augsburg, Erhard Öglin, the first follower of Petrucci in Germany, cut notes on the same plan as the Venetian printer, though they lack the delicacy of the latter's types. In 1507 he published Petrus Tritonius, *Melopoiae sive Harmoniae*, consisting of twenty-two pieces for four voices.

At Rome, Bernardinus Venetus de Vitalibus printed Claudius Ptolemaeus (Ptolemy), *Geographia*. This edition contains 34 copper-plates, including the world map by Joannes Ruysch, among the earliest printed maps showing the New World.

Gershom Soncino, after printing for some five years at Fano, established a press at Pesaro, and by the end of 1514 had issued more than forty books from there. (*See also* 1502.)

Gilles de Gourmont, first cutter of Greek type in France, issued the first work to be printed in Greek from his Paris press. It contained the *Book of Sentences of the Seven Greek Sages*, the *Golden Verses* of Pythagoras, etc. He also printed an *Alphabetum Hebraicum et Graecum*.

The geographer Martin Waldseemüller published at St. Dié, his *Cosmographiæ Introductio*, in which the name Amerige, or America, for the New World was first suggested.

The first privilege recorded in France was that granted in 1507 by Louis XII to Antoine Vérard for his edition of the *Epîtres de Saint Paul*.

1508

In this year Aldo Manuzio entered into partnership with his father-in-law, Andrea Torresano, and their first joint work was the Letters of Pliny the Younger, dated November 1508. (*See* 1505.)

First recorded edition of the famous romance of chivalry, *Amadis de Gaula*. Saragossa: Georgi Coci Aleman (Jorge Coci). There are grounds for thinking that an edition may have been printed in 1496, but no copy of it is known. *Amadis* was a sixteenth-century 'best seller' and was translated into many languages.

Andrew Myllar, with the financial assistance of the merchant Walter Chepman, established the first press in Scotland at Edinburgh. The first pamphlets he printed were a series of ballads including Chaucer's *Maying and Disporte*.

First printing in Rumania, at Tirgoviste, where Makarie printed the Slavonic *Liturgiarion*.

1509

At Venice Paganinus de Paganinis printed Luca Paccioli, *De Divina Proportione*, which contains a chapter on the construction of capital letters. The theories of Leonardo da Vinci, with whom the artist and designer Paccioli worked in Milan, are presumed to have formed the basis for these constructions.

Richard Pynson introduced roman type into England, first using it to print a speech by the Papal Nuncio, Petrus Gryphus. In the same year he combined roman and black letter in a folio edition of *The Ship of Fools* translated by Alexander Barclay from Sebastian Brant's *Narrenschiff*.

The *Aberdeen Breviary* was printed at the expense of Walter Chepman. It came from the Chepman and Myllar press (*see* 1508), but the colophon mentions only Chepman; Myllar may have died before its completion.

The first known printer in York was Hugo Goes, who printed in the Steengate an edition of the York *Directorium*, 1509. He may have been related to the Antwerp printer Matthias van der Goes.

1510

At Erfurt Sebaldus Striblita was the first German printer to use italic.

H. Vietor, who had served his apprenticeship at Cracow under Johannes Haller, set up his own press at Vienna, and in 1510 he printed the first edition of Walafrid Strabo, *Hortulus*. The editor, Joachim Vadianus, had discovered the poem in a manuscript at St. Gall.

Johann Singriener from Öttingen in Bavaria settled at Vienna, where he printed from 1510 to 1545 (for the first four years in partnership with Hieronymus Vietor). He was a type-founder and printed books in French, Greek and Hebrew as well as German and Latin. His mark was a lion bearing two printer's ink balls.

Florian Ungler began to print at Cracow with an *Almanach ad annum 1511* by Stanislaus Aurifaber.

About this year Claude Garamond was apprenticed to the Paris punch-cutter and printer Antoine Augereau (*see also* 1534), who, with Simon de Colines, was one of the first to cut punches for the roman character which gradually replaced the gothic 'black letter'.

Death of Ulrich Gering (*see* 1470), who left a large bequest to the Sorbonne.

A printing press was established at Uppsala by Pawel Grijs, the first printer of Swedish birth. His first book was a *Psalterium* (1510) for the diocese of Uppsala.

1511

Publication at Nuremberg of Albrecht Dürer's three great woodcut books (text by Hieron. Höltzel)—the *Apocalypse of Saint John*, the *Great Passion*, and the *Life of the Virgin*. They were issued with the colophon 'impressum Nurmberge per Albertum Durer pictorem'.

Printing first carried out at Frankfurt-am-Main by Beatus Murner who worked in the monastery of the Discalced Carmelites 1511 to 1512. The first regular printer in this city was Christian Egenolff, who worked there from 1530 to 1555, and his heirs until 1605.

By May, 1511, Ottaviano Petrucci, pioneer of music printing with movable types, had transferred his press from Venice to his native town of Fossombrone. His first production there, dated 10 May, 1511, was a collection of songs with lute accompaniment by Francisco Bossinensis. (*See* 1497: 1501.)

At Paris Gilles de Gourmont published the brilliant satire on universal folly, the *Moriae encomium* of Desiderius Erasmus. It was written during Erasmus's stay in England, at the house of Sir Thomas More.

1512

The earliest engraved title-page appeared in the *Purifica della conscientia* of Thomas Aquinas, printed at Florence.

Bauldrain Dacquin became the first printer at Hesdin, in Artois.

First complete edition of *El Cid*. Burgos: Fadrique Aleman.

About the year 1512 Judah Ghedaliah set up a press at Salonika.

At Targowitz the first book was printed in Old Bulgarian, an edition of the *Gospels*.

1513

The earliest example of true Fraktur, one of the most popular type-faces in Germany, appeared in *Liber Horarum ad usum Ordinis Sancti Georgii* printed at Augsburg by Johann Schönsperger, and compiled under the direction of the Emperor Maximilian I for the use of the Order of St. George, formed in 1469 for the defence of Christendom against the Turks. Among the famous artists whose work decorated this book were Albrecht Dürer, Hans Burgkmair, Lucas Cranach, Hans Baldung Grein, and Jörg Breu. (*See also* 1507.)

At Strassburg, Johann Schott published the most important early edition of Ptolemy's *Cosmographia*, with 27 woodcut maps of the ancient world and 20 based on contemporary knowledge.

It includes Tabula Terrae Novae, the first map specially drawn to show the New World. (*See* 1507.)

At Frankfurt appeared the first edition of Eucharius Rösslin, *Der Swangern frawen und hebammen Roszgarten*, the oldest printed handbook for midwives. Rösslin's son translated the work into Latin as *De partu hominis et quae circa ipsum accidunt* (Frankfurt, 1532), and from this version was made the French translation by Bienassis (1536), and the English one by Richard Jonas, 1540 (*q.v.*). More than 100 editions of the work were published.

Death of the great printer-publisher Anton Koberger of Nuremberg, who had at one time employed twenty-four presses and a staff of over a hundred persons. He was the greatest entrepreneur among printers until the time of Plantin, and had factors in all the important cities of Europe.

First use of Ethiopic type in Potken, *Psalterium Aethiopicum*. Rome: M. Silber.

The first printed edition of *Ausonius* [issued at Paris], by Josse Bade, has on its title-page a representation of part of the interior of an early printing office, showing a pressman and compositor. The cross-beam of the press bears the words *Prelū Ascēsianū*.

The earliest surviving English news-pamphlet, *The Trewe Encountre*—undated, but published shortly after the battle of Flodden, 9 September, 1513, of which it gives an eyewitness account.

1514

Printing intrdoduced into Speyer by Jakob Schmidt, who worked there until *c.* 1536.

Arabic type first used in the *Kitab Selat el Scoua'i* (Book of [Christian] Prayers) printed at Fano by G. de Gregoriis.

Between 1514 and 1517 Arnão Guillén de Brocar printed at Alcalá de Henares (in Latin, *Complutum*) the first of the great Polyglot Bibles. This six-volume folio Bible was produced under the patronage and at the expense of Cardinal Francisco Ximenez de Cisneros (1436–1517), Archbishop of Toledo. The languages employed in this Bible (often referred to as the *Complutensian Polyglot*) were Latin, Greek, Hebrew and Chaldee.

1515

At Venice, died Aldo Manuzio. His father-in-law Andrea Torresano carried on the business on behalf of Aldo's young children.

Hans Holbein the Younger settled at Basel and in this year cut his first title-border for Froben.

Simon Bevilacqua, after printing in several places in Italy, finally established his press at Lyons.

At Cracow, Florian Ungler and Wolfgang Lern printed the first book entirely in Polish—*Raj duszny*, a *Hortulus animae* by Biernat of Lublin.

About 1515, Wynkyn de Worde issued the first (undated) English translation of the *Imitatio Christi*.

1516

At Cologne, Eucharius Cervicornus (Hirtzhorn) began his printing career.

Martin Luther published his first book at Wittenberg—an introduction to the *Theologia Deutsch*, printed by Johann Rau Grunenberg.

Francesco Griffo, known from his birthplace as Francesco da Bologna, founded a press in his native city and in September 1516, issued the first of a series of pocket-size Italian and Latin classics, *Canzionere et triomphi di messer Francesco Petrarcha*. Dated September 20, 1516, it bears the imprint 'Stampato in Bologna per Il Discretto huomo Maestro Francesco da Bologna'. It is printed in minute italic. Six works were printed by this press between that date and 14 January, 1517, after which it seems to have ceased work. We know that Francesco da Bologna was involved in a fatal quarrel in the course of which his son-in-law was killed. Although the fate of Francesco is not recorded, it is thought likely that he was executed some time in 1518. (*See also* 1501.)

Editio princeps of the *Orlando Furioso* of Ludovico Ariosto. Ferrara: Giovanni Mazocco dal Bondeno. This edition, like all those before 1532, has forty cantos. The first definitive version, with forty-six cantos, was printed in Ferrara in 1532 by Francesco Rosso da Valenza.

The earliest purely musical work, *Liber quindecim Missarum* was printed at Rome by Andreas Antiquus de Montona. It contains compositions by Joaquin de Près and others.

At Genoa, Peter Paul Porrus printed a polyglot Psalter, the first to be printed with the characters of each language. This *Psalterium Hebreum*,

Grecum, Arabicum et Chaldeum has Latin glosses for the Hebrew and Chaldee, and a commentary by Justinianus (Agostino Giustiniano), Bishop of Nebbio. (The long note on Psalm XIX contains a biographical notice on Columbus, the earliest bibliographical reference to the great navigator.)

Appearance at Rome of the earliest recorded work of the famous printer Antonio Blado of Asola, *Mirabilia urbis Romae*, dated 21 November, 1516.

Earliest printed edition of the New Testament in Greek. Basel: J. Froben. The text was prepared under the editorship of Desiderius Erasmus, with Greek and Latin in parallel columns. Although a Greek text of the New Testament was printed for the *Complutensian Polyglot* (*see* 1514), this was not published until 1522, so that Froben's was the first in the field. The many errors in the first edition were largely corrected in the second, 1519.

First edition of Sir Thomas More's *Utopia*. Louvain: Thierry Martens (Theodoricus Martinus).

The first press on the continent of Africa was established at Fez about 1516, by Jewish refugees who had worked at Lisbon for the Rabbi Eliezer Toledano. (*See* 1489.)

1517

First printed edition of *Der Teuerdank* (a poetical paraphrase of the life of the Emperor Maximilian), edited by Melchior Pfintzing. Nuremberg: Hans Schönsperger the elder. This rhymed allegorical romance of chivalry relates the exploits of the knight Teuerdank (i.e. 'Valiant hero') and the book was highly successful in unifying engravings and typography. It has 119 wood engravings by Jost von Negker from designs by Hans Schäuffelein, Leonhard Bech and Hans Burgkmair. The type, one of the earliest varieties of Fraktur, was based on the hands of Leonhard Wagner of Augsburg and cut by Hieronymus Andreae. Although the imprint has Nuremberg, it is thought that the book was printed at Augsburg.

Sigismund Grimm set up a press at Augsburg and in the following year started a publishing business in partnership with a rich merchant, Marx Wirsung. He lost his money through an unfortunate experiment in alchemy.

The first *Biblia Rabbinica* (Old Testament) with Aramaic versions was printed at Venice in four folio volumes by Daniel Bomberg (Van Bombergen) who came from Antwerp and set up a Hebrew press at Venice which became famous. This *Biblia Rabbinica* was edited by Felix Pratensis, who dedicated it to Pope Leo X.

At Rome, Jacobus Mazochius published Andrea Fulvio, *Illustrium imagines*, the earliest of a long succession of medal books. It contains 207 heads of Romans, cut after ancient coins and medals.

In this year Franticek Skorina printed books in liturgical Russian at Prague. Skorina chose for the realisation of his publishing plans the centre point of West-Slav cultural life, the Bohemian city of Prague. Between 1517 and 1519 he published twenty-three books of the Old Testament, the first Bible printed in Cyrillic, which contains his woodcut portrait. After that he seems to have ceased work for a time, but in 1525 moved to Wilna. (*See* 1525.)

At Oxford a second press was established by John Scolar, part of whose material seems to have come from Wynkyn de Worde. This second Oxford press is, says Madan, 'peculiar for its short and almost unrecorded work'. Scolar produced only a few books in 1517 and 1518. In 1519 one book was printed by Charles Kyrfoth with Scolar's types, after which the press ceased, and there was a gap of more than sixty years in Oxford printing until Joseph Barnes became the first University Printer in 1585.

1518

Peter Schöffer junior became the first regular printer at Worms, where he worked until 1529. Peter Drach, the printer at Speier, is thought to have printed a Latin and German Psalter at Worms about 1504, but the fact is not proved.

The first printed Greek Bible was issued at Venice by the Aldine Press. It was edited by the father-in-law and brothers-in-law of Aldus Manutius, by whom the press was managed after Aldus's death. Though, like Erasmus's New Testament (*see* 1516), it was anticipated in date of printing by the *Complutensian Polyglot*, it was published earlier.

Editio princeps of Erasmus, *Colloquia*. Basel: J. Froben. Like many of his books it became a best-seller and was frequently reprinted and translated.

Charlotte Guillard succeeded to the business of her late husband Berthold Rembolt, who was for a time in partnership with Ulrich Gering. She married Claude Chevallon in 1520, and was again widowed in 1537. One of the most eminent women printers, she died in 1557.

1519

Johann Neudörfer the Elder issued at Nuremberg the first printed models of writing—6 folio sheets with examples of Fraktur, Chancery and current hands illustrated by woodcuts.

On 10 April, a papal letter granted to Giovanni Francesco Pico della Mirandola a life privilege for the printing of works by his uncle Giovanni and himself. He set up a press at La Mirandola and engaged the printer Giovanni Mazocco, but only two works are known to have come from this press—in 1519, *Liber de veris calamitatum . . .*; and in 1520 *Examen vanitatis doctrinae gentium.*

At Zürich, Christopher Froschauer (*c.* 1490–1564) received the freedom of the city. The printing office which he founded still exists in the shape of the firm of Orell Füssli & Co.

Undated, but probably printed in 1519, the first English translation of *Till Eulenspiegel* was printed at Antwerp by Jan van Doesborch, entitled *Tyll Howleglass.*

Death of Leonardo da Vinci at the Château Clos-Luce, near Amboise. He described a simple process of nature-printing and several new designs for printing presses, one of them with a self-acting to and fro running chariot, but none of these suggestions was put into effect.

The Paris printer Gaspard Philippe became the first recorded printer at Bordeaux.

The *Missale Nidrosiense* printed at Copenhagen by the Canon Poul Raeff, the first Dane to print. The work was undertaken for the Archbishop of Trondhjem, Erik Valkendorf.

1520

Pope Leo X issued the Bull which excommunicated Martin Luther and forbade the printing, distribution, or even possession of his writings.

At Wittenberg, Melchior Lotter printed Luther's tract *An den christlichen Adel deutscher Nation: von des Christlichen Standes Besserung*, which called for the renunciation of the temporal power of the Pope. One of the tracts which helped to set in motion the Reformation.

First complete edition of the Babylonian *Talmud*, issued at Venice in twelve volumes 1520–22 by Daniel Bomberg. The *Tractatus Berachoth* had already appeared separately in 1484.

Sebastien Gryphe (1493–1556), a native of Reutlingen in Swabia, settled at Lyons where he printed more than 400 works in Greek, Latin and Hebrew.

Christopher Plantin was born about 1520 in Touraine, possibly at Saint Avertin, near Tours.

Simon de Colines, printer, bookseller, and engraver, succeeded to the business of Henri I Estienne, whose widow he married.

Thomas More's *Epistola ad Germanum Brixium*, printed by Richard Pynson, is the first dated book printed in England to contain catchwords.

1521

De Architectura, by Marcus Vitruvius Pollio, translated into Italian, was published in a sumptuous edition at Como. The printer, Gotardus de Ponte, was summoned from Milan to Como to print it. In it is found the first mention of the 'camera obscura'.

Christoph Froschauer the Elder set up his press at Zürich, where he worked until his death on 1 April, 1564.

The first printing in French from a Vienna press is the Decree of the Emperor Charles V against Martin Luther, who is called a 'notoire hérétique'. Vienna: Johann Singriener.

By an Edict of 20 October, François I of France forbade the sale of any book until it had been examined by the University of Paris and the Faculty of Theology.

At Cracow, Hieronymus Vietor printed *Rozmowy króla Salomona*, long thought to be the earliest book printed entirely in Polish. But Johann Haller, *Zywot Pana Jezusa Krysta* (Life of Jesus Christ) is now considered an earlier piece of printing. It was translated from the German by Baltasar Opeć of Cracow at the command of the Queen, Elisabeth. There is an edition of this work dated 1522 which is unquestionably not the first, and, although the actual date of the original edition is not known, it is probable that it was printed at Cracow by Florian Ungler towards the end of 1515.

First edition of *Assertio septem sacramentorum adversus Martinum Lutherum*, the reply to Luther by Henry VIII which gained for the English Crown the title of *Fidei defensor*. Printed at London by the King's Printer, Richard Pynson. It is thought that Sir Thomas More had a hand in its composition.

Printing begun at Cambridge by the German printer Johann Lair of Siegburg, known as John Siberch. His first book was the *Oratio* of Henry Bullock, a speech made when Cardinal Wolsey visited the university in 1520. His second book, Augustine, *De miseria ac brevitate vitae*, printed also in 1521, is the rarest of all Siberch's books. Only one copy (bequeathed by John Selden to the Bodleian) is known. The first Greek printing in metal type in England occurs on the title-page of *Cuiusdam fidelis Christiani epistola*, a sermon by Augustine, printed by Siberch in the early part of 1521. A few woodcut words in Greek appear in Wynkyn de Worde's edition of R. Whittinton, *Syntaxis* (1517). In Lucian, *Peri dipsadon* with Bullock's translation, also printed by Siberch, there are four lines of Greek, on the strength of which Siberch proclaimed himself the first printer in both languages in England. But he does not seem to have made use of his Greek type again. Much new information about Siberch is contained in Otto Treptow, *Johann Lair von Siegburg* published at Siegburg in 1964.

1522

Luther's translation of the New Testament into German printed at Wittenberg by Melchior Lotter the Younger with woodcuts by Lucas Cranach the elder. This translation was based mainly on the Greek text of Erasmus, and greatly influenced translations made by other Reformers. It is sometimes called the 'September Testament' because another edition was published in December of the same year.

The first calligraphic copy-book was published in Rome: *La Operina . . . da imparare di scrivere littera cancellarescha*, by the calligrapher, type designer and printer Ludovico degli Arrighi Vicentino. The cursive letters were cut by the goldsmith Lautizio Perugino, and printed from wood blocks.

The jurist Giovanni Nevizzano published at Lyons the first bibliography of law books: *Inventarium librorum in utroque hactenus impressorum*. No name of printer.

Died (in October or November) the printer and bookseller Thielman Kerver I. His wife Yolande, daughter of the bookseller Pasquier Bonhomme,

succeeded him and carried on the business until her death in 1557.

The earliest book on arithmetic printed in England—Cuthbert Tunstall, *De Arte Supputandi*. London: Richard Pynson. Tunstall (1474–1559) became Bishop, first of London and later of Durham.

1523

Died Hans Schönsperger the Elder, who had printed at Augsburg since 1481, when he issued his *Regimen Sanitatis*. He printed an edition of the *Teuerdank* in 1519, two years after its first appearance at Nuremberg. (*See* 1517.)

Hans Lufft set up a press at Wittenberg. (*See also* 1534.)

Printing introduced into Jena by Michel Buchfürer.

Gabriel Kantz became the first printer at Altenburg. In 1526 he went to Zwickau.

Hans Schönsperger the Younger became the first printer at Zwickau, where he worked until 1525.

Publication of the first account of the circumnavigation of the globe, in *Maximiliani Transylvani: Epistola de admirabili et novissima Hispanorum in Orientem navigatione*, etc. Rome: In aedibus Minitii Calvi. Maximilian was one of the survivors of the expedition when on 6 September, 1522, the *Victoria*, with only eighteen men on board, returned to Seville.

This Rome edition was completed in November 1523, and a second edition was printed at Cologne the following January by Eucharius Cervicornus.

Jacques Mareschal was the first recorded printer at Clermont-Ferrand. In this year he published *Les Ordonnances royales*, which has the colophon: 'Nouvellement imprimé à Clermont par Jacques Mareschal. L'an de grâce M.CCCCC.XXiii.' Whether the book was actually printed at Clermont is doubtful. Mareschal, printer and publisher at Lyons 1498–1529, had depôts for the sale of books at Paris and Clermont-Ferrand, and the book cited may have been printed at Lyons.

1524

The first printing at Dresden was the work of a private press known as the Emserpresse which functioned until 1526 in which year Dresden's first regular printer, Wolfgang Stöckel, set up a press after having previously worked at Leipzig.

Stöckel, who printed at Dresden until 1540, was made Court Printer, though without the official title.

Hans Weinreich, who had previously worked at Danzig from *c.* 1520, became the first printer at Königsberg, where he worked until 1553.

Amandus Farckall printed up to this date at Colmar. He soon went to Hagenau and in 1539 came Barthélemy Grüninger from Strassburg.

The calligrapher Giovanni Antonio Tagliente published his writing book *Lo presente libro insegna la vera arte delo excellēnte scrivere, etc.* The first edition, printed at Venice by Stephano de Sabio, was soon followed by others.

Blodius Palladius, *Coryciana*. Rome: Arrighi & L. dei Rotelli. The first book printed by Arrighi and the first to contain swash capitals.

At Vienna Johann Singriener employed the first italic type with sloping capitals.

This year saw the publication of the earliest work so far known to have been printed by Thomas Berthelet, a small tract by Galfredus Petrus, a friar of Bayeux, called *Opus sane de deorum dearumque . . .* printed at the sign of the Roman Lucrece, near the Conduit in Fleet Street, and dated 27 September, 1524.

1525

The earliest (though possibly unfinished) edition of the New Testament in English, printed at Cologne by Peter Quentell from the translation by William Tyndale. Only a fragment now survives, in the Grenville Library at the British Museum. The first 10 sheets had been secretly printed when the editors had to flee to Worms, where the work was begun afresh, most probably by Peter Schöffer. Two copies only of this, the first completed edition, are known: one in the Baptist College Library, Bristol, lacking only the title leaf; the other, in St. Paul's Cathedral Library, London, lacks 71 leaves.

Albrecht Dürer published at Nuremberg his *Underweysung der Messung mit dem Zirckel und Richtscheyt.* Nuremberg: Hieronymus Andreae (for the author). This book, the first printed in a developed Fraktur, and illustrated by the author, was on the theory of perspective and intended for the use of painters, sculptors, and other craftsmen. (*See* 1917.)

Johann Petri of Nuremberg issued a type specimen sheet, and printed in his largest Fraktur a handsome Psalter in German. The specimen, known only in a unique copy, shows three romans, two italics, a Greek, a Hebrew, and two Frakturs. According to his brother-in-law, Johann Neudörffer (in his *Nachrichten*), these types were actually cut by Petri and were not merely his stock.

The unidentified 'A.G.W.' was the first to print at Bremen, where he issued five known works. The first regular press at Bremen was that of Arend Wessell, *c.* 1565–89.

The first press at Lucerne was established there in a monastery by the Franciscan, Thomas Murner, who printed tracts in support of Roman Catholicism from 1525–29. Murner (1475–1537), a bitter opponent of Luther, had set up a press at Strassburg in 1524, but was forced to flee to Switzerland.

Franticek Skorina (*see* 1517) moved his press from Prague to Wilna, where he printed further liturgical works including a Slavonic Psalter and the *Apostol*.

Geoffroy Tory (*c.* 1480–1533) created a new style in Books of Hours with that which he designed in 1525 and which was printed by Simon de Colines. In this the decorative element predominates rather than religious inspiration. Tory became a licensed printer in 1529, and the first book from his press was a 16mo Book of Hours dated 8 February of that year. In 1531 Olivier Mallard took over the printing-house of Tory, who died two years later. (*See also* 1529.)

Guillaume I Le Bé, type-founder and punch-cutter, born at Troyes, where his father was a paper maker. He served his apprenticeship in the type foundry of Robert Estienne, and learned the art of punch-cutting from Claude Garamond. He died in 1598, and the business was carried on by his son Guillaume II Le Bé.

The first work published with the individual imprint of Robert Estienne—an edition of *Apuleii Liber de Deo Socratis.*

Pierre Haultin, French punch-cutter, began to cut his first music punches.

In this year a translation by John Walton of Boethius, *De Consolatione Philosophiae*, was printed at Tavistock, Devonshire, under the title *The Boke of comfort*, by a monk of the exempt monastery, called Thomas Rychard. It was printed at the request of a Cornish gentleman named Robert Langdon, whose arms appear at the end of the book. (*See also* 1534.)

First edition of an anonymous work 'which treateth of ye vertues and proprytes of herbes'. London: Rycharde Banckes. It went through many editions and was known as *Banks's Herbal* from the name of its first publisher.

1526

Chrétien Wechel acquired the business of Conrad Resch in the rue Saint-Jacques, Paris, and set up as bookseller and printer.

A Czech press was founded at Pilsen by Jan Pekk and Jan Fentzl, who came from Nuremberg, where in 1518 they had issued *Enchiridion seu Manuale Curatorum* in Bohemian as well as Latin. Their first joint work at Pilsen was *Erasmus on the Lord's Prayer*.

Editio princeps of the New Testament in Swedish, printed at the Royal Printing Press, Stockholm. The first Royal Printer in Sweden, Georg Richolff the Younger, brought to Stockholm from Lübeck a type foundry, matrices from which were used by later Royal Printers. Richolff the Elder had been a printer in Lübeck from 1501-18, specialising in school books and moral treatises. His son Georg printed at Uppsala in 1525 and in 1526 King Gustav I commissioned him to establish the new Royal Printing House. (*See* 1541.)

1527

At Leipzig, the bookseller Hans Hergot was executed for having published a book inciting to rebellion.

Johann Loersfeld became the first printer at Marburg.

First edition of the first printed Chaldean grammar—Sebastian Münster, *Chaldaica grammatica*. Basel: J. Froben.

At Basel, Johann Froben died through a fall from a book-ladder.

The earliest dated mensural music with text and notes printed from type at a single impression—*Chansons nouvelles en musique, à quatre parties*. Paris: Pierre Attaignant. The punches for the music were cut by Pierre Haultin. Haultin was the first to devise a method of printing music with a single impression, by casting each note on the staves and then fitting them together. Attaignant was the first King's Printer of Music in France.

In Paris, Simon de Colines published the French version of the *Colloques* of Erasmus in an edition of 2,400 copies. When the book was forbidden by the Faculty of Theology, Colines, secretly to dispose of this large edition, simply suppressed the title.

About 1527, the printer John Rastell brought out *A New Interlude and a mery of the Nature of the iiii Elements*, a versified cosmography containing one of the two earliest pieces of mensural music printed in England. The notes and the words to be sung are printed from type by one impression. (A reproduction is shown in A. Hyatt King, *Four Hundred Years of Music Printing*, 1964.)

The first printer at Malmö was Olof Ulrichsson, who had previously worked for Bishop Hans Brask at Söderköping 1523-25. He was active in Malmö 1527-56.

1528

At Venice, the Aldine Press printed Baldassare Conte di Castiglione, *Il Libro del Cortegiano*, which gives the author's idea of the ideal courtier, with rules for gentlemanly behaviour. It is, moreover, a literary masterpiece and was quickly translated into many languages. In 1561 an English translation was published, the work of Sir T. Hoby.

Wynkyn de Worde became the first printer in England to use italic in a Latin translation from Lucian entitled *Complures Dialogi*. There were two sizes and the design is of Netherlands origin, a similar italic having been used at Antwerp by J. Grapheus.

In this year Wynkyn de Worde published an edition of Robert Wakefield, *Oratio de laudibus Trium Linguarum* in which he used some Greek words in movable type as well as some Arabic and Hebrew cut in wood. Reyner Wolfe was the first printer in England to possess a large stock of Greek type.

The early press at Abingdon is represented by a single book—a Breviary printed for the Benedictines of St. Mary's monastery by John Scolar, probably the Oxford printer of 1517-18. It is dated 12 September, 1528. Only one copy is known, lacking two leaves out of 358, and preserved in the library of Emmanuel College, Cambridge.

1529

At Nuremberg, Friedrich Peypus printed the first systematic treatise on the correct writing of the German language—*Lautbüchlein deutscher orthographie*.

The Anabaptist, Melchior Hoffmann, was the first printer at Kiel.

Undated, but probably printed in 1529, is a broadside printed at Vicenza by T. Janiculo—a Paternoster set in the italic of Ludovico degli Arrighi, and designed to illustrate the spelling reform theories of G. G. Trissino as well as the special sorts which Arrighi designed to demonstrate them. The sheet is in itself a specimen of the Arrighi italic.

At Paris, Gilles de Gourmont printed the *Champ Fleury* of Geoffroy Tory (c. 1480–1533). The work is a treatise, part mythological and part geometrical, upon the proportions of the inscriptional lettering of ancient Rome. The figures in *Champ Fleury* are the work of Tory himself, though we do not know whether he engraved them. Although he illustrated comparatively few books, Tory had a great influence on the French school of engraving.

1530

Otto Brunfels (1489–1534), a native of Mainz, was the author of the earliest scientific botanical work. The first part of his *Herbarum vivae eicones* was published by Schott of Strassburg in 1530, and the whole completed six years later. The illustrations are by Hans Weiditz, and the originals were discovered some years ago at Berne.

Christian Egenolff, born at Hadamar, came from Strassburg to Frankfurt-am-Main, where he became the first regular printer (*see also* 1531). He secured the services of Hans Sebald Beham as his illustrator.

La saincte Bible en Francoys, printed at Antwerp by Martin Lempereur (Martin De Keyser). This is the first edition of the complete Bible translated into French by Jacques Le Fèvre d'Etaples (c. 1450–1536), and known from its place of publication as the 'Antwerp Bible'.

Geoffroy Tory appointed King's Printer in France.

Publication of the earliest known collection of music in England. Printed in London 'at the sign of the black Morens', it was for long attributed to Wynkyn de Worde's press. It bears the title *In this boke ar cōteyned XX sōges*, and the songs are by Cornysh, Taverner, Fayrfax, Cowper and others. So far the type has not been found in any other work, and the printer remains unidentified.

1531

At Augsburg, Heinrich Steyner printed the first edition of the *Emblems* of the eminent lawyer Andrea Alciato (1492–1550), a book which had a tremendous success and started the vogue for Emblem Books which lasted until the middle of the seventeenth century. No fewer than 93 editions of Alciato's *Emblems* were published between 1531 and 1600.

About 1531, Christian Egenolff (1502–1555) started his type foundry at Frankfurt. After his death the business passed to his daughter who married first Jacob Sabon, and secondly Conrad Berner. The daughter of this second marriage married Johann Luther in 1629, and he took over the foundry.

Simun Kozicie, Bishop of Modrusc, caused to be printed in his house at Rjeka (Fiume) a number of Slovak volumes in Glagolithic characters. Of these only two are now known: a Roman Missal and a *Life of the Popes and Caesars*. The regular introduction of printing into Rjeka did not take place until 1790 (*q.v.*).

Antoine Augereau printed Andrea Navagero, *Orationes duae*, published at Paris by Jean Petit. Augereau's roman, used in this book was, according to Mrs. Beatrice Warde, 'a type which, considered historically, is the most interesting of all those that followed Estienne's'.

William Rastell printed in London *Registrum brevium* in a calligraphic italic with swash capitals, which A. F. Johnson describes as the best example of a Vicentino italic outside Italy and France.

In this year Thomas Berthelet printed Sir Thomas Elyot, *The Boke named the Governour*, a treatise on moral philosophy which he reprinted several times, and which was popular throughout the sixteenth century. It was aimed at those intended for high office in an endeavour to fit them for their responsibilities.

1532

Editio princeps of Niccolò Machiavelli, *Il Principe*. Rome: Antonio Blado. This edition also contained *La Vita di Castruccio Castracani da Lucca*.

The composer Elzéar Genêt, known as Carpentras from his birthplace, paid for the cutting, under his own supervision, by Etienne Briard of music notes with round heads, but the innovation was not adopted at the time by other punch cutters. Briard's type was used by Jean de Channey of Avignon to print two collections of Genêt's sacred compositions. The first work of his which Jean de Channay printed was a *Liber Missarum*, dated 15 May, 1532. Not only did Briard abandon the traditional square and lozenge form for the breves, semi-breves and minims, replacing them by round-headed notes, but he replaced the complicated system of ligatures by a simple and rational notation representing the real duration of the notes.

At Paris, Robert Estienne printed his superb *Biblia Sacra* in a fount based on the Aldine roman of 1495, probably cut by Claude Garamond.

The Workes of Geffray Chaucer newly printed. London: Thomas Godfray. This was the first collected edition of Chaucer's works, edited by William Thynne, with a dedication to King Henry VIII.

1533

Printing introduced into Stettin by Franz Schlosser, who worked there until 1539.

First press in Transylvania established at Braşov (Kronstadt) by Johann Honter (1498–1549). His earliest known book is *Compendium grammatices latinae*, 1535.

Tomáš Bakalár printed at Pilsen a *Hortulus Animae* in Czech. This was the last book printed at Pilsen during the sixteenth century.

The first extant work printed entirely in Hungarian is an edition of St. Paul's *Epistles* translated from the Vulgate by Benedek Komjáthy. Cracow: H. Vietor.

'An Acte (25 Henry VIII c. 15) concernyng prynters and bynders' forbade the importation into England of foreign-printed books, and abolished the Act of Richard III (*see* 1483). To protect native bookbinders, the Act stated that anyone selling books imported in a bound state was to forfeit 6*s*. 8*d*. for each book sold.

1534

First complete edition of Luther's translation into German of the Bible. Wittenberg: Hans Lufft. Folio. It became at once the most widely read book in Germany and influenced decisively the development of the German language.

At Mainz, Peter Jordan finished the Catholic Bible of Johann Dietenberger with 109 woodcuts by Hans Sebald Beham and Anton Woensam.

At Lübeck, Ludwig Dietz completed a Lutheran Bible in Low German with woodcuts by Erhard Altdorfer.

Death of Thierry Martens, who introduced printing into Alost about 1472. He worked successively at Alost, Louvain and Antwerp for nearly sixty years.

On Christmas Eve the printer and punch-cutter Antoine Augereau was hanged and burned in the Place Maubert, Paris, for his part in the 'affaire des placards'. (A recent account of this tutor of Claude Garamond is given by Mme Jeanne Veyrin-Forrer in *Paris et Ile-de-France*, Vol. 8, 1956.) The British Museum has a copy on vellum of his *Loraison de Cicero*.

The first *Concordance* to the English New Testament compiled by the printer Thomas Gibson.

Death of Wynkyn de Worde, assistant and successor of Caxton. He was buried in the church of St. Bride, Fleet Street.

The first book printed in Iceland—*Breviarium Holense*, printed at Hólar, Iceland, by Jón Matthíasson, known as 'Svenski' (the Swede). The only known copy was destroyed in a fire at Copenhagen in 1728, but two leaves were later found in the binding of a book in the Royal Library in Stockholm.

1535

Editio princeps of the printed English Bible (*sine nota*). The work of Miles Coverdale, it was for long thought to have been printed by Christopher Froschauer at Zurich, but it is now considered more likely to have been printed at Marburg by E. Cervicornus and J. Soter. The initials used in this Bible are found in books issued by these two printers from Cologne, the former of whom established a press at Marburg in 1535.

A Frenchman named Gilibert Nehou introduced printing into Bari with *Operette del Parthenope Suavio in vari tempi et per diversi subietti composte, et da Silvan Flammineo insieme raccolte. . . .* The work is dated 15 October, 1535.

Death of the famous printer Josse Bade (Jodocus Badius Ascensius), born at Ghent about 1462. His daughters were married to three famous printers: Robert Estienne, Michel Vascosan and Jean de Roigny.

Publication of the first French Protestant version of the Bible, translated by Pierre Robert Olivetan. Neuchâtel: Pierre de Vingle. It was called the 'Bible de Serrières', from the village close to Neuchâtel where it was printed.

The first printer at Annecy (Haute Savoie) was the Spaniard Gabriel Pomar, who had previously worked at Lyons and Geneva.

The famous bibliographer of South American printing, José Toribio Medina claimed that a certain Esteban Martín was printing in Mexico from 1535–38, but there is no extant copy of any work by him, and the claim has not so far been substantiated.

First book issued from the Honterus Press, founded at Kronstadt (Brassó, Brasov) by the pedagogue and Reformer Johann Honter (1498–1549). After his death, the press was run by the Kronstadt pastor Valentin Wagner. Honter printed mainly educational and religious works, including his own. In 1546 he set up a paper mill for the use of the press. In 1555 Wagner set up a workshop for engraving on copper and in 1557 brought out an edition of *Imagines Mortis* with engravings after Holbein. The first known book from Honter's press is a *Compendium grammatices latinae* of 1535.

1536

About 1536, Cardinal Pole published his *Ad Henricum VIII pro ecclesiasticae Unitatis Defensione*, privately printed for him at Rome by Antonio Blado (n.d.). A few copies were presented to the Pope and Cardinals, and Henry VIII ordered Cranmer to draw up an answer.

First edition of Johannes Calvin, *Christianiae religionis institutio*. Basel: for T. Platter & B. Lasius. A work of tremendous influence, since published in almost innumerable editions and translations.

Death of the London printer John Rastell.

1537

Johannes Soter, of the famous family of papermakers, became the first printer at Solingen. He set up a press in the paper-mill on the river Wupper, just outside the town. His address was 'Salingaci apud molam chartaceam cis Viperam'. Soter had worked as a printer in Cologne from 1518.

Mathias Apiarius (Biener) introduced printing into Bern, Switzerland. His first work there, dated 18 July, 1537, was a *Compendium musices* by Auctor Lampadius, a cantor of Lüneburg. The most successful of his well-printed books was Pauli's collection of farces, *Schimpf und Ernst* (1542). He had worked at Strassburg, 1533–37.

The first Hungarian printing press established by the magnate Tamás Nádasdy on his estate at Uj Sziget. (*See* 1541.)

First edition of the English Bible known as the *Matthew Bible*. Printed for R. Grafton and E. Whitchurch at Antwerp by Matthew Crom. The name given to the editor, 'Thomas Matthew', is generally considered to be a pseudonym of John Rogers, an intimate friend of Tyndale.

Gerard Mercator started business on his own account as a maker and publisher of globes and maps, with a map of Palestine in six parts. (*See also* 1540.)

Etienne Roffet, called Le Faulcher (d. 1548), was the first Frenchman to be given the title of Royal Bookbinder (*relieur du roi*).

1538

Publication of the first practical dictionary, the *Dictionarium latino-gallicum*, compiled and printed at Paris by Robert Estienne.

There was published the earliest printed edition of the liturgical Epistles and Gospels in English—*The Epistles and Gospels of every Sunday and Holy Day in the Year*. Paris, no printer's name, but assigned to François Regnault.

At Lyons, the brothers Melchior and Gaspar Trechsel printed *Les Simulachres et historiées faces de la mort*, a French version of the *Dance of Death*, with woodcuts generally thought to have been designed by Hans Holbein and executed by H. Lützelberger. (*See* 1543.)

Henry VIII, by a Royal Proclamation of 16 November, banned the importation of English books printed abroad; in particular it decreed that no person 'from hensforth shall printe or bryng into this his realm any bokes of divine scripture in the english tonge with any annotations in the margyn, or any prologe or additions in the calender or table . . . but onely the playne sentence and texte.' No one was to print any English books without due authorisation from the Privy Council or other examining bodies.

1539

Syriac type first used in Teseo Ambrogio, *Introductio in Chaldaicam linguam, Syriacam atque Armenicam*. Pavia: G. M. Simonetta.

First edition of the so-called *Great Bible*, a revision by Coverdale of the *Matthew Bible* of 1537 (*q.v.*) at the instance of Thomas Cromwell. It was printed by Richard Grafton and Edward Whitchurch, partly in Paris, at the printing-house of François Regnault, and partly in London. The second and subsequent editions of the *Great Bible* were often known as *Cranmer's Bible* because they contain a preface by that archbishop. In the same year was issued the version of Richard Taverner in two editions, folio and quarto. London: John Byddell for Thomas Berthelet.

On 12 June, the printer-publisher Johann Cromberger concluded a contract with the Seville printer Juan Pablos (Giovanni Paoli, a native of Brescia) by which the latter, accompanied by his wife and Gil Barbero, his pressman, were to go to Mexico with a printing press. They arrived in Mexico City in September, 1539. (*See also* 1540.)

1540

The glazing- or pressing-hammer, introduced in Germany, replaced the old method of burnishing paper by hand.

First printing press established at Berlin by Johann Weiss from Wittenberg.

Publication of Vannoccio Biringuccio, *De la Pirotechnia*, which contains the earliest account of type-casting. (An annotated translation by Martha Teach Gnudi and Cyril Smith was published by the Columbia Club of Connecticut, New Haven, 1941.) Venice: Venturino Roffinello, for Curtio Navo e Fratelli.

First edition of the writing-book of Giovanni-Battista Palatino—*Libro nuovo d'imparare a scrivere tutte sorte lettere antiche et moderne*, one of the famous writing-books of the sixteenth century. Rome: 'nelle case de M. Benedetto Gionta per Baldassare di Francesco Cartolari Perugino'.

The first book with typeset music printed in the Netherlands, *Souter Liedekens*, which is also the oldest Dutch Psalter with music. Antwerp: Symon Cock. The work is made up of metrical paraphrases of the Psalms by Willem van Zuylen, set to folk tunes. Cock published nine editions

bearing the date 1540, but it is unlikely that all of them were published in that year.

Gerard Kremer, called Mercator, geographer and map-publisher, issued a small manual of 27 leaves, *Literarum latinarum, quas Italicas, cursoriasque vocant, scribendarum ratio*. Louvain: R. Rescius. An edition was also published at Antwerp by Joannes Richard, dated 1540 but probably issued in 1541.

In France, after the death in this year of Conrad Néobar, Royal Printer in Greek, the title was transferred to Robert Estienne, who had been made Royal Printer in Hebrew and Latin in 1539.

Jean de Tournes (Tornasius) set up his printing office at Lyons.

First English edition of *The Byrthe of Mankynde*, the first book on midwifery printed in England, translated by Richard Jonas from Eucharius Rösslin, *De partu hominis*, and dedicated to Queen Catherine [Howard], the wife of Henry VIII. London: Thomas Raynalde. Fifteen English editions of the work were published between 1540 and 1654. The original edition contains three copperplate engravings. (*See* 1513.)

Editio princeps of the Icelandic New Testament. Roskilde (Denmark) Hans Barth. The complete Bible in Icelandic was not printed until 1584.

The first surviving Mexican imprint, the *Manual de Adultos*, was issued by Juan Pablos (Giovanni Paoli) in Mexico City, with the date 13 December, 1540. He is thought to have printed earlier *Breve y mas compendiosa doctrina christiana*, but no trace of this book can now be found.

1541

At Mainz, Franz Behem published Joannes Bergellanus, *De Chalcographiae inventione poema encomiasticum*, a poem on printing and its invention, which displays on the title-page a device which shows a compositor and his case. The case is divided into thirty compartments, in twenty-three of which capital letters are seen; the J, U and W are not present. The author was most probably employed as corrector by Behem. The poem, in which Gutenberg is named as the inventor of printing, may be considered as the first poem on the printer's craft.

At Nuremberg, appeared the first edition of Roger Bacon, *Speculum alchemiae*. The first edition in English, *The Mirror of Alchimy*, was published in London, 1597. Printed by Thomas Creede for Richard Olive.

At Venice, Gabriele Giolito de' Ferrari took over the printing-house established in 1538 by his father Giovanni Giolito. The first book he printed at Venice alone was *Dialoghi Piacevoli di M. Nicolo Franco*, 1541, a reprint of the edition published in 1539 'apud Ioannem Giolitum'. Gabriele, who began his career at Trino, was, with Aldo Manuzio, the best printer in Italy during the first half of the sixteenth century. From 1550 he printed in association with his brothers, and died in 1578, having printed some 850 books.

First edition of the New Testament in Hungarian, printed at the press of Tamás Nádasdy at Uj Sziget, Hungary. Known as the *Sárvár Testament*, it was translated by János Erdösi (Sylvester).

The first to introduce printing into Wesel was Jakob Blawe, who issued three known books in that town, though whether he was a printer or only a publisher has not been established. Johann van Kempen may have worked there in 1545, though the fact has not been proved. The first regular printer at Wesel was Derick van der Straten, who worked there from 1546 to around 1565.

Editio princeps of the Swedish Bible, known as *Gustav Vasa's Bible*. Uppsala: Georg (Jürgen) Richolff the Younger. The cost of production was met by a special contribution of corn from each parish.

1542

At Leipzig, Heinrich Eichbuchler started a printing office which is now represented by the firm of Breitkopf and Härtel.

Editio princeps of Leonhard Fuchs, *De historia stirpium commentarii* Basel: Officina Isingriniana. One of the most celebrated of the early herbals, illustrated by 512 splendid woodcuts, it was followed in the succeeding year by a German edition, called the *New Kreüterbuch*. The woodcuts became familiar to English readers when used on a reduced scale (borrowed from the octavo edition) in both William Turner's *Herbal* and Lyte's *Dodoens*. A number of the woodcuts also appear in other botanical works.

DCP

First edition of the earliest treatise exclusively concerned with physiology, and the first to make use of that term—Jean Fernel, *De naturali parte medecinae*. Paris: Adam Saulnier for Simon de Colines. It was reissued in 1554 as Part One of Fernel's *Medicina* under the title of *Physiologia*.

Jean I de Tournes issued his first book at Lyons—*Le Chevalier Chrestien*, a French version of the *Enchiridion militis christiani* of Erasmus, translated by Louis de Berquin.

The Finnish Primer of Bishop Michael Agricola (d. 1557) printed at Stockholm by A. Laurentsson. This was the first book printed in Finnish, but printing in Finland itself did not begin for another century (*see* 1642). (A fascimile reprint was issued in 1884.)

1543

Johann Petri of Nuremberg published the first edition of *De revolutionibus orbium coelestium*, embodying the researches of Copernicus.

The first press at Hildesheim established by Henning Rüdem, who printed five books there before going to Hanover, into which town he introduced printing at the end of the same year.

Printing introduced into Bonn by Laurenz von der Mülen, who worked there until 1550.

Editio princeps of *De humani corporis fabrica*. Basel: Oporinus. Its author, Andreas Vesalius (André Vésale; André Van Wesele, 1514–64), is regarded as the first scientific anatomist, and this work is a landmark in the history of medicine. The fine woodcut illustrations were for long ascribed to John of Calcar, a pupil of Titian.

Steven Mierdman printed at Antwerp the earliest edition of the New Testament in Spanish, translated from the Greek by Franzisco de Enzinas, a pupil of Melanchthon.

At Paris Robert Estienne published the exceedingly rare *Alphabetum Graecum*, an octavo pamphlet of 16 leaves in which the celebrated Royal Greek types of Garamond were shown for the first time. (*See also* 1544.)

The first Greek book printed in England—a *Chrysostom* edited by Sir John Cheke, the first Greek Lecturer at Cambridge. The printer was Reyner (Reginald) Wolfe, who in 1547 was appointed King's Printer in Latin, Greek and Hebrew, and was the first printer in England to possess Greek types in any quantity. The type for this book was of Basel origin.

Hans Holbein the Younger died in London of the plague. (*See* 1538.)

1544

Publication of Martin Luther's *Geystliche Lieder*, a book of music printed entirely from wood blocks. Leipzig: Valentin Bapst.

The punch-cutter Guillaume Le Bé (1525–98) went to Venice where he cut Hebrew types for the printer Giustiniani.

In Zürich Froschauer published the *Bibliotheca universalis* of Conrad Gesner (1516–65), the first of several bibliographies compiled by Gesner. In it authors are arranged under their Christian names and a list of their books is given. This was the earliest alphabetical general bibliography. A folio of 631 leaves, it lists some 12,000 works in Latin, Greek and Hebrew. In 1548–49 there followed the Subject Index in twenty volumes.

First printed edition of the works of Archimedes edited by Thomas Gechauff Venatorius. Greek and Latin. Latin translation by Jacobus Cremonensis. Basel: Joannes Hervagius.

Hans Kilian, in the service of the Count Palatine, set up a press at Neuburg on the Danube.

The Royal Greek types, designed and cut by Claude Garamond, and based on the handwriting of the Cretan scribe Angelos Vergetios, first appeared in a book in the *Ecclesiastical History* of Eusebius. Paris: Robert Estienne (*but see* 1543). The matrices had a curious history. Robert Estienne took them with him when he fled to Geneva and when they were needed for a further casting under Louis XIII, they had to be redeemed for 3,000 livres because a grandson of the great printer had pawned them in the meantime.

François I appointed a third Royal Printer, Denys Janot, to print in the French language, since he was unwilling for Latin to continue to dominate French printing. Janot succeeded Olivier Mallard as King's Printer in French.

At Sibiu (Hermannstadt) was published the first book in the Rumanian language, a Rumanian Catechism, with a Protestant tendency. This Catechism (of which no copy survives) and the Rumanian Gospels printed at Kronstadt (Brasov) in 1560–61, together with the series of Rumanian and Slavo-Rumanian service books issued by Coresi (*see* 1556) and his successors, reflect the progress of Lutheran Reform in Transylvania.

1545

In the *Corte Instruccye ende onderwijs* by Cornelius van der Heyden, printed by Josse Lambrecht at Ghent, is the first known pictorial representation of a type-caster at work. The same block was used three years later by A. Scoloker in *The Ordenarye for all faythfull Christians*, ostensibly printed at Ipswich.

The Flemish printer, Jacob van Liesvelt was beheaded for having printed a Lutheran Bible. This was the Bible in Flemish which he had printed in 1542, the marginal notes to which were considered heretical by the Inquisitors.

The first work printed for Claude Garamond, and showing for the first time his italic—David Chambellan, *Pia et religiosa meditatio. . . .* Paris: Petrus Gualterus pro Claudio Garmontio. According to Audin, the italic of Garamond was cut shortly before 1545 and the roman after that date, and perhaps after the death of François I.

Compendiosa totius anatomiae delineatio, issued by John Hertford and printed by Thomas Gemini, engraver and printer in London. This had the earliest English example of a title-page with copper-engraved border.

1546

Edict of Charles V concerning books, the circulation of which was prohibited under the censorship of the Faculty of Theology in the University of Louvain. Known as the *Louvain Index*, it was printed at Louvain by Servaes van Sassen.

At Lyons, there came from the press of Balthazar Arnoullet *Epitomes des rois de France en latin et en francoys avec leurs vrayes figures*. This was the first French book decorated with portraits engraved on copper. They were executed by the Lyons artist Claude Corneille, known also as Corneille de La Haye from his native town.

At Paris, Jacques Kerver brought out a French edition of the *Hypnerotomachia*, called *Le Songe de Poliphile*, with illustrations freely adapted from the original Italian cuts, possibly by Jean Goujon (further French editions, 1554, 1561 and 1600). Jacques Kerver, whose active career extended from 1535 to 1583, was the third son of Thielman I Kerver, who worked at Paris 1497–1522, and specialised in Books of Hours.

At Le Mans, Denis Gaignot introduced printing with a splendid *Missale Cenomanensis*.

On 3 August the printer Étienne Dolet (b. 1509) was executed as a heretic on the Place

Maubert, Paris, where a statue to his memory was erected in 1889 and stood until December 1941, when it was melted down to provide metal for the war.

The first book printed in the Welsh language—*Yny lhyvyr hwnn y traethir*. . . . Printed in London by Edward Whitchurch, it was an octavo pamphlet of 16 leaves containing a Calendar, the Creed, the Lord's Prayer, the Ten Commandments, etc. The only known copy is in the National Library of Wales. A facsimile reprint edited by J. H. Davies was issued in 1902.

1547

Eucharius Cervicornus established the first press at Coblenz.

Peter Schöffer the Younger died at Basel, having worked at Mainz, Worms, Strassburg and Venice. He was widely known as a skilful punch-cutter. The parental office at Mainz was carried on by Ivo Schöffer until 1555.

William Salesbury's *Dictionary in Englyshe and Welshe*, the first Welsh dictionary, printed in London by John Waley.

In the first year of his reign Edward VI granted to Richard Grafton a patent for the printing of all statute books.

1548

Publication began of the *Speculum Romanae Magnificentiae*. Rome: Antonio Lafreri. The earliest topographical work of enduring value, its 130 engraved plates formed a conspectus of the surviving monuments of ancient Rome.

First edition of *Un novo modo d'insegnar a scrivere e formar lettre*, etc., by Vespasiano Amphiareo. Venice: Curtio Troiano. This writing book was reprinted at least seventeen times between 1548 and 1620.

Editio princeps of St. Ignatius Loyola (Iñigo Lopez de Recalde), *Exercitia Spiritualia*, translated from the Spanish by A. Frusius. Rome: Antonio Blado.

At Zürich, Christoph Froschauer printed Hans Stumphf's *Swiss Chronicle*, in Volume I of which is an interesting cut of a press at work, showing the forme run out after an impression. The pressman is seen removing the freshly printed sheet.

Jean Crespin (d. 1572), a native of Arras, set up a press in Geneva to print books in the learned languages. From 1556 onwards he began to issue books in English, which included several works of John Knox.

The first press at Innsbruck was established by the Tyrolean government. The first printer was Leonhard Rossnagel, who was succeeded in 1550 by Rupprecht Höller.

Guillaume Roville (b. Tours 1518), after his apprenticeship at Paris, set up as master printer and publisher at Lyons. One of his first books was Alciato, *Emblemata* (1548) printed by Mathias Bonhomme and illustrated by Pierre Vase.

The calligrapher Juan de Yciar together with the engraver Jean de Vingle (son of the printer Jean de Vingle of Lyons) published the writing book *Recopilacion subtilissima intitulada Orthographia Pratica*. Saragossa: Pedro Bernuz. A second, enlarged edition was published in 1550 (*q.v.*).

Establishment of the first press at Lublin. It was a Hebrew press worked by Joseph of Lublin, but no book from this press is known later than 1549.

John Oswen set up his press in the High Street, Worcester, probably at the end of 1548. In January of the following year, he was granted by Edward VI a privilege to print service books for His Majesty's subjects 'of the principality of Wales and the marches thereunto belonging' for the space of seven years.

Antony Scoloker issued, probably in 1548, the *Ordinary for all faithful Christians*, in which is found a woodcut of the interior of a printing office, showing the press being worked. The cut was previously used by Josse Lambrecht at Ghent in a book by Cornelius van der Heyden (1545).

1549

At Cologne, Capar Vopelius published the writing book of Caspar Neff—*Köstliche Schatzkamer der Schreibkunst*.

The Guild of Printers and Booksellers instituted at Venice—the earliest trade association of book-men in Europe. But not until 1571 did it issue a decree forbidding anyone not a member of the Guild from setting up a printing press or opening a bookshop.

In Paris, Arnoul l'Angelier brought out the first edition of *La Défence et Illustration de la Langue Francoyse*—the manifesto of the group of French poets known as the Pléiade.

First English edition of Erasmus, *The Praise of Folie*, translated by Sir Thomas Chaloner and printed in London by Thomas Berthelet.

Several issues of the first Edwardine Prayer Book were printed in this year, both by Richard Grafton and by Edward Whitchurch, to whom in 1547 Edward VI had granted a licence to print 'books concerning divine service . . . being in the english or latin tongue'. Two issues were also printed by John Oswen at Worcester. No two of these various issues agree completely. Whitchurch's first issue is dated 7 March; that of Richard Grafton, 8 March.

The Psalter of David newely translated into Englyshe metre . . . was issued in London with the notice, 'Translated and Imprinted by Robert Crowley . . . and are to be solde in Eley rentes in Holburne'. From typographical evidence it seems probable that this work was actually printed by Steven Mierdman, the Antwerp printer who had recently arrived in England and set up his press. The music, which appears on two pages only, set in four parts, was cut on wood blocks. The fact this this process was seldom used for printing music in England strengthens the probability that Mierdman was the printer.

Edition of the Psalms printed at Canterbury by John Mychell who migrated thither from London, where he had printed at least two books. He continued to print in Canterbury until 1556.

1550

First Italian national bibliography—*La Libraria del Doni, Fiorentino*, by Antonio Francesco Doni. Venice: Gabriel Giolito de Farrari.

Hans Baumann became the first printer at Salzburg, where he worked until 1567.

Robert Estienne published his Greek New Testament in which, for the first time, the chapters were divided into numbered verses.

Publication of *Arte Subtilissima por la qual se ensena a escrevir perfectamente* by the Biscayan calligrapher Juan de Yciar, for which the plates were cut on wood by Juan de Vingles. Saragossa: Pedro Bernuz. (A facsimile of the 1550 edition of the *Arte Subtilissima* with an English translation by Evelyn Schuckburgh, C.B., C.M.G., was first produced by the Lion and Unicorn Press at the Royal College of Art, London, in 1958.)

The first Bible Concordance to be printed—that of Merbecke—was issued from the press of Richard Grafton. A Concordance to the New Testament had been compiled by Thomas Gybson and was published in 1535. John Merbecke was organist to the royal chapel at Windsor.

First printed edition of *The Vision of Piers Plowman* by Robert Langland. London: Robert Crowley.

First printed Bible in Danish, *Biblia . . . paa Danske*, known as *Christian III's Bible* because that King ordered it to be translated from Luther's version. Copenhagen: Ludwig Dietz (of Rostock).

Establishment of a printing-office at Cluj (Klausenburg, Kolozsvár) by Gaspar Heltai senior, a Lutheran preacher, in association with the printer Georg Hoffgreff, who learnt his trade in Nuremberg, probably with Ulrich Neuber. About 1552 the partners quarrelled and for two years Heltai carried on the business alone. In 1554 Hoffgreff again took charge of the office when Heltai went to Wittenberg, but after a few years he is heard of no more, and Heltai took charge of the business until his death in 1574. His widow continued his work until 1584, after which his son, Gaspar Heltai junior succeeded to the business which lasted until the end of the century.

In this year a letter-founder of Seville, Antonio de Espinosa, reached Mexico City, where he cast new type for Juan Pablos.

1551

At Tübingen the printer Ulrich Morhart, from Augsburg, issued the first printed book in the Slovene tongue—a Catechism translated by the Slovak, Primus Trubar. In 1555 Trubar issued, at Tübingen, his *Abecedarium with the Little Catechism*, also in Slovene.

At Florence, died Bernardo Giunta. The business was carried on by his heirs.

At Zürich, appeared the first volume of Conrad Gesner, *Historia Animalium*, published by Forschauer in five volumes, the last appearing in 1587, twenty-two years after the author's death.

Robert Estienne moved from Paris to Geneva.

Charles and Robert Estienne brought out their Greek edition of Appianus Alexandrinus, *Romanarum Historiarum*, set in three sizes of the famous 'grecs du roi', with handsome decorations and initials by Tory. Updike calls it, 'one of the most exquisite books printed from these fonts'.

Printing was introduced into Reims by Claude Chaudière when a university was opened there in 1551. He printed mainly editions of the classics.

Publication of Martin Cortes, *Breve Compendio de la sphera y de la arte de navegar*. Seville: Anton Alvarez. This was the most advanced treatise on navigational science that had so far appeared in print. It has many descriptions of the making of navigational instruments.

First edition in English of Sir Thomas More, *Utopia*. London: Abraham Veale. The printer was possibly Steven Mierdman.

The first part of William Turner's *New Herball* published in London, printed by Steven Mierdman. The second part was published by Arnold Birckman at Cologne, 1562.

Humphrey Powell, the first printer in Ireland, issued the *Boke of the common praier*, the printing of which may have begun in 1550, soon after his arrival in Ireland. Only two complete copies are known; one in Trinity College, Dublin, and the other in Emmanuel College, Cambridge.

1552

A printing-office was established at Prague by Jiřík Rozdálovsky (known as Melantrich), who had been a pupil of Melanchthon at Wittenberg, and later a corrector for Johann Froben at Basel. He designed a type-face known as 'Melantrich-Schwabacher'.

Jakob Bathen, from Louvain, became the first printer at Maastricht.

Robert Ballard appointed by Henri II of France to be King's Music Printer, a title which remained in the family until 1789. The types cut for Ballard by his father-in-law, Guillaume Le Bé, in 1540 remained in use for over 200 years.

Adrien Tournèbe, one of the most learned men of his day, was named French Royal Printer in Greek in succession to Robert Estienne.

At Aix-en-Provence the first recorded press is that of Vas Cavallis, who published in this year *Reiglement des advocats*.

The first printers at Pau were Jean de Vingle and Pierre Poivre, whose first book, in the dialect of Béarn, was *Los Fors et Costumas de Béarn*.

Publication of the Second Prayer Book of Edward VI, the First Prayer Book of 1549 having failed to win general acceptance by the Church. The first of the several editions of the *Second Book of Common Prayer* printed in 1552 and 1553 came from the press of Edward Whitchurch.

Archbishop Hamilton's *Catechisme* was the first book to be printed at St. Andrews, Scotland, and is the first surviving dated book of its printer, John Scot, who came from Edinburgh, where the first mention of him is recorded in 1539, though nothing printed by him in his early years is known.

Printing began at Belgrade, at the press founded by Radisa Dimitrović.

1553

Wolffgang Fugger issued his writing-book, *Nutzlich und wolgegrundt Formular* at Nuremberg. An English translation, the *Handwriting Manual*, translated by Frederick Plaat, with an introduction by Harry Carter, was published in 1960.

The first edition of the Old Testament in Spanish, known as the 'Ferrara Bible': *Biblia en lengua Española*. Ferrara: Duarte Pinel [alias Abraham Usque] at the expense of Jeronimo de Vargas [alias Yom Tob Athias].

At Vienna, Michael Zimmermann took over the printing office of Egidius Aquila, whose widow he married, and began to print books in Arabic and Syriac, being the first German printer to do so.

Publication of Michael Serveto (Servetus), *Christianismi restitutio*, printed clandestinely by Balthasar Arnoullet (though without his name) at Vienne in France. This book formed one of the main charges brought by Calvin against Servetus, who was burned at the stake, together with his book, on October 27. The first disclosure to the world at large of the existence of this book was made in Dr. William Wotton, *Reflections upon Learning, Ancient and Modern* (London, 1694).

The first English translation of Virgil—*The xiii Bukes of Eneados*, translated into Scottish metre by Gavin Douglas, Bishop of Dunkeld. London: [W. Copland?].

John Cawood (1514–72) replaced Richard Grafton as Royal Printer in England. The latter forfeited his post by printing the proclamation declaring Jane, wife of Guilford Dudley, to be Queen.

1554

At Rome was published Ferdinando Ruano, *Sette Alphabeti*, in which he extended the pattern of the mathematical construction of letters to cover italic.

Jan Kosořsky z Kosoře printed *Kozmograffia Czeská*, a Czech translation of Münster's *Cosmographia* of 1536, the finest Czech book of the sixteenth century.

First edition of André Thevet, *Cosmographie du Levant*. Lyons: J. de Tournes and G. Gazeau. It contains 27 fine woodcuts, including one of the author, by Bernard Salomon.

The first printed edition of Anacreon, *Teij Odae*. Paris: Henri Estienne. It shows three sizes of the 'grecs du roi' cut by Claude Garamond.

1555

The first press in Düsseldorf established by Jakob Bathen.

On 9 February died Christian Egenolff who had founded his Frankfurt printing office in 1531. The business passed to his two sons-in-law, Jacob Sabon and Conrad Berner.

Raphael Hoffhalter, engraver, type-founder and bookseller, settled in Vienna, where he joined Kaspar Kraft and established a type-foundry. Hoffhalter, a Pole whose real name was Skrzetuski, had worked for a time in the Netherlands, and later at Zürich. Hoffhalter worked in Vienna until 1563; in 1565 he was at Debreczen, then at Nagyvárad and finally at Belgrade, where he died in 1568. He employed many well-known artists, including Hirschvogel and Lautensack. One of his finest books was Petrus Ranzanus (Bishop of Lucera), *Epitome Rerum Ungaricarum*, 1558. (*See* 1560 *and* 1561.)

Christopher Plantin set up as a master printer in Antwerp. His first book was a bilingual treatise, *La Institutione di una Fanciulla nata Nobilmente: L'Institution d'une Jeune Fille de Noble Maison*, the work of the Venetian pedagogue Giovanni Michele Bruto (1517–92).

Pierre Belon of Mans (1517–64), an early authority on both ornithology and ichthyology, Published *L'Histoire de la nature des oyseaux*. Paris: B. Prevost for G. Cavellat.

Reviving the acts against heresy of Henry IV, Mary I issued a Proclamation forbidding the importation of the writings of 'Martin Luther, Oecolampadyus, Sivinglius, John Calvyn, Pomerane, John Alasco, Bullynger, Bucer, Melancthon, Barnardinus Ochinus, Erasmus Sarcerius, Peter Martyr, Hughe Latymer, Roberte Barnes, John Bale, Justus Jonas, John Hooper, Miles Coverdale, William Tyndale, Thomas Cranmer, Wylliam Turner, Theodore Basyll, otherwyse called Thomas Beacon, John Frythe Roye, and the book commonly called "Halles Cronicles" . . . or any other lyke booke, paper, wrytinge, or worke, made, printed, or set forth by any other persone or persons, conteyning false doctrine, contrarye and agaynste the catholyque faith, and the doctryne of the catholyque churche.'

1556

At Basel, H. Froben and N. Episcopus published Georgius Agricola (Georg Bauer), *De re metallica*, with 273 woodcuts by Hans Rudolf Manuel Deutsch. This treatise on metallurgy and mining is one of the first technological books. The book appeared the year following its author's death.

First edition of *One and Fiftie Psalms of David*, the metrical paraphrase of the Psalms by Sternhold and Hopkins. [Geneva: John Crespin?] This was the first collection of Sternhold and Hopkins to be printed with music.

Printing was introduced into Liège by Henri Rochefort.

In L. G. Gyraldio, *Pinax iconicus*, a book illustrated with nine finely executed copperplate engravings, the Lorraine engraver Pierre Woeiriot (1532–96) inserted a portrait of himself which is possibly the oldest French portrait engraved upon copper.

The first French edition of Marco Polo's travels—*La Description Géographique des Provinces et Villes plus Fameuses de l'Inde Orientale*. Paris: E. Groulleau. Strangely enough, although the work was originally written in old French at Marco Polo's dictation, this first printed edition in French is a translation of a Latin version, itself a re-translation of an Italian version of a Latin translation of an Italian version of the original.

Death of Sebastian Gryph (Greyff, Gryphius), who had worked at Lyons as printer-publisher since 1520. He was a native of Reutlingen. In 1532 he printed Rabelais' edition of the writings of Hippocrates and Galen. He was a friend of the martyred printer Étienne Dolet. After the death of Sebastian Gryph, his son Antony took over the business.

Death of Charlotte Guillard, a celebrated woman printer, who was the widow of two well-known printers, having married first Berthold Rembolt and secondly Claude Chevalon.

Independently of the Honterus Press (*see* 1535) another printing office started work at Kronstadt (Brasov) producing a number of service books in Rumanian under the direction of the Deacon Coresi and in part financed by the mayor of the city, Johann Benker. The Gospels in Rumanian appeared in 1561. Most of the Rumanian and Slavo-Rumanian books printed at Kronstadt are exceedingly rare, and many may have been later destroyed by the Orthodox clergy as being tainted with heresy.

The *Ordinary* printed at Mexico City by Juan Pablos was the first book with music to be printed in the New World.

Fray Juan Diez, *Sumario compendioso*, was printed by Juan Pablos in Mexico. This was the first mathematical book printed in the New World.

Printing entered India for the first time at Goa, when João Bustamente, who in that year joined the Society of Jesus, printed for the Jesuit missionaries *Conclusões e outras coisas*, of which no copy is now known.

1557

Johann Schirenbrand and Peter Schmidt set up the first press at Mulhouse. From 1559 to 1564 Schmidt printed on his own.

The first official *Index* of prohibited books published by the Roman Pontiffs was printed by Antonio Blado, but suppressed before publication. A second edition was published in 1559.

At Geneva, Conrad Bade printed Whittingham's New Testament with a preface by Calvin. It was the first English edition to introduce Estienne's division into verses. (*See* 1550.)

Arrival at Basel of Thomas Guarin, who had fled there from Tournai. He later married the daughter of Michael Isingrin, to whose business he succeeded. He has a long career as printer and publisher. The artist Tobias Stimmer worked for him.

At Lyons, Robert Granjon published *Dialogue de la vie et de la mort* by Innocenzio Ringhieri, translated by Jean Louveau, set in a new script type which had been cut by Granjon and to which

he gave the name 'Lettre françoise'. This form of letter became known as *civilité*, since it was largely used in courtesy books such as *La civilité puérile* of Erasmus and its many adaptations.

At Lyons, Jean de Tournes printed *La Métamorphose figurée* of Ovid, one of the most charming books of the period. It was illustrated with 178 vignettes delicately drawn and set within varied borders, the work of the celebrated Bernard Salomon, known as 'le Petit Bernard'.

The first press at La Rochelle was established by Barthélemy Berton.

Richard Tottel (*c.* 1530–1593) printed and published the celebrated anthology of poetry called *Songes and Sonettes written by the right honorable Lorde Henry Howard late Earle of Surrey and other*, but generally known as *Tottel's Miscellany*. It was the first anthology of lyric verse to be published in England and contained 271 poems, none of which had previously been printed. Eight editions had been published by 1587.

First edition of Robert Recorde, *The Whetstone of Witte*, in which algebra was for the first time introduced into England. Recorde, the first English author of books on arithmetic and geometry, is said to have been the first to use the sign $=$.

On 4 May the Stationers' Company of London received its Royal Charter of Incorporation (the history of the Company is given in detail in *The Stationers' Company* by Cyprian Blagden (1960)).

First edition of Thomas Tusser's *Hundreth Good Poyntes of Husbandrie*. (It was reprinted in 1834 by Charles Clark at his private press, Great Totham, Essex, for Longman & Co.)

1558

At Nuremberg, Christoph Heussler published the first volume of Hans Sachs' collected works, *Sehr Herrliche Schöne und warhaffte Gedicht. . . .* The fifth and final volume was published in 1579.

Luigi Cornaro (1475–1566) published at the age of 83 the treatise which immortalised his name, *Trattato de la vita sobria*. Padua: G. Perchacino. This defence of moderation in everything was translated into English (from a Latin translation) by the poet George Herbert and published at Cambridge in 1634.

At Geneva, Jean Crespin printed John Knox, *The First Blast of the Trumpet against the Monstrous Regiment of Women*, the violent diatribe of the Scottish Calvinist against Mary Queen of Scots, in which he argued that government by a woman is contrary to natural law.

A press was founded at Ovár (Altenburg) by the zealous Reformer, Gál Huszár, under the patronage of the Archduke Maximilian. He was for a time associated with the printer Raphael Hoffhalter, then working in Vienna, and is thought to have been helped by the latter in establishing his press at Ovár. In the early part of 1560 he left Ovár for Kassa (Kaschau) where he printed a Protestant Hymn-book. For religious reasons he fled from Kassa at the end of that same year and went to Debrecen (Debrezin) where he printed five known works between 1561 and 1562. He reappears as a printer at Komjáti in 1574 where he issued a fine Hymn-book with more than fifty decorated initials.

In the year following the first publication of a book set in *civilité* type (*see* 1557) Philippe Danfrie and Richard Breton published F. de Corlieu, *Brieve instruction pour tous estatz* at Paris, also set in this form of script type. According to Robert Brun (*Le Livre Français*) the type was cut by Granjon, who granted a concession for its exploitation to Danfrie. But Harry Carter and H. D. L. Vervliet (*Civilité Types*) are of the opinion that the type was cut by Philippe Danfrie, who was a metal-worker skilled in making astronomical and mathematical instruments as well as bookbinders' tools. (*See also* 1559.)

1559

The first allowed papal *Index Auctorum et Librorum Prohibitorum* (*see* 1557) issued by Pope Paul V and printed at Rome by Antonio Blado. At the close of the *Index* appears a list of sixty-one printers with a prohibition of all works printed by them.

Inauguration at Rome of the first Vatican Press under the style of *Tipografia Camerale*. This press, under the direction of the Florentine printer Antonio Blado de Asola, was not installed within the Vatican palace. (*See* 1587.)

The Zürich printer Andreas Gesner issued one of his finest productions, *Imperatorum Romanorum omnium imagines*, an extra large folio containing woodcut portraits $11\frac{1}{8}$ inches in diameter, based upon the woodcuts of medals first published by Strada in his *Thesaurus Antiquitatum* (Lyons, 1552). The publishers suggested that purchasers could remove leaves at their choice to be framed as wall decorations. Andreas and Jakob Gesner were both well-known Zürich printers, working sometimes together and sometimes separately. Andreas also worked occasionally in conjunction with Rudolf Wyssenbach.

On 7 September, Robert Estienne died at Geneva.

Alexander Leopold set up the first press at Graz, where he worked until 1562.

In the Netherlands, the Antwerp type-founder and printer Ameet Tavernier brought out a *civilité* type based on the contemporary Flemish hand. It is first seen in a Flemish version of Erasmus *De Civilitate* entitled *Goede manierlijcke seden*. Antwerp: Jan de Laet.

First complete edition of the *Heptameron*, by Marguerite de Navarre (1492–1549). Paris: Benoit Prévost. These tales were first printed in an incomplete form in 1558 under the title *Histoires des Amans Fortunez*.

At Paris was published P. Ramée, *Scholae Grammaticae*, the first work to make the systematic distinction, in printing, between U and V.

Probably in this year, Jón Matthíasson (*see* 1534) printed the first book in Icelandic at Breidabólsstadur. It was a translation of sermons by Antonius Corvinus, printed for Olafur Hjaltason, first Lutheran bishop of the see of Hóar.

1560

At Rome, Blado published the *Essemplare di piu sorti Lettere* of the writing master Giovanni Francesco Cresci.

First edition of the so-called *Geneva Bible*, because produced in that city by the Marian exiles and printed there by Rowland Hall. It was the first English Bible printed in roman type, and the first English printed text with division into verses. The translators were William Whittingham, Anthony Gilby and Thomas Sampson, and Miles Coverdale may have also had a hand in it. This version is also known as the 'Breeches' Bible from its rendering of Genesis iii, 7.

At Vienna, Raphael Hoffhalter (*see* 1555) brought out one of the finest books on tournaments—Hans Francolin, *Rerum praeclare gestarum, intra et extra moenia civitatis Viennensis. . . .* It contains eight magnificent large folding engravings by Hans Sebastian Lautensach.

An anonymous press was at work in Debreczen, Hungary.

First edition of the collected works of Pierre de Ronsard (1524–85). 4 vols. Paris: Gabriel Buon. This edition is described by Brunet as a 'prodigious rarity'. Four copies are known, of which only two are complete.

Nicolas Bacquenois, a well-known printer from Reims, set up the first press at Verdun. His first book was *Pour l'entière majorité du Roy très chrestien*.

The Paris printer Martin l'Homme was hanged for printing a pamphlet against the Guises, and in particular the Cardinal de Lorraine. Its title was *Epistre envoyée au Tigre de France*.

First edition of *Liber Precum Publicarum . . .* , the Latin translation of the English Prayer Book authorised by letters patent of Queen Elizabeth I. The printer was Reginald Wolfe, the Royal Printer in the learned tongues.

1561

At Rome, Pope Pius IV established the first papal printing office under the technical management of Paolo Manuzio, the son of Aldo. (*See* 1562.)

First edition of Francesco Guicciardini, *La Historia di Italia*. Florence: Lorenzo Torrentino. For the first time it showed Italy in the larger context of European politics as a whole.

At Haarlem was published Cicero, *De Officiis*, translated by Dierick Coornhert. In the dedicatory epistle from the translator to the Burgomaster and Aldermen of Haarlem occurs the first printed account of the Coster legend. (*See also* 1588.)

Death of Bernard Salomon (b. 1508), the celebrated woodcutter known as 'le Petit Bernard' who worked mainly for Jean de Tournes at Lyons. He was one of the finest artist-engravers of his day.

First Bible printed in Polish, known as the *Cracow Bible* or the *Leopolita Bible*. Cracow: N. and S. Scharffenberger.

Robert Lekprevik began printing in Edinburgh. His first dated book was *Ane oration . . .* by Theodore Beza (9 September, 1561).

The first work printed in India to have survived (*see* 1556)—the *Compendio spiritual da Vida Christãa*, completed 2 July, 1561 at Goa by João Quinquencio and João de Endem. The author was Dom Gaspar de Leão, first Archbishop of Goa.

1562

The first production of the papal printing office at Rome (*see* 1561) was Cardinal Pole's posthumous *De Concilio*.

The Bohemian Brothers, under their leader, Jan Blahoslav, founded a press at Eibenschitz, and in 1564 issued their first book, a Czech New Testament. (*See also* 1578.)

Printing began at Scutari when the printer known as Stefan of Scutari, who had worked with Vicenc Vuković at Venice, where he worked on the first part of the *Triod Cvetni*, 1560–61, returned to his native town to complete it on a press he had set up with the help of Camillo Zanetti.

Thomas Cromwell's *Great Bible* was reprinted in a quarto edition by Richard Harrison.

Reyner Wolfe printed the *Apologia* of Bishop Jewel, edited by Archbishop Matthew Parker.

1563

At Bruges, Hubert Goltzius published *Julius Caesar, sive Historiae Imperatorum Caesarumque Romanorum, ex antiquis numismatibus restitutae*, the first volume of a history of classical numismatics of which Marcus Laurinus was the sponsor. Goltzius (*c.* 1526–83) combined in this work his talents as author, artist, printer and publisher. The book contains a fine engraved portrait of Goltzius by Melchior Lorichius of Flensburg (1527–*c.* 1594). Hubert Goltzius, who had been a pupil of the Liège artist Lambert Lombard, published in 1557 *Icones imperatorum romanum*, which was later reprinted by Plantin.

The first press at Douai was set up by the Louvain printer Jacques Boscard, who inaugurated it by printing a Latin speech delivered at the recent opening of the university.

By Letters Patent of Charles IX of France (Mantes, 10 September), it was forbidden for any French printer to print without permission under penalty of being hanged or strangled.

At La Rochelle, Barthélemy Berton printed the celebrated treatise of the potter, Bernard Palissy: *Recepte véritable par laquelle tous les hommes de la France pourront apprendre à augmenter et multiplier leurs thrésors*. Part of the edition is dated 1564.

Jean de Tournes printed a handsome edition of the Psalms in the version of Clément Marot, so beloved of the Reformers of Geneva, for Antoine Vincent at Lyons.

At Brest-Litovsk was printed a Polish Bible (the second edition of the Bible in Polish) known as the *Radziwill Bible* because the Polish prince Nicholas Radziwill (1515–65) was responsible for collecting the band of scholars who translated it.

The first book on architecture to be published in England—*The First and Chief Grounds of Architecture* by John Shute, an architect and painter in the service of John Dudley, Duke of Northumberland. London: Thomas Marshe.

On March 27, a Bill brought into the House of Commons authorised the translation of the Bible and the divine service into Welsh. (*See also* 1567.)

Queen Elizabeth I granted a patent for seven years to William Salesbury of Llanrwst and the London printer John Waley for the printing of Bibles, Prayer-books, and other church service books in the Welsh tongue. In 1547 Salesbury had issued a *Dictionary in Englyshe and Welshe* printed in London by John Waley (*q.v.*).

First edition of John Foxe, *Acts and Monuments of these Latter Times touching Matters of the Church*, commonly known as *Foxe's Book of Martyrs*. London: John Day.

The first Russian press set up in Moscow by Ivan Fedorov and Peter Timofeiev Mstislaveć. (*See also* 1564.)

1564

Georg Willer, an Augsburg bookseller, brought out the first catalogue of the Frankfurt Fair—the first comprehensive book catalogue printed in Germany. This trade fair was held at Frankfurt during Lent and Michaelmas and flourished during the sixteenth and seventeenth centuries. The title of this catalogue was: *Novorum librorum quos nundinae autumnales, Francoforti anno 1564 celebratae, venales exhibuerunt, Catalogus*, etc. It was a quarto pamphlet of 10 leaves, listing 256 books. Willer's catalogues were issued regularly until his death, and were continued by his sons until 1627. (*See also* 1592.)

Gerard Mercator published his map of Great Britain in eight sheets. Three copies are known: one each at Wrotslaw (Breslau), Perugia and Rome.

Death of Jean de Tournes. The business was continued by his son.

Robert Lekprevik printed the Psalms in Edinburgh—the earliest example of music printing in Scotland.

Henry Denham, former apprentice of Richard Tottel, set up his own printing house in White Cross Street, Cripplegate, but moved the following year to Paternoster Row, where he remained, at the Sign of the Star, for many years. He printed for many of the well-known London booksellers.

The first dated book appeared in Russia, the *Apostol* (Acts and Epistles of the Apostles) printed by Ivan Fedorov at Moscow and richly decorated with woodcuts. He is thought to have brought the press and types from Poland. Ivan Fedorov, together with his partner, Peter Timofeiev Mstislaveć, worked in Moscow only until the end of 1565, when they disappeared for reasons unknown. But in 1568 we find a Psalm Book printed at Moscow by Neveza Timofeiev. The two earlier Moscow printers turned up a few years later in Zabludowo, near Bialystok, where they printed an edition of the Gospels.

1565

First edition of *The History of the Churche of Englande* by the Venerable Bede (673–735) translated by T. Stapleton from Bede's *Historia Ecclesiastica Gentis Anglorum*, completed in 731. Antwerp: J. Laet.

In Paris died Jean Grolier de Servier, Vicomte d'Aguisy (b. 1479), who held several high offices including that of Treasurer-General of the Duchy of Milan. A friend of Aldo Manuzio, he was one of the earliest of the great bibliophiles of France, and was renowned for the handsome manner in which his great collection of books was bound.

A wandering printer, Gosuin Goeberi, was the first to print at Sedan. In this year he printed for a local poet *Le Dieu-Gard de Navyere*, 'à l'imprimerie Sédanoise'.

The *Chasovnik*, a Book of Hours, printed by Ivan Fedorov at Moscow, was the earliest Greek Orthodox liturgical book to be printed in Russia, and the second earliest dated volume printed in that country. (*See* 1564.)

1566

Printing was introuced into Gotha by Thomas Rebart from Jena, who worked there until the following year. There was then a long gap in

Gotha's printing history until Peter Schmidt began to print there in 1640.

The last folio edition of the *Great Bible*, known as the *Rouen Bible* from the imprint which runs: 'At Rouen, at the coste and charges of Richard Carmarden. Cum privilegio. 1566.' It does not resemble any previous issue, the text being printed in larger and more heavily leaded type.

Nicolas Hierosme became the first regular printer at Nancy.

About the year 1566 printing began at Norwich after the arrival there of a printer from Brabant, named Anthony de Solen (Solempne) who printed several books in Dutch for the benefit of the religious refugees from the Low Countries who had settled in that city. He was made a freeman of Norwich on 11 December, 1570. The Psalms in Dutch came from his press in 1568, but the only specimen known of his printing in English is a broadside entitled *Certayne versis written by Thomas Brooke*, which has the colophon: 'Imprinted at Norwiche in the Paryshe of Saynct Andrewe by Anthony de Solempne. 1570.' He continued printing until 1579, but most of the products of his press have not survived.

At Copenhagen appeared Matthaeus Richter (Judex), *De typographiae inventione, et de praelorum legitima inspectione*, a treatise on the invention of printing and the proper manner of supervising a printing office.

1567

Paracelsus (Theophrastus von Hohenheim, 1493–1541) wrote the first treatise devoted to an occupational disease—*Von der Bergsucht und anderen Bergkrankheiten* (on miners' diseases), published posthumously at Dillingen by S. Mayer in 1567.

The earliest account of the working of a press appeared in a bilingual treatise, *La Première, et la Seconde Partie des Dialogues Francois, pour les Jeunes Enfans: Het Eerste ende Tweede deel van de Francoische t'samensprekinghen, overgheset in de nederduytsche spraecke*. Antwerp: Christopher Plantin. Two of the dialogues deal with writing and printing; the former was probably contributed by the writing master Pierre Hamon, while the latter was probably the work of Plantin himself, and contains much useful information concerning the technology of printing in the middle of the sixteenth century. (An English

translation with notes, by Ray Nash, was printed by D. B. Updike at the Merrymount Press in 1940 for the Department of Printing and Graphic Arts, Harvard College Library. It was reprinted in 1964 under the title *The Plantin Dialogue on Calligraphy and Printing in the 16th Century* by the Stinehour Press, Lunenburg, Vermont.)

Christopher Plantin, at Antwerp, issued the *Index, sive Specimen Characterum Christophori Plantini*, showing forty-one specimens of type used in the Plantin printing-house. (A facsimile with notes was published at New York by Douglas C. McMurtrie in 1924.)

Editio princeps of Lodovico Guicciardini, *Descrittione di tutti i Paesi Bassi*. Antwerp: Willem Silvius. This book was an early precursor of Baedeker and the Blue Guides. In the same year, a French translation was issued by the same printer; in 1580, a German version was printed at Basel by Sebastian Henricpetri; and in 1581, an augmented edition of the original Italian version was printed at Antwerp by Christopher Plantin. The first Dutch translation (by Kiliaen) appeared in 1612.

Anglo-Saxon type made its first appearance in Ælfric's *A Testimonie of Antiquitie*, printed by John Day under the direction of Archbishop Matthew Parker. Harry Carter and Christopher Ricks, in their foreword to Edward Rowe Mores's *A Dissertation upon English Typographical Founders and Founderies* (Oxford, 1961) doubt the assertion contained in the anonymous preface to Asser's *Ælfredi regis res gestae* (in which the type is again used) that Day cut the letters himself, and think it likely that the roman letters were of Flemish origin and that the runes mixed with them were made in London by one of Day's foreign journeymen.

First New Testament in Welsh issued. London: Henry Denham, at the cost and charges of Humphrey Toy. The translators were William Salesbury, Thomas Huet, and Dr. Richard Davis.

In the archives of Norwich is an entry from an aliens' register (reproduced in the *Proceedings of the Norfolk Archaeological Society*, Vol. 5, p. 78): 'Anthonius de la Solemme tipographus cum uxore et duobus pueris ex Brabantia huc venit.' (*See* 1566.) Another printer, Albert Christian, came from Holland in this year, but no work of his is known. He may, perhaps, have worked for Anthony de Solemne.

Death of Iceland's first printer, Jón Matthiasson,

who was succeeded by his son, also Jón. (*See* 1534, 1559.)

1568

The famous Frankfurt publisher Sigmund Feyerabend brought out Jost Ammann, *Eygentliche Beschreibung aller Stände*, more commonly known as *Das Ständebuch*, with 114 woodcuts by Jost Ammann depicting various trades and crafts, including those of paper-maker, type-founder, and bookbinder, each accompanied by rhymed verses from the pen of Hans Sachs (a facsimile reprint was published by Insel-Verlag, Leipzig, in 1960). Simultaneously with the German edition, Feyerabend brought out a Latin version *Πανοπλια, omnium illiberalium, mechanicarum aut sedentariarum artium genera continens*, of which the text was by the poet Hartmann Schopper. The order of the illustrations varies sometimes from that of the German edition. Moreover, the Latin edition has some extra pictures and verses depicting military ranks from Kaiser to Landsknecht, possibly at the request of Schopper who had fought against the Turks in Hungary.

On 9 July Pope Pius V issued an apostolic brief ordaining that the new revised Breviary, redrafted in accordance with the decision of the Council of Trent in 1563, should be adopted as soon as copies were ready. The privilege for the publication of this Tridentine Breviary was granted to Paolo Manuzio, printer to the Papal Court.

At Florence was published *Due Trattati* by one of the most famous of all goldsmiths, Benvenuto Cellini. These two treatises were the only works of Cellini published during his lifetime, for the famous autobiography was not published until 1728.

Publication, in Milan, of *Athrauaeth Gristnogaul*, the Catechism in Welsh, translated by Morys Clynoc, first Rector of the English College in Rome. Only one copy is known, in the Newberry Library, Chicago (a facsimile was published in 1880).

First illustrated and complete edition of Giorgio Vasari, *Le vite de' piu eccellenti pittori, scultori, ed archietti*. Florence: I. Giunta. The book was first published in 1550.

On 6 July, died Johannes Oporinus, one of the most famous of the early German printers, born at Basel in 1507. In 1569 was published Andreas Jociscus, *Oratio de ortu, vita, et obitu Johannis Oporini Basiliensis, typographorum Germaniae principis*, to which was added a list of books which came from the press of Oporinus.

Between 1568 and 1572 the second of the great Polyglot Bibles was published in eight folio volumes by Christopher Plantin at Antwerp under the general editorship of the Spanish theologian, Benito Arias Montano (1527–98). This work, one of the greatest typographical undertakings of the sixteenth century, was printed in five languages—Latin, Greek, Hebrew, Syriac and Chaldee.

At Antwerp Christopher Plantin printed Peter Heyns, *ABC, oft Exemplen om de kinderen bequamelick te leeren schryven*, set in Robert Granjon's *civilité* types.

First edition of the Bible sponsored by Archbishop Matthew Parker and known as the *Bishops' Bible*. London: Richard Jugge. It was sanctioned by Convocation and a copy was presented to Queen Elizabeth on 5 October, 1568.

1569

Gerard Mercator (Kremer) published at Duisburg his celebrated map of the world for seafarers, engraved on 24 large copper plates.

Thomas Guarin printed at Basel the earliest edition of the Bible in Spanish, translated by Cassiodoro de Reina.

At Paris, was published the writing book of Jacques de la Rue, *Exemplaires de plusieurs sortes de Lettres*.

John Day printed *Christian Prayers and Meditations*, often called *Queen Elizabeth's Prayer Book* from the figure of that queen which serves as frontispiece. (*See also* 1853.)

At Copenhagen, Laurentz Benedict printed *Den Danske Salmebog*, edited by Hans Thomisson (Thomesen). The musical notation in this book of Psalms was the first music printing from movable type in Denmark. Benedict was a prominent printer at Copenhagen, where he produced many fine service books, and was the first Danish printer to use German Fraktur types. He was also an artist who made several of the handsome woodcuts which decorate some of his books.

1570

First edition of Bartolomeo Scappi, *Opera*, one of the most famous cookery books of the sixteenth century, the result of Scappi's long experience in the kitchens of the Popes. Venice: M. Tramezzino. There are 27 engravings and a portrait of the author, who calls himself 'cuoco secreto di Papa Pio V'.

At Venice, Domenico de Franceschi published *I quattro libri dell' architettura* by the famous architect Andrea Palladio. The first English translation, by Giacomo Leoni, published 1715–16, incorporated the notes made by Inigo Jones in his copy of Palladio's book.

First edition of the *Theatrum Orbis Terrarum* by the geographer Abraham Ortels (Ortelius). Antwerp: Ægidius Coppenius Diesth (Gilles Coppens of Diest). Ortelius (1527–98) was appointed Royal Cosmographer to King Philip II of Spain in 1573. His atlas was translated and reprinted many times between 1570 and 1612.

In the latter part of this year (the exact date is not known), died the Antwerp punch-cutter and type-founder Ameet Tavernier. He was born *c.* 1522 at Belle (Bailleul) and learned punch-cutting at Ghent with Joos Lambrecht. In 1556, he became a citizen of Antwerp having already spent some years in that city. His types began to make their appearance in Antwerp-printed books from 1550 and spread to many countries. Best known of the characters which Tavernier engraved is a series of *civilité* types based on the current Flemish secretary hand, and the counterpart of Robert Granjon's 'lettre françoys'. Ameet Tavernier was also a printer, and around fifty books came from his press. The first book in which Tavernier's *civilité* is used is the *Civilité puérile* which he himself printed for Jean Bellère, 1559.

Death of the punch-cutter François Guyot, a Parisian who had settled in Antwerp and became a freeman of that city in 1539. He supplied Plantin and other Antwerp printers with type.

The first edition of Euclid in English—*Elements of Geometrie*. London: John Day.

The Huguenot refugee, Thomas Vautrollier, a Frenchman from Troyes who was granted letters of denization on 9 March, 1562, printed his first book, the writing-book entitled *A Booke containing divers sortes of hands* by Jean de Beauchesne and John Baildon. As far as is known, it was the first writing-book to have been published in England. The British Museum copy is dated 1571, but a copy is known, possibly unique, dated 1570.

1571

Pope Pius V instituted the Congregation of the Index for the purpose of enforcing the Tridentine Index and of dealing with questions relating to the prohibition or expurgation of books.

A *civilité* type called *Median geschreven* (Pica script) cut by the Ghent type-founder and punch-cutter Hendrik van den Keere, made its first appearance in A. Adrianensens, *Van ghehoorsaemheyt*. . . . Louvain: H. Welle.

At Dordrecht, Jean Canin issued the first edition of the Dutch Reformed Bible (*Deux-aes Bible*) to be printed in the Low Countries. (Earlier editions had been printed at Emden.)

In May, Charles IX of France issued the Edict of Gaillon, the first royal regulation in France regarding the book trade as a trade. The Edict, which contained twenty-four clauses, made apprenticeship obligatory in order to become a journeyman. The term of apprenticeship was qualified simply as 'un temps suffisant', but the minimum period from then onwards was three years, increased to four years in 1615. The Edict also required a master printer to be certified as capable by two sworn booksellers and two other master printers. Prior to this enactment, anyone could set up as a master printer in France.

On 3 April, Frédéric I Morel was appointed 'Imprimeur du Roi'.

Publication of the first New Testament in the Basque tongue—*Iesus Christ gure Iavnaren Testamentu Berria*. Rochellan: Pierre Hautin Imprimiçale. A translation from the Geneva version by Jean Leiçarraga, a Calvinist of Driscous.

At Madrid, the first edition of Francisco Lucas, *Arte de escrivir*.

Robert Henryson's adaption of Aesop, *Morall Fabillis*, printed at Edinburgh by Thomas Bassandyne in Robert Granjon's first script type.

In that year Robert Lekprevik went from Edinburgh to Stirling, where the Court then was, and introduced printing into that city with *Ane Admonition Direct to the trew Lordis mantenaris of the Kingis Graces Authoritie*. M.G.B. [George Buchanan]. Lekprevik returned to Edinburgh in 1573, after printing a few works at St. Andrews, and continued to work there until 1582.

The first known fount of Irish type was presented by Queen Elizabeth to John O'Kearney, treasurer of St. Patrick's Cathedral, Dublin, for the printing of the Scriptures in Irish. The earliest appearance of this fount (a hybrid one containing only seven distinctively Irish sorts) is in a broadside *Tuar Ferge Foighide*, a poem by Philip O'Huiginn, printed in 1571 and sent over to the Archbishop of Canterbury, presumably as a specimen of the type. In the same year it was used for a *Church Catechism and Articles*.

1572

Henri II Estienne, son of Robert Estienne, printed and published at Geneva his famous *Thesaurus Graecae Linguae* in five volumes folio (Vol. 5 appeared in 1573). The immense labour involved in this work impaired both his health and his fortune, but in 1579 Henri III awarded him a pension of 300 livres.

Death, at Geneva, of Jean Crespin, a native of Arras who embraced the reformed religion and went to Geneva where he gained a great reputation as a printer.

The famous printer Andreas Wechel narrowly escaped death during the Massacre of Saint Bartholomew. He fled from Paris and settled at Frankfurt-am-Main.

In London, on 1 April, died John Cawood, an original member of the Stationers' Company and Master in 1561, 1562 and 1566. He was appointed Queen's Printer jointly with Richard Jugge.

First edition of the great Portuguese epic *Os Lusiadas* by Luis de Camoẽs. Lisbon: Antonio Gonzalves. Two editions were printed in 1572. The one with the pelican's head on the border turned to the left is considered the earlier; in the other edition the bird's head is turned to the right.

1573

Printing first introduced into Aachen by Hans de Braecker, who had previously printed at Wesel 1558 to 1567.

The Medicean Press was established by Ferdinand I de' Medici, one of three cardinals charged with the task of endeavouring to reconcile the dissident Eastern churches. He commissioned the French punch-cutter, Robert Granjon, to engrave punches for various exotic types. The finest work of the Medicean Press, which closed in 1596 when its patron, after becoming Grand Duke of Tuscany, left Rome for good, was a lavishly illustrated edition of the Gospels in Arabic, issued 1590–91.

The first press at Orange (Vaucluse) was established by Adam du Mont from Avignon whose first book there was *Dialogus quo multa exponuntur quae Lutheranis acciderunt*.

Death of Reyner Wolfe, a printer who came to England about 1530 and obtained letters of denization 1533, in which he is described as a native of Gelderland. Wolfe was the first printer in England to possess a large stock of Greek type and later held a patent for printing in Greek. His Greek type seems to have been of Basel origin. He was Master of the Stationers' Company in 1560, 1564, 1567 and 1572. In April 1547, he was granted by Edward VI a patent for life as King's typographer and bookseller in Latin, Greek and Hebrew.

Death of the printer Richard Grafton. He left four sons and one daughter, who married the printer Richard Tottel.

The first book of the famous Danish astronomer Tycho Brahe (1546–1601), *De nova stella*, was published at Copenhagen. It was translated into English as *Astronomicall coniectur of the new and much admired star which appeared in the year 1572* (London, 1632).

1574

Leonhard Thurneysser zum Thurn (1530–96), doctor, goldsmith, alchemist, astrologer and adventurer, was a native of Basel. He became in 1571 physician-in-ordinary to the Elector Johann Georg who helped him to set up a press in the Grey Monastery at Berlin. On this he printed his own works and those of others. He owned many types, especially Oriental ones, and employed from time to time as many as 200 workmen. But through a series of misfortunes he was obliged in 1577 to sell his printing office to his compositor Michael Hentzke.

Publication of Giulio Antonio Hercolani, *Essemplare utile*, at Bologna. This writing-book was printed from engraved copper plates.

On 6 April, died Paolo Manuzio, third son of the elder Aldo Manuzio. He was born at Venice, 1512.

Henri Estienne published his book on the famous Frankfurt Fair, *Francofordiense Emporium* (it was reprinted, together with a French translation by Isidore Liseux, at Paris, 1875).

Thomas Vautrollier issued the second writing-book from his press: *A newe booke of copies, containing divers sortes of sundry hands*. The only known copy is in the Bodleian Library at Oxford.

Between the years 1574 and 1579 appeared the well-known maps of English counties by Christopher Saxton, known as 'the Father of English Cartography'. His complete atlas was published 1579.

The second Russian edition of the *Apostol* (*see* 1564) was printed at Lvov by Ivan Fedorov. On the last 5 leaves of this edition is an account by the printer of the destruction of his Moscow press.

1575

The Frankfurt punch-cutter Jacob Sabon, son-in-law of Christian Egenolff, was granted a privilege by the Emperor for the five sizes of Fraktur which he had cut, and anyone copying them was liable to a heavy fine.

The Provost Nikolaus Telegdy set up a press in his own house at Nagyszombat and so began a printing establishment which was the forerunner of the Royal Hungarian University Press founded at Budapest in 1777.

Queen Elizabeth granted a patent, dated 22 January, 1575, to the musicians Thomas Tallis and William Byrd for the publishing of music (apart from metrical Psalters) for the space of twenty-one years. Tallis died in 1585, and two years later Byrd assigned the privilege to the printer Thomas East.
Publication of Thomas Mors, *The Mariners Boke, containing godly and necessary orders and prayers to be observed in every ship, both for the mariners, and all other, whatsoever they be, that shall travaile one the sea, for their voyage*. London: Henry Bynneman.

1576

On 4 November, and the two following days, Antwerp was sacked by the Spanish soldiery in what has become known as 'The Spanish Fury'. Many printers were ruined, including Christopher Plantin who nine times over was forced to ransom his property, and at the age of nearly sixty had to set to work to retrieve the fortunes of his famous printing house. Only by his indomitable energy and the generous help of his friends was he able eventually to rebuild his business.

Publication of Loys le Roy, *De la vicissitude ou variété des choses en l'univers*. Paris: Chez Pierre l'Huillier. In Book Two of this work there is an early reference to the art of printing (it was reprinted in translation, 1955, as *Loys le Roy on the Art of Printing*. Oxford: New Bodleian Library.) A complete translation in English, by Robert Ashley, of Le Roy's work was published in 1594 by Charles Yetsweirt under the title: *Of the interchangeable course or variety of things in the whole world*.

Androuet Du Cerceau began the publication of *Les plus beaux bastiments de France*, with full page copper-plate engravings of the châteaux of the kings and nobility of France.

The first press at Posen (Poznán) set up by Melchior Nering.

William Lambarde published the first English county history, his *Perambulation of Kent*. It was several times reprinted in the sixteenth and seventeenth centuries, and a reprint of the second edition (1579) with a Life of Lambarde was published at Chatham in 1826 by W. Burrill.

1577

Willem Silvius appointed Printer to the University of Leyden. His son Charles succeeded him in 1580 but only exercised his craft for a year. He sold the business in 1583.

The New Testament in Polish printed at Cracow by Alexis Rodecki.

First edition of Holinshed; *Chronicles of England, Scotlande and Irelande*. London: Henry Bynneman. Additional matter appeared in a new edition of 1586–87, which was probably the edition used by Shakespeare to supply the facts for his English historical plays.
Dissatisfied members of the Company of Stationers drew up a 'Complaint of diverse of their hynderance by grauntes of privilidges' (Lansdowne MS. 48) in which it was stated that 'the privilidges latelie granted by her Majestie . . . hath and will be the overthrowe of the Printers and Stacioners within this Cittie, being in number 175'.

Andronik Timofeev went with Ivan Fedorov to Alexandrovkaya Slovoda and set up a small printing office where in 1577 they printed a Psalter.

At Amballakkadu, near Trichur, the first 'Malabar' (a term then used to signify both Malayalam and Tamil) types were cut by Joannes Gonsalves. No example of Amballakkadu printing survives, following the devastation caused by Tippoo's invasion of Travancore and Cochin.

1578

The first known printing at Ravenna—*Rime di diversi eccellenti autore* . . . printed by Cesare Cavazza.

The first press at St. Gallen was set up by Leonhard Straub.

At Antwerp, Christopher Plantin printed the *Masses* of Georges de la Hèle, one of the finest examples of music printing in any century. The music type was designed and cut by the Flemish punch-cutter Henrik van den Keere (Henri du Tour).

First printing at Nîmes. In this year Sébastien Jacquy printed *Questionnaire des tumeurs contre nature*.

At London, Christopher Barker printed the first large folio edition of the Geneva version of the Bible.

1579

Frédéric II Morel appointed 'imprimeur ordinaire du roi' not only for books in French, but also in Hebrew, Greek and Latin.

The Bible in the vernacular was printed for the first time in Scotland. The New Testament had been completed by Thomas Bassandyne, then in partnership with Alexander Arbuthnet, in 1576, but in January 1577, as the result of legal action, Bassandyne had to hand over to his former partner the printing house and the Bible as far as it had been printed. Bassandyne died on 18 October, 1577, and Arbuthnet completed the Bible, a reprint of the second folio edition of the *Geneva Bible*, at Kirk o' Field, Edinburgh, in 1579. Robert Lekprevik had obtained a licence in April 1568, to print the Bible in the Geneva version, but as far as is known he never made use of this privilege. Arbuthnet's slowness in producing the Bibles he had licence to print led the General Assembly to recommend that the London printer, Thomas Vautrollier, should be given permission to establish a press in Scotland.

First edition of Thomas North's famous translation of Plutarch's *Lives of the Noble Grecians and Romans*, one of Shakespeare's source books. The translation was made from that of Jacques Amyot, published in 1559, with additions from other writers. London: Thomas Vautrollier & John Wight.

First English edition of Marco Polo's Travels: *The most noble and famous travels of Marcus Paulus*. The translation is by John Frampton. London: for Ralph Newbery.

1580

The first book on football was printed at Florence by the Giunti. It was called *Discorso sopra 'l giuoco del calcio Fiorentino*, by Giovanni de' Bardi and details the somewhat complicated rules of the game as played in Florence in the sixteenth century. A plate shows a match taking place in front of Santa Croce.

Louis Elsevier settled in Leyden as bookbinder, later becoming bookseller and (1586) publisher. His son Isaac was appointed official publisher to the University of Leyden in 1620.

Editio princeps of Michel Eyquem de Montaigne, *Essais*. Bordeaux: S. Millanges. Two volumes 8vo. This first edition of Montaigne's *Essays* contained only two books, and the essays were shorter than in their final form. The first Paris edition was published by Jean Richer in 1587.

William Bullokar, one of the first Englishmen to propose a system of simplified spelling, published *Bullokars booke at large for the amendment of orthographie for English speech*. It was printed by Henry Denham. He also translated what he entitled *Aesop's fables in true ortography*, *with grammer notz*, published by John Jackson and Edmund Bollifant (1585).

1581

Death of Andreas Wechel, the son of Christian Wechel, and like his father a well-known printer of the Greek and Roman classics. It was at the house of Andreas Wechel that Sir Philip Sidney stayed when he was at Frankfurt.

First edition of Vincentio Galilei, *Dialogo . . . della musica antica e della moderna*. Florence: Giorgio Marescotti. Two of the musical examples in this book are printed from an engraved copper plate—the earliest known application of copper engraving to the printing of music.

The first press was established in Assisi by Jacques de Bresse, but no work from his press is now known.

Jean des Preyz set up the first press at Langres (Haute Marne). (*See* 1588.)

Printing was introduced into Malines by Jacobus Heyndricx, who had previously worked at Antwerp. The first book he printed at Malines was an account of the sack of the town by the Spaniards in 1572. Heyndricx died in 1582 and his printing office was taken over by Gilles van Cranenbroeck.

First edition of the Bible in Slavonic, known as the *Ostrog Bible* because it was prepared under the auspices of Konstantin, Prince of Ostrog. It was printed in folio by the Moscow printer Ivan Fedorov. The Psalms were published separately at Wilna the same year. A copy of the *Ostrog Bible* in the British Museum is thought to have belonged at one time to Ivan the Terrible.

1582

Printing was introduced at Middelburgh with the publication of an English work, Robert Browne's *A booke which sheweth the life and manners of all true Christians*. Middelburgh: R. Painter. The author was the founder of the sect called 'Brownists'.

The first Roman Catholic version of the New Testament in English was printed at Rheims by John Fogny. The translation was made for English Catholics by William Allen (later Cardinal, and Archbishop of Mechlin), Gregory Martin, and Richard Bristow, with notes by Thomas Worthington.

Publication of Baltasar de Beaujoyeulx, *Balet Comique de la Royne* printed with types cut by Guillaume Le Bé, who was the father-in-law of one of the publishers, Robert Ballard. Paris: Adrian le Roy, Robert Ballard & Mamert Patisson. This work was an important forerunner of French opera.

The first press at Calais was set up by Abraham Le Maire who in this year printed *Entrée, estat ou répertoire des deniers et marchandises estrangères*.

1583

Michael von Aitzing (Eytzinger) (1535–98) published at Cologne the first of his *Messrelationen*, the oldest half-yearly account of trade fairs with the market prices at Cologne, Aachen and the Low Countries. These 'Accounts of the Fairs' were at first semestrial, later annual.

Christopher Plantin appointed Printer to the University of Leyden.

ECP

Louis Rabier from Orléans, who called himself 'printer to the King of Navarre' set up the first press at Orthez (Basses-Pyrénées), where he began by printing a book in the dialect of Béarn *Los Psalmes de David*.

Publication of Sir Thomas Smith, *De republica Anglorum. The maner of government of England*, a book described by A. F. Pollard as, 'the most important description of the constitution and government of England written in the Tudor age'. London: H. Midleton for G. Seton. Eleven editions were published in England in less than sixty years, and it was translated into Latin, Dutch and German. In 1589 the title was changed to *The Common-welth of England*.

Thomas Thomas was appointed first official printer to the University of Cambridge.

Death of the London printer Henry Bynneman, whose first book came from the press in 1566.

On 17 December, died Russia's prototypographer, Ivan Fedorov. Originally a scribe, he founded at Moscow the earliest press established in Russia (*see* 1564). He did not remain in Moscow for long; being accused of heresy he fled to Lithuania and set up another press near Vilno. He later went to Lvov, where he set up a third press and printed another edition of the *Apostol*, with which he had made his début at Moscow. He left Lvov to settle at Ostrog, which owes to him the fourth press established in Russia, and one which became famous for the production of the *Ostrog Bible*. (*See* 1581.)

A missionary, Father Ruggieri, caused to be printed in xylogravure at Tchao-kin his *Catechism* in the Chinese language. This was the first book of apologetics in Chinese and the first book printed by Europeans in China. 1,200 copies were printed, of which only two seem to have survived.

Printing introduced into Angra, capital of Tercera, one of the Azores. In the Bodleian Library, Oxford, is the only known copy of *Relación de la jornada, expugnación, y conquista de la isla Tercera*, etc. The colophon reads: 'Fecha en la ciudad de Angra de la isla Tercera, a onze de Agosto, mil y quinientos y ochenta y tres.'

1584

First edition of *Ierusalem . . . brevis descriptio* by Christiaan van Adrichem (1533–85). Cologne: Godfried van Kempen. This description of

Jerusalem was reprinted many times and was translated into most of the European languages.

First edition of the Slovene Bible. Wittenberg: Heirs of H. Krafft.

On 2 September, died Hans Lufft, prominent printer of Reformation books and known as 'the Bible printer' because between 1534 and 1574 he printed more than 100,000 Bibles.

The Eliot's Court Press issued its first book, Edmund Bunny's edition of Robert Parsons, *Booke of Christian Exercise*. This press was formed by a syndicate of four men—Edmund Bollifant, Arnold Hatfield, John Jackson, and Ninian Newton—who set up as printers to the trade in Eliot's Court, Little Old Bailey, London. The press took as its device the caduceus.

At the Castle of Uranienborg, on the little island of Ven, the astronomer Tycho Brahe established, together with an observatory, a press and a paper mill, thereby becoming the first paper-maker in Sweden. His printing office was later transferred to Wandsbeck, near Hamburg.

First edition of the complete Bible in Icelandic printed at Hólar by order of Gudbrand Thorlakson, Bishop of Hólar and under the auspices of Frederick II, King of Denmark. The printer was Jón Jónsson.

Printing revived in Moscow by Andronik Timofeev.

The first press in South America and the second in the New World was established at Lima, Peru, by Antonio Ricardo. The first product of that press was *Pragmatica sobre los diez dias del año*, containing instructions from the King of Spain regarding the reformation of the calendar by Pope Gregory XIII. Ricardo, a native of Turin, came to Lima from Mexico, where he had set up a press in 1577.

1585

The first known appearance of Chinese characters in a Western book is in Juan Gonzalez de Mendoza, *Historia de las cosas mas notables [sic.], rites y costumbres del gran Reyno de la China*. Rome: V. Accolti. The characters in this book are, however, very badly formed and the first proper printing of Chinese characters is seen in Martinus Martini, *Novus Atlas Sinensis*, published at Amsterdam in 1655 by J. Blaeu.

At Graz, Georg Widmanstetter set up a printing office which through successive generations of the family became famous, and is today continued by the Steiermark Gauverlag & Druckerei.

First edition of Simon Stevin, *De Thiende*. Leyden: Christopher Plantin. The book which introduced the decimal system.

In this year was published the best known of all the maps of Gerard Mercator—the first part of his celebrated collection of maps, to which he gave the name of *Atlas*. Part 2 appeared in 1590 and Part 3 in 1595, in which year the three parts were also published together (107 maps).

Establishment of the third press at Oxford, with Joseph Barnes, an Oxford bookseller, as Printer to the University. The first book issued was John Case, *Speculum moralium quaestionum in universam Ethicem Aristotelis*.

Richard Tottel unsuccessfully petitioned the government for a grant of land on which to establish a paper mill.

1586

The first music intended for performance to be printed from engraved copper plates: an anthology of songs called *Diletto spirituale*. Rome: Simon Verovio. The engraver is thought to have been Martin van Buyten. In the same year Verovio issued another book with engraved music—Jacopo Peetrino's *Primo libro delle melodie spirituale*.

Formation at Paris of 'Compagnie de la Grand Navire' composed of Baptiste Dupuis, Jacques Dupuis, Sébastien Nivelle, and Michel Sonnius. It was formed for the financing of big publishing projects. (*See also* 1622.)

Decree of the Court of Star Chamber 'for orders in printinge', requiring all printers to declare the number of presses in their possession to the Master and Wardens of the Stationers' Company and forbidding all provincial presses except one each at Oxford and Cambridge. The Wardens of the Stationers' Company were given powers to search for and carry away all presses and printing material used for printing unlicensed works contrary to the Queen's injunctions of 1559.

The first Greek book printed at Oxford by the University Press—St. John Chrysostom's Homilies edited by John Harmar and printed by Joseph Barnes.

In January, died John Walley, a London printer who began to exercise his craft about 1546, was an original member of the Stationers' Company, Renter from 1554 to 1557, and three times

Warden. He was followed in the business by his son Robert, who was brought on the livery of the Company in 1585.

1587

The first printed version of the Faust legend—*Historia von D. Johann Fausten dem weitbeschreyten Zauberer unnd [sic] Schwartzkünstler*. Frankfurt-am-Main: Johann Spies. The first English edition, translated by P. F. Gent, was published at London in 1592 under the title: *The historie of the damnable life and deserved death of Dr. John Faustus.*

The Vatican Press was installed within the palace by Pope Sixtus V on 27 April, 1587 by the Bull *Eam semper.* (*See also* 1559.)

The Typographia Medicea founded by Cardinal Ferdinand de' Medici and placed under the management of G. B. Raimondi. Robert Granjon cut several Oriental founts for this press.

First edition at Edinburgh of Andrew Simson, *Rudimenta grammatices.* An MS. note in Herbert's annotated edition of Ames: 'This book in some measure superseded the *Grammar* of Despauter . . . and was so grateful to the youth that it was long the only institute which was much studied in the Scottish schools.'

The first Almanac printed in Ireland by William Farmer at Dublin.

1588

Printing introduced into Riga by the German Niklas Mollyn, who in 1590 obtained from Sigismund III a privilege for himself and his heirs.

Pope Sixtus V ordered the Congregation (*see* 1571) to draw up a new and enlarged edition of the Tridentine Index.

Publication at Antwerp by Christopher Plantin of *Batavia*, a history of Holland in Latin by Hadrianus Junius (Adraen de Jonghe) in which occurs the story of the invention of printing by Laurens Janszoon Coster, a native of Haarlem, about 1440. Although the claim of Holland to have been the cradle of printing had already been put forward in the *Cologne Chronicle* of 1499 and in Jan Van Zuren's *Dialogue on the first . . . invention of printing* printed some time between 1549 and 1561, Hadrianus Junius was the first to mention Coster by name. Although there is good ground for believing that a crude form of printing from movable types was practised in

Holland very early, there is very little evidence in support of the theory that Coster was its inventor (the chief upholder of his claim was Dr. J. H. Hessels in, *inter alia, Haarlem the birthplace of printing, not Mentz* (1887). *But see* V. Scholderer on 'The Invention of Printing' in *The Library*, June, 1940).

At Langres, Jean des Preyz issued a classic of the ballet, the *Orchesographie* of Thoinot Arbeau (i.e. Jehan Tabourot). It was translated into English by Cyril Beaumont, who himself published it in 1925.

In October Robert Waldegrave printed on a secret press at East Molesey, Surrey, the first of what are known as the *Marprelate Tracts*, reputed to have been written by one John Penry, a Welsh Puritan, and attacking the episcopacy. They appeared under the pseudonym of Martin Marprelate. Waldegrave, who was twice imprisoned for printing Puritan pamphlets, moved his press from place to place, but in the end, to escape further imprisonment he fled to La Rochelle, and thence, in 1590 to Edinburgh, where he was appointed King's Printer to James VI. When James succeeded to the English throne Waldegrave returned to London, where he died in 1604. The Marprelate press was, after the flight of Waldegrave, carried on by others.

First edition of the Bible in Welsh, translated by William Morgan—*Y Beibl Cyssegr-lan.* London: Deputies of Christopher Barker.

At London, printed by J. Windet, appeared the first edition of Timothy Bright (*c.* 1551–1615), *Characterie, an Arte of shorte, swifte, and secret writing by Character.* This early shorthand book was reprinted in 1888, edited by J. H. Ford.

John Legate was appointed printer to the University of Cambridge in succession to Thomas Thomas, who died in 1588. (*See also* 1591.)

On 18 June, died Robert Crowley, scholar, preacher and a member of the Stationers' Company. His imprint appears on many books, but they were mostly printed by others. A Protestant, he went to Frankfurt on the accession of Queen Mary. After her death he returned to England and held a number of ecclesiastical preferments, among them the living of St. Giles's, Cripplegate, where he was buried. (*See also* 1549.)

First printed book in a European language to be issued in Macao—*Christiani pueri institutio adolescentiaeque perfugium*, by Joannes Bonifacius, S.J., 'Apud Sinas in Portu Macaensi in Domo Societatis Iesu'.

1589

On 1 July, died Christopher Plantin and was buried in the apse of Antwerp Cathedral. The Antwerp business was carried on by his son-in-law Jan Moerentorf (Moretus), and the Leyden printing office by another son-in-law, François Raphelengien. The Antwerp office functioned until 1867.

Queen Elizabeth granted a concession for paper-making to John Spilman (Spielmann), a German, later knighted, who had acquired Bicknor Manor, near Dartford, Kent, with its wheat and malt mills. He established a paper mill there, having been granted a monopoly, 'for the gathering of all maner of linen ragges, skr lles, or scraps of parchment, peaces of Lyme, Leather, Shreddel and Slippinges of Cardes and oulde fishinge Nettes, fitte and necessarie for the makinge of anie sorte of white wrightinge paper'. After a century or so the business declined as others entered the field, and in 1732 the decayed mill became a gunpowder factory.

Publication of the second Danish Bible, known as *Frederick II's Bible*. Copenhagen: Matz Vingaard. The illustrations are similar to those in the *Bishops' Bible* of 1568 (*q.v.*).

1590

At Frankfurt-am-Main appeared the first volume of the topographical work *Collectiones peregrinationum in Indiam orientalem et Indiam occidentalem* by Theodore de Brye (1528–98) assisted by his sons Johann Theodore (1561–1623) and Johann Israel (1570–1611). Six volumes were published in Theodore's lifetime, but the whole work was not completed until 1634 with the publication of Vol. 25.

First edition of the complete Magyar Bible, translated by Gaspar Karoli (1529–91), pastor of Göncz in Upper Hungary. Visoly: Valentine Mantskovic. The costs of this Bible were defrayed by Sigmond Rákóczi (later Prince of Transylvania) and István Báthori.

First edition of Christopher Marlowe's *Tamburlaine the Great*. London: R. Jones.

Publication of the first three books of Edmund Spenser, *The Faery Queene*. London: [J. Wolfe] for W. Ponsonby. The second three books were published in 1596, printed for Ponsonby by Richard Field.

The first paper mill established in Scotland by a German paper-maker named John Groot Heres at Dalry, Edinburgh. The concession was granted by the Lords of Council, and Heres had the financial backing of a Scottish merchant, Mungo Russell, and his son Gideon.

1591

First book printed at Teramo—Mutio de Mutii, *Il padre de famiglia*, printed by Is. & Lepido Facio Fratelli.

Editio princeps of the Gospels in Arabic. Rome: Typographia Medicea. The editor was J. Baptista Raimondi, the director of the printing office.

The French ambassador at Constantinople, François Savary, Comte de Brèves, had an Arabic fount cut there in three sizes; they were finished in Paris by Le Bé, and were used to print an Arabic version of the Psalter in Rome in 1614. Other oriental types were cut for Savary de Brèves by Jacques de Sanlecque, Le Bé's pupil. (*See* 1596.)

John Legate, printer to the University of Cambridge, printed the first Cambridge Bible—an octavo edition of the Geneva version. He was the first printer to use the Cambridge emblem on his title-page. Legate married the daughter of the printer Christopher Barker.

A document in the Land Revenue Records, London, reads: 'Fenclifton, Co. Cambridge—lease of a water mill called paper mills, late of the bishopric of Ely, to John George, dated 14 July, 34th Eliz.'

The first book printed in Japan with European characters and in the Japanese language was *Flos Sanctorum o vida de los Santos: Sanctos No Go Sanguio no Uchi Nuqigaqi*. These two little volumes of 8 and 9 leaves respectively were printed at the Seminary of Cazzusa, belonging to the kingdom of Arima, whose ruler had become a Christian. In 1592, the Seminary was transferred from Cazzusa to the island of Amacusa, where several other works were printed, including a Portuguese-Japanese dictionary.

1592

The Egenolff-Berner type-foundry at Frankfurt-am-Main issued its first specimen sheet—this is apparently the earliest surviving sheet of type-founder's specimens issued in Europe, and an extremely valuable source of information regarding early types, since their designers are designated.

The first collected edition of the Georg Willer catalogues of the Frankfurt Fair from 1564 to 1592 was published at Frankfurt by Nicolaus Basse, who came from Valenciennes. (*See also* 1564.)

Publication at Rome of the Clementine Vulgate, which is still the official Roman Catholic Bible.

Hans Konrad Waldkirch became the first printer at Schaffhausen. He had previously worked at Basel, to which city he returned after having printed only one known book at Schaffhausen, *Christliche Ordnung und Brauch der Kirchen zu Schaffhausen. . . .* It may well be that he was called in especially to print that particular book. After his departure, Schaffhausen remained without a printer for more than half a century.

The first book printed in England to employ Hebrew type in any quantity—the *Cambro-brytannicae Cymraecaeve linguae institutiones* of J. D. Rhys, printed by Thomas Orwin. (In 1528 De Worde had made use of a few words of Hebrew roughly cut in wood for Wakefield's *Oratorio*.)

1593

Printing introduced into Hanau by Wilhelm Antonius, who worked there until 1611. The business was carried on by his heirs until 1615.

Editio princeps of Shakespeare, *Venus and Adonis*. London: Richard Field. The presumably unique copy of this edition is in the Bodleian Library, Oxford.

John Norden (1548–1625) published his first cartographic work, the *Speculum Britanniae* Part I—a descriptive account of Middlesex, with a map of the county.

1594

First catalogue of books displayed at the Leipzig Fair published by Henning Gross.

Louis Elsevier (b. Louvain in 1546 or 1547) was, on 8 August, admitted a burgess of Leyden. He was the first of that name to achieve fame as publisher and bookseller.

Jean Gillet introduced printing into Montpellier with a *Discours de la défaite de Soissons*.

Shakespeare's *Rape of Lucrece* printed by Richard Field for John Harrison.

1595

On 19 April, died Gilles Beys the Parisian printer and son-in-law of the Antwerp printer Christopher Plantin, whose youngest daughter, Madeleine, he had married. His widow later married the printer Adrien Périer.

Pierre Mascaron printed the first book at Marseilles—*Obros et rimos prouvenssalos* by the Provençal poet Louis Bellaud de la Bellaudière (Loys de la Bellaudiero). There was another issue the same year with an 'Avertissamen as letours'.

Publication of the first part of the *Catalogue of English Books*. London: John Windet for Andrew Maunsell. The second part was issued the same year, printed by James Roberts. This was the first catalogue intended primarily for the English book trade. A reprint was published in 1966 by the Gregg Press. The first volume listed 2,639 theological works written in or translated into English; the second listed 321 books dealing mainly with science, mathematics and medicine. Maunsell announced his intention of publishing a third volume devoted to law, history, poetry and other subjects, but he died in 1596 and the projected third volume was never issued.

First edition of Sir Philip Sidney, *An Apologie for Poetrie*. London: [J. Roberts] for H. Olney. An edition under the title *The Defence of Poesie* was printed in the same year for William Ponsonby. Publication was posthumous, Sidney having died in 1586.

1596

First edition of Jan Huygen van Linschoten, *Itinerario*. Amsterdam: Cornelius Claesz. This book first pointed out to the Dutch the importance of trade with the East Indies and by its influence stimulated the formation of the Dutch United East India Company.

Jacques de Sanlecque, punch-cutter and typefounder, and pupil of Guillaume Le Bé, started a foundry in Paris. He gained a measure of celebrity as engraver of the oriental types cut for the scholar Savary de Brèves for his printing office in Rome. These types returned to Paris and were used by the printer Antoine Vitré for the Polyglot Bible of Le Jay, ten volumes, Paris 1628–45.

1597

Printing introduced into Kassel by Wilhelm Wessel, who worked there until 1626. He was also an engraver. His son Johannes followed him in the business from 1626 until 1639.

Death of Aldo Manuzio the grandson, with whom the famous printing dynasty came to an end.

On 20 July died François Raphelengien, printer to the University of Leyden, and son-in-law of the Antwerp printer Christopher Plantin, whose daughter Margaret he had married. His wife had died in April 1594. Two of his sons, Christopher and François, followed their father's profession.

Publication of Thomas Morley, *A Plaine and easie Introduction to practicall Musicke*. London: Peter Short. The most famous of Elizabethan treatises on music, this book went through several editions and was reprinted as late as 1771.

Peter Short printed John Dowland, *First Booke of Songes and Aires*.

John Gerard published his *Herball or Generall Historie of Plantes*. London: John Norton. This folio contained 2,146 woodcut illustrations, most of which are from the blocks with which Tabernaemontanus illustrated his *Eicones* (1590).

Editio princeps of Shakespeare's *Richard II* and *Richard III*. London: Valentine Simms for Andrew Wise. Also the first garbled edition of *Romeo and Juliet*. London: [John Danter].

Editio princeps of the *Essays* of Francis Bacon. London: J. Windett for H. Hooper. The first edition contains only ten essays; that of 1612 has thirty-eight; and that of 1625 has fifty-eight.

1598

At Lyons died Henri II Estienne.

First edition of Shakespeare, *Loves Labours Lost*. London: William White for Cuthbert Burbie.

The first edition of Chapman's Homer— *Seaven Bookes of the Iliades of Homer. . . .* London: John Windet.

First edition of John Stow, *A Survey of London*. London: John Wolfe.

1599

The first known book-auction catalogue was issued, describing the library of Philipp van Marnix of St. Aldegonde, Dutch statesman and writer, secretary to Prince William I and to the States-General. The sale probably took place under the direction of Louis Elsevier in Leyden. Only two copies of this catalogue are known to have survived, in Amsterdam and Copenhagen.

Willem Janszoon Blaeu started business in Amsterdam as a publisher of maps, globes and books.

Death of the famous French punch-cutter Guillaume Le Bé, born at Tours in 1525.

First edition of the Bible translated into Polish by J. Wujek, which became the standard Roman Catholic version of the Bible in Polish. It was printed at Cracow at the press of Lazarus Andrysowicz at the cost of the Archbishop of Gniezno (Gniesen).

First edition of King James VI of Scotland, *Basilikon Doron*, containing his instructions to 'his Dearest Sonne, Henry the Prince'. The volume was privately printed by Robert Waldegrave, who was sworn to secrecy, and according to James only seven copies were printed. One copy is now in the British Museum (G. 4993).

On 29 November, died Christopher Barker, printer to Queen Elizabeth I. He was buried in St. Mary's Church, Datchet, near Windsor.

The Swedish antiquary Johannes Bureus published at Uppsala a large single sheet folio of runic inscriptions engraved by himself on copper. He later designed, and possibly cut, runic types cast at Stockholm by Andreas Gutterwitz for Bureus's alphabet book of runes, 1611.

1600

At Hamburg, a publishing firm was founded by Georg Ludwig Froben, a relative of the famous Basel printer.

The first opera to survive in printed form: Jacopo Peri, *Euridice*. Florence: Giorgio Marescotti. The first performance took place at the Pitti Palace, Florence, on 6 October, 1600.

Without precise date, but probably between 1600 and 1610, appeared the oblong quarto picture book entitled *Nova Reperta* which contains the often reproduced engraving by Stradanus (Jan van der Straet, 1523–1605) of a contemporary printing office. The book went through several editions, of which at least one edition was published by Philip Galle and another by Jean Galle. All are undated, and some are heterogeneous copies made up of engravings from the Philip Galle and Jean Galle editions. In fact the series was often republished, with some variants, by several members of the Galle family. Jean Galle was the eldest son of Theodore Galle and Catherine Moerentorf (Moretus).

First editions of Shakespeare, *A Midsummer Nights Dream*. London: James Roberts for Thomas Fisher; *Henry V*. Thomas Creed for Thomas Millington and John Busby; *The Merchant of Venice*. James Roberts; *Much Ado About Nothing*. Valentine Sims for Andrew Wise and William Aspley.

First edition of William Gilbert, *De Magnete . . .*, a book which has been described as the first major original contribution to science that was published in England. London: Peter Short. (An English version, *On the magnet . . .* was published in London in 1900, translated by Silvanus P. Thompson.)

First edition of *England's Helicon*, one of the best anthologies of English lyric writing of the Elizabethan period. London: I. R. [John Roberts] for John Flasket.

1601

First printed edition of the *Myrobiblion* of the Patriarch of Constantinople, Photius (815–891), an industrious lexicographer of the Byzantine Age. Augsburg: Hans Schulter the Elder. This work (in Greek) is a nomenclature of books read and commented upon by this enlightened scholar, who revealed in this way numerous texts which have since disappeared.

First edition of *Animadversiones in historiam generalem plantarum* by the botanist Gaspard Bauhin (Caspar Bauhinus). Frankfurt: Melchior Hartmann.

The Herzog Friedrich Wilhelm von Sachsen, who had a press built in his castle at Torgau, took it to Weimar, into which city printing was thus introduced. Unhappily the first printing from this Weimar press was the announcement of the Duke's death in 1602.

1602

The heirs of Andreas Wechel (d. 1581), his son-in-law Claude de Marne and his daughter Margaret, widow of Jean Aubry, transferred their press to the headquarters of the Calvinist colony at Neu-Hanau.

First edition of Shakespeare, *The Merrie Wives of Windsor*. London: Thomas Creed for Arthur Johnson.

Publication in London of John Willis, *The Art of Stenographie*. To Willis is generally given the credit of inventing the first English stenographic alphabet.

On 8 November, the Bodleian Library, Oxford, was first opened to the public. The first librarian was Thomas James.

John Franckton printed in Dublin the first Irish New Testament, making use of the Irish fount of Queen Elizabeth. (*See* 1571.)

The first European press in the Philippines was set up by the Dominicans at Binondo.

1603

First printing press at Groningen set up by an East Frisian savant named Ubbo Emmius, whose works were printed on it (1603–5) by Groningen's first printer, Gerhard Ketelius.

1604

First press at Goslar established by Johann Vogt (d. 1625), who printed there, *inter alia*, an illustrated folio Bible.

First edition of Christopher Marlowe, *Tragical History of Dr. Faustus*. London: V. S. [Valentine Sims] for Thomas Bushell.

A Japanese *Vocabulary* was printed by the Jesuit Fathers at Nagasaki, on the island of Ximo.

1605

At Nuremberg the engraver Johann Sibmacher published his famous *Wappenbuch*. Many editions were printed, including one with historical, genealogical and heraldic tables and notes, in eight volumes (Nuremberg, 1856–1936).

Printing introduced at Darmstadt by Balthasar Hofmann, who worked there from 1605 to 1622. The first product of this press was *Ein Christliche Predigt von dem erschrecklichen Chasmate*, by the minister, Heinrich Leuchter.

Johann Maximilian Helmlin became the first printer at Rottweil.

Nikolaus Hampel, who in 1602 married Anna Judith, daughter of the Marburg printer Paul Egenolff, introduced printing into Giessen.

At Prague, Peter Loderecker published his *Dictionarium Septem Diversarum Linguarum*, the seven languages being Latin, Italian, Dalmatian, Bohemian, German, Polish and Hungarian. Prague: 'E Typographaeo Ottmariano'.

Jan van den Velde published at Amsterdam his *Spieghel der Schriftkonste*, which had a great influence on calligraphy in Germany and Scandinavia.

Editio princeps of Part I of Miguel de Cervantes Saavedra, *El Ingenioso Hidalgo Don Quixote de la Mancha*. Madrid: Juan de la Cuesta. 664 pp. quarto. The Second Part, 584 pp. quarto, was published at the end of 1615. (A facsimile of the original editions of Part 1 and Part 2 was brought out at Barcelona in 1872.) (*See also* 1612.)

1606

Cantrell Legge was appointed Printer to the University of Cambridge. He died in 1625, and was succeeded by Thomas Buck, said to have been 'a quarrelsome man but a good printer'.

The edition of the Gospels printed in Church Slavonic at Moscow by Onisim Mihailov Radishevski, who had been with Ivan Fedorov's press at Ostrog, contains the first important example of Russian book illustration.

1607

At Padua, the architect Vittorio Zonca brought out a technical work, *Nuovo teatro di machine ed edificii*. It was reprinted at Padua in 1621, 1640(?) and 1656.

Editio princeps of the *Diodati Bible* in Italian— the version made by Giovanni Diodati (1576– 1649) 'di nation Lucchese' [Geneva]. In its modern form it is the official Bible of Italian Protestants. Some copies bear the imprint *In Geneva* and *Apresso Johanne Tornesio* (Jean II de Tournes).

John Franckton printed at Dublin the *Book of Common Prayer* in folio in Irish type. It was subsidised in part by the Government, and probably also by William Daniel, or O'Donnell, consecrated Archbishop of Tuam in 1609.

An edition of Camden's *Britannia* was published by George Bishop and John Norton which included a series of county maps.

1608

At Breslau, the learned Oriental traveller Peter Kirsten set up a press in his house and printed from Arabic manuscripts. The first to appear was *P. Kirstenii . . . Decas Sacra Canticorum et Carminum Arabicorum ex aliquot MSS.*[is] [1609].

The first appearance of tied notes in music printing was in Gabriel Bataille, *Airs de differents autheurs mis en tablature de luth*. Paris: Pierre

Ballard. It also has round-headed notes instead of the more usual diamond-shaped notes. The Ballard family enjoyed almost a monopoly of music-printing in France for more than a century.

1609

In this year appeared the two first regular numbered and dated news-books, both of which appeared in January. They were: the *Avisa, Relation oder Zeitung*, probably printed at Wolfenbüttel by Julius Adolph von Söhne; and the *Relation: aller Fürnemen und gedenkwürdigen Historien*, printed at Strassburg by Johann Carolus. The *Avisa* was founded and in part written by Duke Heinrich Julius as part of his attempt to reconcile the Protestant and Catholic factions.

First edition of Johannes Kepler, *Astronomia nova* $A\widetilde{\iota}\tau\iota o\lambda o\gamma\eta\tau os$ [Heidelberg: E. Vögelin]. In this book, and in his *Harmonices mundi* (1619), Kepler put forward his three laws of planetary motion. Only a few copies of the *Astronomia nova*, which was produced at the expense of the Emperor Rudolph II, were printed. The blocks for the plates were executed in Prague.

The first Roman Catholic version of the whole Bible in English was printed at Douai by Laurence Kellam (two volume quarto). Like the Rheims New Testament (*see* 1582) it rendered into English the text of the Vulgate.

Editio princeps of *Shake-speares Sonnets. Never before imprinted*. London: G. Eld for T. T[horpe].

James I acquired for Prince Henry the library of Lord Lumley (*c.* 1534–1609) which contained some 2,200 printed books and 400 manuscripts. The majority of these books can be identified in the British Museum library today.

1610

Death of Jan Moerentorf (Johannes Moretus) the son-in-law and successor of Christopher Plantin at Antwerp.

The first volume appeared of the magnificent edition of St. John Chrysostom printed at Eton, nominally by John Norton, but in fact by Melchissidec Bradwood* of the Eliot's Court Press, at the expense of, and under the direction of Sir Henry Savile, Provost of Eton. The

* Although this printer's surname is written Bradwood in most works of reference, in the Parish Register of St. Giles, Cripplegate it is given as 'Broadway' on nine occasions, and 'Bradwoode' only twice.

Great Primer Greek type used for the main text is a close copy of the famous 'Grecs du Roi' (*see* 1544), and its origin is uncertain. It is a French type, purchased possibly at Frankfurt. The whole work, in eight folio volumes, was completed in 1613 and is reputed to have cost Savile £8,000.

John Speed began the publication of the best-known of all early county maps of Britiain. In 1611 he issued a collection known as the *Theatre of the Empire of Great Britain*.

1611

In France, appeared for the first time the news-book *Le Mercure français* which continued until 1648. Paris: Jean Richer.

Jean Jannon, a former workman of Robert III Estienne, set up a printing office at Sedan. He cut, or had cut, a small letter used for the first time in 1625 in a Virgil in Latin; the face became popular under the name of 'petite Sédanaise'. (*See also* 1621.)

Editio princeps of the King James's Bible, commonly known as the *Authorised Version*. London: Robert Barker. There are three issued assigned to the year 1611, about which, *see* F. Fry, *A Description of . . . the Editions, in large folio, of Authorized Version . . .* (1865). The first quarto edition was printed in roman letter in 1612.

The first Hall of the Stationers' Company established at Bergavenny House, at the north end of Ave Maria Lane. This building was destroyed in the Great Fire of 1666. The present Hall was completed in 1670 and, though damaged by air raids during the Second World War, was afterwards restored.

Runic type was first used at Stockholm in J. T. Bureus, *Runa A.B.C. Boken* printed by A. Gutterwitz. They are said to have been cut at the expense of King Gustav Adolphus. A second edition was printed at Uppsala in 1624 by E. Mattsson, the successor of Gutterwitz.

1612

First edition of Antonio Neri, *L'Arte Vetraria*. Florence: Nella Stamperia de' Giunti. This early glazier's handbook, dealing with the colouring of glass, was reprinted several times, and as late as 1817 at Milan.

Publication of Andres Brun, *Arte muy provechoso para aprender de escrivir perfectamente*. Saragossa: Juan de Larumbe.

First edition of John Brinsley, *Ludus Literarius: or The Grammar Schoole*. London: for Thomas Man. The first English textbook for teachers and a source book for the history of Elizabethan education.

The first English translation of *Don Quixote* —*The History of the Valorous and Wittie Knight Errant Don Quixote of the Mancha*, translated by Thomas Shelton. London: William Stansby for Ed. Blount and W. Barret. The first part, a small quarto of 598 pp., was issued in 1612; one copy only seems to have survived. It was reprinted in 1620 together with the second part.

William Hole engraved for Dorothy Evans an anthology of virginal music entitled *Parthenia*. This was the first music book in England to be printed from copper plates. Although undated, it was probably issued some time between November 1612 and February 1613, since it was published to celebrate the betrothal of Elizabeth, daughter of James I, to Frederick, Elector Palatine of the Rhine.

Thomas Finlason of Edinburgh appointed King's Printer for Scotland on 17 June, in succession to Henry Charteris. In 1602 he had purchased the privileges, stock and plant of Robert Smyth.

1613

At Eichstätt, was published Basilius Besler, *Hortus Eystettensis* (two volumes folio), described by Sir Thomas Browne as the 'massiest' of herbals, illustrated with 374 plates, the work of at least six engravers, the most famous of whom was Wolfgang Kilian of Augsburg. They portray more than a thousand flowers, representing 667 species. Besler was in charge of the gardens of Johann Konrad von Gemmingen, Prince Bishop of Eichstätt, after whom the work was named.

Peter Paul Rubens began his association with Balthasar Moretus. He designed a number of title-pages for the Plantin Office. (These were reprinted in an album *Titels en Portretten gesneden naar P. P. Rubens voor de Plantijnsche Drukkerij*, published at Antwerp in 1877.)

The first printing of any work by Xenophon in Greek in England was his *De Cyri Institutione*, printed in the Greek type used by Sir Henry Savile for the Eton St. Chrysostom (*see* 1610). The Xenophon bears the caduceus device of the Eliot's Court Press.

On 28 January, died Sir Thomas Bodley (b. 1544), founder of the Bodleian Library,

Oxford, formally opened on 8 November, 1602. He was buried in the chapel of Merton College.

Stockholm's last sixteenth-century printer, Andreas Gutterwitz (d. 1610) had left a type-foundry, inventoried in 1612. In 1613 Eskil Mattsson received a royal privilege as Printer to Uppsala University, and the Crown purchased the remainder of Gutterwitz's material and allowed it to be taken to Uppsala; the Crown had previously owned half of the Gutterwitz printing office.

1614

The first book printed at Pistoia: *Capitoli sopra l'offitio de' Fiumi e Strade di Pistoia*. Pistoia: Salviano e Andrea Felici. The only known work of these printers.

Publication of Crispijn de Passe's *Hortus Floridus*. Printed at Utrecht, the engravings and letterpress of all parts except Part II by the author, that of Part II by Hermann Borculo for the Arnhem bookseller Jan Jansson. In 1615 an English edition was published in Utrecht (S. de Roy for de Passe) under the title *A Garden of Flowers* illustrated with the plates of the original edition. Editions were also published in French and Dutch of this example of early 'florilegia', which contains some of the best copperplate figures of plants ever produced.

Editio princeps of Sir Walter Raleigh, *Historie of the World*. London: for W. Burre. It was written while Raleigh was imprisoned in the Tower of London, and although its historical value is slight, it contains many magnificent passages of Eliza-bethan prose.

First issue of the first twelve books of Homer's *Odyssey* translated into heroic couplets by George Chapman (1559–1634). The other twelve books were issued later in the same year bound up with sheets of the first twelve. London: R. Field for Nat. Butter.

1615

First volume issued of *Syntagma musicum* by Michael Praetorius (1571–1621). Wittenberg: Johannes Richter. This encyclopaedia is a basic source-book on all aspects of Baroque music, and is especially valuable for its illustrations. The work was planned to be in four volumes, but only three were completed before the author's death, the last one appearing in 1620.

The first printing-house established at Linz, on the Danube, by the Nuremberg printer Johann Planck. The press acquired a certain fame for printing the works of the astronomer Kepler during his years spent in Linz. Planck worked at Linz until 1627.

First edition of Pedro Diaz Morante, *Arte Nueva de Escribir*. The only known copy of the original edition of this well-known writing-book is in the library of the Escuela Normal at Madrid. It has 21 plates, including the frontispiece. Other editions followed.

1616

Georg Leopold Fuhrmann of Nuremberg pub-lished his specimen book, the introduction to which gives an account of the origin of printing. The types shown are good examples of those employed at the beginning of the century in a well-known German printing office.

Printing introduced into Königgrätz by Martin Kleinwächter who had previously worked at Wiltschütz where he was also the first printer, 1614.

First edition of Théodore Agrippa d'Aubigny, *Les Tragiques*, a satirical poem published anony-mously, with the imprint 'Donnez au public par le Larcin de Promethée. L.B.D.D. au Dezert' [Geneva].

First printed edition of the New Testament in Arabic. Leyden: Thomas Erpenius.

1617

Martin Mann became Osnabrück's first printer.

Death of Louis Elsevier. He was buried on 4 February, in St. Peter's church, Leyden, beside his wife, Mayke Duverdyn.

The famous engraver Hendrik Goltzius died at Haarlem.

John Minsheu the lexicographer published his *Ductor in Linguas, the Guide into the Tongues*, a dictionary in eleven languages. This is said to have been the first book in England published by subscription. The names of the subscribers were printed in the work.

John Bill began to issue twice yearly (April and October) a London edition of the Frankfurt *Mess Katalog* the publication of which continued for about eleven years.

A press was set up at Kiev, in the Kievopetcher-skoi monastery, where books for the Greek

Church continued to be printed until the beginning of the nineteenth century.

1618

Stefano Paolino printed at Rome *Rudimentum Syriacum*, a veritable specimen book of the Syriac characters which Savory de Brèves had had engraved at Constantinople when he was ambassador there. The types eventually went to the Imprimerie Royale, Paris. (*See* 1591.)

Appearance of the first newspaper properly so-called—the undated coranto in Dutch printed at Amsterdam by Joris Veseler, probably about 16 June, and published by Caspar van Hilten.

9 July, an Edict was issued in France by Louis XIII leading to the formation of a Syndical and Royal Chamber of Booksellers, Printers and Binders of Paris with monopolistic powers. Though initially applied only to Paris, it was in 1626 extended to cover the whole of France.

At Paris, Etienne Durand printed anonymously *La Riparographe*, a defamatory libel against the king, for which the author was burned alive at Paris.

First edition of *The Pen's Excellency or Secretary's Delight* by Martin Billingsley. London: no printer's name. One of the earliest English 'copy books', it contains a portrait of the author.

Peter van Selow arrived in Stockholm from Germany as 'Russian' printer to the Crown, to cut Russian type for service books to be used in the recently conquered Russian-speaking provinces. Later he cut and cast many other kinds of type and supplied them to practically every printer in Sweden. They included Fraktur, Schwabacher, roman, etc., as well as Greek and Hebrew types. (An inventory was made by his successor (*see* 1648) and is shown in Bengt Bengtsson, *Svenskt stilgjuterei före år 1700*; Stockholm: 1956.)

Oloff Oloffson printed at Stockholm a new Bible under the patronage of Gustav Adolf, King of Sweden 1611–32. It was a revision of the *Gustavus Vasa Bible*. (*See* 1541.)

1619

The first press was installed at Nice by François Castello from Turin. The first known book printed by him was *Decisiones synodales* by Bishop Martinengo, which was published in 1620.

Sir Henry Savile, Provost of Eton, presented to Oxford University the matrices for the Great Primer Greek types used in his famous edition of St. John Chrysostom. (*See* 1610.)

1620

The first press at Aachen of which we have definite knowledge was started by Heinrich Hulting, although Hans de Braecker may have printed there in 1573 and Hans Schwarzenbach in 1591.

At Prague, was published Dalemile, *Bohemian Chronicle*, the work of one of the oldest poets and historians of Bohemia.

The first newspaper in the English language—an English translation of a Dutch coranto, *The new tydings out of Italie*, published in Amsterdam by Pieter van den Keere and printed by Joris Veseler. (*See* 1618.)

First edition of Francis Bacon, *Instauratio magna*, the author's greatest work, in which he put forward his ideas as to the true method of advancing knowledge. The second part of this work, the *Novum organum* contains the exposition of his new system, and led him to be described by Voltaire as 'the father of experimental philosophy'. London: John Bill.

The first complete English translation of *Don Quixote*, by Thomas Shelton, was published in London, two volumes quarto, printed for Edward Blount. (*See also* 1612.)

Death of John Legate, Printer to the University of Cambridge (*see* 1591). His apprentice, Cantrell Legge had been appointed Printer in 1606 but Legate still continued (apparently justly) to exercise the title since he is named Printer in a document of 1617 together with Legge and Thomas Buck. (*See* 1625.)

1621

Publication of Jean Cinquarbres (Johannes Quinquarboreo), *Linguae Hebraicae Institutiones*. Paris: Guillaume Le Bé. An important book inasmuch as it contains a representative selection of the types of the Le Bé foundry, and has moreover a notice by Le Bé in which he writes of his types.

Publication of *Espreuve des caractères nouvellement taillez. A Sedan, Par Jean Jannon Imprimeur de l'Academie. M.DC.XXI.* The specimen comprises eleven romans, eight italics, one Hebrew and a set of two-line initials. Jeannon was a master printer in Paris until 1610, when his

Protestant sympathies took him to Sedan where the Calvinist Academy gave him work. He was, however, forbidden to print for anyone other than the Prince of Sedan and the Academy. He remained there for twenty years and then, after a quarrel, he returned to Paris. Apart from the specimen book of Le Bé in the Bibliothèque Nationale, this is probably the earliest French founder's book of type specimens. While at Sedan, Jannon cut some very small roman faces which he used for the little 'Sedan' editions of the classics. Jannon's types were used by the Imprimerie Royale (*see* 1640) which acquired them in 1642 and called them 'caractères de l'université'. (A facsimile of Jannon's *Espreuve de caractères* was published in Paris in 1927, edited, with an introduction, by Paul Beaujon [*i.e.* Mrs. Beatrice Warde].)

On 24 September, appeared the first newspaper in English printed in England—*Corante, or newes from Italy, Germany, Hungarie, Spaine and France, 1621*. It was 'printed for N.B.', which might stand for Nicholas Bourne or Nathaniel Butter, both well-known stationers. Most authorities think it was the latter.

Editio princeps of Robert Burton, *The Anatomy of Melancholy*. Oxford: John Lichfield and James Short for Henry Cripps. Subsequent editions contained additional matter and not until the sixth edition, 1651, was the final form achieved.

Jerónimo de Contreras, who was progenitor of one of the most famous printing families in Latin America, and who had printed at Seville in 1618, emigrated to Peru where he printed at Lima from 1621 to about 1640, when the business was carried on by his son José de Contreras, who managed it for forty-seven years. In 1621 Jéronimo de Contreras printed a 4-page news sheet, *Nuevas de Castilla*.

1622

Formation in Paris of the 'Compagnie de Libraires du Palais, aux Cinq Sources d'Eau'. This comprised six of the most important booksellers of the city, and resembled the later Printing Conger set up in England around 1719. This association of a number of booksellers for the publication of works entailing a considerable outlay was practised on the Continent much earlier than in England.

Thomas Archer and Nicholas Bourne began a weekly series of quarto news-books, printed by John Dawson. The first number in this, the first series of numbered and dated news-books to appear in England, was probably dated 14 May, but no copy now exists. The second issue was dated 23 May. The first copy to bear a number was the issue of 15 October (Novo 1). The series ran for fifty issues, the last being dated 2 October, 1623.

At London, John Bellamie published the first account of the voyage of the *Mayflower* and the settlement of Plymouth, New England—*A Relation or Journall of the beginning and proceedings of the English Plantation setled at Plimoth in New England*. Edited by G. Mourt, this book is usually referred to as 'Mourt's Relation', and a copy of the first edition fetched £5,714 in 1967.

First edition of Shakespeare, *Othello*. London: N.O. [Nicholas Okes] for Thomas Walkley.

Edward Raban went from St. Andrews, where he had been printer to the University, to Aberdeen, where he started the first press in that town, remaining there during the rest of his business life. He was printer to both town and university, and adopted the town's arms as his device. He was, as he tells us in his book *Rabans Resolution against Drunkenness* (1622), at one time employed by a printer of Leyden. He was of German descent.

Peter von Selow printed a Catechism in Russian at Stockholm. (*See* 1618.)

1623

Editio princeps of William Shakespeare, *Comedies, Histories, and Tragedies*. London: Isaac Jaggard and Ed. Blount. This first collected edition of Shakespeare's plays, commonly known as the *First Folio* was published seven years after the author's death. It is regrettable that one of the most famous books in the world is also one of the worst printed.

First edition of *The Duchess of Malfy*, the powerful tragedy by John Webster (c. 1580– c. 1625). London: N. Okes. The play was first performed in 1616.

1624

The first book printed by the brothers Johann and Heinrich Stern at Lüneburg—*Cryptomenytices et Cryptographiae*, by Gustavus Selenus, the pseudonym of Herzog Augustus the Younger of Braunschweig-Wolfenbüttel.

Publication of the first sizeable work in English

concerning the North American continent, Captain John Smith, *The Generall Historie of Virginia, New England, and the Summer Isles.* London: Printed by I. D[awson] and I. H[aviland] for M. Sparke.

William Turner appointed Printer to the University of Oxford in succession to James Short.

The first printed book in an African native tongue—a Catechism in Kixicongo dialect printed at Lisbon.

At Strengnäs was issued the first Swedish news-book, *Hermes Gothicus.*

1625

Bonaventura and Abraham Elsevier, who had formed a partnership in 1622, took over the printing office of Thomas Erpenius, at his death the only printer in the Netherlands who possessed founts of Oriental characters. The business was purchased from the widow of Erpenius for 9,000 florins.

At Lyons, G. Savary and B. Gaultier published François Desmoulins, *Le Paranimphe de lescriture ronde financiere et italienne.* . . . This is the first book to illustrate the 'ronde financière', so called because used by the clerks of the French Treasury.

Guillaume II Le Bé, punch-cutter and founder, admitted as printer and bookseller.

1626

In this year appeared the first Berlin news-book, a weekly (which survives only in a fragment) to which was added a secret insert in italic which contained the news to which the Court might have taken exception.

The Congregatio de Propaganda Fide, founded in 1622, set up its own printing press to print books for missionary work. Its first director, Stefano Paolino, was himself a punch-cutter by profession. A catalogue of the publications of the press was issued at Rome in 1773. In conjunction with its press, the Congregatio established a type-foundry which became the most complete polyglot foundry in Europe. It soon acquired the matrices of other type-foundries, including that of the Stamperia Vaticana, established in 1587. The foundry began to issue specimens of exotic type made for missionary presses in 1629, and continued to do so until the latter half of the nineteenth century, some fifty in all.

Bonaventura and Abraham Elsevier were appointed official printers to Leyden University.

Publication of the complete version of Ovid's *Metamorphoses* in the translation of George Sandys. London: William Stansby. The first five books of the translation had been published by William Barrett in 1621, but no copy of this edition seems to have survived.

1627

First edition of Johann Kepler, *Tabulae Rudolphinae.* Ulm: Jonas Saur. These Rudolphine Tables were a great aid to astronomical observation for more than a century. In 1936, Max Caspar published at Munich a *Bibliographia Kepleriana* listing 162 items from 1590 to 1930. The engraved allegorical frontispiece to Kepler's *Tables* shows Kepler himself in his study and the astronomers Hipparchus, Ptolemaeus, Copernicus, and Tycho Brahe whom Kepler succeeded as Imperial Mathematician to the Emperor Rudolph.

The celebrated Augsburg engraver Lucas Kilian published in that city his *Newes ABC Buechlein,* with 25 copper plates.

Gabriel Naudé (1600–53), librarian to Cardinal Richelieu, and later to Cardinal Mazarin and Christina, Queen of Sweden, published his popular *Advis pour dresser une Bibliothèque,* which went into numerous editions and was translated into English and Latin. In 1633 he published at Venice his *Bibliographica politica,* which also went into several editions and was translated into French in 1642.

As early as 1627 a press was in operation at Constantinople for the printing of Greek books. It was organized by Nicodemus Metaxas under the patronage of the Greek Church.

1628

First edition of William Harvey, *Exercitatio anatomica de motu cordis.* Frankfurt: Sumptibus Guilielmi Fitzeri. With this book, modern physiology may be said to have begun. Harvey (1578–1657) collected a vast amount of material on comparative anatomy which was destroyed during the Civil War in 1642, when Harvey's London lodgings were wrecked by a mob.

The first type specimen, *Indice de' caratteri,* was issued at Rome by the Stamperia Vaticana, showing a wide range of roman, italic, exotic and music types. Robert Granjon cut many founts for this press.

At Haarlem, Pieter Schrijver published a book dealing with the claims of Laurens Coster to be the inventor of printing. This book, *Laure-Crans voor L. Coster van Harlem, eerste vinder vande Boeck-Druckerey*, printed by Adriaen Rooman, is notable for what is possibly the first authentic representation of a printing press engraved from a drawing by Pieter Zaenredam.

The Antwerp historian François Sweerts (1567–1629) published *Athenae Belgicae*, a folio of 708 pp., describing the work of some 2,000 authors. Antwerp: Guil. a Tungris.

A further Royal Charter was granted to the University of Cambridge by Charles I which encouraged Thomas Buck to proceed with the printing of the first Cambridge edition of the *Authorized Version* of the Bible. (*See* 1629.)

At Stockholm Ignatius Meurer printed a Swedish book, *Swerikes Rikes Stadzlagh*, for the first time in roman, an example which was not followed at the time.

1629

In Madrid, was published the first bibliography of America—Antonio de Leon Pinelo, *Epitome de la Bibliotheca Oriental y Occidental; nautica y geografica*. The author, born in Peru, was called 'the Chronicler of the Indies'.

First edition of the *King James's Bible* to be produced outside London was printed at the University Press at Cambridge by Thomas Buck. (*See* 1606.)

Miles Flesher, John Haviland, and Robert Young, in association, secured the assignment of the lucrative law-book patent. In 1632, they purchased a 21-year lease of Roger Norton's grammar patent, and set the seal to their monopolistic tendencies in 1634 by obtaining the lease of the patent of King's Printer in England, which gave them both the Bible and the *Book of Common Prayer*.

First edition of John Parkinson's herbal *Paradisi in Sole Paradisus Terrestris* (a punning title on the author's name). London: Humfrey Lownes & Robert Young.

Died, Henrik Waldkirch, who, since 1598, had one of the largest printing businesses in Denmark.

1630

Printing introduced into Heilbronn by Christophe Krause, who plied his craft there until the year of his death, 1654. In 1634 he received permission from the authorities to print the weekly *Avisen*, or news-sheets. He came from Kempten where he was printer to the Fürststiftische Hofdruckerei from its foundation in 1609 until around 1630.

Death of Frédéric Morel II, one of the most learned printers of his time. He united in his person the offices of Professor Regius and Architypographus Regius.

Antoine Vitré, the Paris printer, appointed by patent of 7 April, 1630, Royal Printer in Oriental languages. (*See also* 1645.)

1631

Appearance of the oldest regular French newspaper. The brothers Eusèbe, Isaac, and Théophraste Renaudot founded the *Gazette de France*, for which they obtained a privilege from Louis XIII, who established a special press for this sheet, placed under the direction of Théophraste Renaudot. Published at first once or twice a week, from 1792 it appeared daily.

First appearance of Samaritan type in J. Morin, *Exercitationes ecclesiasticae in utrumque Samaritanorum Pentateuchum*, printed at Paris by Antoine Vitré. This type was probably based on the manuscript of the Samaritan Pentateuch purchased at Damascus by the traveller Pietro della Valle in 1616, and deposited in the Oratory, Paris, in 1623.

Publication of the so-called *Wicked Bible*, from the word 'not' having been omitted from the Seventh Commandment (*Exodus* xx, 14). London: R. Barker and the Assignes of J. Bill.

1632

First edition of Galileo Galilei, *Dialogo . . . sopra i due massimi sistemi del mondo, Tolemaico e Copernicano*. Florence: Gio. Batista Landini. This is the book in which Galileo maintained that the earth moves round the sun. Published in January 1632, its sale was forbidden in August of that year. In October its author was haled before the Inquisition. The book remained on the *Index* until 1823.

At Rome was published the first edition of Famiano Strada, *De Bello Belgico*, a remarkable history of the Low Countries during the first part of the reign of Philip II (1555–79). The second edition appeared at Antwerp in 1635, printed by Jan Cnobbaert. The work was completed by a *Decas secunda* for the years 1579–90, which was published at Rome in 1647. The book had a great success and was translated into Flemish, Italian, English, Spanish and Polish.

1633

Willem Janszoon Blaeu (1571–1638), the celebrated Dutch publisher and map-maker, was appointed cartographer to the Dutch East India Company.

Posthumous publication of the collected *Poems* of John Donne (1573–1631). London: Miles Flesher for John Marriot.

1634

At Oxford, was printed Charles Butler, *The History of Bees*, in which phonetic symbols were used for the first time in English.

A citizen of London, named John Day, was granted a privilege for the space of fourteen years to enjoy the sole printing of weekly bills of the prices of all foreign commodities, a practice which, states the Patent, had been discontinued near three years, 'to the great hindrance of the merchants in their commerce and correspondance, to the disgrace of the City of London, and to the prejudice of the Customs'.

1635

At Frankfurt-am-Main, was published the first volume of Matthäus Merian, *Theatrum Europaeum*. This enormous chronicle of contemporary events in twenty-one volumes, with innumerable copperplate engravings, was not completed until 1738.

Christoph Reussner, from Rostock, became the first printer at Reval.

In January, by Letters Patent of Louis XIII, the Académie Française was officially constituted.

Charles Morel was appointed 'Imprimeur du Roi'.

Death at Nancy of the famous French illustrator Jacques Callot.

Francis Quarles, the best remembered of all the English writers of Emblem Books, published the first edition of his *Emblemes*. Very popular and frequently reprinted during the seventeenth and eighteenth centuries, Quarles's book derived from two books sponsored by the Jesuits—Herman

Hugo's *Pia Desideria* (1624) and the anonymous *Typus Mundi* (1627).

Henrik Keyser, a German who settled at Stockholm in 1633, became Sweden's Royal Printer. The Keyser family, for three generations, was prominent in Swedish typography.

1636

The Congregatio de Propaganda Fide at Rome issued a specimen showing a fount of Coptic characters, which are the first known to have been cut. In that same year the press issued Kircher, *Prodromus Coptus*. No fount was available in England until 1672, when Dr. Fell bought Coptic matrices for the Oxford University Press. From these were cast the type used in David Wilkins's edition of the New Testament, 1716.

First Italian news-book published at Florence by Lorenzo Landi and Amatore Massi. It was untitled.

Georg Decker of Eisfeld in Thuringia appointed University Printer at Basel.

Antoine Vitré, Royal Printer for Oriental Languages in France, published at Paris his specimen, *Linguarum orientalium . . . alphabeta*. Among the types shown are many of the oriental types formed by Savary de Brèves, French ambassador to Constantinople, and purchased by Vitré for Louis XIII.

The first officially recorded bookbinder in America was John Sanders, who took the Freeman's Oath in 1636 and in the following year opened a shop in Boston.

1637

First edition of the Dutch Bible as authorised by the States-General. Leyden: P. Aertsz van Ravesteyn. It became the standard Bible of the Dutch Reformed Church.

First edition of René Descartes, *Discours de la Méthode*, the first and most important of its author's works. Leyden: Jan Maire.

Decree of the Court of Star Chamber limited the number of printers in England to twenty-three and the number of type-founders to four. The thirty-three clauses of this decree severely restricted the freedom of the press, and was one of the most drastic of all the repressive acts concerning printing, though it lost much of its force a few years later, when in 1641 the Long

Parliament abolished the Court of Star Chamber. The four men appointed as authorised founders were John Grismond, Thomas Wright, Arthur Nicholls, and Alexander Fifield.

The right granted by Royal Charter to Oxford University to print 'all manner of books' was curtailed when the privilege of printing Bibles, Almanacs and Grammars was surrendered in 1637 to the Stationers' Company in return for an annual payment of £200. It was not until 1673 that the restrictions on Bible-printing at Oxford were removed.

Introduction of *The Booke of Common Prayer and Administration of the Sacraments . . . for the use of the Church of Scotland* (Edinburgh: Robert Young).

1638

Louis Elsevier, son of Joost Elsevier, established the Amsterdam branch of the famous firm of Elsevier. He managed the business alone until joined by his cousin Daniel in 1655.

The folio Bible printed at Cambridge by Thomas Buck and Roger Daniel. One of the finest Bibles ever printed at Cambridge. It remained the standard text until 1762.

George Anderson, a former Edinburgh printer, moved to Glasgow in 1638 and set up the first press in that city. His first book was Thomas Abernethie, *The Abjuration of poperie*. His son Andrew was appointed King's Printer in Scotland in 1671. (*See also* 1644.)

The first press in North America was set up at Cambridge, Massachusetts, by Stephen Daye. The press had been purchased by the Rev. Jose Glover and taken with him when he embarked for Massachusetts in 1638, but he died on the journey and the press and material became the property of his widow. The working of the press was entrusted to Stephen Daye, a native of Cambridge, England, who had accompanied the Glovers, and he was assisted by his son Matthew. The first products of the press, of which no copies survive, were a broadside, *The Freeman's Oath*, and Peirce's *Almanack* for 1639. (*See also* 1640.)

1639

A printing press was set up in Newcastle upon Tyne when Charles I, during his march north against the Scots, established his headquarters there. The Lord General of the Army, the Earl of Arundel, wrote to the Secretary of State asking for a printer and press to be sent to that town to print the King's daily commands for his Court and Army, and John Legatt, son-in-law of the King's Printer, Robert Barker, arrived to print proclamations and pamphlets.

1640

Bicentenary celebrations of the invention of printing took place in many German cities, and commemorative publications were issued in Leipzig, Mainz, Cologne, Dresden, Breslau and Strassburg.

The Society of Jesus celebrated the first hundred years of its history by issuing their great emblem book *Imago Primi Saeculi Societatis Jesu*. Antwerp: Ex Officina Plantiniana.

Foundation at Paris of the Imprimerie Royale, which evolved from the king's private press at the desire of Cardinal Richelieu. The first director was Sébastien Cramoisy, and the first book to come from the royal printing house was an edition of Thomas à Kempis, *De Imitatione Christi*.

Cardinal Richelieu set up a private press at his château in Touraine.

On 3 November, the bookseller George Thomason began his collection of the fugitive literature of the Civil War period, now known collectively as the 'Thomason Tracts'. The collection, of inestimable value for the history of the period, comprises 22,255 items, including 7,216 issues of newspapers and 97 manuscripts, and passed into the custody of the British Museum, a gift from George III, in 1762.

On 3 November, the Long Parliament assembled. It abolished the Court of Star Chamber (*see* 1637), the decrees of which became a dead letter. For a while there was free trade in printing and existing rights were everywhere infringed.

The first existing book printed in what is now the United States came from the press of Stephen Daye at Cambridge, Massachusetts. It was *The Whole Booke of Psalmes*, familiarly known as the *Bay Psalm Book*, edited by Richard Mather. The actual printer was probably Stephen Daye's son, Matthew. Only five perfect copies are now known to exist, and a facsimile was published in New York, with an introduction by Wilberforce Eames, in 1903. In 1947 a copy of the original edition fetched $151,000 at auction.

1641

At Nuremberg, Wolfgang Endter printed the first edition of the *Kurfürstenbibel*, so-called on account of the frontispiece with portraits of Electors of Saxony.

Michael Sparke published his exposure of the evils of monopoly in a tract entitled *Scintilla or a Light Broken Into Dark Warehouses*, in which he attacked the holders of patents, such as Miles Flesher and Robert Young, whom he mentions by name, and the monopolists of the Stationers' Company by implication. The imprint of the book runs: 'Printed, not for *profit*, but for the Common Weles good: and no where to be *sold*, but some where to be given.'

1642

This year appeared the first volume of Merian's *Topographia*, the twenty-one volumes of which were completed in 1672, forming a precious pictorial record of seventeenth-century towns, with its 2,142 illustrations and 92 maps. (*See* 1635.)

Ludwig von Siegen, the inventor of mezzotint, issued his first dated specimen, a portrait of the Landgräfin Amalie Elisabeth.

On 25 March, a decree was signed by the King of France (confirmed 20 July, 1663) forbidding all casting of type without royal consent, and all exportation of matrices outside the kingdom. In this age of religious struggles, a handsome type became an important factor in the promulgation of theological dogma.

Pierre Moreau, calligrapher and type-designer, specialised in the engraving of books of Hours, for which he engraved both type and illustrations. He cut punches for script types of his own design and dedicated his first work with them (1642) to Louis XIII, who accorded him the title of 'Imprimeur du Roi'. Moreau's script types, for which he had a privilege, met with scant success.

The Bible in Finnish appeared for the first time, printed at Stockholm (*see also* 1685) by Henrik Keyser I, a native of Germany and head of a family associated for years with Swedish printing. (*See* 1635.)

Printing in Finland began with the establishment by the University of Åbo, founded in 1640, of the first press, the printer being Petrus Wald (Peder Eriksson Wald), from Västerås (1602–53). Peter von Selow supplied all the founts. The

FCP

first book from that press was a dissertation of M. O. Wexionius, *Discursus politicus de prudentia*. A second press was set up in Åbo in 1668 by Bishop Gezelius, and was managed by the printer Johan Winter.

Permission to establish a press in Malta granted on 7 June to Pompeo de Fiore; but no printed matter is known which bears his name.

1643

At Antwerp, the Belgian Jesuits began the publication of the *Acta Sanctorum*, a critical study of the lives of the Christian saints. The work is still in progress, some seventy great folios having appeared to date. This may justly be regarded as one of the most remarkable collective scholarly publications of any age.

Pierre Moreau, a Paris calligrapher, printed an edition of *L'Imitation de Jésus Christ* in a script type of his own design. This was one of a number of books which he printed in script types, and which, after passing through several hands, were eventually bought by the Imprimerie Royale in 1787. (*See also* 1642.)

Publication of Sir Richard Baker, *Chronicle of the Kings of England* of which at least ten editions had been issued by 1730. Commonly known as *Baker's Chronicle*, it was to be found in the library of every country gentleman with pretensions to literary awareness. Sir Roger de Coverley was always reading and quoting from it.

First appearance, in January, of *Mercurius Aulicus*, the first Royalist counterblast to the Parliamentary news-books which poured from the presses during the Civil War. It was printed at Oxford by Henry Hill and edited by Sir John Birkhead. On 29 August, the same year, appeared *Mercurius Britannicus*, the first formal and open opponent of *Mercurius Aulicus*.

Norway had its first printing press when the Copenhagen printer Tyge Nielsen was summoned to Christiania (Oslo) to print Christen Bang, *Postilla catechetica*. In the same year Nielsen was granted a royal privilege for printing school texts and almanacs. In the following year, however, as the result of a legal action by Bang, who had advanced money to the printer, Nielsen lost his press. Printing then ceased at Oslo until 1647, when Melchior Martzan, the University printer at Copenhagen, set up a branch establishment at Oslo.

First known printing in Malta—*I Natali delle Religiose Militie . . .* by Fra Geronimo Marulli. It was probably printed by the second printer in the island, Paolo Bonacota.

1644

The first book printed in Scotland using Hebrew type—*Hebraeae Linguae Institutiones* etc., by John Row. Glasgow: George Anderson.

First edition of John Milton, *Areopagitica*—a plea 'for the Liberty of Unlicenc'd Printing'. It carried neither printer's nor bookseller's name, and was both unlicensed and unregistered. Addressed directly to Parliament, this famous plea for the freedom of the press was the outcome of Milton's disapproval of the various repressive measures against liberty of expression embodied in the Star Chamber decree of 1637 and that of 1643.

In Russia the Moscow printing house had been destroyed when the Poles set fire to a large part of the city in 1611. Printing was not resumed until 1644 when Mihail Fedorovich set up his press there.

1645

Completion of the great Paris Polyglot Bible (ten volumes folio) printed by Antoine Vitré, King's Printer for Oriental languages, and published by Guy Michel Le Jay. The printing was begun in 1628. The original idea was conceived by Cardinal Du Perron, but he died in 1617, and Le Jay became the patron of the project, and is said to have expended 100,000 *écus* on the undertaking. This Polyglot is in seven languages—Greek, Latin, Hebrew, Samaritan, Chaldee, Syriac and Arabic. It contains the Samaritan Pentateuch for the first time, printed from manuscripts brought into Europe around 1620. The printer spells his name Vitray on the frontispiece and Vitré at the end.

At Paris the engraver Abraham Bosse brought out his *Traicté des manieres de graver en taille-douce*, a book on the theory of engraving which went through many editions and had considerable influence upon several generations of artists. (It was republished, 1937, at Bologna, with an Italian translation by Luigi Servolini.)

On 10 January, died Robert Barker, the King's Printer, who had spent the last ten years of his life in the King's Bench Prison for debt. His financial difficulties had been largely brought about by the calling in and burning of his

edition of the Bible in 1631, known as the *Wicked Bible* on account of the distressing omission of the 'not' in the Seventh Commandment.

1646

At Caen, was published Samuel Bochart, *Geographiae Sacrae*, financed by a rich merchant of Caen, Pierre Cardonnel, who got the Sedan punch-cutter Jean Jannon to cut special type for it. The punches were seized during a police perquisition in 1644, and although Cardonnel's book finally appeared in 1646, with the imprint 'Cadomi; Typis Petri Cardonalli', he was not allowed to print anything else.

William Bentley, a printer at Finsbury, in London, issued a new and cheap edition of the Bible, Parliament having at that time opposed the monopoly of Bible printing. In doing so, he incurred not only the wrath of the Company of Stationers, but also that of the printer John Field, who had become Printer to Parliament and was soon to be Printer to the Protector, Cromwell. He was himself anxious to secure what had been the old King's Printer's patent.

The Royalist printer Stephen Bulkley, a York printer, set up a press at Newcastle upon Tyne while Charles I was in that city during the Civil War, and there printed *A message from his majestie to the Speaker of the House of Peeres, Pro Tempore*.

1647

A book by Simon Morin called *Pensées* was published, without imprint, probably at Amsterdam. The book and its author were later burned on the Place de Grève, Paris.

On 30 September, was published an ordinance against unlicensed or scandalous Pamphlets and for the better Regulating of Printing. This was directed mainly against the vast number of unlicensed news-books, the spread of which had been encouraged by the Civil War. The freedom with which they commented upon politics, often in the most scurrilous terms, drove the government into repressive measures.

The first secular work to be published in Russia was a book on the art of war, *Ulozenie i chytrost ratnago strojenia piechotnych lieudei*.

1648

Christoffel van Dijk, who had hitherto worked as a freelance punch-cutter, established his own foundry in Amsterdam, where he designed many type faces (including Hebrew and Armenian) which exerted considerable influence on type design. He became the leading Dutch type-founder and supplied most of the punches for the Elseviers, as well as some to Dr. Fell for the Oxford University Press. Many of his punches are still preserved at the Enschedé foundry at Haarlem.

Gilles Dubois appointed book-binder to the king of France, an office he held conjointly with Claude le Mire.

Death of the punch-cutter and type-founder Peter van Selow (*see* 1618). His business was acquired by the printer at Strängnäs, Sweden, Zacharias Brockenius.

1649

In France, an Edict of Louis XIV on the subject of printing enacted that apprentices were to be young, of good conduct, Catholic and of French birth, industrious, knowing Latin well and able to read Greek, under penalty to the master of a fine of 300 livres and cancellation of his *brevet*. In the same year, by Letters Patent of 20 December, it was forbidden to print any book without first obtaining the royal privilege.

First edition of *Eikon Basilike*. London: William Du Gard for Richard Royston. It bears the date (Old Style) M.DC.XLVIII. Although put forth as the work of Charles I, it is thought to have been written by John Gauden, Bishop of Worcester. It appeared the day after the king's execution.

In England, was passed an Act against 'unlicensed and scandalous books and pamphlets' which embodied a lengthy list of press regulations.

A Platform of Church Discipline, commonly known as the 'Cambridge Platform', was a defence of the system of self-government in Church affairs drawn up by the Puritan churches in New England. It was printed at Cambridge, Massachusetts, by Samuel Green, the successor to Stephen and Matthew Daye. A copy of the first issue of this early American printing, one of the two known copies, was sold at the Parke-Bernet Galleries in New York in April 1967, for £28,572.

1650

At Amsterdam, Jan Blaeu began publishing the *Atlas Magnus* completed in eleven folio volumes in 1662.

At Paris, appeared Jacobus Mentel, *De Vera Typographiae Origine Paraenesis*, dedicated to Bernard Malinkrot, and published by Robert Ballard.

Du Gard, the friend of Milton, was appointed editor of an official gazette in French for readers on the Continent, *Les Nouvelles ordinaires de Londres*. It lasted for several years.

John Durie, Keeper of the Royal Library from the death of Charles I until the Restoration, published *The Reformed Librarie Keeper*, the first book in English on library economy.

A printing press was for the first time established at Göteborg by Amund Grefwe. In that year he printed Jos. Stegmann, *Christelige nyårhts—gåfwors apoteek*, the Psalms in Swedish verse and Luther's *Catechism*.

1651

The first book in French propounding a system of shorthand—*Méthode pour escrire aussi vite qu'on parle* Paris, *chez l'auteur.*, by the Abbé Jacques Cossard.

First edition of *The English Dancing Master* published by John Playford the elder. By 1728, eighteen editions had been published. It is an invaluable record of English popular melodies of the period.

Evan Tyler, an Edinburgh printer, set up the first printing press at Leith. Later he went to London where he worked in Ducket Court, Aldersgate Street, until the Restoration, when he returned to Edinburgh.

1652

Stephen Bulkley established the first press in Gateshead, Durham, whence he had moved from Newcastle upon Tyne. (*See also* 1646.)

Samuel Chidley's pamphlet *Cry against a crying Sinne*, printed throughout in red ink to show that, to quote the author, 'Parliament's sins were sins red as scarlet.'

1653

First edition of Izaak Walton, *The Compleat Angler*. London: Richard Marriott. Published at eighteen pence, a copy of the first edition of this book was sold in New York in 1946 for $4,400.

John Field, Printer to Cambridge University, printed a diminutive version of the Bible, commonly called the *Pearl Bible*. It is memorable for its blunders, as for instance *I Corinthians vi.* 9:

'Know ye not that the unrighteous *shall inherit the earth*?'

Printing of the first volume of the London Polyglot Bible begun at the press of Thomas Roycroft in Bartholomew Close. (*See* 1657.)

First public library in the United States founded at Boston.

1654

First edition of John Playford, *A Breefe Introduction to the Skill of Music*. A popular treatise of which at least nineteen editions had been published by 1730. The Playfords, father and son, were the great publishers of music in England in the second half of the seventeenth century. (*See also* 1651.)

1655

Johann Rist (1607–67), a pastor at Mecklenburg, published his version of the German morality play *Depositio Cornuti Typographici*, a ceremony which took place in Germany when a printer's apprentice had served his term. In the words of Blades 'the quondam apprentice did not at once take his place among the workmen, but was called a "Cornute"—an amphibious animal, neither apprentice nor workman, but a horned beast full of all kinds of wickedness, from which he could be freed only by the saving ceremony of the Depositio'. The first printed version of the *Depositio* was made by a Danzig printer, Paul de Vise, and published at Lüneburg in 1621. But Rist's is the best-known version, printed and published by the Stern printing house at Lüneburg in 1655. (This firm brought out a reprint of the original edition in 1886, edited by Karl Theodor Gaedertz. William Blades published an account of the *Depositio* together with a rhythmical translation in 1885, published by Trübner and Co., and this in turn was reissued by Maximilian Editions Ltd. in 1962.) The German version has been printed many times, at Frankfurt in 1677, at Sultzbach in 1684, at Lübeck in 1714 and at Nuremberg in 1721 and 1733.

The first book of pastry recipes—*Le Patissier François*. Amsterdam: L. & D. Elsevier.

At Paris, Louis Barbedor published his writing-book *L'Escriture financière dans sa naifveté*; 'sine nota'.

The first Hebrew book in Hebrew type to be printed at Oxford—Edward Pocock's *Porta Mosis*. Double column—Hebrew and Latin. Oxford: H. Hall. Pocock was Professor of Hebrew and Arabic at Oxford.

Jørgen Hantsch, whose press was associated with the Soro Academy founded by Christian IV, issued the first Danish type specimen book.

1656

At Haarlem, Abraham Casteleyn founded the news-sheet *Weeckelycke Courante van Europa*.

First edition of the most famous of seventeenth-century 'Utopias' *The Commonwealth of Oceana* by James Harrington the elder. London: J. Streater for Livewell Chapman.

1657

Editio princeps of *Les Lettres Provinciales* by Blaise Pascal (1623–62). Cologne: Pierre de la Vallé. Of this book Lytton Strachey wrote, 'In the *Lettres Provinciales* Pascal created French prose.'

First edition of the *Romansche* or *Grison Bible*. Zürich: Heinrich Hamberger. Translated into the Lower Engadine Romansch by Joan Pitschen Salutz.

The Polyglot Bible of Brian Walton (*c.* 1600–61), begun in 1653, was completed in six folio volumes. This *Biblia Sacra Polyglotta*, one of the four great Polyglot Bibles issued during the sixteenth and seventeenth centuries, was printed in London by Thomas Roycroft and exemplifies seventeenth-century printing at its best. For his skill and trouble, Roycroft was allowed to assume the title 'Orientalium Typographus Regius'. The exotic founts employed, Hebrew, Latin, Greek, Aramaic, Syriac, Samaritan, Ethiopic, Arabic, and Persian, appear to have been furnished by the four English type-founders nominated under the Star Chamber decree. The work is therefore a landmark in the history of letter-founding in England, since never before had a work of importance been printed in this country in any of the learned characters other than Latin and Greek. The Samaritan type was probably cut under the supervision of Archbishop Ussher, who had tried unsuccessfully to acquire the Samaritan type of Thomas Erpenius. (*See* 1625.)

First issue of William London, *A Catalogue of the most vendible Books in England*. Re-issued with a supplement in 1658, the whole recording 3,096 titles divided into subjects.

At Copenhagen, appeared the first regular Danish newspaper, *Ordinarie Wochentliche Zeitung* in German.

1658

At Nuremberg, Wolfgang Endter published *Orbis sensualium pictus*, by the Czech pedagogue Johann Amos Comenius (Jan Komenski: 1592–1670), a school-book for teaching Latin with pictures to impress the words upon the child's memory. There were many editions and translations. In the following year an edition was printed at London for J. Kirby in Latin and English, called *Commenius's Visible World*, and in 1666 Michael and Johann Frederick Endter published a polyglot edition in German, Latin, Italian and French.

The first Oxford Architypographus or Controller of the Press, authorised by the Laudian Statutes, was elected. He was Samuel Clarke, M.A.

William Bradford, who became the first printer in Pennsylvania, was born at Leicester. His parents were Quakers who emigrated to America in 1682. William Bradford served his apprenticeship in London with Andrew Sowles of Gracechurch Street, whose daughter Elizabeth he married.

1659

Foundation by decree of the Great Elector of the 'Chürfürstliche Bibliothek zu Cölln an der Spree' now the Prussian State Library in Berlin.

At Hamm, in Westphalia, a printing office was founded which was the origin of the present-day Grote'sche Verlagsbuchhandlung, Berlin.

Johann Georg Cotta acquired by marriage a bookselling business at Tübingen.

Publication of the *Biblia sacra Hebraea . . .* Amsterdam: Joseph Athias. This was a famous edition by the learned Jewish Rabbi and printer Joseph Athias, which became the standard version. The Hebrew title-page is dated 1659; the Latin, 1661. It was Athias who acquired the amalgamated foundry of Van Dijck and Daniel Elsevier after the latter's death in 1680. The Hebrew types of Athias were later bought by the firm of Ploos van Amstel and were eventually acquired by Johannes Enschedé en Zonen of Haarlem.

Anton Janson, a Dutch type-founder and engraver, trained in Amsterdam by Christoffel van Dijck, established the first independent type-foundry in Leipzig. (*See also* 1934.)

At Smyrna, the Jewish printer Abraham ben Jedidiah Gabbai took over the press 'La Stampa del Caf Nahat' which his father, Jedidiah ben Isaac Gabbai had founded at Leghorn around 1650. Abraham worked at Smyrna printing Hebrew books until 1680.

1660

On 1 January, Timothy Ritzsch brought out the first number of the *Leipsicer Zeitung*.

Printing began at Bolzano, with the *Elenchus encomiorum . . .* of Bonaventura O'Connor. Bulsani: Car. Girardus. In 1658 O'Connor had published *Quintuplex Pantekaedechyris Mariana* at Trento.

Samuel Mearne appointed bookbinder to Charles II. He later held a similar royal appointment under James II.

1661

The first Spanish news-book, *Relación o Gaceta de algunos casos particulares*, appeared this year.

Robert Sanders, a Glasgow bookseller, set up a printing press in that city. In 1684, he purchased George Swintoun's share in the King's Printing House.

Foundation of the Kongelige Bibliothek in Copenhagen.

Printing of the New Testament translated into the Indian tongue by the Rev. John Eliot (1604–90) begun by Samuel Green at Cambridge, Massachusetts, and completed with the assistance of Marmaduke Johnson (*see* 1663). There exist trial printings of *Genesis* as early as 1655.

1662

First edition of Georg Andreas Böckler, *Theatrum machinarum novum*. Cologne: Sumptibus P. Principis. One of the copperplate engravings in this book shows the complete process of making paper by hand.

Passing of an Act (13 & 14 Charles II, cap. 32, 33) for, 'preventing the frequent abuses in printing seditious, treasonable and unlicensed books and pamphlets, and for regulating of printing and printing presses.' By this Act, the number of master type-founders was again reduced to four, as in the Star Chamber decree of 1637 (*q.v.*)—abrogated by the dissolution of that Court in

1640. This restriction continued in force until 1695, when it expired. Another clause in the Act restricted the number of master printers, which had gradually increased under the Commonwealth, to twenty.

John Ogilby published *The Entertainment of His Most Excellent Majestie Charles II, in His Passage through the City of London to his Coronation, containing an exact Accompt of the whole Solemnity.* London: Thomas Roycroft for the author. This folio volume contains a series of folding plates depicting the procession, and a frontispiece of the arms of Charles II engraved by Wenzel Hollar.

The earliest secular music printed in Scotland —a collection of *Songs and Fancies,* commonly known as Forbes's *Cantus.* Aberdeen: John Forbes. There were later editions in 1666 and 1682.

The privilege granted in 1657 to Glasgow University for printing Bibles was cancelled.

Editio princeps of Thomas Fuller (1608–61), *The Worthies of England.* Fuller was one of the best writers of 'characters' at a time when character writing was much in vogue.

1663

The Hamburg poet and theologian Johann Rist started the learned periodical *Monatsgespräche.*

An Act was passed one clause of which directed that, 'every printer should send three copies of every book new printed, or reprinted with additions, to the Stationers' Company, to be sent to the King's Library, and the Vice-Chancellors of the two Universities of Oxford and Cambridge'.

Sir Roger l'Estrange (1616–1704) appointed 'Surveyor of the Imprimery' by Charles II. In the same year he published his *Considerations and Proposals in order to the Regulation of the Press.* London: printed by A.C. June 3, M.DC. LXIII.

In Denmark, appeared in this year the *Europaeische Woechentliche Zeitung,* printed in German. In 1672 came *Extraordinaires maanedliges Relationes.*

At Cambridge, Mass., Samuel Green and Marmaduke Johnson issued the Rev. John Eliot's Bible in the Algonquin tongue, known as the *Eliot Indian Bible,* the first Bible printed in the Western hemisphere. The New Testament had appeared in 1661. (*See* 1661.)

1664

Philippe Labbé published in Paris his *Bibliotheca bibliothecarum.* Editions were published at Rouen in 1672 and 1678.

Richard Atkyns, a London printer, in order to support his claim to certain exclusive privileges of printing under the King's patent, published a tract called *The Original and Growth of Printing,* in which he claimed that printing had been introduced into England and established at Oxford in 1468 by a certain Frederick Corsellis, who had been privily taken from Haarlem to Oxford for that purpose. No evidence has ever been found to corroborate Atkyns's story, which is no longer believed.

The London printer John Twyn, of Cloth Fair, Smithfield, was arrested for attempting to print a pamphlet *A Treatise of the Execution of Justice* and tried for treason on the grounds that the work was intended to foment a rebellion. He was executed at Tyburn. (A report is in Cobbett's *State Trials,* Vol. 6.)

First edition of Thomas Mun (1571–1641), *England's Treasure by Forraign Trade.* London: J.G. for Thomas Clark. This treatise, by a merchant who has been described as England's first political economist, was written about 1630 and published posthumously by his son John.

Publication of *A Compendium of the Usuall Hands,* 'written and invented by Richard Daniel, and engraved by Edward Cocker', London.

At Cambridge, Mass., Samuel Green and Marmaduke Johnson printed Richard Baxter, *A Call to the Unconverted,* translated into the Massachusetts Indian language by John Eliot, from the edition printed in London, 1657. Only one copy is now known—a presentation volume from Governor Winthrop.

1665

At Dordrecht, Franciscus Juntus printed at his own expense and for the first time the *Codex Argenteus,* an important memorial of the old Gothic tongue. He had special type cut with several new letters, among them a runic script, for the setting of the extensive commentary.

In France, Denis de Sallo (under the pseudonym of Sieur d'Hédouville) started the *Journal des Scavans,* of which 111 volumes were issued between 1665 and 1792. It still appears.

On Wednesday, 15 November, appeared the

first number of *The Oxford Gazette*, printed by Leonard Lichfield, the forerunner of *The London Gazette*. No. 21 (22–25 January, 1665/6) was the last number printed at Oxford, and ever since that date the *Gazette* has been printed at London, but the title of *Oxford Gazette* was retained for two more numbers, the first to bear the title *The London Gazette* being No. 24 (1–5 February, 1665/6).

The Royal Society (founded in 1660) began to publish its *Philosophical Transactions* in which have been published many important contributions to human thought. It was begun as a periodical publication by Henry Oldenburg.

Nicholas Nicholls, in a petition to the King for 'the place of Letter Founder to your Majesties Presses', gave a tiny specimen of his types, One can hardly call it a specimen sheet, since it measures no more than $8\frac{1}{2} \times 4\frac{1}{2}$ cms., and Moxon was the first English founder to issue a full specimen of his types. (*See* 1669.)

1666

At Frankfurt-am-Main, Johann Andreae acquired the printing house which had once been that of the Wechel family. The firm enjoyed a considerable reputation during its long existence as printing house, publishing firm and typefoundry.

Göttingen had its first printer, Justus Nithmann. The press was established by Magister Heinrich Tolle.

First collected edition of the *Plays* of Molière published. Paris: Louis Bilaine & Gabriel Quinet.

On 22 September, the Hall of the Company of Stationers was destroyed in the Great Fire of London. Pepys was told by the bookseller Joseph Kirton that over £150,000 worth of books belonging to the booksellers who dwelt around St. Paul's were consumed in the fire. A new Hall was completed by 1670.

On 23 October, was published *The Case and Proposals of the Free Journeymen Printers in and about London*, which gave the number of working printers who had served a regular apprenticeship, then resident in and about London, as amounting to 140.

An edition of the New Testament in the Turkish language was printed by H. Hall, Printer to the University of Oxford. It was translated by William Seaman under the patronage of the Hon. Robert Boyle, who contributed £60 towards its cost, the remainder being provided by the Levant Company.

Publication of Aesop's *Fables* in English, French and Latin, illustrated by Francis Barlow. The English text by Thomas Philipott; the French and Latin by Robert Codrington. London: William Godbid for Francis Barlow. (*See also* 1687.)

The first newspaper printed in Danish, *Den Danske Mercurius*, printed by Jørgen Gøde, University printer and first manager of the Danish Royal Press, established in 1660. It was edited by the poet Anders Bording. (*See* 1657.)

1667

On 27 April, the poet John Milton executed the contract by which he disposed of the copyright of his *Paradise Lost* to Samuel Simmons for the sum of £5 down and a further £5 when the first edition of 1,300 copies should have been sold, and two similar sums at the end of the second and third editions if called for. In 1680, the poet's widow resigned the full copyright to Simmons for a third and final payment of £8, and Simmons himself, at the end of 1680 or beginning of 1681 resold it for £25 to Brabazon Aylmer, a bookseller of Cornhill. The first issue of the first edition bears the imprint 'Printed, and are to be sold by Peter Parker . . . and by Robert Boulter . . . and Mathias Walker'. London, 1667.

2 May, death of the poet and pamphleteer George Wither (b. 1588) to whom James I had in 1623 granted a monopoly for fifty-one years of his *Hymns and Songs of the Church*—a monopoly bitterly resented by the Stationers' Company, since the grant required all stationers to insert the work in every copy of the *Psalms in Metre*, the rights in which had previously been granted to the Company. They petitioned Parliament in 1624 and that part of the grant was recalled.

Dr. John Fell began to acquire, through his agents abroad, Dutch punches and matrices for the University Press at Oxford. (*See* 1672.)

1668

At Florence, the physician and naturalist Francesco Redi (1626–97) published his most famous work, *Esperienze intorno alla generazione degli insetti*. Five editions were published during the next twenty years. An English translation by Mab Bigelow was published in 1909.

In Italy, Francesco Nazzari launched in Rome the first number of the *Giornale de' Letterati*.

Editio princeps of the six first books of the *Fables* of Jean de la Fontaine (1621–95). Paris: Claude Barbin. 4to. In the same year, a two-volume 12mo edition was published at Paris by D. Thierry and C. Barbin.

At Paris, the writing-master and engraver Louis Senault published a folio volume *Les rares Escritures financières et italienne-bastardes nouvellement à la mode*.

John Starkey published the first of the book trade catalogues known as *Term Catalogues* because they were issued four times a year, in the middle of the Law terms of Michaelmas, Hilary, Easter and Trinity. This catalogue was called *Mercurius Librarius*. The complete series consists of 159 issues (1668–1709).

Birth of Michael Maittaire (1668–1747), author of *Annales Typographici* (*see* 1719). His parents were Protestants, and after the Revocation of the Edict of Nantes they came to England, where the young Maittaire was sent to Westminster School. He later became one of the masters there.

Printing introduced into the episcopal town of Lund in Sweden by Vitus Haberegger from Malmö.

The oldest surviving piece of printing at Batavia (Dutch East Indies) is *Naerder artyculen ende poincten* . . . (A Treaty of Peace between Admiral Cornelius Speelman and the Sultan of Macassar). No printer's name is given and it was probably set and printed by Government personnel.

1669

First edition of Hans Jacob Christoffel von Grimmelshausen, *Abentheurliche Simplicissimus*. The author concealed his identity under the pseudonym of G. Schleifheim von Salsfort, and the book bore the fictitious imprint 'Mompelgart, bey Johann Fillion'. New editions were immediately brought out by Georg Müller at Frankfurt-am-Main, and by Wolff Eberhard Felsecker at Nuremberg, of whom the former must have been the publisher of the original edition.

Editio princeps of Blaise Pascal, *Pensées de M. Pascal sur la Réligion*. Paris: Guillaume Desprez. Of the first issue, dated 1669, only one copy is now known; all others are dated 1670. A counterfeit edition was published the same year.

Editio princeps of Molière, *Le Tartufe, ou L'Imposteur*. Paris: Jean Ribou.

The earliest full specimen of types issued by an English type-foundry: *Proves of several sorts of Letter cast by Joseph Moxon. Westminster. Printed by Joseph Moxon, in Russell Street, at the Signe of Atlas: 1669.* (The specimen is reproduced in the reprint of Moxon's *Mechanick Exercises* edited by Herbert Davis & Harry Carter (1958) from the only recorded copy in the Bagford Collection in the British Museum (Harl. 5915, No. 459).) (*See also* 1665.)

The first dated English mezzotint—a portrait of Charles II by William Sherwin. Francis Place may have been the first English mezzotint engraver, but he did not produce a dated print prior to that of Sherwin.

Publication at Cambridge, Mass. (presumably by Marmaduke Johnson), of the Rev. John Eliot's *Indian Primer*. Only one copy is known.

1670

About 1670, Reinhard Voskens, a native of Amsterdam who had started a type-foundry in Frankfurt-am-Main, issued a specimen *Proben von mayner mit eigener Handt geschnittenen Schrifften, Buchstaben*, etc. (It is reproduced in G. Mori, *Die Schriftgiesser Bartholomäus Voskens in Hamburg und Reinhard Voskens in Frankfurt a.M.* (1923).) Soon afterwards the Voskens foundry in Frankfurt was acquired by Johann Adolph Schmidt, at one time an employee in the Luther foundry in that city.

Publication of Benedict de Spinoza, *Tractatus Theologico-Politicus*, the only major work of its author published during his lifetime. It emphasised the need for freedom of thought in the well-ordered State. 'Apud Henricum Künrath; Hamburgi' [Amsterdam]. It was printed without the author's name.

Editio princeps of Molière, *Le Bourgeois Gentilhomme*. Paris: Pierre Le Monnier.

1671

Oxford University leased the privilege of printing to four members of the university, Dr. John Fell, Thomas Yate, Sir Leoline Jenkins and Joseph Williamson. The new company was to pay the university £200 a year for the privilege.

Andrew Anderson of Edinburgh appointed King's Printer in Scotland for a period of forty-one years.

1672

One of the fathers of Spanish bibliography, Nicolas Antonio (1617–84) published his *Bibliotheca Hispana Nova* (Rome, two volumes: *Ex officina N. A. Tinassii*) which dealt with writers from 1500 onwards. (*See also* 1783.)

Publication of *Magnum in Parvo, or the Pens Perfection*—'Invented, written and engraven in silver' by Edward Cocker, London.

In August, Dr. John Fell received from the Rev. Thomas Marshall, his agent for the purchase of punches and matrices in Holland, a final consignment of material, much of which was the work of two famous Dutch punch-cutters, Dirck Voskens and Christoffel van Dijck. (*See also* 1667.)

1673

At Paris, was published Christian Huygens, *Horologium oscillatorium*, a description of the pendulum clock, invented by the author in 1656. It is also a treatise on the motion of bodies and various principles of mechanics, and is generally considered to be the Dutch mathematician's *magnum opus*.

The agreement of the Oxford University Press with the Stationers' Company (*see* 1637) lapsed, and Oxford was able to exercise its former right to print Bibles. (*See* 1675.)

1674

About this year, a type-foundry was established in Angel Alley, Aldersgate Street, London, by James and Thomas Grover. The foundry eventually came into the possession of John James in 1758.

1675

At Vienna, the Court interpreter of Oriental languages, Franz Meninski von Mesgnien, established with his own money an Oriental press and later got Johann Lobinger of Nuremberg to cut Arabic characters for his *Thesaurus linguarum orientalium* (three parts, 1680–87).

The Oxford University Press began its printing of Bibles with a quarto English Bible. The printing began in 1673, but it was not published until 1675. In that same year the Press issued its first Greek New Testament (the text of which was a reprint of the second Elsevier edition of 1633), as well as a quarto *Book of Common Prayer* and a quarto Psalter.

Eustace Burnaby received a royal patent for 'the art and skill of making all sorts of white paper for the use of writing and printing, being a new manufacture never practised in any our kingdoms or dominions'. The location of Burnaby's mill is thought to have been in the Windsor area, either at Stanwell or Cranborn. The art of making white paper in England had lapsed since the closing of Spilman's mill. (*See* 1589.)

John Foster, born at Dorchester, near Boston Mass., in 1648, set up the first press in Boston. In 1674, Marmaduke Johnson had received permission from the General Court of the colony to remove his press from Cambridge to Boston and, although he established himself in that city, he died on 25 December, 1674, before the press could be put into operation. Foster purchased his equipment and printed in Boston until his death in 1681.

1676

The first recorded book auction in England was the sale of the library of Dr. Lazarus Seaman, held by the bookseller and publisher William Cooper, in business at the sign of the Pelican in Little Britain. The sale was held in the house of Dr. Seaman in Warwick Court, Paternoster Row, and Cooper issued a *Catalogus variorum et insignium Librorum . . . clarissimi doctissimiq. Viri Lazari Seaman, S.T.D.*—the first sale catalogue of a book auction published in England.

The punch-cutter Peter de Walpergen arrived at Oxford from Holland at the invitation of Bishop Fell. He cut a number of types for the University Press, and on the death of his patron he set up in business on his own. He died in 1703.

On 4 September, died John Ogilby (b. 1600), geographical printer to Charles II, an account of whose coronation he published in a folio volume with plates. (*See* 1662.)

1677

The scholar Franciscus Junius made an important gift of type and matrices to the University Press at Oxford. The collection included Runic, Gothic, Saxon, Icelandic, Danish and Swedish types.

In this year was published the first English directory, Samuel Lee's *A Collection of the Names of Merchants living in and about the City of London*.

First Edition of Cocker, *Arithmetic*; the 56th

edition was published in 1767. (*See* Sir Ambrose Heal, *Cocker's Arithmetic*, 1929.)

Jacob Tonson I, first publisher of Dryden and Pope, opened his bookshop in Fleet Street.

Death of the Czech artist Wenzel Hollar in London.

The first illustrated book from an American press —William Hubbard, *Narrative of the Indian Wars*, printed at Boston by John Foster.

1678

Johann Peter von Ghelen (Jan van Ghelen) son of the famous Antwerp printer, acquired a printing office and became University Printer. He was appointed Court Printer in 1701.

First edition of John Bunyan, *The Pilgrim's Progress* (Part I). London: Printed for Nathaniel Ponder at the Peacock in the Poultry near Cornhill. It was an immediate success and eleven authorised editions, as well as some pirated ones, appeared during the author's lifetime. The book has been translated into some 150 languages.

Printing began at Bucarest with a work called *Cheia intelescelui* (The Key of Agreement).

1679

At Frankfurt-am-Main appeared C. A. Ramsay, *Tacheographia*—the first German shorthand book.

At Paris the bookseller Laurent Houry published his first Court Almanac—the *Almanach Royal*.

1680

At Frankfurt-am-Main, Moritz Georg Weidmann founded a publishing firm which eventually became the Berlin firm of Weidmannsche Verlagsbuchhandlung.

On 13 October, died Daniel Elsevier, the head of the Amsterdam house of the Elseviers, and one of the most famous publishers in Europe. His death meant the extinction of the Amsterdam house, although his widow published a few books in 1681.

A Proclamation by Charles II of 12 May for suppressing 'the printing and publishing of unlicensed news-books and pamphlets of news. London: J. Bill.

On 7 October, the printer Robert Everingham issued the first number of the *Weekly Adverisement of Books*.

In England regular parliamentary printing began with the printing in this year of the *Votes & Proceedings* of the House of Commons.

1681

Editio princeps of the New Testament in Portuguese. It was translated by João Ferreira d'Almeida, a minister at Batavia, for the use of Portuguese living in the East Indies. Amsterdam: For the widow of J. V. Someren.

At Paris, Louis Bilaine printed Jean Mabillon, *De re diplomatica*, which Magliabecchi called 'an immortal work'. The author, Jean Mabillon (1652–1707), the famous French scholar and Benedictine preacher was offered by Colbert, to whom it was dedicated, a pension of 2,000 livres, which he refused. This book laid the foundations for the documentary study of palaeography and contains 58 finely engraved plates, copied from ancient manuscripts and diplomatic documents. A second edition was published 1704–09.

William Penn wrote his account of the natural resources and political constitution of the Quaker province of Pennsylvania, published in London 1681 as *Some Account of the Province of Pennsilvania in America*.

Death of Thomas Newcombe, aged 53, printer to King Charles II.

Death of John Foster who established the press in Boston. (*See* 1675.)

1682

At Stuttgart, August Metzler founded the still existing Metzler printing and publishing firm.

The breaker-washer, known as a 'Hollander' first made its appearance in Dutch paper mills, a fact which gave it its name. It replaced the hammers of the stamping-mills hitherto used for macerating the rags.

At Paris, appeared the first edition of the complete works of Molière, in eight volumes 12 mo., D. Thierry, C. Barbin, & P. Trabouillet. A two-volume edition of *Les Œuvres de Monsieur Molière* was published at Paris in 1666 and a seven-volume edition in 1674–75. But the 1682 edition contained 'les Œuvres posthumes de Monsieur de Molière, imprimées pour la première fois en l'année 1682'.

Foundation of the Advocates' Library at Edinburgh, formally inaugurated in March 1689. In 1925, after the passing of the National Library of Scotland Act, the Advocates' Library became in name what it had for long been in fact, the National Library of Scotland.

The printer William Nuthead established a press in Virginia, but in the following year he was prohibited from printing after he had published certain Assembly papers without permission of the Governor and Council. A press was not permanently established in Virginia until 1730.

1683

Peter Schröder became the first printer at Schwerin. He had previously worked at Parchim from 1671 until 1681. He died around 1695.

Publication of the second volume of *Mechanick Exercises, or the Doctrine of Handy-Works*, by Joseph Moxon (1627–1700). This second volume, which began to come out in parts in 1683, was devoted to printing and type-founding, and was the earliest practical manual of printing in any language (it was reprinted at New York in 1896 edited by Theodore Low De Vinne, and in 1958 and 1962 the Oxford University Press issued a critical edition edited by Herbert Davis and Harry Carter).

During the winter the Thames froze, and souvenir cards were printed at printing booths set up on the ice.

1684

Founding of the Stamperia del Seminario at Padua. The foundry which adjoined the printing house was famous, and elicited the praise of Bodoni.

A new Charter to replace that destroyed in the Great Fire of 1666 was granted to the Stationers' Company by Charles II.

1685

At Amsterdam, was published a Hungarian Bible, the masterpiece of the Hungarian printer and punch-cutter Miklós Misztótfalusi Kis, who learnt his trade as punch-cutter at the Blaeu printing office in Amsterdam. Later he set up in business on his own and furnished matrices to his customers in many European countries. He came to England from Amsterdam between 1680 and 1689.

Editio princeps of the Old Testament in Irish, translated by William Bedell, Bishop of Kilmore (1571–1642), assisted by Murtagh O'Ciong and Dennis O'Sheriden. London. No printer's name.

An English printer, William Bradford, established the first press in Philadelphia. He may have chosen the chief town of the recently founded Friends' Colony because he himself was the son-in-law of the Quaker printer Andrew Sowle of London.

William Nuthead set up the first press in Maryland at St. Mary's City.

1686

In France, by an Edict promulgated at Versailles in August and registered in Parliament on 7 September the number of printing offices in Paris was limited to thirty-six. (In 1645 there were no fewer than seventy-six printing offices in Paris.) Jurisdiction over them passed from the University of Paris to the Government. No bookseller could apply for a printing office if he had not been registered as a printer before the Edict was published.

First edition of the Bible in Lett. Riga: Johann Georg Wilcke[n]. The New Testament title-page is dated 1685, but the general title bears the date 1686.

1687

First edition of the *Philosophiae naturalis principia mathematica* by Isaac Newton (1642–1727). London: Joseph Streater for Samuel Smith. The work which established a conception of the universe unchallenged until Einstein.

At London appeared *Aesop's Fables with his Life* in English, French and Latin, illustrated with delightful etchings by Francis Barlow. The French text is set in roman, the Latin in italic, while below the illustrations are English verses composed by Mrs. Aphra Behn. Printed by Henry Hills junior for Francis Barlow. (*See also* 1666.) This edition has the 112 illustrations of the 1666 edition with an additional 31 for the Life of Aesop.

1688

First edition of *Les Caractères de Théophraste* by Jean de la Bruyère (1645–95). Paris: Estienne Michallet.

A new edition of John Milton, *Paradise Lost*, 'adorned with Sculptures' was printed by Miles

Flesher for Richard Bently and Jacob Tonson, who had acquired the copyright. (*See also* 1667.)

At Skálholt, in Iceland, were published *Islendingabók* and *Landnámabók*, the two primary sources of the earliest history of Iceland.

Editio princeps of the Bible in Rumanian, printed at Bucarest. It was translated by Nicolae Milescu and others.

1689

The Paris printer Jean de la Caille published his *Histoire de l'Imprimerie et de la Librairie*. Paris: Pierre Le Mercier, at the expense of the author.

Birth of François Didot (d. 1757) founder of the illustrious family of printers, publishers, type-designers and paper-makers of that name.

Bishop Petrus Bång established the first press at Wiborg.

1690

Edward Jones, printer to William III, accompanied the king to Ireland and set up a press 'at the King's Hospital in Oxman-Town'. He printed a *Form of Prayer* for use during the king's stay in Ireland. Jones died in London, 16 February 1706.

First edition of the Irish Bible contained in one 12mo volume. London: R. Everingham.

A German named William Rittenhouse (originally Wilhelm Rittinghausen), by trade a paper-maker, was put in charge of the first paper-mill in America, built in that year near Germantown, Pennsylvania, by William Bradford and Samuel Carpenter.

1691

Jean Anisson (1642–1740), brother of the Lyons printer Jacques Anisson (d. 1714) became Director of the Imprimerie Royale du Louvre, a position which remained in the family until 1792 (*q.v.*).

Death of Thomas Newcombe the younger, King's Printer to Charles II, James II and William III.

1692

The King of France ordered new characters to be made for the Imprimerie Royale. These were engraved by the titular punch-cutter of the royal printing house, Philippe Grandjean, but the complete founts were not finished for half a century. Grandjean, who had begun the work died in 1714 and was replaced by his widow, who in turn was succeeded by Jean Alexandre. They were eventually completed by Alexandre's son-in-law and successor, Louis Luce. However, the first bodies, cut by Grandjean (especially the Saint-Augustin and Gros Romain) were inaugurated in the celebrated folio *Médailles sur les principaux événements du règne de Louis le Grand* on which work started in 1694. (*See* 1702.)

The first trade newspaper in England—*A Collection for Improvement of Husbandry and Trade*, founded by John Houghton, F.R.S.

1693

At Oxford, was printed at the Sheldonian Theatre *A Specimen of the Several Sorts of Letter given to the University by Dr. John Fell late Lord Bishop of Oxford. To which is added the Letter given by Mr. F. Junius*. This book contains specimens of the Dutch and French types procured by Dr. Fell for the Oxford University Press, with an appendix by the antiquary Franciscus Junius (François du Jon). This was the earliest of the eight known printed specimens of types issued by the University Press at Oxford. The others were issued in 1695, 1706, 17— (undated, but between 1706 and 1768), 1753, 1768 (together with two supplements dated 1770 and 1775), 1786, and 1794. (*See also* 1753.)

William Bradford appointed Royal Printer for the Province of New York—a post he held for half a century. He died 1752, aged 90.

1694

Printing introduced into Wetzlar by Georg Ernst Winckler. His son Nikolaus Ludwig succeeded him in 1729 or earlier.

Jan and Kasper Luyken published in Amsterdam *Het menselyk bedryf*, illustrating in 100 engravings various trades and crafts. (*See also* 1568.)

At Paris, Pierre le Petit published the first edition of the *Dictionnaire de l'Académie Française*.

A librarian at the Sorbonne, André Chevillier (1636–1700) published *L'Origine de l'Imprimerie de Paris*. Paris: J. de Laulne.

1695

The first printer at Bristol was William Bonny who in this year set up a press in Tower Lane and printed for the Bristol merchant John Cary his

An Essay on the State of England in relation to its Trade, its Poor, and its Taxes.

On 29 November, died Anthony Wood, celebrated antiquary and author of *History and Antiquities of the Colleges and Halls in the University of Oxford* and of the *Athenae Oxonienses*.

1696

Publication at Oxford of Heinrich Wilhelm Ludolf (1655–1712), *Grammatica Russica*, the first surviving grammar of the Russian, as distinct from the Slavonic, language. Oxford: *E Theatro Sheldoniano*. An edition of the Latin text of this book, together with a Russian translation by B. Larin, was published at Leningrad in 1937. (*See also* 1755.)

On 4 August, appeared the first issue of *Dawks's News Letter*, set in a script type, which was the first English news-lettter to be published thrice weekly. Its publisher states that 'it does undoubtedly exceed the best of the *written news*, contains double the quantity, is read with abundance more ease and pleasure, and will be useful to improve the younger sort in writing a curious hand'.

The first regular press at Shrewsbury was set up there by Thomas Jones, formerly a London bookseller, who printed many books in Welsh from 1696 to 1713.

A press was set up for the first time at Plymouth by D. Jourdaine.

1697

At Paris, Marie-Anne Didot, wife of the bookseller Nyon, was admitted to the Guild of Booksellers. She was the first of the famous Didot family to become a member of the trade.

The first book known to have been printed at Belfast is either Robert Craghead, *Answer to the Bishop of Derry's Second Admonition*, John M'Bride, *Animadversions*, or the same author's *Answer to a peaceable and friendly Address*. All three were printed in 1697. Printing is thought to have begun in Belfast in 1694, but no book earlier than 1697 is known.

In Uppsala, the Swedish scholar Olaus Rudbeck completed on his own press the third volume of his great work *Atlantica*. Other volumes are said to have been destroyed in the great fire of 1702.

At Copenhagen, Justin Hog issued Thormod Torfesen, *Orcades*, the first notable work on the Orkneys and Hebrides.

1698

At Antwerp, the designer and engraver Jacob Harrewijn (1662–after 1732) published a charming lettering book, *De XXV letteren van het ABC*. In 1701 appeared his illustrations for *La vie et les aventures de Lazarille de Tormes*, published at Brussels.

First edition of John Ayres, *A Tutor to Penmanship*. London: Sold by the author.

The University of Cambridge assumed direct control of its printing press and a Syndicate was appointed to supervise its management and working, consisting of the Vice-Chancellor, the heads of houses, the professors, and twelve named members.

The 9th edition of the *Bay Psalm Book* (*see* 1640) was the first to appear with tunes in two-part harmony, constituting the earliest music printing in the U.S.A. Boston: B. Green and J. Allen for Michael Perry. The only known copy is in the possession of the Massachusetts Historical Society.

1699

B. Stein founded the first printing office in the town of Lingen, where a university had been opened in 1697.

The widow of Claude Barbin published in Paris the first (incomplete) edition of François de Salignac de la Mothe Fénelon, *Télémaque*. When the edition had reached page 208 the police seized all the copies already in possession of the booksellers and tried to suppress the work. But the manuscript was sold to a Hague bookseller, Adrian Moetjens, who at once published an edition with many errors. He published a more perfect edition in 1701. In 1717 the greatnephew of the author published a new edition from a copy corrected by Fénelon himself, and this is held to be the *textus receptus*.

1700

In this year, even before the raising of Prussia to the status of a kingdom, Ulrich Liebpert of Berlin called himself 'Royal Prussian Court-Printer'.

Publication of *Vox Stellarum* by the so-called astrologer Francis Moore. This book of prognostications was the direct ancestor of *Old Moore's Almanack*.

John Ayres published *The Accomplisht Clerk or Accurate Penman.* (*See also* 1698.)

Printing began in Paraguay with a *Martyrologium Romanum* issued from a mission press in 1700, according to F. Antonio Sepp, *Continuatio laborum apostolicorum . . . in Paraquaria* (Ingolstadt: 1710). It was probably printed at Loreto, but no copy is now known, nor has the second edition, 1709, survived. The founders of the mission press were the Jesuit Fathers Juan Baptista Neumann of Vienna and José Serrano of Antequera in Andalucia.

1701

At Halle, the first German directory was printed —*Das ietzlebende Leipzig*, 48 pages.

At Erfurt, Johann Georg Starke printed the first hundred-year Calendar (1701–1801).

The Lutheran minister Johann Müller, in conjunction with the Leyden firm of Van der Mey, invented a method of stereotyping, and in this year printed the first book using this process, a small prayer-book. Müller then went into partnership with the Dutch bookseller Samuel Luchtmans and several books bearing their joint imprint were printed from stereotype plates. One such plate, used for printing a Dutch Bible issued by Müller's sons and Luchtmans & Co. in 1718, is preserved in the British Museum. Johann Müller died 1710.

Schnurrer, in his *Bibliotheca Arabica*, states that a printing press was set up in the monastery of Snagof, near Bucarest, by the abbot Antim Ivireanul, and in 1701 a Greek and Arabic Missal printed there. The earliest recorded book from this press is of 1696.

The first printing at Norwich since the departure of Solemne 120 years previously (*see* 1566). This was Francis Burges, *Some Observations on the Use and Origin of the Noble Art and Mystery of Printing*. No copy of this pamphlet is now known, but it was reprinted in the *Harleian Miscellany*. In it the author declares 'the first day that ever printing was at Norwich was Saturday, 27 September, 1701', and that the pamphlet in question was the first work printed in that town. Burges probably started the first Norwich newspaper, *The Norwich Press*, in the same year. He died 1706. From Burges's book it appears that the paper came from mills at Tabram (Taverham), Norfolk, where a paper mill was active until around 1811.

1702

From the Imprimerie Royale at Paris, came the magnificent folio *Médailles sur les Principaux Événements du Règne de Louis Le Grand*, in which appeared for the first time the 'Romain du roi' of Philippe Grandjean, officially 'premier Graveur du Roi pour son Imprimerie du Louvre'. The new type cut for Louis XIV for the exclusive use of the Imprimerie Royale was based upon the lengthy studies, both historical and geometrical, of a committee chosen by the Académie des Sciences, and consisting of the Abbé Nicolas Jaugeon, M. Des Billettes and M. Sébastien Truchet. 'Each separate character of the complete alphabet and all accents, in roman and italic, were decoratively engraved by L. Simonneau upon copper plates and finally handed over for the punch-cutter to follow' (Stanley Morison, *The Typographic Arts*). Grandjean died in 1714, and his work was continued by N. Alexandre, his friend and pupil and by Louis Luce, Alexandre's son-in-law. When finally completed in 1745, the 'romains du roi' had been cut in twenty-one sizes of roman and italic. These types, although exclusive to the Imprimerie Royale, were very closely imitated by other French typographers. (*See also* 1692.)

On Wednesday, 11 March, was published the first number of the *Daily Courant*, the first daily newspaper published in England. The first number was printed on one side of the sheet only.

Between 1702 and 1704, were published the three volumes of *The History of the Rebellion and Civil Wars in England*, by Edward Hyde, Earl of Clarendon. Each chapter of the three folio volumes, printed at the Sheldonian Theatre, Oxford, has an initial letter, head-piece and tail-piece, line engraved on copper by Michael Burghers, a Dutchman who worked for the University Press at Oxford from c. 1673 until his death in 1727.

The earliest example of copperplate engraving in the English Colonies of N. America appeared —the portrait of Increase Mather in that author's *Ichabod*. Boston: Timothy Green.

On 1 January, died Samuel Green, founder of an extensive family of printers in N. America. For some fifty years he managed the press of Harvard University at Cambridge, Mass.

1703

Johann van Ghelen printed at Vienna the first regular newspaper in German to appear in Vienna—the *Wiener Diarium* (afterwards renamed the *Wiener Zeitung*), which was the official organ of the Government.

Izaak Enschedé (1681–1761) set up as a printer in Haarlem, thus founding a firm of printers and type-founders which is in the same family to this day. The firm was incorporated as a joint stock company in 1932.

At Moscow, Peter the Great founded and edited the first Russian news-sheet, *Vedomosti*.

1704

At Frankfurt-am-Main, died the philologist Hiob Ludolf who had paid for the cutting of an Ethiopian fount. The matrices, together with the Ethiopian books he had printed, he bequeathed to the people of Abyssinia.

In France, a decree was issued on 21 July fixing the maximum number of printing offices in each town. In all, 274 establishments were authorised.

The first technical dictionary published in England was *Lexicon Technicum: or an Universal English Dictionary of Arts and Sciences*, by John Harris (*c.* 1666–1719), an eminent member of the Royal Society. The text was well illustrated and a second volume was published 1710.

Publication of Sir Isaac Newton, *Opticks*. This appeared without the author's name on the title-page, although his initials are to be found at the end of the advertisement. London: For Sam. Smith & Benj. Walford.

Publication of the first volume of the *Foedera* of Thomas Rymer. The last of the twenty-folio volumes appeared in 1735. Lowndes called it 'an invaluable work, equally interesting to the antiquary and historian'. London: A. & J. Churchill and J. Tonson.

On 19 February Daniel Defoe began publication in London of his *Weekly Review of the Affairs of France* whilst imprisoned on a conviction for publishing a satirical pamphlet, *The Shortest Way with the Dissenters* (1702).

The *Boston News Letter* founded in that city by John Campbell. This was the earliest permanent newspaper in North America. The first number was dated 17–24 April, and the newspaper continued with occasional changes of name for seventy-two years. Benjamin Harris had printed *Publick Occurrences* in 1690, but this publication was banned after one issue.

1705

First newspaper (in Latin) published in Hungary: *Mercurius Hungaricus*. (*See also* 1780.)

The Royal Society printed John Bagford, 'An Essay on the Invention of Printing', in Vol. 25 of *Philosophical Transactions*.

On 19 February, appeared the first number of *The Edinburgh Courant*, printed by James Watson. After fifty-five numbers it was transferred to Andrew Anderson, 'printer to the Queen, the city, and the college'.

The *Dublin Gazette* founded.

Earliest surviving book printed in Paraguay— Juan Eusebio Nieremberg, *Diferencia entre lo temporal y eterno*, a small folio of 438 pp., double column, printed probably at Loreto. (*See also* 1700.)

1706

The first to print at Worcester since the departure of John Oswen (*see* 1548) was Stephen Bryan. In 1709 he started the local newspaper *The Worcester Postman*.

A press was set up in Aleppo, under the direction of Athanasius, patriarch of the Greek Melchites. The first book printed was an Arabic Psalter.

1707

On 16 February, Claude Rigaud, brother-in-law of Jean Anisson, became director of the Imprimerie Royale, Paris.

Isaac Watts, founder of modern English hymnody, published his *Hymns and Spiritual Songs*. London: John Lawrence.

A new press was established in Moscow and, because Peter the Great ordered a radical simplification of the Cyrillic characters, Mihail Efremov began casting from Dutch matrices three new founts of Russian type brought into Russia. The first book in the new 'grazhdanski' (lit. 'civic') type was a quarto *Geometry* dated 1708. This was the first time that modern Russian type was used in place of the old Cyrillic.

At Batavia, in Java, A. L. Lodetus, printer to the Dutch East India Company, printed a Malay vocabulary in two volumes, which amalgamated the older vocabularies of De Houtman (1604) and Wiltens and Danckaerts (1623).

1708

At Nuremburg, Johann Leonhard Buggel, a German writing master published the *Schreibkünstler*.

At Paris, was published Bernard de Montfaucon, *Palaeographia Graeca,* the first book on the history of Greek letters and writing. Montfaucon (1655–1741), a Benedictine monk, wrote and edited many learned works, including the complete works of Saint Athanasius (1698).

The first complete decorated fount known to typography in Western Europe is an English design from the Grover foundry and was called Union Pearl. Its earliest known use is in 1708. It had no immediate successors.

John White, a native of York, set up as a printer at Newcastle upon Tyne, and became one of the biggest printers of chap-books in the North of England. He had an immense stock of quaint old cuts, inherited from his father, who had been a printer in York. Some of these were undoubtedly the battered remnants of blocks originally cut for early printers such as Wynkyn de Worde and Richard Pynson.

Died William Rittenhouse, the first paper-maker in America (*see* 1690). He was born Wilhelm Rittinghausen in 1654 at Mülheim in the Ruhr, and learned his trade in the Rhineland and Holland, emigrating to N. America in 1688.

1709

At Antwerp, was published the *Bibliotheca sacra* of Jacques Le Long (1665–1721), librarian of the Oratory, listing all the editions of the Bible, as well as the works of its commentators. It was republished at Paris in 1723 and at Halle 1778–90, in a greatly enlarged edition, six volumes.

Passing of the Copyright Act in England, with effect from 1 April, 1710. For the first time in the history of printing in Britain, legal recognition was accorded to the rights of the author and the conception of permanent copyright was ended.

The first evening newspaper appeared in England—the thrice-weekly *Evening Post.*

12 April, *The Tatler* was begun by Richard Steele under the pseudonym of Isaac Bickerstaff. It was published three times a week and lasted until 13 January, 1711.

John Moncur, who printed at Edinburgh

1707–26, is the first known Scottish printer to have issued a specimen of the types in his printing house. They were all of Dutch origin.

Thomas Short from Boston set up the first press in Connecticut at New London. Two products came from his press in June, 1709—*Proclamation for a Fast* and *An Act for Making and Emitting Bills of Publick Credit.* The latter was probably the earlier, according to Lawrence C. Wroth.

First printing office founded in Georgia at Tiflis. The first printings were of Rumanian books in Georgian characters.

1710

Paùl Pater (1656–1724) published *De Germaniae Miraculo . . . typis literarum earumque differentiis dissertatio,* the first knowledgeable and scientific treatise on printing types. Leipzig: J. F. Gleditsch.

Charles Hildebrand, baron of Canstein, established at Halle, Germany, a printing office called the Canstein Bible Institution for the purpose of printing and selling Bibles and New Testaments at moderate prices. By 1805 more than three million copies had come from the press of the institution, and by 1910 some seven million copies had been circulated.

Publication in London of George Shelley's *Alphabets in all the Hands;* a writing-book which is said to have influenced Baskerville. The examples were engraved by G. Bickham. This oblong folio is undated, but probably 1710.

John Barber succeeded Samuel Roycroft as printer to the City of London.

1711

At Rome, Francisco Gonzaga published *Catalogus Bibliothecae Josephi Renati Imperialis.* the great library known to all the scholars of Europe. Cardinal Imperiali had inherited this rich library from his uncle, Cardinal Lorenzo, and he later acquired many rare books of Cardinal Slusius.

Publication of Richard Bentley's edition of Horace—a landmark in classical scholarship. Cambridge: at the University Press.

On 1 March, appeared the first number of the *Spectator* conducted by Joseph Addison (1672–1719). It appeared daily, Sundays excepted.

1 August saw the first number of the *Newcastle Courant,* printed and published by John White.

It was the first newspaper in England to be printed north of the Trent.

A Government printing house was established at St. Petersburg through the influence of Peter the Great. The manager was Mihail Petrovich Avramov, and the first product of his press was *Marsovaja kniga* (The Book of Mars). A second printing house was set up in 1720 in the Nevski Monastery for the printing of religious books, but both were closed in 1727. To replace these two, in 1727 was opened the printing house of the Academy of Science which, as the oldest printing house in Russia for scientific works, is still renowned today.

1712

Stamp Duty upon newspapers introduced into England. A duty of a half-penny was levied on all newspapers contained in a half sheet or less, and a penny on every copy between a half sheet and a whole sheet (4 pages). Pamphlets paid duty at the rate of two shillings for every edition. The Stamp Duty was raised several times during the ensuing years and was not abolished until 1855.

Thomas Short, the first printer in Connecticut (*see* 1709) died and was succeeded by Timothy Green.

The first press in what was later British India was set up at Tranquebar, in the Tanjore district of Madras, by Danish missionaries, the area being then under Danish sovereignty. In charge of the press was the Danish missionary Bartholomaeus Ziegenbalg, who issued the first work, *On the Damnable Character of Paganism*, in 1713.

1713

François Didot (1689–1759), printer-bookseller and founder of the family celebrated in the annals of French typography, set up as a bookseller in Paris at the sign of the *Bible d'Or*, having been received that year as a member of the 'corporation des libraires'. Much later he became a printer (Lottin says 30 January, 1754). (*See also* 1689.)

Publication at Edinburgh of James Watson, *History of the Art of Printing*, the first history of the subject in the English language, though much of it is a translation of Jean de la Caille, *Histoire de l'Imprimerie*, Paris: 1689. (A reprint was issued in 1966 by the Gregg Press.)

Publication began of Carl Gustaf Warmholtz, *Bibliotheca Historica Sveo-Gothica*, etc. It was

not completed until 1889, and became, in effect, the national bibliography of Sweden. (A reprint, in sixteen volumes, was published 1966–67.)

1714

Thomas Ruddiman (1674–1757) published his classic textbook *Rudiments of the Latin Tongue*. Edinburgh: Robert Freebairn.

In September died Thomas Britton, 'the musical small-coal man'. He was a great collector of clients among the nobility. At his death, he left a large collection of books, manuscript and printed music, and musical instruments. Lord Somers gave £500 for his collection of pamphlets.

1715

The Regent of France, wishing to bring to the attention of scholars the numerous Chinese works in the Royal Library, ordered the making of Chinese types which later served to print the *Chinese Dictionary* of Basile, published in 1813 by order of Napoleon. The characters were cut under the supervision of the Orientalist, Etienne Fourmont (1683–1745), after whose death the work was suspended until 1811, when it was resumed under M. de Guignes *fils* for the printing of Basile's *Dictionary*.

William Bowyer I (1663–1737) completed the printing of Miss Elizabeth Elstob's *Anglo-Saxon Grammar*. This work was begun in 1712, but the Saxon type used was destroyed in a fire at Bowyer's premises on 28 January, 1713, before the work was completed. A new fount was designed by Humphrey Wanley and cut by Robert Andrews.

In 1715, Thomas Ruddiman set up as printer and publisher, taking his younger brother Walter (1687–1770) as partner. The firm devoted itself mainly to school books. In 1730 Thomas Ruddiman was appointed chief librarian to the Society of Advocates at Edinburgh, where he had been assistant librarian since 1702. From January 1724 onwards, he printed (and later owned) the *Caledonian Mercury* (first issued 28 April, 1720). (His *Life*, by George Chalmers, was published at London in 1794.)

Completion, at Tranquebar, of the New Testament in Tamil—the earliest edition of the New Testament printed in a language of India. It was translated by Bartholomaeus Ziegenbalg, a missionary of the Danish Lutheran church. The press and paper were a gift from the S.P.C.K. (*See also* 1712.)

1716

Publication at Nuremberg of Johann Conrad Zeltner, *Correctorum in typographiis eruditorum centuria, speciminis loco collecta*. It contains the lives of ninety-nine celebrated correctors of the press. It was printed by Adam Jonathan Felsecker.

Death of John Bagford (b. *circa* 1650), famous (or notorious) for his collection of title-pages and detached fragments of books and manuscripts acquired for the purpose of assisting him in the writing of a history of printing, paper-making, and binding, which he never completed. His collection, of great interest to historians of printing, was bought after his death by Robert Harley, Earl of Oxford, and eventually came to rest in the British Museum as part of the Harleian Collection. (*See also* 1705.)

First issue of *The Nottingham Post*, printed and published by John Collyer. It was discontinued in 1732.

1717

Giovanni Antonio Volpi and his brother, the Abbé Gaetano, founded a printing house at Padua, the director of which was the printer Giuseppe Comino. The first production of the press was Joannis Poleni, *De motu aquae mixto*, 1717. Most of the Cominian publications bear the inscription, 'Excudebat Josephus Cominus Vulpiorum aere'. After the death of the brothers Volpi the business passed to Ange Comino, son of Giuseppe.

J. Baskett printed a large folio Bible in two volumes, called the *Vinegar Bible* from the mistake in the headline of *Luke*, which reads 'The Parable of the Vinegar' instead of 'Vineyard'. Apart from this error the book is well printed and has several good copperplate engravings. There were two issues, each containing the same mistake. The first has the date 1717 on the first title-page and 1716 on the New Testament title, whereas the second issue has the date 1717 on both title-pages.

An edition of the *Book of Common Prayer* appeared with the following imprint: 'London: Engraven and Printed by Permission of Mr. John Baskett, Printer to the Kings most Excellent Majesty. 1717. Sold by John Sturt Engraver, in Golden-Lion-Court in Aldersgate Street.' This edition was engraved throughout on 188 silver plates by John Sturt (1658–1730), who had engraved many of John Ayres's books on calligraphy. Each page has an ornamental border, there are a number of vignettes in the text, and the frontispiece has a portrait of George I on which are inscribed in minute characters the Creed, the Lord's Prayer, the Commandments, the Prayer for the Royal Family and the Twenty-first Psalm.

The architect Colin Campbell published the first volume of his *Vitruvius Britannicus, or the British Architect*. This folio work was completed in three volumes, 1717–25. With this work there began a great period of book production for craftsmen in England.

First issue of *The Kentish Post, or Canterbury Newsletter* dated 23 October, 1717, printed by Thomas Reeve, the second known printer at Canterbury (*see* 1549). After a few issues the printing was undertaken first by James Abree and W. Aylett, and then by Abree alone. Abree printed a number of books and pamphlets at Canterbury from 1718 to 1740, and died in 1768.

1718

C. L. Thiboust published at Paris his Latin poem on the excellence of printing, *Typographiæ excellentia*, which gives a description of letter-founding in France at that period, accompanied by a curious engraving showing casters at work.

Isaac Carter set up what is thought to have been the first printing press in Wales at Trefhedyn in Cardiganshire. About 1725 he moved his press to Carmarthen.

1719

Bernhard Christoph Breitkopf (1695-1777) acquired the Leipzig printing business originally established in 1542 by Heinrich Eichbuchler. In 1795 Gottfried Härtel became a partner in the firm, which specialised in music printing, and from that time it became known as Breitkopf and Härtel.

At Strassburg, Johann Heinrich Heitz founded the printing firm still run by his descendants.

A foundry was established at Milan by a printer named Bellagata, who, according to Fournier, had bought the punches and matrices belonging to a wandering type-cutter and founder named Ignace Antoine Keblin. It was for long the only type foundry in Milan.

Publication was begun of the *Annales Typographici* by Michael Maittaire (1668–1747). The work was completed in 1741, and a supplement was issued by Michael Denis in 1789. The *Annales* includes in chronological order printed literature published up to 1664.

On 25 April, appeared the first edition of Daniel Defoe, *Robinson Crusoe*, for which the author received £10. By 6 August, four editions had already appeared in England, together with at least two pirated editions, and in the following year it was translated into French, Dutch and German (a facsimile reprint of the first edition was published in 1883 with an introduction by Austin Dobson).

The first Manchester newspaper issued in January—the *Manchester Weekly Journal*, printed by Roger Adams. Adams later went to Chester, where he was responsible for the *Chester Courant* from 1730 until his death.

Samuel Richardson (1689–1761), his apprenticeship with John Wilde completed, set up as master printer in a small court off Fleet Street, London.

The first American arithmetic—*Hodder's Arithmetick: or that necessary Art made most easy*, by James Hodder, Writing-Master. Boston: James Franklin. This book was produced at the time when Benjamin Franklin was working as apprentice to his brother James, and so he may have had a hand in setting it.

1720

Publication of George Frederick Handel, *Radamisto*. London: Richard Meares and Chr. Smith. Engraved throughout by Thomas Cross, and one of the finest examples of his work.

28 April, first issue of the *Caledonian Mercury*, printed at Edinburgh by William Adams junior for the proprietor, William Rolland. It was the first newspaper in Scotland to print literary articles as well as political news. 589 issues were printed by Adams until the printing was handed over on 17 January, 1724 to Thomas Ruddiman. (*See also* 1715.)

In May appeared the *Leeds Mercury* printed and published weekly by John Hirst.

In May, also, appeared the *Northampton Mercury* (2 May but not numbered) printed by Robert Raikes and William Dicey. (*See also* 1722.)

William Caslon cut an Arabic type for the S.P.C.K. for their New Testament and Psalter.

1721

Johann Heinrich Gottfried Ernesti (*see also* 1733), proprietor of the Endter printing house at Nuremberg, issued a printing handbook, *Die Wol-eingerichtete Buchdruckerey*, in which are type specimens of Greek, Hebrew (both Rabbinic and German-Hebrew), Samaritan, Estranghelo, Syriac, Arabic, Coptic, Russian, Cyrillic, Armenian and other exotic characters. At the end of the book is a reprint of Rist's version of the *Depositio Cornuti*. On the title-page of a later edition (1733) are engravings of early printers from 'Coster' and Gutenberg to Plantin, as also of the interior of a printing office. (*See* 1655.)

Editio princeps of Montesquieu, *Lettres Persanes*, published in Holland with the fictitious imprint 'Cologne, chez Pierre Marteau'.

First edition of Nathan Bailey, *An Universal Etymological English Dictionary*. London: for E. Bell and others. In 1802 the 30th edition was published.

Publication of Henry Purcell, *Orpheus Britannicus*. This posthumous work, in two volumes, is an anthology of Purcell's finest songs. It passed through several editions before the middle of the eighteenth century, the best and most complete being that published by William Pearson in 1721.

The first American music book of which copies (though only two) have survived—Thomas Walter, *The Grounds and Rules of Musick Explained*. Boston: James Franklin. Probably it is also the first music engraved in America. This book is thought to have been preceded in the same year by the first music textbook printed in America, John Tufts, *An Introduction to the Singing of Psalm-Tunes*, but no copy of the original edition of this book is now known, nor is its exact title recorded. It went through eleven editions between 1721 and 1744, but the fifth edition, printed at Boston by Samuel Gerrish in 1726, with the title quoted is the earliest in existence.

1722

The first known musical periodical was *Critica musica*, a weekly magazine published at Hamburg 1722–25 by Johann Mattheson.

The first press at Gloucester was established by Robert Raikes (father of the philanthropist) and William Dicey, for the printing of the *Gloucester Journal*.

At Lisbon was published Manoel de Andrade de Figueiredo, *Nova escola para aprender a ler, escrever, e contar.*

At Uppsala was published the first edition of Johannes Olaus Alnander (1694–1737), *Historiola artis typographicæ in Svecia*, a second edition of which appeared at Rostock in 1725.

1723

At Saint-Omer, France, was published *La Science pratique de l'Imprimerie*, by Martin Dominique Fertel (1672–1752). He was the first to mention the lack of uniformity in sizes of type current in his day. Updike says: 'It is the first treatise written in French, the aim of which was to show how to arrange a book clearly and attractively. It is admirably done, and should be consulted by any one wishing to reconstitute French typography of the early eighteenth century.' (It was reprinted, with additions by Annoy van de Wyder, at Brussels in 1822.)

Rules for the conduct of printing and bookselling in Paris were drawn up by the Chancellor, D'Aguesseau, and promulgated by the Conseil du Roi on 28 February, 1723. They contained 123 clauses.

In March John Wilford began to issue his *Monthly Catalogue* of English and foreign books. This was the first really successful trade periodical and lasted until 1730.

The first known printing by the first Cuban printer, Carlos Habré, possibly a Frenchman, was *Tarifa general de precios de medicina*, printed at Havana (it was reprinted in facsimile by Manuel Pérez Beato in 1936 (*La primera obra impresa en Cuba*)).

1724

The printer Samuel Negus wrot the curious *Compleat and private List of all the Printing-houses in and about the Cities of London and Westminster*, published by William Bowyer I. In this work Negus arranged the printers under various classifications such as, 'Well Affected to King George', 'Nonjurors', and 'Said to be High Flyers'. According to his own account, Negus had been a printer for twenty-three years, but a master for only two, in which time, he declares, 'I have suffered very much for want of employ.'

At London, the score of Handel's *Julius Caesar* was published, printed on punched pewter plates engraved by Cluer—a method originated about 1710 by John Walsh and John Hare.

Thomas Longman (1699–1755) bought the publishing business of the late William Taylor (publisher of the *Robinson Crusoe* of 1719) and thus founded a firm which has remained ever since in the hands of the Longman family. Thomas Longman became one of the shareholders in Chambers' *Cyclopedia* and Johnson's *Dictionary*. A New York branch of the firm was founded in 1887.

Thomas Gent (1693–1778), who had been employed for a time in London by Samuel Richardson, set up in York as a master printer. He was a remarkable character (though a poor printer) who, from being a runaway apprentice, ended up as a master printer, and historian of several towns in the north of England. The three topographical works which he both wrote and printed are *The Antient and Modern History of the City of York* (1730), *History of the Loyal Town of Ripon* (1733), and *History of the Royal and Beautiful Town of Kingston-upon-Hull* (1735). He died at York in his eighty-seventh year, and his amusing autobiography was published posthumously in London by Thomas Thorpe in 1832, with an engraved portrait of the author by Valentine Green.

Benjamin Franklin arrived in London and obtained employment as a printer first with Samuel Palmer and later with John Watts.

1725

Jakob Christof Le Blon (1667–1741) published *Coloritto, or the Harmony of Colouring in Painting . . . L'Harmonie du Coloris dans la peinture. . . .* This book was incorporated into his posthumously published *L'Art d'imprimer les Tableaux. . . .* Paris: A. Gautier de Montdorge. 1756. *Coloritto* is undated, but from the Sloane MS. 3972, Vol. 6, folio 73, we find that Sir Hans Sloane acquired his copy in 1725. Le Blon, a native of Frankfurt, invented a colour mezzotint process which consisted in printing successively, and in register, from three mezzotint plates inked in red, blue and yellow. His book contained nine full page mezzotints in colour; but the proper exploitation of the trichromate process had to wait until the invention of photography and the subsequent half-tone process. Later he used also a fourth plate for black and so became the first to make use of the four-colour process.

First edition of the *Lettres* of Marie de

Rabutin-Chantal, Marquise de Sévigné (1626–96). Troyes: Jacques Lefevre. The original edition contains only thirty-one letters. Augmented editions followed in 1726.

Louis-Laurent Anisson became director of the Imprimerie Royale, Paris. He resigned in 1733.

In October, at the age of 63, William Bradford (*see* 1685) established the weekly *New York Gazette*, the first published in that city.

1726

At Nuremberg and at Altdorf, Friedrich Roth-Scholz published his *Icones Bibliopolarum et Typographorum*, containing a collection of engraved portraits of famous printers and publishers. Part I and Part II (1726, 1779) were published by the Heirs of J. D. Taubers and each contains fifty portraits. Part III was published by Lochner & Rothgängel in 1742, and has thirty portraits.

Completion of the Imperial Library at Vienna, built in the reign of Charles VI by Johann Bernhard Fischer von Erlach. The Imperial collection of books and manuscripts was begun in 1498 under the Emperor Maximilian.

The first of the six folio volumes of the *Diccionario de la Lengua Castellana*, the first dictionary published by the Academia Española, and known as the 'Dictionary of the Authorities'. Madrid: Francisco del Hierro. It was completed in 1739.

First edition of *Travels into Several Remote Nations of the World by Lemuel Gulliver* (by Jonathan Swift). London: Benjamin Motte. Swift's name was not associated with the work until the definitive text was issued in 1735 by Faulkner, 'the Prince of Dublin Printers'.

John Selden's *Works* were published by John Walthoe, a bookseller of Cornhill, London. The types used were, until fairly recently, ascribed to Caslon. Actually they are those of Christoffel van Dijck and Johannes Kannewet of Holland.

1727

The Maryland Gazette, the first permanent newspaper in Maryland, was established by William Parks.

James Franklin, elder brother of Benjamin, took his press from Boston to Newport, Rhode Island, to become the first printer in that colony. His first-known imprints (1727) were *John Hammett's Vindication and Relation*, and Poor Robin's *Rhode Island Almanack* for 1728. In 1732 he began publication of the short-lived *Rhode Island Gazette*.

The Sultan Achmet III issued an edict permitting the establishment of printing presses in the Ottoman empire. Previously printing had been forbidden to the Turks by the command of the Sultans Bajazet II in 1483 and Selim I in 1515. (*See further* 1729.)

1728

At Nuremberg, the Heirs of J. D. Taubers published Danielis Molleri, *Dissertatio de Typographia*. On the verso of the last leaf is an advertisement for the *Buchhändler Lexicon* of Friedrich Roth-Scholz.

Publication of the *Cyclopedia* of Ephraim Chambers, *An Universal Dictionary of Arts and Sciences*. Two volumes. It was largely an adaptation of the dictionaries of Louis Moréri (*Le Grand Dictionnaire Historique*, 1674) and Pierre Bayle (*Dictionnaire Historique et Critique*, 1697). The French *Encyclopédie* of 1751–65 was originally planned as a translation of Chambers's work. A five-volume edition, refounded and augmented by Abraham Rees, was published 1786–88. Vol. 3 contained a *Specimen of printing types* from the Wilson foundry at Glasgow, and Vol. 5 contained specimens of type by William Caslon and by Joseph Fry and Sons.

A *Form of Prayer* for 11 June, 1728, is the earliest known specimen of stereotype printing by William Ged's process. Ged, a goldsmith by profession, began experimenting with stereotype plates around 1725. (*See also* 1739.)

Benjamin Franklin established his printing office in Philadelphia.

The *St. Petersburg Zeitung* founded at what is now Leningrad; it was issued in German by the publishing department of the Russian Academy of Sciences until the revolution of 1917.

1729

In March, on the death of Mr. Rolland, the proprietor of the *Caledonian Mercury*, the property was transferred to Thomas Ruddiman (*see* 1715 and 1720). From No. 1396 it was printed for and by Thomas and Walter Ruddiman, and the proprietorship of the paper remained with the family of Ruddiman (though under occasional modifications) until May 1772.

The first Turkish press was founded at

Constantinople by a Hungarian convert to Islam, who adopted the name of Ibrahim Muteferrika. He was aided by Zaid Agha, the son of Mehemmet Tchelebi, who had been ambassador to France, and by a Jesuit, Jean-Baptiste Holderman. In 1729 he printed an Arabic-Turkish vocabulary in two volumes, by Muhammed Ben Mustapha.

1730

On 8 January, the *Grub Street Journal* made its appearance. In 1737 its name was changed to the *Literary Courier of Grub Street*. Its founder was a non-juring clergyman named Russel, and Pope was one of its early contributors.

The first issue, 3 February, of *The Daily Advertiser*, which maintained a separate existence until 1807. In 1754 it appeared in a 4-column format which became the standard for the English newspaper until in 1808 *The Times* added a fifth column.

William Parks set up the first press in Virginia at Williamsburg.

David Harry, a printer formerly employed at Philadelphia by Samuel Keimer, set up a press at Bridgetown, Barbados. There, according to Franklin, he employed his old master as a journeyman. In the same year, Benjamin Franklin took over the business of his former employer, Samuel Keimer. In 1748 he was joined by David Hall.

1731

Edward Cave (1691–1754) brought out his highly successful periodical miscellany *The Gentleman's Magazine*. Cave began his career as a printer at St. John's Gate, Clerkenwell, where he printed under the name of 'R. Newton'. In addition to periodical literature, his press turned out a number of learned books, such as Halde, *History of China* (1736) and Newton's *Compleat Herbal* (1752).

A disastrous fire at Ashburnham House, Westminster, damaged a large portion of the famous Cottonian Library collected by Sir Robert Cotton (d. 1631). The library was stored for a time at Westminster School until transferred to the British Museum in 1753.

George Webb set up the first press in South Carolina at Charleston. The government of the colony had offered a subvention to help the first printer who would consent to move his press to Charleston. Soon three printers arrived in that town, Eleazer Phillips Jr., Thomas Whitemarsh, and George Webb. It was Phillips who became the official printer to the colony, but he died in July, 1732. Thomas Whitemarsh, his successor, printed a broadside headed *Charlestown, South Carolina* dated 27 November, 1731, and published at some subsequent date. But the American historian of printing, Douglas C. McMurtrie discovered in the Public Record Office at London a pamphlet describing council proceedings, *Anno Quinto Georgii II Regis*, bearing the imprint, 'Charles Town. Printed by George Webb.' Undated, it bears at the end the 'permission' of the Governor, dated 4 November, 1731. It is therefore considered probable that George Webb was actually the first printer in the colony.

1732

One of the largest encyclopaedias ever published began to come from the press in 1732 and was not completed until 1750. This was Joh. Heinrich Zedler, *Grosses vollständiges Universal-Lexicon aller Wissenschaften und Künste*, in sixty-four volumes. Four supplementary volumes also appeared between 1751 and 1754. In Zedler's *Lexicon*, a staff of editors was employed for the first time, each of whom dealt with particular subjects. It was also the first encyclopaedia to include biographies of living persons, and is therefore still useful for the information it contains concerning minor figures and institutions of the eighteenth century.

The city of Vienna built a large paper mill at Rammersdorf, south of the capital, so that Austria should not be dependent on imported paper.

Samuel Palmer published his *General History of Printing*, and died the same year. Had he lived, it was his intention to follow it with another volume on the practical aspects of printing. Palmer, who had a printing office in Bartholomew Close, was assisted in the preparation of the work by George Psalmanazar. London: A. Betterworth.

On 8 January, appeared the first issue of the *South Carolina Gazette*, printed at Charlestown by Thomas Whitemarsh. In the same month, Eleazer Phillips Jr. is thought to have issued *The South Carolina Weekly Journal* for about six months, until he died; but no copy of the newspaper has yet been found.

1733

In Germany during the eighteenth century a number of books were illustrated by 'nature printing'. In this year Johann Michel Funcke printed Hieronymus Kniphof (1704–63), *Botanica in originali*, by this method with the assistance of the author. An augmented edition was published in twelve parts at Halle and Magdeburg 1757–67, printed by Johann Gottfried Trampe.

Jacques Anisson-Duperron became director of the Imprimerie Royale at Paris.

Between 1733 and 1737 John Pine (1690–1756), said to have been a pupil of the famous French engraver Bernard Picart, published a Latin edition of the works of Horace printed entirely from engraved plates, text as well as ornament. It is supposed that the text was first set in type and transferred to the plate before it was engraved.

Between 1733 and 1741 was published, in parts, *The Universal Penman* by George Bickham —an influential writing-book.

Publication of Jethro Tull, *Horse-hoeing husbandry*, a book which marked the beginning in Britain of modern scientific agriculture. Tull invented (around 1701) a machine drill which enabled seeds to be planted in rows, as opposed to the customary broadcast hand-sowing. He also invented the horse-hoe for cleansing the soil by keeping it friable and free from weeds.

1734

At Paris, Pierre Prault published the first volume of a six-volume edition of Molière. with 35 plates, mostly by Laurent Cars after François Boucher, and more than 200 vignettes.

William Caslon (1692–1766), English punch-cutter and type-founder, issued his first dated specimen sheet, containing samples of thirty-eight founts, including Greek, Saxon, Gothic, Coptic, Armenian, Samaritan, Hebrew, Syriac, and Arabic. All but three of the founts shown in this specimen were cut by Caslon himself. (*See also* 1720 and 1728.)

Lloyd's List was started by the Corporation of Lloyd's of London. With the exception of the *London Gazette* it is the oldest London newspaper still published, and was also the first London newspaper to become a daily paper.

The earliest known Jamaican imprint is a copy of a Sheet Almanac, 19 in. by $15\frac{1}{2}$ in. printed by John Letts in 1734, with no address, but probably Kingston.

1735

At Göttingen, the Dutch bookseller Abraham van den Hoeck founded the firm which is today Vandenhoeck & Ruprecht.

Karl Linnaeus (1707–78) published at Leyden his most important work, *Systema naturae regnum vegetabile*, in which the great Swedish naturalist developed the modern classification of living things into genera and species, the binomial nomenclature which has remained in use ever since.

Izaak Enschedé and his son Johannes bought the printing house 'De Blye Druck' where the the widow Casteleyn printed the *Oprechte Haerlemsche Courant* as well as municipal acts and ordinances, and purchased the goodwill of her business. At her death the Enschedés were granted for twenty years the sole rights of printing the *Courant* and the official acts of the city.

At Cambridge, appeared *A Dissertation concerning the Origin of Printing in England*, by the Rev. Conyers Middleton. This work was written to disprove Atkyns's theory of the introduction of printing into England by Corsellis in 1468. A second edition appeared in 1775, and the work was translated into French the same year.

In the same year was printed at Cambridge Richard Bentley, *Eight Sermons preached at the Honourable Robert Boyle's Lectures 1692*, the only book printed at Cambridge with the imprint of a woman, Mary Fenner, the widow of William Fenner.

Christopher Sauer (Sower) the Elder established a press at Germantown (Pennsylvania), which was later developed by his son, Christopher Sauer II, of whom Isaiah Thomas notes, in his *History of Printing* that 'his was by far the most extensive book manufactury then, and for many years afterwards, in the British American colonies.' (*See also* 1743.)

1736

Pierre-Simon Fournier le Jeune (1712–68) began working on his own in the family trade. A prolific designer, he cut during his lifetime some 60,000 punches for 147 complete alphabets of his various type-faces, in sizes ranging from 5 to 84 point.

He also designed about 400 rules and printers' flowers. (*See also* 1764.)

First edition of a celebrated religious polemic, *The Analogy of Religion, Natural and Revealed*. by Bishop Butler. It defended the Christian against the prevalent Deism or 'natural religion' of the early eighteenth century.

Thomas James, the type-founder, died. When he came out of his apprenticeship to Robert Andrews in February 1708, he went to Holland where he acquired matrices and moulds necessary to start a successful foundry in London, for he found that the Dutch letters were superior to anything he could obtain at the time in England. He started his foundry in Aldermanbury, moving thence to Town Ditch, and finally to Bartholomew Close. His son John James succeeded to the business after his death.

William Parks, who had set up the first press at Williamsburg, Virginia, in 1730, began the first newspaper in that colony, *The Virginia Gazette*.

1737

Pierre-Simon Fournier le Jeune published for the first time his point-system or *Tables des proportions des différens caractères de l'imprimerie*. He specified a series of bodies approximating to those in common use but all multiples of a unit which he termed a 'point typographique', based on a scale of 144 points. In size it was 0·955 of the later 'Didot' system. (*See* 1775.)

First edition of Cruden's *Concordance of the Holy Scriptures*, the best known of all the Bible Concordances published in England, and of which many editions followed.

One of the finest of all English illustrated song-books, *The Musical Entertainer*, was issued in parts between 1737 and 1739. The parts were later issued in two volumes, Vol. I 'printed for and sold by George Bickham', and Vol. II, 'printed for C. Corbett'. Text, music and illustrations were engraved by George Bickham (*see* 1733), who published in 1738 *An Easy Introduction to Dancing*, with illustrations giving the positions of the dancers.

A press was set up at Colombo, in the island of Ceylon, at the instigation of the governor, Baron Imhof. The first book, issued in 1737 was a Prayer Book, followed in 1738 by a short *Confession of Faith*, and in 1739 by an edition of the *Four Gospels*. The press was run by missionaries of the Dutch Church.

1738

Bishop Giovanni Bragadino established the Stamperia del Seminario at Verona.

On 14 January, the printing house and dwelling of the King's Printer, John Baskett, in Blackfriars, were totally destroyed by fire.

The first recorded Bogotá imprint—*Septenario al corazôn doloroso de Maria*, by Father Juan Ricaurte y Terreros, printed at Santa Fé de Bogotá by the Jesuit printing office. Ten items have been recorded as coming from this press between 1738 and 1742, after which date there is no further record as to its ultimate fate.

1739

In this year appeared the earliest known specimen from the type-foundry of Bernhard Christoph Breitkopf at Leipzig. 158 specimens on 15 pages.

Also in this year, the earliest specimen of the Erhardt foundry: *Gegenwartige Hollandische Schriften, und andere mehr, in Ehrhardtischen Giesserey zu bekommen*. 29 specimens on 8 pages.

Gabriel Nicolaus Raspe (1712–85), the celebrated bookseller-publisher at Nuremberg, took over in this year the Nuremberg bookshop of Johann Stein. In 1744 he married Stein's daughter and developed a publishing and bookselling business in conjunction with Johann Ad. Stein, the son of Johann Stein, as the firm of Stein & Raspe (1744–53). After the death of his wife, Raspe separated from his brother-in-law, who continued the retail bookselling business, while Raspe himself developed a prosperous publishing business, specialising in historical and scientific books. Two which became standard works are Martini & Chemnitz, *Conchylien-cabinets*, with 406 plates (1769–95) and J. Sibmacher, *Wappenbuch*, with 1,556 plates (1772–86).

J. F. Foppens (1689–1761), professor of theology at Louvain, brought up to date the labours of Aubert Le Mire, François Sweert, and Valère André, with his *Bibliotheca Belgica*, published at Brussels in two volumes of 1,233 pp.

On 27 January, in France, the Conseil d'Etat du Roi issued a proclamation regarding the manufacture of paper. Its sixty-one clauses enter minutely into details regarding manufacture, composition, weight, dimensions, watermarks, etc.

William Ged (*see* 1728) published an edition of Sallust which bears on the title-page an announcement in Latin to the effect that it was printed, 'by William Ged, Goldsmith of Edinburgh, not with movable type, as is commonly done, but with cast plates'. This, and the reissue of 1744, were printed entirely from Ged's stereotype plates. Ged was later implicated in the 1745 rebellion and narrowly escaped execution. He later went to Jamaica.

William Strahan (1715–85), after having served his apprenticeship in Edinburgh, went to London and set up as a master printer with two journeymen. Admitted to the freedom of the Stationers' Company by redemption in 1737, and Master in 1774, he was actively engaged in printing until his death (*see also* 1776). By the exercise of sound literary judgment allied to industry and business acumen, William Strahan built up one of the greatest printing houses in London, including a share in the patent of King's Printer. His granddaughter married John Spottiswoode who succeeded as King's Printer on the death of Strahan's son Andrew in 1818.

That winter there was printing on the Thames during the great frost.

1740

At Leipzig, was published the first volume of Christian Friedrich Gessner. *Die so nöthig als nützliche Buchdruckerkunst und Schriftgiesserey*, the fourth and final volume of which appeared in 1745. The book embraces the history of printing, lives of the printers, printers' marks, specimens of exotic types, a dictionary of printing terms, and a list of German printers working in 1740. The frontispiece shows the interior of a pressroom of the period. It was an eighteenth-century German counterpart of Fournier's *Manuel Typographique*.

At Augsburg, publication of Giuseppe Galli Bibiena, *Architetture e Prospettive*, a book of designs which had a wide influence on architecture and scene painting. This folio volume, dedicated to the Emperor Charles VI, has 54 plates.

At Hamburg (sumptibus C. Heroldi), publication of Johann Christian Wolf (1690–1770) *Monumenta Typographica*. Four volumes.

At Bremen, was published *Abhandlung von der Buchdruckerkunst* . . . a treatise on printing and the early products of the printing press. Bremen: Brauer & Jani.

Foundation of the Stamperia Reale at Turin. It continued until 1873 (after the capital of the kingdom had been moved from Turin to Florence and finally to Rome), when the establishment was taken over by Paravia, an educational publisher, whose firm still exists.

Publication, at The Hague, of P.M. [Prosper Marchand], *Histoire de l'origine et des premiers progrès de l'imprimerie*. According to Brunet, this book was for long considered the best work on the subject. A supplement by B. Mercier de Saint Léger was published at Paris, 1775, printed by P. Denys Pierres.

At Paris, the engraver Louis Luce, of the Imprimerie Royale, cut a 4-point roman and italic which he called 'Premier Alphabet'.

About 1740, Robert Urie established his printing office in Glasgow, and early made use of type from the Camlachie foundry of Alexander Wilson. Urie printed for Robert Foulis (*see* 1743) before the latter set up his own press. He died at Glasgow 1770.

James Whatman I (1702–59), who had married Ann, widow of Richard Harris, became joint owner with his wife of the Turkey Mill at Hollingbourne, near Maidstone. This was originally a fulling-mill, where the cloth known as Turkey Red was treated; but near the end of the seventeenth century it had been converted for the making of paper. On the elder Whatman's death he was succeeded by his son James Whatman II. (*See* 1759.)

The first circulating library was established in London at 132 Strand by a bookseller named Wright.

The first press in Monmouthshire was set up at Pontypool by Samuel and Felix Farley, printers at Bristol, at the instigation of the Baptist minister, Miles Harri.

Foundation of Philadelphia University Library.

1741

At Leipzig, Johann David Köhler published *Ehren-Rettung Johann Guttenbergs*, in which the history of the invention of printing and the lives of its initiators are treated for the first time on the basis of authentic documents.

First edition of Samuel Richardson, *Pamela or Virtue Rewarded*, the first modern novel of character, told in the form of letters (four volumes. Vols. 1, 2 dated 1741; Vols. 3, 4 dated 1742). In the same year was published a parody on this work, entitled *An Apology for the Life of Mrs. Shamela Andrews*, by Conny Keyber. The author was almost certainly Henry Fielding, and the pseudonym under which this burlesque was written hints at Conyers Middleton and Colley Cibber.

On 16 November, was published the first number of *The Birmingham Gazette, or the General Correspondent*. It was printed and published by the printer Thomas Aris, who may have been a relative of Samuel Aris, the London printer who worked in Creed Lane.

1742

Pierre-Simon Fournier issued his type-specimen *Modèles des caractères*.

At St. Andrews, Alexander Wilson, Professor of Astronomy at Glasgow University, in association with John Baine, established the first type-foundry in Scotland. In 1744 they moved the business to Camlachie, near Glasgow, owing to the increasing demand for their types.

On 22 May, died John Baskett, King's Printer, and Master of the Stationers' Company in 1714 and 1715.

1743

Publication of C. G. Gessner, *Der in der Buchdruckerei wohl unterrichtete Lehr-Junge: oder bey der löblichen Buchdruckerkunst nöthige und nützliche Anfangsgründe*. Leipzig: C. F. Gessner. It is of considerable interest to type historians because it contains specimens of two German foundries of the eighteenth century: Ehrhardt and Zinc. One of the plates shows in detail a printing press of the period. The book contains also a history of printing, above all of Leipzig printers, and an account of the 1740 celebrations in connection with the 300th anniversary of the invention of printing. At the end of the work is added the *Depositio Cornuti Typographici*. (*See* 1655 *and* 1721.)

Izaak and Johannes Enschedé bought the material of the Amsterdam type-founder Henrik Floris Wetstein, which formed the nucleus of the present type-foundry in Haarlem. In this year the German punch-cutter J. M. Fleischman, a native of Nuremberg, began his long association with the Enschedé foundry for which he worked almost exclusively until his death in 1768. Type from Fleischman's matrices is still used for finely printed editions from the Enschedé presses.

Mozet's specimen book: *Épreuves des Caractères de la Fonderie de Claude Mozet, Fondeur et Graveur de Caractères d'Imprimerie. A Paris, rue de la Parcheminerie, au coin de la rue des Prêtres Saint Séverin*. Mozet had already issued a specimen in 1736, and in 1754 he issued another from Nantes.

Robert Foulis, who began printing and publishing on his own account in 1741, printed his first Greek text, Demetrius Phalerus, *De Elocutione*, and submitted it with an application for the post of Printer to the University of Glasgow, a post to which he was nominated that same year.

Christopher Sauer the Elder of Germantown, issued his great German Bible, said to have been printed on paper made in a mill operated by the Seventh Day Baptist community at Ephrata, Maryland.

1744

The first printed book in England intended for children (apart from school books) was *A Little Pretty Pocket Book* published at sixpence by John Newbery. It was advertised in the *Morning Post* of 18 June, 1744. In 1922 the American *Publishers' Weekly* inaugurated the Newbery Medal for the best juvenile book of the year.

First appearance in print of the British National Anthem. It was included in *Thesaurus Musicus. A Collection of two, three, and four part songs several of them never before printed*. London: John Simpson at the Bass Viol and Flute in Sweetings Alley. Dr. John Bull (1563–1628) has been regarded as the composer, but the air was probably traditional.

The famous firm of Sotheby & Co., the oldest existing book auction house in England, was founded by a bookseller, Samuel Baker. In 1767 he was joined by George Leigh, and in 1778 John Sotheby, Baker's nephew, joined the firm.

What is thought to have been the first book printed with Wilson and Baine's Glasgow type was the 1744 edition of *The Spectator*, printed for Andrew Staleker and John Barry by one of the best Scottish printers of his day, Robert Urie.

At Philadelphia, Benjamin Franklin issued a translation of M. T. Cicero's *Cato Major, or his Discourse of Old Age*. Bruce Rogers has called it Franklin's handsomest book. The translation was made by James Logan, first Chief Justice of the Supreme Court of Pennsylvania. It was issued in London in 1778, and as a piece of sales promotion the London publisher added the mention 'with explanatory notes by Benjamin Franklin, LL.D.' on the title-page, though in fact Franklin did no more than print the first edition.

1745

The first press was set up at Karlsruhe, then a young town, by Johann Ludwig Held.

Completion at The Hague of the monumental ten-volume folio edition of Thomas Rymer, *Foedera*—8,800 pages in all. This was the third edition of the work (*see* 1704) and is the most complete edition. Its documentation runs from 1101 to 1654. This edition was begun in 1739.

1746

The first press at Lugano started by the brothers Agnelli.

In April, *The Aberdeen Journal, or North British Magazine*, printed and published by the Aberdeen University printer James Chalmers, contained the first account of the Battle of Culloden.

At Copenhagen, Laurids de Thurah published the first volume of his *Den Danske Vitruvius*. The second folio volume appeared in 1749. This work, the text of which is in Danish, French and German, is a source book for the history of Danish architecture. In 1748, Laurids de Thurah published *Hafnia hodierna*, a description of Copenhagen with 110 copperplate engravings.

1747

Foundation of the Biblioteca Nazionale Centrale at Florence.

In January was published the first number of *The Universal Magazine of Knowledge and Pleasure*, the only successful rival of the *Gentleman's Magazine* (*see* 1731). It ran until 1802, and was published monthly.

Printing in Brazil was started at Rio de Janeiro by Antonio Isidoro da Fonseca, whose first book was *Relaçaõ da entrada que fez O. Excellentissimo . . . Senhor D. F. Antonio do Desterro Malhevro, Bispo de Rio de Janeiro*.

1748

First edition of Charles Louis de Secondat, Baron de Montesquieu, *De l'Esprit des Loix*. Geneva: Barrillot & fils.

Between 1748 and 1759 was published *Plantae et Papiliones Rariores* the most important engraved work of the botanical artist Georg Dionysius Ehret (1708–70). A native of Heidelberg, he lived in England from 1736 until his death. In 1757 he was made a Fellow of the Royal Society, and is acknowledged to be one of the finest botanical artists of the eighteenth century.

Between 1748 and 1758 was published the most important anthology of English verse printed in the eighteenth century: *A Collection of Poems in Six Volumes. By Several Hands*. London: J. Hughs for R. and J. Dodsley.

Publication of *Bibliotheca Britannico-Hibernica* by Thomas Tanner (1674–1735), Bishop of St. Asaph. London: G. Bowyer.

Robert Foulis (1707–76) took into partnership his brother Andrew (1712–75). Of the many fine books they produced, the four-volume *Homer* probably represents the summit of their achievement. (*See* 1756.)

The first printed book in the Manx tongue—the *Gospel of St. Matthew*. Lunnyng: Ean Oliver.

1749

Frederick the Great set up a private press in his palace of Sans-Souci at Potsdam on which Christian Friedrich Henning printed a number of fine books with the address 'Au donjon du Château'. The first work, the King's poem 'Palladion', was published in 1750 as *Œuvres du Philosophe de Sans-Souci*.

Jacques-François Rosart invented at Haarlem for the first time a means of printing music from movable types. Rosart's claim was for long disputed until evidence to justify it was found in 1908 by Charles Enschedé. Rosart, who came from Brussels, was a skilful punch-cutter and type-founder. A type specimen book issued at Brussels in 1768 has an engraved portrait of Rosart.

Publication in Paris of the first three volumes of the monumental *Histoire naturelle . . .* by Georges Louis Le Clerc, Comte de Buffon (1707–88). The work was completed in 1804 with the publication of Vol. 44. The work went through many editions, was translated into several languages, and remained a standard natural history for the greater part of the nineteenth century.

Joseph Ames (1689–1759) published *Typo-graphical Antiquities . . . an historical account of Printing in England*. It was later revised and enlarged by William Herbert. Ames was the first to discard the long ∫ in favour of the short *s* in this book, though his example was not followed until some thirty-five years later.

First edition of Henry Fielding, *Tom Jones*. It was published in six volumes by Andrew Millar.

On 3 January, appeared the first issue of the Copenhagen newspaper *Berlingske Tidende* (Berling's Gazette), thus called after the name of its founder.

James Davis set up the first press in North Carolina at Newbern. He was appointed Public Printer and continued in that capacity until 1777. His first imprint, 1749, was probably *The Journal of the House of Burgesses*. . . .

1750

At Leipzig, Johann Friedrich Gleditsch published the first volume of Christian Gottlieb Jöcher, *Allgemeines Gelehrten Lexicon*, describing the lives and works of some 70,000 writers and scholars. The fourth and final volume was published 1751.

Publication of *Parentalia, or Memoirs of the Family of Wren, but chiefly of Sir Christopher Wren*. This collection of notes, documents and reminiscence was compiled by the architect's son, Christopher, and published by Stephen, the grandson of Sir Christopher. A source book for the life of the great architect.

Thomas Harrison and Edward Owen founded the firm of Harrison & Sons Ltd., and were soon engaged in Government printing, including the *London Gazette* from 1760 onwards. In 1911 the firm received a contract for the printing of British postage stamps.

The *Universal Magazine* of June, 1750, illustrated an article on type-founding with an engraving of part of Caslon's foundry.

1751

Václav Jan Krabat set up his type-foundry at Prague.

Publication begun at Paris of that landmark in the history of European thought, the *Encyclo-pédie, ou Dictionnaire raisonné des Sciences, des Arts, et des Métiers*. The editor-in-chief was Denis Diderot (1713–84) and he was assisted by d'Alembert and some of the most brilliant

scholars of the age. The first edition, consisting of 17 volumes of text plus 4 supplementary volumes and 12 volumes of plates, as well as a 2-volume Index, was published between 1751 and 1780 by Briasson, David, Le Breton, Durand and Panckoucke. Folio.

The earliest violin 'method' in English, *The Art of Playing on the Violin*, by Francesco Geminiani (1687–1762), violinist and composer, and pupil of Arcangelo Corelli. A native of Lucca, he died in Dublin. The engraved musical examples and exercises were the work of the music engraver and publisher John Philips, and the book was printed in London for the author by J. Johnson.

James Davis began publication of the *North Carolina Gazette*, the first newspaper in that colony. (*See also* 1749.)

The Boston printer Bartholomew Green established the first press at Halifax, Nova Scotia.

1752

A small 16-page pamphlet was published by T. Legg at Green Arbour Court, London, called *An Essay on the Original Use and Excellency of the noble Art and Mystery of Printing*. Its only interest is in the fact that it bestows high praise on one Stephen Baylis, of St. Anne's Lane, a maker of printing ink. This branch of the printing trade is so seldom noticed.

On 7 November, John Hawkesworth brought out the first number of *The Adventurer*, published twice weekly. It ran for 140 issues, to twenty-nine of which Samuel Johnson contributed.

Dr. William Dodd (later executed for forgery) brought out the first Shakespeare anthology—*The Beauties of Shakespeare*. This anthology is notable for the learning displayed in the notes.

The first music book printed from movable type in the United States came from the press of Christopher Sauer at Germantown, Maryland: a German hymn-book entitled *Fünff schöne geistliche Lieder*.

On 23 March, John Bushell published the first number of *The Halifax Gazette*, the oldest known piece of Canadian printing. The press had been taken to Halifax in 1751 by Bartholomew Green the Younger, who died soon after his arrival, whereupon Bushell, who had been his partner in Boston took charge of the business. Bushell was Government Printer at Halifax until his death in 1761, when he was succeeded by

Anthony Henry. The earliest surviving Halifax imprint is Nathans & Hart, *Price Current*. John Bushell, 1752.

1753

The University Press at Oxford issued a specimen of Anglo-Saxon types known as the 'Elstob Leaf'. An Anglo-Saxon fount was cut in order to print Miss Elizabeth Elstob's *Anglo-Saxon Grammar* (1715) and the small fount shown on the specimen was possibly cast from the matrices which William Bowyer II presented to Oxford through the intermediary of Edward Rowe Mores. The specimen exists in two versions, both dated 1753. One version, noting the lack of four punches, exists in a unique copy now in the St. Bride Institute Printing Library, London; of the other version there are two copies at Oxford, one in the Bodleian Library and the other in archives of the Printer to the University. The date of 1753 is the year in which Bowyer made his gift, and not necessarily the year of printing.

The British Museum was constituted by Act of Parliament. The Act also provided for the transfer to the new institution of the famous library of Sir Robert Cotton (d. 1631).

Birth of Thomas Bewick (d. 1828), restorer of the art of wood engraving. He was born at Cherryburn, near Newcastle upon Tyne, and as a lad was apprenticed to an engraver named Ralph Beilby. After a year in London at the end of his apprenticeship, he returned to Newcastle and went into partnership with his former master, and his younger brother, John Bewick, became their apprentice.

1754

Johann Gottlob Immanuel Breitkof (1719–94) invented a new method of printing music with movable and interchangeable characters. After several years of research, he decided to divide the customary single type-unit into separate pieces for note-head and stem, whilst the stave was cast in segments of different lengths. At the end of the stem could be fitted another portion with one, two, or three hooks for notes of different time-values. The types were thus made infinitely variable. His first work with the new method, issued in 1754, was an *Aria*, which Breitkopf presented to the Electress of Bavaria, who was so impressed that she confided to him the printing of her pastoral drama *Il Trionfo della fedelta*, which was published in 1756.

Montague House was purchased and the collection of Sir Hans Sloane (1660–1753), with certain others, was placed therein to form the nucleus of the British Museum.

First edition of George Washington's first published work, *The Journal of Major George Washington*. Williamsburg: William Hunter. Only six copies are now known. Hunter had succeeded William Parks as Public Printer of Virginia.

James Parker set up the first press at Woodbridge, New Jersey, and printed first *Votes and Proceedings of the General Assembly of the Province of New Jersey*.

1755

Between 1755 and 1759 was published the magnificent four-volume folio edition of *Fables Choisies* by Jean La Fontaine, with illustrations from originals by the animal painter Oudry, redrawn by Charles-Nicolas Cochin, who, with others, engraved the plates. Paris: Published jointly by Durand and Desaint & Saillant. It was printed by Charles-Antoine Jombert, who, starting as a Paris bookseller in 1736, was active as a printer from 1754 to 1760.

Publication of Samuel Johnson, *Dictionary of the English Language*. London: William Strahan. The printing of this work actually began before 1750, and the book was financed by a syndicate of booksellers, the chief of whom was Robert Dodsley.

First edition in book form of John Smith, *Printer's Grammar*, after initial publication in parts (a new edition was published by the Gregg Press in 1966). An abridged edition was issued in 1787.

At St. Petersburg was published the first grammar written in Russian. This was the *Rossiskaya grammatika* of Lomonosov. (*See also* 1696.)

The first press in Ecuador was set up in the Jesuit college at Ambato, about seventy-five miles south of Quito. Here the Jesuit printer Juan Adán Schwartz, who had arrived in Quito in 1754, produced his first book. St. Bonaventure, *Piisma erga Dei genetricem devotio*. In 1759 the press was moved to Quito.

1756

Leopold Mozart (1719–87), father of the celebrated Wolfgang Amadeus Mozart, published his famous work *Versuch einer gründlichen Violinschule*, which was issued in many editions and several transactions, and was for some time the only fundamental violin method in use.

At Vienna, Johann Leopold Kaliwoda printed *Dissertatio . . . de Calligraphiae Nomenclatione, cultu praestantia utilitate,* by the writing master Johann Georg Schwandner, a comprehensive introduction to calligraphy. The plates were cut by Caspar Schwab.

At Paris, Gautier de Montdorge published *L'Art d'imprimer les tableaux,* describing the method of colour printing introduced into France by Jakob Christof Le Blon of Frankfurt. It contains samples of the new method of colour printing. (*See* 1725.)

Pierre-Simon Fournier (1712–68), known as 'Fournier le Jeune', engraver, punch-cutter and type-founder, printed a type specimen called *Essai d'un nouveau Caractère de fonte pour l'Impression de la Musique,* of which only twelve copies were printed, and of which only one copy has apparently survived. It is now in the Royal Library of Sweden. The new type aimed at giving the impression of copperplate engraving. In 1765 he published a *Traité historique . . . sur les Caractères de Musique.* (*See also* 1737 *and* 1764.)

The Foulis Brothers (*see* 1748) published at Glasgow 'one of the finest monuments of Greek typography which our nation possesses'. It was a four-volume folio *Homer,* the magnificent fount for which was cut by Alexander Wilson. Its trial use was in the Callimachus, *Hymni et Epigrammata,* of 1755.

The Fann Street letter foundry was established by Thomas Cottrell, a former apprentice of William Caslon I. It was acquired around 1800 by Robert Thorne, and after his death in 1820 it was bought by W. & F. Thorowgood, who in 1827 merged it with Fry's foundry.

On 4 May, died the engraver John Pine. (*See* 1733.)

Daniel Fowle set up the first press in New Hampshire at Portsmouth. His first imprint, apart from *Proposals for the publication of a Weekly Gazette,* was *Ames's Almanack for the Year 1757.* In 1756, also, he printed the first issue of *The New Hampshire Gazette.* He died 1787.

1757

The chief work of the doctor and scholar Albrecht von Haller, *Elementa physiologiae corporis humani,*

was published at Lausanne 1757–1766 in eight quarto volumes. (*See also* 1774.)

At Paris appeared *Épreuves des Caracteres du Fond des Sanlecques.* This was the foundry of Jean Eustache Louis de Sanlecque (d. 1778), a descendant of Jacques I de Sanlecque (1558–1648) a pupil of Guillaume Le Bé. After the death of Jean de Sanlecque, his foundry, carried on for a while by his widow, passed to Maurice Joly.

Also in 1757 was published *Épreuve de la Première Partie des Caractères de la Fonderie de François Gando le Jeune.* He issued other specimens in 1758, 1760 and 1763. (Gando's Cicero Italique is shown in Updike, Vol. 1, Fig. 191.)

The first book from the press of John Baskerville (1706–75), a quarto edition of Virgil, *Bucolica, Georgica et Aeneis,* was published by Dodsley, and at once established Baskerville's reputation as a printer.

The old Royal Library was presented to the nation by King George II and housed in the British Museum.

On 16 July, William Robinson began to print the first work issued from Horace Walpole's private press at Strawberry Hill, Twickenham. This was an edition of two Odes by Thomas Gray, *The Progress of Poetry* and *The Bard.*

On 1 January, appeared *The London Chronicle: or, Universal Evening Post,* started by the bookseller Robert Dodsley.

In Sweden, an *English and Swedish Dictionary* by Jacob Serenius was printed at the Royal Press by Peter Momme, one of Sweden's finest printers in the eighteenth century. In 1768 the press descended to his son, but the privilege as Royal Printer was acquired by his son-in-law, Henrik Fougt. (*See* 1767.)

1758

The first daily paper in Spain—*Diario noticioso, curioso, erudito y comercial publico y economico.* The title was later changed to *Diario de Avisos de Madrid.*

On 15 April, Samuel Johnson started *The Idler,* a periodical which was not printed singly, but appeared weekly on Saturdays in the *Universal Chronicle.* It ceased in 1760 after 103 numbers had been issued. A collected edition was published in 1761.

On 7 October, died Joseph Ames, F.R.S., Secretary to the Society of Antiquaries, and author of *Typographical Antiquities*. (*See* 1749.)

A bookseller named Timothy Toft set up what was probably the first printing press at Chelmsford, in Essex.

1759

In 1759 and 1760 Louis-Antoine de Caraccioli brought out *Le Livre à la Mode* (printed in green ink); *Le Livre à la Mode, Nouvelle Edition* (printed in red ink). In 1757 he had issued *Le Livre des Quatre Couleurs* (printed with sections in yellow, green, magenta and orange inks).

Editio princeps of *Candide, ou L'Optimisme*, by François Marie Arouet de Voltaire. It was supposedly translated from the German of Dr. Ralph.

Although John Baskerville's *Virgil* (*see* 1757) has been described as the first book to be printed on wove paper, that work was printed partly on wove and partly on laid paper. The *Paradise Regained* of 1759 seems to have been the first book which Baskerville printed throughout on wove paper, and there is still some doubt as to whether this book, or Edward Capell's *Prolusions*, also published in 1759, was the first wholly printed on wove paper. The wove paper was made by James Whatman at the Turkey Mill at Hollingbourne, Kent.

In June, appeared the first number of *The Annual Register*, printed for R. and J. Dodsley. For some years the historical portion was written by Edmund Burke.

The first known printing at Halifax, Yorkshire, was *A Treasury of Maxims*, printed by P. Darby, who, in 1760, issued *A Pocket Companion for Harrowgate Spaw*.

On 15 January, the British Museum was opened to the public.

1760

At Augsburg, was published Johann Heinrich Lambert, *Photometria*, in which Lambert propounded his system for the scientific measurement of the strength of light. He invented the photometer, described in this work.

Publication of J. D. Schöpflin, *Vincidiae Typographica*, in which the records of the lawsuit between Gutenberg and his partners at Strassburg in 1439 were first printed. The originals of the documents it reproduced were destroyed when the Prussians bombarded Strassburg in 1870.

1761

Charles Joseph Panckoucke (1736–98) set up as a bookseller in Paris after having acquired the stock of Michael Lambert. The publisher, with Beaumarchais, of the Kehl edition of Voltaire, Panckoucke was the outstanding French bookseller-publisher of the latter part of the eighteenth century. A scholar, he translated Ariosto, Tasso and Lucretius, *inter alia*, and was the founder of the *Journal de Politique et de Littérature* and publisher of the edition of Racine's works illustrated by Gravelot. In 1781 he began his *Encyclopédie méthodique* (q.v.). He died shortly after he had founded the *Moniteur Universel* which, from 1800 to 1869, was the official journal of the French government.

On 4 July, died Samuel Richardson (b. 1689), author and printer. He served his apprenticeship with the London printer John Wilde and, in 1719, after a period as journeyman and corrector of the press, he set up his own business in a court off Fleet Street. He became Master of the Stationers' Company, 1754. After his death, the business was carried on by his nephew, William Richardson.

James Adams, born in England, and previously a journeyman in the employ of Franklin and Hall, Philadelphia, set up the first press in Wilmington, Delaware. The first printing from his press was either *The Child's New Spelling Book*, or Evan Ellis, *Advice of Evan Ellis to his daughter when at Sea . . .* both of which were printed in 1761.

1762

The Palatine Library at Parma founded by Philip of Bourbon.

Fortunato Bartolomeo de Felice (1723–89) left his native Rome in 1757 and went to Berne and entered the 'Typographische Gesellschaft' founded there in 1758. In 1762 he went to Yverdon (Ifferten) and there set up a printing office. His chief work is the *Encyclopédie d'Yverdon*, in fifty-six volumes, 1770–80, an imitation of the French *Encyclopédie*.

At Amsterdam, appeared the first edition of Jean-Jacques Rousseau, *Du Contrat Social*, in which the author proposed to base all government on the direct or implied consent of the governed. Amsterdam: Marc Michel Rey. The first copies off the press carried the title *Du Contrat Social*; in later copies is added to this title, *Ou Principes du Droit Politique*. There were two printings in 1762.

Publication of Jean de La Fontaine, *Contes et Nouvelles en Vers*, with 80 plates by Charles Eisen (1720–78) and 53 *culs-de-lampe* by P. P. Choffard. This famous edition, possibly Eisen's masterpiece, is known as the 'Fermiers généraux' edition from the fact that this body defrayed the costs of publication. Amsterdam [in fact Paris]: Barbou. This is one of the most beautiful illustrated French books of the eighteenth century.

Publication at London of the important collection of songs and cantatas entitled *Clio and Euterpe, or British Harmony*. Engraved throughout, the three volumes contain nearly 600 songs (sold by the proprietor, Henry Roberts).

On 5 June, appeared the first issue of *The North Briton*, started by John Wilkes in opposition to *The Briton*, edited by Tobias Smollet which appeared on 29 May. Its life was a stormy one, often interrupted by warrants and the imprisonment of Wilkes, who was committed to the Tower in respect of No. XLV of *The North Briton* and expelled from the House of Commons. (*See also* 1763.)

James Johnston went from Britain to establish the first press in Georgia at Savannah, as Printer to the Government at an annual salary of £100. His first known publication is *An Act to prevent stealing of Horses and neat Cattle*, which was promulgated in March 1759. On 7 April, 1763 Johnston started *The Georgia Gazette*.

1763

The *Gothaischer Hof-Kalendar*, or *Almanach de Gotha*, made its first appearance. The early numbers are exceedingly rare, and the earliest issue in the British Museum is dated 1774.

At Paris, J. B. Despilly began publication of the *Catalogue hebdomadaire ou liste alphabétique des livres tant nationaux qu'étrangers*, the ancestor of the *Bibliographie de la France*.

The Paris bookseller and collector Guillaume François De Bure published the first volume of his *Bibliographie instructive, ou Traité de la connoissance des livres rares et singuliers*. The seventh and final volume appeared in 1768.

Baskerville issued his magnificent folio Bible printed under licence from the Cambridge University Press. It is dated 1762. This is one of the finest Bibles ever printed in England, set in a handsome Great Primer shown in the specimen of 1757. It was a financial failure.

The punch-cutter and type-founder Joseph Jackson (1733–92), who had been apprentice to William Caslon I, and had worked for a time under Thomas Cottrell, set up for himself as a type-founder in a small house at Cock Lane. His business grew and he soon moved to Dorset Street, off Fleet Street. His first specimen sheet is no longer extant, but is thought to have been issued about 1765. He cut the type for the facsimile of *Domesday Book* (*see* 1783) as well as the fine fount of two-line English roman for Macklin's Bible (*see* 1800). In 1790 his foundry was destroyed by fire, and this calamity hastened Jackson's death.

John Wilkes (*see* 1762) set up a private press in his own house in George Street, Westminster, with Thomas Farmer as printer.

At Christiania appeared *Norske Intelligenz-Seddeler*, the first regular Norwegian newspaper.

1764

At Leipzig, was founded the Zeichnungs-, Malerey-, und Architecktur-Academie, the first director of which was the polymath Adam Friedrich Oefer.

Pierre-Simon Fournier le Jeune (1712–68) published his *Manuel typographique, utile aux gens de lettres, & à ceux qui exercent les différentes parties de l'art de l'imprimerie*. Paris: Barbou. Two volumes. 1764–66. The first volume of the *Manuel* deals with the art of type-founding and contains 16 engraved plates showing instruments used by the type-founder; the second volume (1766) shows a vast range of type specimens, each enclosed within a border.

In this year was published José Luis de Cisneros, *Descripción exacta de la provincia de Benezuela*, with the imprint 'Impresso en Valencia año de M D CCLXIV'. This was for long considered to have been the first recorded printing in Venezuela, issued at Nueva Valencia. But after careful investigation, the Spanish bibliographer Pedro Grases considers that the book was published at San Sebastian, Spain, by Lorenzo Riesgo y Montero, printer to the Real Compañia Guipuzcoana de Caracas. (*See* 1808.)

Joseph Fry and William Pine of Bristol established a type-foundry in that city attached to the printing office of Pine, who was the first printer of the *Bristol Gazette*. The foundry, known as Fry and Pine's, with Isaac Moore as manager, moved to London in 1768. Moore's connection with the firm came to an end about 1776, when the firm became J. Fry & Co. In 1782 Joseph Fry took his sons Edmund and Henry into partnership, and in that same year the Frys acquired much of the material from the sale of the James foundry. In 1787 Joseph Fry retired and the business was carried on by Edmund Fry.

On 24 March, appeared *The Newcastle Chronicle*, printed and published by Thomas Slack.

Samuel Johannson Alnander (1731–72), in conjunction with Peter Kindahl, published at Uppsala *Historia librorum prohibitorum in Svecia*, of which only one volume appeared.

The first press was set up at New Orleans, Louisiana, by Denis Braud. The earliest known imprint of the New Orleans press is the *Extrait de la lettre du Roi à M. Dabbadie*, announcing the cession of the colony to Spain.

James Davis, who had set up the first press in North Carolina (*see* 1749), started the *North Carolina Magazine*.

On 21 June, was issued the first number of the *Quebec Gazette*, printed by William Brown and his partner Thomas Gilmore. Brown had printed for three years at Bridgetown, Barbados, but had to leave that country for health reasons. Gilmore died in February 1773 and Brown continued as sole proprietor of the paper until his death in 1789. The paper ran until 1874, with only two short interruptions in 1765 and 1775.

1765

The naturalist Jacob Christian Schäffer (1718–90) published at Regensburg the first part of *Versuche und Muster, ohne alle Lumpen Papier zu machen*. The six parts were completed in 1772. The work is concerned with Schäffer's experiments in quest of new material for paper-making, and shows specimens of paper made from a wide range of natural substances, including varieties of wood, vines, hemp, moss, bark, straw, potatoes, reeds and even wasps' nests. In 1768 the Royal Society of Arts awarded him a silver medal for his work.

At Leipzig, Philipp Erasmus Reich founded the first German booksellers' organisation—the Buchhandlungsgesellschaft.

At The Hague, Van Daalen published G. Meerman, *Origines typographicae*. In its day it was one of the best works dealing with historical investigations into the history of printing.

The Englishman George Cummings took out the first patent for coating paper. The coating was made up of white lead, plaster of Paris, and stone lime, mixed with water to a suitable consistency. At that time the coating had to be applied by hand. Coating machinery was introduced about 1850.

Publication at Oxford of William Blackstone, *Commentaries on the Laws of England* (four volumes, 1765–69), a general history of English law which still remains one of the standard authorities. The work grew out of Blackstone's lectures at Oxford as first Vinerian Professor of English Law.

On 27 December, appeared the first number of *The Liverpool General Advertiser*.

Nicolaus Møller appointed Printer to the Royal Court of Denmark.

Nicholas Hasselbach, a one-time journeyman with Christopher Sauer I, set up the first press at Baltimore. The first product of his press was John Redick, *A Detection of the Conduct and Proceedings of Messrs. Annan and Henderson at Oxford Meeting-House, April 18, 1764*. The only known copy of this book is undated, but the preface bears the date 12 February, 1765.

The first substantial volume printed at Quebec was *Catéchisme du Diocèse de Sens*, by Monseigneur Jean-Joseph Languet, Archbishop of Sens. Quebec: Brown & Gilmore. This was the first book of any size from this firm, which had hitherto printed broadsides and government ordinances.

Printing introduced into Dominica by William Smith, who printed and published the *Dominica Gazette* at Charlotte-Town (Roseau) in July 1765.

The first printer at Guadeloupe was Jean Bénard, who set up a press at Basse-Terre with a printer's licence delivered by Louis XV on 21 June, 1764.

1766

First edition, Berlin, of Gotthold Ephraim Lessing, *Laoköon, oder über die Grenzen der Malerei und Poesie*, a famous critical discussion of the limitations of all forms of art.

HCP

The Hamburg printer Johann Schwarz brought out the first professional trade paper, the weekly *Der Buchdrucker*, which met with immediate success.

At London the famous animal painter George Stubbs (1724–1806) published his *Anatomy of the Horse*, with 24 engraved plates.

On 23 January, died William Caslon I, called by Rowe Mores 'the Coryphoeus of letter-founders'. He was buried in the churchyard of St. Luke's, near Chiswell Street, London, where his foundry was situated. In fact, St. Luke's was the church of the parish in which his three foundries were all situated. (For an account of his life and work see Talbot Baines Reed, *A History of the old English Letter Foundries*; new edition revised and enlarged by A. F. Johnson. London: Faber & Faber. 1952.)

The first printing in Argentina was at Córdoba de Tucumán by a German Jesuit, Pablo Karrer, a printer by profession, who used a press brought over from Europe by Father Carlos Gervasoni about 1758. The first surviving imprint of this press, dated 1766, is *Laudationes Quinque*—five panegyrics on Dr. Ignatio Duarte y Quirós, a great benefactor of the University of San Ignacio, as the Jesuit Colegio Máximo de Córdoba became in 1622. The members of the Order were expelled in 1767 and the press and material were sent to Buenos Aires in 1780.

1767

The earliest dated specimen book of the Amsterdam type-foundry of Ploos van Amstel.

Charles-Pierre Mame (1746–1825) began his career as a printer at Angers. One of his sons, Armand (b. 1775), founded a press at Tours in 1796, which was continued by his son Alfred (1811–93) together with his nephew and son-in-law Charles Ernest. Alfred Mame, who went to Paris 1835–36, returned to Tours and made the firm of Mame important both for printing and publishing. The plant was almost completely destroyed during the battles of June 1940.

At Edinburgh, was published a translation of the New Testament into Gaelic, made by Rev. Charles Stuart, minister of Killin.

Henrik Fougt, the Swedish printer, obtained an English patent (24 December, 1767) for his invention of, 'certain new and curious types . . . for the printing of music notes'. In 1764 Fougt

had been granted a privilege by the Swedish Government for printing music and books. In 1771, Fougt succeeded Peter Momme as Royal Printer, and for many years his press was one of the best known in Sweden. Fougt, a Laplander by birth, was a great Anglophile, and much of his typographic work was based on ideas received during his stay in England around 1767. While in England he published a considerable amount of music printed in his music type, the first, published in 1768, being Francesco Uttini, *Six sonatas for two violins and a bass*.

At Stockholm, was founded the first Swedish national daily newspaper, *Dagligt Allehanda*.

The Quebec printers Brown and Gilmore issued *The Trial of Daniel Disney*, the first book printed in the English language in Lower Canada.

1768

At the invitation of Ferdinand, Duke of Parma, Bodoni took over the management of the private ducal press, the Stamperia Reale at Parma, where he remained for twenty years, becoming one of the most influential punch-cutters and book designers of his time. Giambattista Bodoni (1740–1813), the son of a Piedmontese printer, was about to set out for England to seek his fortune when he was asked to take charge of the Stamperia Reale.

On 27 May, died J. M. Fleischman (b. 1701), the outstanding punch-cutter of the Netherlands in the eighteenth century. In the same year the Enschedé foundry at Haarlem, for which he worked, issued a specimen book, a classic in typographical literature. In addition to notes on the provenance of the older founts, it contains a tribute to Fleischman. This *Proef van letteren . . .* was supplemented in 1773.

Publication of J. B. L. Osmont, *Dictionnaire typographique, historique, et critique des livres rares, singuliers, estimés, et recherchés, en tous genres*. Paris: chez Lacombe. Two volumes 8vo.

The first edition of the *Encyclopædia Britannica* was published in numbers (at 6d each, or 8d on fine paper) between 1768 and 1771. This, the most famous of all the encyclopaedias in the English language, was conceived by the printer Colin Macfarquhar and his friend Andrew Bell the engraver, both of Edinburgh. The planning of the publication was due to the antiquarian and one-time compositor William Smellie, who wrote a great part of it himself. It was 'sold by Colin

Macfarquhar, at his printing office in Nicolson Street' [Edinburgh].

At Glasgow, Robert and Andrew Foulis printed the *Poems* of Thomas Gray—the first book set in Alexander Wilson's beautiful fount of Double Pica roman.

First edition of Laurence Sterne, *A Sentimental Journey through France and Italy*.

The old-established business of William Sandby in Fleet Street, London, was bought by a retired officer of Marines named John Mac-Murray. Dropping the prefix 'Mac' (the Scots were unpopular in England at the time), he became the founder of the great publishing firm of John Murray.

A Connecticut silversmith and lapidary named Abel Buell (1742–1822) was the first to cut and cast type in the American Colonies, and in 1768 he produced the first American type specimen. The lettering is pica roman, very crudely cut, but nevertheless of historical interest. The only known copy of this small specimen is in the form of a proof taken from a stick of type and sent to the Rev. Ezra Stiles of Newport by Dr. Benjamin Gale, a friend of Buell. It is now among the Stiles Papers at Yale University. (For details of Buell's career, *see* Lawrence C. Wroth, *Abel Buell of Connecticut*, 1958.)

The first press on the Ile de France (now Mauritius) was set up at Port-Louis by the Burgundian, Pierre Saunois. The first product of his press was *La Presse. A Madame la Dauphine*—a short poem by Saunois dedicating the new press to the Dauphine of France, Marie Josèphe de Saxe.

1769

The Rev. James Granger (1723–76) produced his five-volume *Biographical History of England*, completed in 1774, which led to such a vogue for 'extra-illustrating' that this practice became known as 'grangerising'.

Death of Henry Woodfall, Master of the Stationers' Company in 1766. In the same year his son, Henry Sampson Woodfall began to print the political tracts known as the *Letters of Junius*.

Establishment at Lisbon of the Impressão Regia, or Royal Printing House (now the National Printing House).

The first press made by an American craftsman was the work of Isaac Doolittle, a clock- and watch-maker of New Haven, Conn. It was,

according to an announcement in the *Massachusetts Gazette and Boston Weekly News-Letter* of 7 September, 1769, 'a Mahogany Printing-Press of the most approved Construction' and was supplied to the Philadelphia printer William Goddard.

1770

At Mainz, Bernhard Schott founded the music-publishing firm now B. Schotts Söhne.

By order of the Imperial Court at Vienna, Joseph Lorenz Kurzböch set up a press for printing in Slavonic, Greek and Oriental tongues.

Publication of Philip Luckombe, *A concise history of the origin and progress of printing*. A reissue followed in 1771 with the title changed to *The History and Art of Printing*. The work was published anonymously, and is based largely on Ames's *Typographical Antiquities* for the historical part, and on Moxon for the technical portion. The most important part of the work for present-day students of printing lies in the 40-page specimen of the types of William Caslon II.

Publication at London (printed for the author) of *Critical Observations on the Art of Dancing*, by Giovanni Andrea Battista (n.d. [1770]), with 54 engraved plates of music. In 1772, the same author published *A Treatise on the Art of Dancing* which, though largely based on Cahusac's *La Danse ancienne et moderne* (The Hague, 1754), can claim to be the first serious book in English on the art of the dance.

First newspaper in Welsh—*Eurgrawn Cymraeg*.

The Society of Antiquaries began the publication of *Archaeologia*.

1771

Bodoni issued his specimen book *Fregi e Majuscole incise e fuse*.

At Paris, J. Barbou printed the *Essai d'une nouvelle Typographie* by Louis René Luce, type designer and punch-cutter at the Imprimerie Royale, Paris. Louis Luce was the son-in-law of Jean Alexandre, who had been a pupil of Philippe Grandjean. The *Essai* is made up of fifteen bodies of roman and italic type, as well as a collection of vignettes and ornaments.

Epreuve de Caractères de la Fonderie de Perrenot et Fils. Avignon, Place St. Didier. Another edition of the *Épreuve* was issued in 1784, and *Lettres taillées sur différens corps* was published without a date.

The first known printer at Rochester, Kent, printed a *Poll Book for the City of Rochester*. This was Thomas Fisher, who in 1772 issued *The History and Antiquities of the Town of Rochester*.

At Darlington, County Durham, J. Sadler, presumably the first printer there, published M. Raine, *English Rudiments*.

On 30 September, died the London printer John Hughs (b. 1703), since 1763 printer of the parliamentary papers and journals of the House of Commons. A printer for just over forty years, he printed most of the books published by the Dodsleys.

1772

At Berlin, was published Johann Gottfried Herder, *Abhandlung über den Ursprung der Sprache*, a book from which sprang the scientific study of language.

Publication of Sallust, *La Conjuración de Catalina y la Guerra de Jugurta*. Madrid: Joaquin Ibarra. One of the most magnificent books printed by the Spanish Court printer, Ibarra (1725–85), with types cut by Antonio Espinosa. Like Baskerville, Ibarra hot-pressed his paper and made his own printing ink. The engraved title-page was designed and cut by E. Monfort; the majority of the plates and ornaments were designed by M. S. Maella. The Spanish translation was made by the Infante Don Gabriel Antonio de Bourbon, second son of Charles III.

First type specimen of Alexander Wilson & Sons. In 1760 Wilson placed the control of the foundry in the hands of his two sons, who traded under the style of the Glasgow Letter Foundry of Alexander Wilson & Sons.

The London newspaper *The Morning Post* first appeared in this year. The earliest surviving issue is No. 4, Thursday, 5 November, 1772.

Death of John James, last of the old school of type-founders; William Caslon I being the first representative of the new school. After James's death, much of his material was acquired by Rowe Mores.

1773

In this year, Goethe and his friend Johann Friedrich Merck themselves published the first edition of *Götz von Berlichingen*. Goethe procured the paper and Merck paid for the printing, which was done by Johann Wittich of Darmstadt.

At Berlin, Joachim Pauli published the first of the seventeen volumes of the *Oeconomischen Encyclopädie* by J. G. Krünitz.

The specimen *Vermeerdering van meest nieuw gesnedene . . . letteren 1768–1773* was issued from the Haarlem foundry of Johannes Enschedé. It contained a folded broadside showing the interior of the foundry and various processes, drawn by Van Noorde, 1768. (*See also* 1768.)

A specimen book of the foundry of Louis Delacolonge; *Les Caractères et les Vignettes de la Fonderie du Sieur Delacolonge*. Lyons, 'Montée et près les Carmelites'. Louis Delacolonge was the son of Alexandre Delacolonge, who set up a foundry at Lyons in 1720.

Joseph Gillé published at Paris an interesting specimen, *Épreuves des Caractères de la Fonderie de Joseph Gillé*. His son, J. G. Gillé *fils*, issued in 1808 a folio specimen, *Recueil des Divers Caractères, Vignettes et Ornemens*. . . .

Publication at Paris of Jaubert, *Dictionnaire des Arts et Métiers*, in five volumes, printed by Didot le Jeune.

Death of Hubert François Gravelot (b. 1699), possibly the most elegant book illustrator of the eighteenth century. A pupil of Boucher, he spent some fifteen years in London, during which time he illustrated Shakespeare and Fielding's *Tom Jones*. He returned to Paris in 1745. His best work is probably contained in the *Decameron* of 1757, which also has plates by Boucher, Cochin and Eisen, and his art is seen at its most gracious in the *Contes Moraux* of Marmontel (1765).

James Whatman II, at the demand of the Society of Antiquaries, fashioned a mould which would give a sheet of paper $52\frac{3}{4} \times 31\frac{3}{4}$ inches, destined for the printing of an engraving by Basire of the meeting between Henry VIII and François I at the Field of the Cloth of Gold. To handle a mould of this size a special lifting device had to be made and the normal vat crew was increased from three or four to eleven. This size of paper, the largest made by hand in Europe, was termed 'Antiquarian'.

The first Manx version of the Old Testament was published in two 8vo volumes. Whitehaven: John Ware & Son for S.P.C.K. A complete Manx Bible was printed in a small edition in 1775, by the same printer. (*See also* 1748.)

The first newspaper printed on the island of Mauritius—*Annonces, Affiches et Avis divers pour les colonies des Iles de France et de Bourbon*. The printer was Nicolas Lambert.

In November appeared the first periodical worthy of the name to be published in Iceland. It was *Islandske Maaneds Tidender,* printed at Hrappsey. It ran as a monthly publication for three years, and was then discontinued through lack of funds.

1774

First edition of Goethe's *Werther (Die Leiden des jungen Werthers).* Within two years some sixteen German editions had appeared, and the book was translated into almost every European language. Leipzig: In der Weygandschen Buchhandlung.

At Venice, A. Zatta published Jacopo Morelli, *Della publica libreria di San Marco in Venezia dissertazione historica,* a history of the famous Bibliotheca Marciana at Venice by the man who was its curator from 1778 to 1819.

At Zürich, between 1774 and 1777, was published the *Bibliotheca anatomica . . .* of Albrecht von Haller (1708–77). known as the founder of medical and scientific bibliography. (*See also* 1757.)

By the decision of the House of Lords in the case of Alexander Donaldson, attempts by the booksellers to invoke Common Law rights to perpetual ownership of copyright were defeated. Donaldson had made a test case of his reprint of James Thomson, *The Seasons.* When legal action was taken, he lost his case, but on taking it to the House of Lords he obtained judgment by a majority of twenty-one votes to eleven.

First edition of *The Origin of Printing* by William Bowyer (1699–1777).

On 24 February, at Carnbee, in Fifeshire, was born Archibald Constable the Elder, one of the most eminent of Scottish publishers. He was apprenticed to the Edinburgh bookseller Peter Hill and set up as a bookseller on his own account in the Scottish capital in 1795. In 1798 he founded the publishing firm of Constable and in 1812 became proprietor of the *Encyclopædia Britannica.* His firm was caught up in the commercial crisis of 1825 and failed—a failure which also involved Sir Walter Scott as well as the printing firm of James Ballantyne and Co., which had been largely financed by the author of the Waverley novels. Archibald Constable died 21 July, 1827. The firm was refounded by his son Thomas in 1847, and again in 1890 by his grandson, Archibald Constable the Younger.

Jacob Bay, a former Swiss silk weaver, set up as a type-founder at Germantown, Pennsylvania. It is recorded that he was also a punch-cutter. He cast type for Christopher Sauer's great Bible of 1776.

First American edition of *Robinson Crusoe.* (*See also* 1719.)

1775

At Vienna, Josef Gerold took over the printing office of Leopold Kaliwoda. In the following year he completed the *Hortus Botanicus Vindobonensis* of Nikolaus Joseph Jacquin (1727–1817), Director of the University Botanic Garden at Vienna. It has 300 coloured engravings. This was the beginning of the Viennese firm of Carl Gerold's Sohn.

Although Fournier le Jeune had proposed a constant unit of type measurement (*see* 1737), it was not until 1775 that François-Ambroise Didot succeeded in imposing a unit of type, later named the 'Didot point' in France, where it was generally adopted. German type-founders also adopted it between 1840 and 1879. Didot's point system was obtained by relating the body size of the type to the legal standard of measurement then in force, the royal foot, the 'pied du roi'. This resulted in an augmentation of Fournier's point by a twelfth, 12 point Didot being the equivalent of 13 point Fournier.

About this year the first of the new Didot types were cut. They have been attributed to the punch-cutter Pierre Louis Waflard, but there is no documentary proof of this, and A. F. Johnson writes in his *Type Designs* that, 'possibly this man has been given too much prominence in the history of the Didot types'.

At Vaasa in Finland, the first press was established by Georg Wilhelm Londicer, who began printing in 1776.

On 7 April, appeared the first number of Story & Humphreys's *Pennsylvania Mercury,* the first work printed with types manufactured in America. The maker of the type is not known with certainty, but it was probably either Jacob Bay or Justus Fox, as there were no other founders then in the district. In the issue of that paper for 23 June, appeared an advertisement for a book called *The Impenetrable Secret,* 'just published and printed with types, paper and ink, manufactured in this Province'. Unfortunately no copy is known to exist of this first completely American book.

Isaiah Thomas, the first printer at Worcester, Massachusetts, started the *Massachusetts Spy* on 3 May, 1775. In the same year he printed *A Narrative of the Excursion and Ravages of the King's Troops under the command of General Gage* . . . During his long career Thomas published more than 400 works, and is now remembered as the author of a *History of Printing in America.* (*See* 1810.)

The earliest known copy of the *Jamaica Gazette* is dated 1775. It was printed at Kingston by Joseph Weatherby.

1776

François Barletti de Saint-Paul published his *Nouveau système typographique,* the first to advocate the casting of logotypes, or type-metal slugs forming commonly occurring words or syllables, thus expediting composition—or so it was claimed.

John Bell (1745–1831) brought out his neatly printed *British Theatre* in twenty-one volumes (1776–78). In 1785 he became the first since Ames to discard the long ∫ in favour of s.

First volume published of Edward Gibbon, *The History of the Decline and Fall of the Roman Empire.* London: W. Strahan and T. Cadell. The work was not completed until the sixth volume appeared in 1788.

First edition of Adam Smith, *The Wealth of Nations.* London: W. Strahan & T. Cadell. Two volumes. The book which ushered in the age of the doctrine of *laissez-faire.*

Death of Robert Foulis, the celebrated Glasgow printer and publisher. He attempted, without success, to establish in Scotland an academy for the cultivation of the fine arts. His brother and partner, Andrew Foulis, died in 1775.

First Russian bibliography published at Moscow—Kaminski, *De notittia librorum Russicorum.* It lists 700 printed books.

Philip Astley, *The Modern Riding Master,* probably the first illustrated American sporting book, was published at Philadelphia by Robert Aitken. The first edition had been published in London by the author, 1775.

Fleury Mesplet (*c.* 1735–94), a native of Lyons, who learned printing there, and in 1773–74

worked as a printer in London, with an office in the vicinity of Covent Garden. He went to Philadelphia in 1774 where he printed in French with scant success. In 1776 he was invited to go to Montreal and there he established the first French press in Canada. In that same year he printed *Réglement de la Confrérie de l'Adoration perpetuelle du Saint-Sacrement et de la Bonne Mort,* and also a play *Jonathan et David* by the Jesuit Father Desbillons, as performed by the students of Montreal College. One of these two pieces was the first printing produced at Montreal, where he worked until his death on 29 January, 1794.

The earliest surviving imprint from Chile—*Modo de ganar el jubileo santo* (1776). Nothing is known concerning the printer and only one copy is extant, now in the Biblioteca Nacional at Santiago de Chile. The German Jesuit, Father Carlos Haimhausen, brought a press to Santiago in 1748, but no work of his has been discovered. He himself died in 1767.

1777

At Leipzig, Johann Gottlob Immanuel Breitkopf published his *Ueber den Druck der geographischen Charten.*

On 26 May, died Jacques François Rosart (b. 1714), the famous Netherlands punch-cutter whose first type specimens appeared about 1740. His son, Matthias, was also a punch-cutter.

France received its first daily newspaper, the *Journal de Paris.*

Pierre-François Didot (1732–95), licensed as bookseller in 1733, became printer to the Comte de Provence (later Louis XVIII). In addition to printing many well-produced books, in 1789 he purchased the important paper mill at Essonnes which contributed as much to the renown of the family as the typographic prowess of its other members.

First edition of John Howard, *The State of the Prisons,* a work which sought to improve the dreadful conditions of prison life at that time. The author himself died of prison fever in 1790, but his book ran through many editions and sowed the seeds of penal reform. Warrington: W. Eyres.

On 18 November, died William Bowyer II (b. 1699) who has been called 'the most learned printer of the eighteenth century'. He was elected a Fellow of the Society of Antiquaries, to which body he became the official printer in 1736.

At Dublin was printed the first edition of Richard Brinsley Sheridan, *The School for Scandal*.

1778

Death of Charles Eisen (b. Valenciennes 1720), one of the great French book illustrators of the eighteenth century. His masterpiece was the celebrated 'Fermiers-généraux' edition of the *Contes* of La Fontaine. (*See* 1762.)

A printing press was set up aboard the French warship *Languedoc* which in 1778 sailed to North America, and a call to the French in America was printed on it.

First edition of *A dissertation upon English typographical founders and founderies* by Edward Rowe Mores (1730–78). On its subject this book remains an essential text. (It was reprinted for the Grolier Club, New York, in 1924, and in 1961 the Oxford Bibliographical Society issued a critical edition with introduction and notes by Harry Carter and Christopher Ricks.) The original edition seems to have been printed by Mores himself at his home.

At Huddersfield, W. Moorhouse's *Sermon* is the earliest extant work of the town's first printer, J. Brook.

The famous Scottish publishing firm of Oliver and Boyd founded.

The first English printing in India took place at Hoogly, where Charles Wilkins (later Sir Charles) printed *A Grammar of the Bengal Language* by Nathaniel Brassey Halhed. The Bengali and Sanskrit words are in Bengali script from types engraved and cast by Wilkins, at that time in the service of the East India Company.

1779

At Leipzig, Johann Gottlob Immanuel Breitkopf published his *Ueber die Geschichte der Erfindung der Buchdruckerkunst.*

The first Sunday newspaper in Britain, the *British Gazette and Sunday Monitor*, was begun by a woman, Mrs. Elizabeth Johnson.

On 1 January at Chichester was born William Clowes, founder of the vast printing establishment of William Clowes & Sons Ltd. His apprenticeship over, William Clowes came to London in 1802 and worked as a compositor with Henry Teape, a printer in George Street, Tower Hill.

About the end of 1803 he started his own printing office in Villiers Street, Strand. When he died in 1847 he left behind a gigantic establishment and was, in the words of Samuel Smiles, 'the greatest multiplier of books in his day'.

1780

Johann Friedrich Unger (1753–1804) opened a printing office in Berlin, to which in 1791 he added a type-foundry. In 1788 he was appointed printer to the Akademie der Künste und mechanischen Wissenschaften. Unger was also the publisher of many German classic authors—Goethe, Schiller and Schlegel amongst others. Unger was also an engraver and designed the still-popular Unger-Fraktur, which he issued in its final form in 1794.

First Hungarian newspaper in the Magyar tongue, *Magyar Hirmondó*, printed at Pozsony (Bratislava) by Mathias Ráth.

The Madrid printer Joaquin Ibarra printed a four-volume quarto edition of *Don Quixote* for the Biblioteca Real, set in roman and italic designed by Geronimo Gil. The book is considered the finest *Don Quixote* produced in Spain.

Judah Padock Spooner and Timothy Green set up the first press in Vermont at Westminster. The first product of their press was a *Thanksgiving Proclamation*, probably printed in October 1780, and on 14 December of the same year they printed the first Vermont newspaper, *The Vermont Gazette*.

Charles Wilkins, who had printed at Hoogly in 1778 (*q.v.*), printed at Malda, Bengal, a *Compendious Vocabulary English and Persian*, compiled for the use of the Hon. East India Co. by Francis Gladwin.

The first book printed at Bombay of which we have certain knowledge is a Calendar for 1780 'printed by Rustom Caresajee in the Buzar'.

The first newspaper press was established at Calcutta, and on 29 January, 1780, appeared the first number of *Hickey's Bengal Gazette or Calcutta General Advertiser*, printed by J. A. Hickey. The first book printed there was G. Dallas, *Guide to India*.

What was probably the first Buenos Aires imprint came from the press of the Niños Expósitos (Foundling Hospital) and was probably printed by one Augustín Garrigós of Alicante. It was a small broadside—*Letrilla, que llevaba por registro en su Breviario le Seráfica Madre Santa Teresa de Jesús.* Fifteen separate imprints from this press have been recorded for 1780, sixty-one for 1781, and ninety-five for 1782. Most of these were official broadsides.

1781

At Stuttgart, J. B. Metzler published Schiller's *Räuber* at the author's expense.

The publishing firm of Hoffmann and Campe founded at Hamburg.

At Vienna was established an Institute for the Deaf and Dumb, at which was composed and printed by the inmates, among other things, the first libretto of Mozart's *Don Giovanni.*

The French publisher Charles-Joseph Panckoucke began the publication of the *Encyclopédie Méthodique* designed to replace the Encyclopaedia of Diderot. It was a colossal work in 192 quarto volumes which took half a century and was then never completed and contained 6,439 illustrations.

Simon-Pierre, son of Fournier Le Jeune cut for Benjamin Franklin—perhaps based on his writing—an English script type.

At Riga was published Immanuel Kant, *Critik der reinen Vernunft* (The Critique of Pure Reason).

John Nichols edited and published *Biographical Memoirs of William Ged*; it was later reprinted at Newcastle (*see* 1819). About this time the Scotsman Alexander Tilloch, editor of the *Philosophical Magazine*, had invented, in conjunction with the printer Andrew Foulis, and without any knowledge of Ged's work, a method of producing stereotype plates, and in 1784 the two men took out a patent for the process. Later the invention was purchased from them by the 3rd Earl Stanhope, who further developed it in association with the printer Andrew Wilson, who set up the Stereotype Office in Duke Street, Lincoln's Inn Fields.

On 23 June, appeared the first number of *The Manchester Chronicle*, printed and published by Charles Wheeler.

Charles Wilkins printed at Calcutta *A Translation of a Royal Grant of Land by one of the ancient Raajaas of Hindostan* . . . The translation was made by Wilkins at the command of Warren Hastings.

1782

At Mannheim, Johann Michael Götz published the first compositions of the 12-year-old Beethoven.

At Vienna, Christian Friedrich Wappler published Michael Denis, *Wiens Buchdruckergeschichte bis M.D.LX.* The title-page has an engraving of the Bibliotheca Garellia of which Denis was curator.

First edition of *Les Liaisons Dangereuses* by Pierre-Ambroise-François Choderlos de Laclos (1741–1803). Amsterdam & se trouve à Paris, chez Durand.

Le Prince Aîné, Inspecteur de la Librairie for the Chambre Syndicale at Paris published *Essai historique sur la Bibliothèque du Roi*, a detailed history of what is now the Bibliothèque Nationale. (A new edition, revised and augmented by Louis Paris was published in 1856.)

At Philadelphia, Robert Aitken published the first English Bible printed in America.

1783

Étienne-Alexandre-Jacques Anisson published at Paris *Description d'une nouvelle presse*, . . . the press which became known as the Anisson press. Its great advantage at the time was the fact that it printed at one pull of the bar.

At Madrid, the Royal Printer, Joaquin Ibarra, published the first volume, folio, of Nicolas Antonio, *Bibliotheca Hispana Nova*. Ibarra died in 1785, and the second volume was published by his widow and heirs. There was a second issue of Vol. 1 in 1788, with an advice to the reader dated 1787, but still having the 1783 title-page. The author, a Canon of Seville, was the father of Spanish bibliography: the original edition had been published at Rome 1672–96. (*See* 1672.)

Domesday Book, edited by Abraham Farley, F.R.S., was published in two folio volumes by John Nichols in facsimile of the original. The work took ten years to print, and the fount of facsimile types was cut by Joseph Jackson after a fount by Cottrell had been rejected. An introduction and glossary was published in 1788. Unfortunately the type was destroyed in a fire which swept through Nichols's printing office at Red Lion Court in 1808.

John Walter, proprietor of *The Times*, published Henry Johnson, *An Introduction to Logography.* Johnson was a compositor at *The Times* and wrote the book to recommend to the public Walter's Logographic Press. (*See* 1785.)

J. Briscoe, the first known printer at Douglas, in the Isle of Man, issued the Acts of Tynwald, his earliest surviving work.

John Wells, a printer of Charleston, left that town for St. Augustine, Florida, where, in partnership with his brother William C. Wells, he began publication of the *East-Florida Gazette* on 1 February, 1783. The existence of this newspaper is known only through the fact that the issues for 1 March, and 3 and 17 May were found in the Public Record Office, London. According to the issue of 1 March, the paper was printed, 'by Charles Wright for John Wells, jun.'. Nothing, however, is known of this printer, who yet remains the first printer connected with East Florida.

1784

Printing for the blind was introduced for the first time by Valentin Haüy, founder of the Asylum for Blind Children in Paris. He used a heavily embossed script character which could be read by touch. His pupils did the printing, and they were also taught to do ordinary letterpress printing.

The prospectus (Avis aux Souscripteurs) for a new edition of Tasso's *Gerusalemme Liberata* was printed in a new type-face cut in the foundry of F. A. Didot—a roman which A. F. Johnson, in his *Type Designs* (1934 and 1959) calls 'a modern face and the first of its class'. (A reproduction is shown in Geoffrey Dowding, *An Introduction to the History of Printing Types* (1961).) The prospectus was printed on *papier vélin*, a highly finished wove paper similar to that used by Baskerville.

Between 1784 and 1790 was published the celebrated Kehl edition of the works of Voltaire, printed in Baskerville types from the matrices bought by Pierre-Augustin Caron de Beaumarchais (1732–99) who bought also the copyright of all Voltaire's works from the publisher Panckoucke, and superintended the planning and production of the two editions, which consisted of seventy volumes 8vo or ninety-two volumes 12mo. In all 28,000 copies were printed on five different qualities of paper.

The type-founders Perrenot et Fils issued at Avignon an *Épreuve des Caractères de la Fonderie de Perrenot & Fils*. Antoine Perrenot, the father, who died in 1786 had bought the foundry in 1747 from a certain M. Legrand. (*See also* 1771.)

John Walter I bought the property in Blackfriars which had once been the King's Printing House until Charles Eyre and William Strahan, who had acquired John Baskett's patent, removed the printing office to new premises which they built in New Street, near Gough Square. John Walter purchased this property in Printing House Square to house his Logographic Press. (*See also* 1785.)

Johann Christian Ritter established the first press at Cape Town.

1785

Foundation at Leipzig of the publishing firm of Georg Joachim Göschen (1752–1828), who came there from Bremen. He was the publisher of works by Schiller, Goethe and Wieland. The firm was taken over by J. G. Cotta of Stuttgart in 1838.

Philippe Denis Pierres published at Paris *Caractères de l'Imprimerie de M. Pierres, Imprimeur Ordinaire du Roi*, etc., etc. Each specimen of type shown has the name of the foundry from which it came. Updike says it is, 'the first specimen book (that I have seen) which appears to be intended by a printer for the use of his customers'. Hitherto they had been issued by typefounders for the use of printers. Pierres started his career in the printing house of his uncle, Augustin Martin Lottin.

First edition of Beaumarchais, *La Folle Journée, ou le Mariage de Figaro*. Paris: Ruault. The first performance of the play took place on 27 April, 1784.

Death of the famous Spanish printer Joaquin Ibarra, born at Saragossa in 1723 (*see* 1772, 1780 *and* 1783). As a printer, his reputation equalled that of Baskerville and Bodoni.

On 1 January, was issued the first number of the *Daily Universal Register*, the title of which was changed on 1 January, 1788, to *The Times*. Its founder was John Walter I (1738–1812) who had started it to advertise his Logographic Press (*see* 1783), which in 1784 began to reprint a series of English classics, the first being Watts, *Improvement of the Human Mind*. But for general printing the process proved too cumbersome, since four enormous cases were needed for the fount. Walter abandoned his logotypes in 1792.

The earliest directory of the English book

trade, *The London and Country Printers, Booksellers, and Stationers Vade Mecum* was printed and published by J. Pendred.

Death of the letter-founder Thomas Cottrell. His foundry became the property of Robert Thorne in 1794, though what happened to it in the intervening years is not known.

The first press in Maine was set up at Falmouth (now Portland) by Benjamin Titcomb and Thomas B. Wait who issued the *Falmouth Gazette* (afterwards, when Falmouth became Portland, called the *Cumberland Gazette*).

The first newspaper in Delaware was the *Delaware Gazette*, first issued in June 1785 from the Wilmington printing office of Jacob A. Killen. No trace has been found of the *Wilmington Courant* mentioned by Isaiah Thomas.

From Worcester, Massachusetts, came *A Specimen of Isaiah Thomas's Printing Types*, advertised as, 'As large and complete an assortment as is to be met with in any one printing office in America. Chiefly manufactured by that great Artist, William Caslon Esq. of London.'

Matthew Carey (b. Dublin 1760), as the result of a meeting with Franklin in Paris, whither Carey had fled to escape prosecution for his attacks on the Irish penal code, emigrated to Philadelphia, where he soon became a successful printer and publisher. He began the *Columbian Magazine* and later the very successful periodical *The American Museum*. The firm Carey founded is today, as Lea and Febiger, the oldest surviving publishing house in the U.S.A.

On 25 August, Fleury Mesplet, the French printer of Montreal (*see* 1776) brought out the first number of the bilingual *Montreal Gazette: Gazette de Montréal*, which has survived to this day.

1786

A small volume of poems 'chiefly in the Scottish dialect', by Robert Burns, was printed by an obscure printer named John Wilson at Kilmarnock. The edition was 600 copies and the book is now extremely rare and much coveted by lovers of Burns.

Richard Austin began his career as a punchcutter employed by John Bell, and later worked for S. and C. Stephenson. Hansard writes that he cut most of the modern founts both for Wilson of Glasgow and Miller of Edinburgh. About 1808 he cut the Greek type sponsored by Richard Porson of Cambridge. About 1819 he started the

Imperial Letter Foundry in the management of which he was succeeded by his son George in 1824.

Her Majesty's Stationery Office was founded as a stationery supply service for all government departments.

Many experiments were being made with a view to finding a substitute for the linen rags then used for paper-making. In 1786 the *Œuvres du Marquis de Villette* was printed in London, 156 pages, on the bark of the lime tree. At the end of the volume are samples of paper from the nettle, hopbine, moss, reeds, conifers, couch grass, hazel tree bark, mallow, oak, poplar, spindle-tree and water willow. In the dedication to the Marquis Ducrest the author writes: 'J'ai soumis à la fabrication de papier toutes les plantes, les écorces, et les végétaux les plus communs.'

1787

Johann Friedrich Cotta (1764–1832), later Freiherr von Cottendorf, took over the declining bookselling business of his father at Tübingen, and made it into one of the leading establishments in the country. His main achievement was the founding of the *Allgemeine Zeitung* which was published at Stuttgart in 1798, Ulm in 1803, and at Augsburg in 1816.

Giambattista Toderini published his *Letteratura Turchese*, Part 3 of which deals with the *Istoria dell'arte impressoria Turchese*. It was translated into French and German. Venice: Giacomo Storti.

In Venice, was published the six-volume catalogue of the library of the Italian bibliophile, Maffeo Pinelli (1736–85), edited by Jacob Morelli. (*See* 1789.)

The first edition of Beckford's *Vathek*, in the original French, was published at Lausanne by Isaac Hignou & Co. The first edition in English had been published the previous year by J. Johnson.

At Vienna, Johann Trattner published his *Specimen Characterum Latinorum*.

At Paris, appeared *Essai historique sur l'origine des Caractères Orientaux de l'Imprimerie Royale, sur les ouvrages qui ont été imprimés à Paris en Arabe, en Syriaque, en Arménien, etc., et sur les Caractères Grecs de Francois Ier appelés communément Grecs du Roi*. By M. de Guignes.

The first printed edition of the famous *Paston Letters*, written between 1422 and 1509, was published in four volumes by John Fenn, 1787–89. A fifth volume was added by Frere in 1823. Many of the letters remained undiscovered until 1865 when they were published with introductions by James Gairdner, 1872–75.

At London, the British Museum published *Librorum impressorum qui in Museo Britannico adservantur catalogus*. Two volumes folio. This catalogues some 70,000 works.

The *Botanical Magazine*, which has continued publication down to the present day, was founded by William Curtis (1746–99).

John Bradford, the first printer in Kentucky, with financial help from the town of Lexington, set up his press there, and on 11 August, 1787, brought out the first issue of the *Kentucke Gazette*. The earliest known book printing from his press is *The Kentucke Almanack for 1788*. (*See* D. C. McMurtrie, *John Bradford, Pioneer Printer of Kentucky*, 1931.)

1788

The Leipzig printer Christian Gottlob Täubel published a textbook on printing, *Orthotypographisches Handbuch*.

First edition of the *Manuale Tipografico* of Giambattista Bodoni. (*See also* 1818.)

Étienne-Alexandre-Jacques Anisson became Director of the Imprimerie Royale, Paris (*see also* 1783). He held the post until 1794, when he was guillotined during the French Revolution.

The first English 'modern' face (cut by Richard Austin), appeared in *The Poetry of Anna Matilda*, published and printed by John Bell.

John Bell issued the first specimen sheet of his British Letter Foundry, established the year before in the Strand, London, near Exeter Exchange.

The first daily evening paper in Britain, the *Star*, made its appearance.

1789

Johann Gottlob Immanuel Breitkopf endeavoured to assemble Chinese characters on separate cast bodies, and published his attempts, which he soon gave up, in *Exemplum typographiae sinicis*.

Pierre Didot l'Aîné (1761–1853) succeeded his father, François-Ambroise. He became Royal Printer in France in 1791, and his publications became so famous that the government, deciding to honour the printer's craft in his person, ordered the transfer of his presses to the Louvre in 1797. It was there that he printed the handsome series of classics known as the 'Editions du Louvre' (*see* 1797). The three-volume *Racine* was set in type cut and cast by his brother Firmin. Pierre Didot was also a writer, and in 1799 published a specimen book with types displayed in various poems from his pen.

At Paris, 'De l'Imprimerie de Monsieur', Pierre-François Didot le Jeune published *Paul et Virginie* by Bernardin de Saint Pierre, which bears on the title-page the mention that it was printed on 'paper vélin d'Essones'. Pierre-François Didot had purchased the paper mill at Essones, and was the first to introduce 'papier vélin', or wove paper, into France. One of his daughters was married to Bernardin de Saint-Pierre.

M. Lottin Aîné, 'Imprimeur Libraire du Roi', published his *Catalogue chronologique des Libraires et des Libraires-Imprimeurs de Paris depuis l'an 1470 . . . jusqu'à présent*. Paris: chez Jean-Roch Lottin de S. Germain. Still a most useful work.

The French bookseller-publisher Charles-Joseph Panckoucke set up a printing office to produce the *Gazette Nationale* or *Moniteur Universel* which he had just founded, and which became (An VIII) the *Journal Officiel* of the French Republic.

At Paris Joseph Gillé took over his father's foundry at the latter's death in 1789 and increased its reputation with the cutting of various versions of the Didot style.

Sale by auction at London of the Pinelli Library and publication of the catalogue, *Bibliotheca Pinelliana*.

Publication of Richard Gough's new and revised edition of Camden's *Britannia*, in three folio volumes, dedicated to George III.

First edition of *The Natural History of Selborne*, by Gilbert White (1720–93).

After serving his apprenticeship with a Coventry printer, Charles Whittingham the Elder came to London and set up as a jobbing printer in Fetter Lane. In 1797 he removed to larger premises in Dean Street. By 1807 he had premises in Goswell Street, and three years later, after taking into partnership his foreman, Robert Rowland, left the city business in the latter's hands and went to Chiswick, where he set up a press and also started a paper pulp manufactory. Here he worked until his death in 1840.

John Bell founded the daily newspaper *The Oracle*.

A Dutch type-founder named Adam Mappa, who had his own foundry at Delft, emigrated to New York taking with him a large amount of material, and established the first type-foundry in that city. His type-founding equipment is said to have belonged formerly to Reinhard Voskens of Amsterdam.

1790

At Leipzig, the first edition of the first published version of Goethe, *Faust, ein Fragment*, was published by Georg Joachim Göschen. It was another twenty years (1808) before the completed *Faust, Part I* came from the press.

By decree dated 14 August, 1790, the French National Assembly appointed a commission charged with making an inventory of the material at the Imprimerie Nationale, Paris. The members included Jacques Anisson, the director of the printing house.

Death of Charles-Nicolas Cochin (b. 1715), the celebrated French engraver and illustrator. His work is seen to best advantage in the works of Boileau (1747), Ariosto, *Orlando Furioso* (1773) and Dionis du Séjour, *L'Origine des Grâces* (1777).

William Nicholson of London (*c.* 1755–1815), author, schoolmaster, and inventor, took out a patent for several inventions relating to printing, and his specifications embodied many of the essential features of later printing machines. His ideas for printing from a flat forme by means of a cylinder round which the paper was fed, foreshadowed the later invention of König (*see* 1810). He also proposed a rotary machine with two cylinders, one for the type and the other for the paper, but failed to indicate how the type should be secured to the impression cylinder. Perhaps from lack of capital, he never put his ideas to a practical test. A description of his proposed printing press appeared in the *Repertory of Arts*, Vol. 5.

Joseph Bramah (1748–1814) invented a hydraulic press for extracting the superfluous water from newly formed sheets of paper fresh from the vat. Previously screw presses had been used. It was patented in 1795.

John Catnach (1769–1813) set up a press at Alnwick, Northumberland, and although others had printed there before him, yet he is the first Alnwick printer whose works have survived. He published at Alnwick about 1796, selections from Buffon entitled *The Beauties of Natural History* with 67 wood-engravings by Thomas Bewick. In 1808 he went to Newcastle upon Tyne, but his business there failed, and he was imprisoned for debt. On his release he went to London to try his fortune, but soon after opening a business in Wardour Street, he died after an accident.

Printing introduced into Rjeka (Fiume) by Laurent Aloysius Karlecki.

America passed the first Federal Copyright Act. This protected the rights of Americans only.

1791

Johann Friedrich Unger (1750–1804) issued at Berlin his *Schriftproben der Didotschen und gewöhnlichen Lettern*. Unger's foundry contained most of the ancient material from the old Luther foundry at Frankfurt-am-Main.

The famous Italian typographer Bodoni printed an edition, in English, of Walpole's *Castle of Otranto* for the bookseller J. Edwards, of Pall Mall.

In France, following the Revolution, the ancient corporations were abolished and whoever so wished, could set up as printer or bookseller on payment of a patent fee by the Decree of March, 1791.

William Bulmer (1757–1830) began publication of his handsome edition of Shakespeare, illustrated with plates in the possession of the art publishers Messrs. Boydell, and which gained for Bulmer recognition as a printer of fine books. In 1790 he had established the Shakespeare Printing Office in Cleveland Row, St. James's. The Shakespeare was set in type cut by William Martin of Birmingham.

On 13 March, appeared the first part of Thomas Paine, *The Rights of Man*, a reply to Burke's *Reflections on the Revolution in France* (1790). It was eagerly read, especially when the government endeavoured to suppress it. In it Paine laid down the basic principles of fundamental human rights. London: J. Johnson.

On 16 May, was published James Boswell, *The Life of Samuel Johnson, LL.D.* This date was the anniversary of Boswell's first meeting with Johnson.

On Sunday, 4 December, appeared the first issue of the *Observer*, founded by W. S. Bourne, the oldest London Sunday newspaper still in existence. (*For the earliest see* 1779.)

At Leningrad, appeared the first music engraved in Russia, in a music drama called *The beginning of the rule of Olega*, the words of which were by Catherine the Great, and the music by Giuseppe Sarti, V. Pashkevich and C. Cannobio. It was printed at the press of the Mining School.

The first press in Tennessee was set up at Rogersville (then a little village known as Hawkins Court House) by two printers from North Carolina, George Roulstone and Robert Ferguson. They printed here while waiting to move into the new capital, Knoxville, which was still being built. On 5 November, 1791, they brought out the first number of the *Knoxville Gazette* and in October, 1792 were at last able to move into that town.

1792

At Paris, L'Imprimerie du Louvre became L'Imprimerie Nationale Exécutive. Its director, Anisson, was arrested as a conspirator and guillotined. The printing house was exploited for the benefit of the State, and a special room was set aside for the printing of *assignats*. During the Year 3, under the name of Imprimerie Nationale, the ancient printing house of the Louvre was transferred to the rue de La Vrillière, where it was still situated when the Empire was proclaimed 18 May, 1804.

Vincent Figgins who had worked for many years for Joseph Jackson, established his own type-foundry in Swan Yard, Holborn Bridge. When he retired in 1836 (he died 1844), the business was carried on by his sons Vincent and James. In 1865, the foundry was situated in Ray Street, Farringdon Road, and the premises were greatly enlarged in 1876, at which time it was the wealthiest and most extensive of the English foundries. In 1793, Figgins brought out his first type specimen.

Louis Roy, French-Canadian printer, appointed Government Printer at Newark (*now* Niagara-on-the-Lake). The 8-page pamphlet he issued in January 1793—*Speech of His Excellency John Graves Simcoe*—was the first formal piece of printing in the Province of Upper Canada.

1793

At Leipzig, Johann Gottlob Immanuel Breitkopf published *Ueber Bibliographie und Bibliophilie*.

The Leipzig publisher Wilhelm Heinsius brought out the first volume of his *Allgemeines Bücher-Lexikon*, a list of books printed in Germany and neighbouring countries, for the use of booksellers. It continued until 1892.

At Nuremberg, between 1793 and 1803 were published the eleven volumes of Georg Wolfgang Panzer, *Annales Typographici*, covering the period from the invention of printing to 1536.

At Parma, Bodoni printed the *Poems* of Thomas Gray. He printed several English books on commission for London booksellers, and this is a fine example of his printing. (*See also* 1791.)

Antoine François Momoro (1756–94) published his *Traité élémentaire de l'imprimerie, ou le manuel de l'imprimeur*. With 36 engraved plates. Paris: Tilliard frères. Momoro was born at Besançon, of Spanish origin. He married the daughter of Fournier le Jeune. He was guillotined on 24 March, 1794. He is the presumed author of the device 'Liberté, Egalité, Fraternité' which, as member of the Conseil Municipal of Paris, in 1793 he had incised on all the public monuments.

At Madrid, from the office of D. Benito Cano, came *Muestras de los grados de letras y viñetas que se hallan en el obrador de fundicion de la Viuda e Hijo de Pradell*. José Edualdo Mariano Pradell (1721–88) was possibly the best punch-cutter and type-founder in Spain during the latter part of the eighteenth century.

On 28 June, was held the first 'General Meeting of Letter-Founders', which took place at the York Hotel, London, and led to the formation of the London Society of Master Letter-Founders, which existed until 1820.

The Cambridge Intelligencer established by Benjamin Flower, a strenuous advocate of the liberty of conscience, which often led to his prosecution and imprisonment.

On 6 November, died John Murray, the founder of the publishing firm of that name. (*See* 1768.)

The first book printed in Greenland—*Tuksiautit akioreeksautikset* (*lit.* Songs for several persons). The printer was an amateur, a missionary named Jesper Brodersen, who, after studying theology at the University of Copenhagen, was sent in

1786 to Neu Herrnhut, near Godthaab, Greenland. The copy of this book (imperfect) in the Royal Library, Copenhagen, is the only one known. No further printing seems to have taken place until 1855.

The first press in Ohio was established at Cincinnati by William Maxwell, who had previously been a printer at Lexington, Kentucky. On 9 November he issued the first number of *The Centinel of the North-Western Territory*. His first book printing seems to have been *The Laws of the Territory of the United States North-West of the Ohio*, which came from his press in 1796.

The first press at Saint-Denis, capital of Bourbon, now known as Reunion Island, was set up by a priest named Louis Delsuc. Its first products were currency notes, and the earliest printed specimen now extant is a pamphlet, *Code Pénale Militaire* with the imprint 'De l'Imprimerie Coloniale'.

A printing press was established at Scutari, Anatolia, by the Sultan Selim III, which came to an end with the assassination of that ruler in July 1808.

1794

J. F. Unger completed in Berlin the fifth and final design of his new Fraktur, which was cut by Johann Christoph Gubitz. He first used it in Karl Philipp Moritz, *Neue Cecilia*.

From Venice came *Saggi dei Caratteri, Vignette e Fregi della nuova fonderia di Antonio Zatta e Figlio, tipografi, calcografi, e librai Veneti*—a specimen book from the firm of A. Zatta & Son, which for more than a century was one of the leading Venetian firms of publishers and type-founders.

Bartolomeo Conte Giuliari (1761–1842) founded at Verona the Stamperia Giuliari, a private press which functioned until 1827, in which year the material was sold to the printing firm of Valentino Crescini, which had moved from Padua to Verona. The Stamperia Giuliari was founded mainly with the aim of producing a sumptuous work, *Ittiolitologia Veronese*, 1796–1809.

In London, F. Faulder published *A View of the Evidences of Christianity*, by William Paley, Archdeacon of Carlisle. This was a prescribed book at Cambridge until well into the twentieth century.

Samuel Bagster (1772–1851), founder of the present publishing firm of Bagster & Sons, started business as a general bookseller in the Strand, London, on 19 April, 1794. Although the production of the English Bible was a monopoly in Britain, it had, however, been decided that the patent did not apply to Bibles printed with notes and to polyglot editions, and Samuel Bagster decided to specialise in this field (*see* 1816, 1831, 1841). On his death he was succeeded by his son Jonathan Bagster (1813–72).

Robert Thorne purchased Thomas Cottrell's type-foundry at Barbican, London.

1795

About 1795, was perfected the French process of 'Polytypage', subsequently used almost everywhere for the production of casts from wood engravings. The apparatus was originally designed for the printing of *assignats* issued by the Constituent Assembly. These had to be printed in immense quantities on a considerable number of hand presses, and no engraver could have produced dozens of absolutely identical blocks. The 'machine à polytyper', or 'mouton' as it was nicknamed, was devised by a committee which included Firmin and Henri Didot, the punch-cutters Frieze and Gérard, and the engravers Gatteaux and Tardieu. The engraving was suspended over a tray on to which hot metal was poured. The engraving was released to fall with considerable but even pressure on to the fluid metal. In 1818 A. Applegath obtained an English patent for a polytyping machine.

William Bulmer produced one of his finest examples of elegant printing in the *Poems* of Oliver Goldsmith and Thomas Parnell—a quarto volume set in types cut by William Martin, on paper from the Whatman mills, and with woodcuts by Thomas Bewick. In the 'advertisement' to this volume, Bulmer emphasises that the productions of his Shakespeare Printing Office were, 'particularly meant to combine the various beauties of Printing, Type-founding, Engraving, and Paper-making'. Even the ink was prepared by Bulmer from a recipe of Robert Martin, to whom Baskerville had imparted the secret of preparing a rich black ink.

Rudolf Ackermann (1764–1834), a native of Schneeberg in Saxony, opened his print shop in the Strand, London. He was brought up to the trade of a coach-builder and coming to England shortly before the French Revolution he continued in London for a time the profession of a carriage draughtsman, which led to his acquaintance with artists and eventually to his setting up as a dealer in prints and ultimately to the publishing of art books. One of the most famous of his publications was the *Microcosm of London* (1808–11) with its splendid aquatint plates. A large staff of artists (many of them children) coloured by hand 104,000 aquatint plates for this work. Ackermann called his shop the Repository of Arts, and in 1809 brought out a magazine which he called *The Repository of Arts, Literature, Commerce, Manufactures, Fashions and Politics*. He also introduced into England the Continental vogue for annuals, his first being called *Forget-me-not*, published in 1825. In 1830 he transferred his business to his three sons and to his principal assistant Mr. Walton.

First edition of Lindley Murray, *English Grammar*. York: Wilson, Spence & Mawman. This book met with a phenomenal success; in addition to over 600 printings in English in various parts of the world, it was translated into Dutch, Danish, Swedish, German, Russian and Japanese.

Isaiah Thomas printed at Worcester the *Elegiac Sonnets* of Mrs. Charlotte T. Smith first published at London in 1784. This is the first known example of printing on wove paper in America.

Formation of the Typographical Society of New York, the first organisation of working printers. It existed for two and a half years and was followed, 1799–1804 by the Franklin Society of Journeymen Printers.

The Scotsman, Archibald Binny went to America, where he settled in Philadelphia and established there a type-foundry. In association with another Scot, James Ronaldson, he formed the firm of Binny & Ronaldson, which was the first type-foundry in the United States to achieve permanency. Later they acquired the foundry begun by John Baine and Grandson in 1788, and later still the foundry set up in 1791 by the Dutch founder A. G. Mappa. After various changes of ownership the foundry was absorbed into the American Type Founders Co. in 1892. Binny and Ronaldson were the first type-founders to cast a dollar sign, and they originated the Oxford type chosen by D. B. Updike for his *Printing Types*. (*See* 1809.)

In November, printing was carried out for the first time at Sydney, New South Wales, by George Hughes, though nothing of that year survives.

1796

Between 1796 and 1808, was published by Friedrich Arnold Brockhaus at Leipzig the first edition of the *Konversationslexikon*, one of the most successful of European dictionaries. Many editions of 'Brockhaus' have since been published.

Justus Erich Walbaum set up as a type-founder at Goslar. Early in 1803 he moved his business to Weimar, where it soon became one of the most famous foundries in Germany. In 1836 he sold the business to F. A. Brockhaus, the Leipzig printer and publisher, and the foundry was moved to that city. In 1918 it was acquired by the firm of H. Berthold, in whose possession remain Walbaum's original punches and matrices. Walbaum, whose son predeceased him, died on 21 June, 1837. His Antiqua has been described as, 'the most *human* of the neo-classic faces'.

At Leipzig, Karl Christoph Traugott Tauchnitz (1761–1836) bought a small printing office and founded the famous firm which still bears his name. In 1798 he started to publish, and in 1800 added a type-foundry.

At Valencia, Benito Monfort published José Villaroya, *Disertación sobre el origen del nobilisimo arte tipografico*. . . .

James Ballantyne (1772–1833) founded at Kelso the press named after him. He was a school friend of Sir Walter Scott, who later became a partner in the business. About 1805 the Ballantyne Press moved to Edinburgh, one of the first products of the press in that city was the first quarto of Scott's *Lay of the Last Minstrel*. Shortly after Ballantyne's death, the firm became Ballantyne, Hanson & Co. In 1915 the goodwill of the business was purchased by Spottiswoode & Co.

Simon and Charles Stephenson issued a type specimen book, the first part of which appeared in 1796 and the whole book in 1797.

On 1 May, was issued the Sunday newspaper *Bell's Weekly Messenger*, founded by John Bell.

The first press in Michigan was set up at Detroit by John McCall in 1796, in which year he printed *An Act passed at the First Session of the Fourth Congress of the United States . . . the seventh of*

December, 1795. Apart from this small book, nothing is known of the printer.

The earliest known surviving specimen of Australian printing is *Instructions to the Watchmen of Town Divisions,* dated Sydney, 18 November, 1796, printed by George Hughes on the first press brought to New South Wales.

1797

At Berlin, J. F. Unger published the first volume of August Wilhelm Schlegel's translation of the works of Shakespeare.

At Tübigen, Johann Friedrich Cotta published the first part of Friedrich Hölderlin, *Hyperion.* The second part appeared in 1799.

In France, the Ministry of the Interior put at the disposal of Pierre Didot l'Aîné the rooms in the Louvre formerly occupied by the Imprimerie Royale. There he printed, from 1798 to 1802, his editions of *Virgil* (1798), *Horace* (1799) and *Racine* (1801), which were proclaimed to be amongst the most perfect pieces of printing of any age or any country.

Thomas Bensley printed a handsome edition of James Thomson, *The Seasons* with engravings by F. Bartolozzi and P. W. Tomkins after originals by W. Hamilton, R.A. The type was designed by Vincent Figgins, and Reed called this book, 'one of the finest achievements of English typography'.

The first volume appeared of *A History of British Birds,* with illustrations by Thomas Bewick. The second volume was published in 1804. The value of this book rests less on the text, of slight value, than upon the quality of Bewick's delightful wood engravings.

On 20 November, died Roger Payne (b. Windsor, 1739), the celebrated bookbinder. He learned his trade from a Mr. Pote, bookseller to Eton College.

John Hatchard founded the bookselling firm of Hatchards at the age of 29.

1798

The Bavarian, Aloys Senefelder (1771–1834), invented the planographic method of printing known as lithography or, as he himself termed it, 'polyautography'. After securing patent rights at Munich, Senefelder patented his process in London in 1800, and in Paris in 1801. Before he died, Senefelder saw his invention develop into a flourishing branch of the printing industry in many European countries. Senefelder wrote a manual of lithography in German, which was translated into English and published in London in 1819 by Rudolf Ackermann.

The German firm of Reinicke & Hinrichs published the first complete and accurate catalogue of books published during the previous year. This was called *Verzeichnis Neuer Bücher.*

At Berlin, Hans Friedrich Vieweg published *Taschenbuch für Frauenzimmer von Bildung,* in which, with engravings by Chodowiecki, Goethe's *Hermann und Dorothea* first appeared.

A Hungarian printer named Samuel Falka began experiments in stereotyping at Vienna. Refused a privilege for exploiting his method he left Vienna and became printer at the University of Buda, in Hungary.

At Brussels, Pierre Lambinet (1742–1813) published *Recherches sur l'origine de l'imprimerie en Belgique.*

At Paris, the printer Bertrand Quinquet published his *Traité de l'Imprimerie.* 'Imprimerie de l'Auteur. An VII.'

At Madrid, the widow of Joaquin Ibarra published the writing-book of Torquato Torio, *Arte de Escribir,* which contains a history of the early calligraphers.

Richard Austin cut the decorated face known as Fry's Ornamented, used primarily as a titling type.

Publication of Edward Jenner, *An Inquiry into the Causes and Effects of Variolae Vaccinae . . .,* a pamphlet in which Jenner announced his discovery of the connection between cowpox and smallpox, and led to immunisation by vaccination.

Publication of *An Essay on the Principle of Population* by Thomas Malthus, a work which exerted a strong influence on the study of economics and social theory in general.

The firm of Thomas Nelson & Sons Ltd. was founded by Thomas Nelson, a native of Throsk, near Stirling. After acquiring some experience of the publishing business in London, he started as a bookseller in a small way of business at the corner of West Bow, Edinburgh, about 1798. His eldest son William developed the business considerably, and was later joined by his younger brother Thomas, who originated the extensive series of school books for which the firm soon gained a reputation. A printing office was added to the business within about thirty years from its inception. An American branch of the firm was established at New York in 1854.

Printing presses were suppressed in Russia by order of the Tsar, Paul I (1754–1801).

Andrew Marschalk, at the Walnut Hills fort near Vicksburg, established the first press in Mississippi. Marschalk was an army officer who had taken with him to the fort a small press for personal use, on which he printed a ballad by William Reeves called *The Galley Slave*. Later he moved to Natchez where he took up printing professionally.

A printing office was set up at Scarborough, on the island of Tobago.

Between 1798 and 1799, during his Egyptian campaign, Napoleon Bonaparte established presses at Alexandria, Cairo and Gizeh.

In September, the missionary William Carey set up a press at Madnabati, India. The printing press was a gift from Mr. Udny, an indigo planter. The press was later transferred to Serampore. (*See* 1800.)

1799

Nicolas-Louis Robert invented about 1799 at Essonnes, in France, a machine for making a continuous sheet of paper on an endless wire web which was to replace the slow and tedious hand process. Financial difficulties, due to the unsettled state of the country after the French Revolution, prevented Robert from bringing his invention into practical form, and he sold the patent to St. Leger Didot. It was later taken up by the brothers Henry and Sealy Fourdrinier in England. (*See* 1804.)

Publication began of Robert John Thornton, *The Temple of Flora*, one of the most famous of all printed florilegia. This large folio work was first advertised in 1797, and was issued in parts between 1799 and 1807. It was one of the most sumptuous botanical publications ever published and many distinguished artists were engaged to make paintings for the plates. There were various editions and issues of this work, for which see G. Dunthorne, *Flower and Fruit Prints of the Eighteenth and early Nineteenth Centuries* (1938).

William Savage (1770-1843) who began his career as a printer and bookseller at Howden,

Yorks., in 1790, came to London a few years later, and in 1799 was appointed printer to the Royal Institution. (*See also* 1819.)

Death of the Rev. Clayton Mordaunt Cracherode (b. Taplow, 1730), F.R.S., F.S.A., and a Trustee of the British Museum. During his lifetime he had accumulated a magnificent library, remarkably rich in rarities, and with the exception of two books, he bequeathed his entire collection to the British Museum.

1800

Part I of Friedrich von Schiller (1759–1805), *Gedichte*. Leipzig: Crusius. Part II was published in 1803.

At Leipzig, the composer Fr. Anton Hoffmeister and the organist Ambrosius Kühnel founded a music-publishing firm out of which grew the modern firm of music publishers, C. F. Peters.

Publication of *Fleurs dessinées d'après nature*, by Gerard van Spaëndonck (1746–1822), Paris. The 24 stipple engravings, printed in colour and finished by hand, are, says Wilfrid Blunt, 'probably the finest engravings of flowers ever made'. Pierre-Joseph Redouté (*see* 1817) was a pupil of van Spaëndonck.

Pierre Didot l'Aîné printed at Paris the *Constitution de la République* in the specially large type designed for it by his brother Firmin Didot.

Charles Mahon, 3rd Earl of Stanhope, made the first hand press to combine an iron frame (instead of a wooden one), compound lever action, and a platen large enough to cover the forme. Lord Stanhope did not patent his press, which was built by several engineers. The first models were not strong enough to take the strain of the increased pressure from the system of leverage employed, and the press was soon redesigned. The illustration in Johnson's *Typographia* (1824) shows a Stanhope press of the second design.

Thomas Macklin's *Holy Bible, embellished with Engravings from Pictures and Designs by the most eminent Artists* (seven volumes folio) printed by Thomas Bensley. It embodied a very fine fount of two-line English roman cut for Bensley by Joseph Jackson in the Figgins foundry.

The first issue of the *Post Office London Directory*, started by two inspectors of the Inland letter-carriers named Ferguson and Sparkes.

Library of Congress established at Washington, D.C.

16 August, saw the first number of *The Cape Town Gazette & African Advertiser*, printed by Walker and Robertson. Before the end of the year their press was bought by the government, and there was no further independent printing at Cape Town until George Grieg, from H.M. Printing Office in London, arrived there and began printing the *South African Commercial Advertiser* at the end of 1823. The paper was suppressed in May 1824.

First press established at Serampore, north of Calcutta, by the Baptist missionary, William Carey.

1801

At Meersburg-am-Bodensee, Bartholomäus Herder founded the publishing firm which continues to this day at Freiburg.

In England, John Gamble patented a machine for the manufacture of paper in a continuous sheet. In 1804, the patent was reassigned to Henry and Sealy Fourdrinier.

In England an Act was passed in 1800 for the taking of the first English Census. In the following year was published *Abstract of the Answers and Returns to the Act for Taking Account of the Population of Great Britain*.

1802

Etienne Gabriel Peignot published his *Dictionnaire raisonné de Bibliologie*. Paris: an X (1802), two volumes. A supplementary volume appeared in 1804.

This year saw the publication of the first of the eight magnificent volumes of Pierre-Joseph Redouté, *Les Liliacées* (1802–16). Printed for the author by Didot Jeune. (*See also* 1817.)

First edition of *Le Génie du Christianisme* by the Vicomte de Châteaubriand (1768–1848). Paris: Migneret. Five volumes.

Armand-Gaston Camus (1740–1804), who wrote a number of books on printing and bibliography, published his *Histoire et procédés du polytypage et du stéréotypage*. Paris: A. A. Renouard.

Foundation of the *Edinburgh Review*, published by Archibald Constable. It lasted until 1929.

1803

Justus Erich Walbaum (1768–1839) moved his type-foundry from Goslar to Weimar, and soon afterwards produced the roman letter named after him, one of the most important German type-faces of the nineteenth century. In 1836 his foundry was acquired by F. A. Brockhaus and in 1918 merged with H. Berthold.

Adam von Bartsch, Viennese engraver and calligrapher, published at Vienna the first volume of *Le Peintre Graveur*, which provided a basis for the scientific study of the graphic arts. The twenty-one volumes were published between 1803 and 1821.

The Hartleben Verlag founded at Budapest by Konrad Adolf Hartleben (1778–1863), a native of Mainz. The firm moved its head office to Vienna in 1844. (*See also* 1882.)

Jean-Joseph Marcel (1776–1854) printed *Alphabet irlandais, précédé d'une notice historique, littéraire et typographique*. Paris: Imprimerie de la République (Nivose, An XII). The types belonged originally to the Propaganda Fidei at Rome, and were seized by Bonaparte during his campaign in Italy. Marcel became director of the Imprimerie Royale in 1814.

After the 3rd Earl Stanhope had purchased the patent of Alexander Tilloch and Andrew Foulis for a method of making stereotype plates, he further developed the process in association with the printer Andrew Wilson, who in this year founded the Stereotype Office in Duke Street, Lincoln's Inn Fields, London.

Richard Taylor (1781–1858) established himself as a printer, in partnership with his father, at Blackhorse Court, Fleet Street. He later removed to Shoe Lane, and subsequently to Red Lion Court, where the firm of Taylor and Francis still carries on business. Dibdin described him as 'a judicious, sensible, unostentatious, and scholastic printer'. Taylor was a member of several learned bodies and printed many important scientific works as well as the scientific monthly *The Philosophical Magazine*.

The newspaper *The Globe* was started as the organ of the Whig party.

William Clowes, founder of the firm of William Clowes & Sons Ltd., started his own printing office at 20 Villiers Street, London.

Robert Hoe (1784–1833) arrived in New York from England. By trade he was a working carpenter, and began his career in the U.S. in 1805 as partner of Matthew Smith (Smith & Hoe) in the manufacture of furniture. He married Smith's daughter, and when his partner died formed another partnership with his brother-in-law, Peter Smith, the constructor (1822) of the Smith press. Later, Hoe bought the patents of the press designed by Samuel Rust (1829). The combination of the two presses resulted in the 'Washington' press, which became even more popular than the 'Columbian'. When Peter Smith died (1825), the firm became R. Hoe & Company. Robert Hoe died 1833, and his son, Richard March Hoe (1812–86), became head of the firm. (*See* 1846.)

On 5 March, appeared the first number of *The Sydney Gazette and New South Wales Advertiser*, founded by the printer George Howe (1769–1821) who introduced printing into Australia and became the first Government Printer in New South Wales. He was born at St. Kitts, where his father and brother were printers. As a young man he was employed in the printing office of *The Times*.

1804

Publication at Breslau of J. E. Scheibel, *Geschichte der seit dreihundert Jahren in Breslau befindlichen Stadtbuchdruckerey* . . . containing a chronological history of the Breslau Stadtbuchdruckerey from Conrad Baumgarten, 1504, to the firm of Grass and Barth, 1804.

Vincenz Degen's printing house at Vienna was transformed into an Imperial Court and State Printing Office under Degen's management. From it grew the later Vienna State Printing House.

Publication of *The Gospel according to St. John . . . in Mohawk and English*. London: Phillips & Fardon. The earliest edition of a book of the Bible in any language published by the British and Foreign Bible Society after its foundation in 1804. The translation into Mohawk was by John Norton, a Cherokee by birth, but who had lived from infancy among the Mohawks.

Publication of Vol. 1 of William Cobbett's *Parliamentary Debates*. This was the beginning of what is now *Hansard*. These reports of proceedings in Parliament were started by Cobbett and the rights were sold by him to Hansard in 1812.

Henry and Sealy Fourdrinier purchased the patents of Didot and Gamble in the paper machine invented around 1799 by the Frenchman, Nicolas Louis Robert. Improvements led to the engineer Bryan Donkin successfully completing the first Fourdrinier paper-making machine. First experiments were made at Boxmoor, and a second machine was built at Two Waters. By 1840 there were 280 Fourdrinier machines at work in the United Kingdom.

Elihu White began making type at Hartford, Connecticut. In 1810 he moved to New York and in 1812 issued his first specimen book. He prospered and opened branches in Boston, Cincinnati and Chicago, which he later sold. The last owners of the N.Y. type-foundry of Elihu White before it was merged into A.T.F. Co., were Farmer, Little & Co.

1805

Friedrich Arnold Brockhaus (1772–1823) founded his publishing house at Amsterdam. It was moved to Altenburg in 1811, and in 1817 was transferred to Leipzig. The firm was greatly developed by his son Heinrich (1804–74), printer, publisher and type-founder. The foundry, which no longer exists, issued specimens in 1846, 1854 and 1859.

On the occasion of the visit of Pope Pius VII to its premises, the Imprimerie Imperiale executed the *Oraison Dominicale en 150 langues* printed in all the exotic types available to the Director, Marcellin Legrand, types which for the most part had been looted from the Stamperia Vaticana by the French Republican Armies which captured Rome in 1798 and, despite strong representations, were never afterwards returned to the Vatican.

Joseph Bramah (1748–1814) took out a patent (No. 2840 of 1805) for making paper in 'endless sheets of any length'. This involved stationing a vat of stuff over a gauze drum and letting the stuff drop in any required quantity on the drum. The principle was developed and improved upon by John Dickinson (1782–1869) who invented his cylinder machine in 1809 (Patent No. 3191).

The first type-casting machine invented in the U.S. patented by William Wing of Hartford, Connecticut. The patent was sold to Elihu White, but the invention was finally abandoned.

The earliest newspaper in the Straits Settlement, the *Prince of Wales's Island Gazette* founded. It lasted for 22 years.

1806

At Heidelberg, Mohr & Zimmer published the first volume of the collection of old German folk poetry known as *Des Knaben Wunderhorn*, gathered together by Achim von Arnim and Clemens Brentano. Three volumes, 1806–08.

At Leipzig, Benediktus Gotthelf Teubner took over a small printing office, working himself as compositor, pressman and corrector. It later grew into the large firm of B. G. Teubner.

Between 1806 and 1808 were published the four volumes of the *Dictionnaire des ouvrages anonymes et pseudonymes* by Antoine Alexandre Barbier. A third edition, revised and augmented by O. Barbier, was published in 1872.

Anthony Francis Berte took out a patent for a type-casting machine in which the casting was performed by applying the mould to an aperture in the side of the metal pot through which the hot metal was ejected into the mould with force. This seems to be the first suggestion in England of the hand-pump subsequently adopted by all the founders. Berte took out another patent in the following year in which several improvements were made on the former patent.

George Cruikshank (1792–1878) published his first work as a book illustrator, at the age of 14— a coloured title-page for John Fairburn's *Description of the popular and comic new pantomime*.

William Balston (1759–1849) established his own paper mill at Springfield Mill, Maidstone. In 1774, he had begun as apprentice to James Whatman II at Turkey Mill. When that was sold in 1794 to the Hollingworth Brothers, Balston, with the financial aid of Whatman, bought a partnership in the firm, which became Hollingworths and Balston. Today the firm exists as W. & R. Balston Ltd., making writing and drawing papers.

1807

Publication of John Thomas Smith's *Antiquities of Westminster*, printed by Thomas Bensley— the first book published in England with a lithographic illustration. The stone being ruined during the printing, only the first 300 copies of the book contain the lithograph.

The Bible Society published its first Gaelic Bible.

John Brown took out a patent (3047) for certain improvements in the construction of a printing press which foreshadowed the later platen machines.

Founding of Hodgsons, an auctioneering business in London confined solely to the sale of books and literary property. In 1968 they were purchased by Sotheby's.

The publishing firm of John Wiley & Sons Inc., founded in New York by Charles Wiley, bookseller and printer.

The first printing office in Uruguay was opened at Montevideo.

1808

Publication of the first part of Goethe's *Faust* by Johann Friedrich Cotta (1764–1832). The second part was published in 1832, the year of Goethe's death.

The Italian music-publishing firm of Ricordi founded at Milan by Giovanni Ricordi (1785–1853), who on 13 January opened a small shop and office in the Via di Pescaria Vecchia. From these premises came the first product of the Casa Ricordi—*Le Stagioni dell'Anno*, four sonatas for French guitar by Antonio Nava.

First edition of Caleb Stower's *The Printer's Grammar*. Although based on Smith and Luckombe, the book has much new material, and its chapters on rates of pay and the pricing of printing work are of considerable interest to the historian of printing.

The first printers known definitely to have worked in Venezuela were the Englishmen Matthew Gallagher and James Lamb, who came there from Trinidad, and set up a press at Caracas, where they issued the first number of the *Gazeta de Caracas* on 24 October, 1808. (*But see* 1764.)

1809

First edition (in six volumes) of the well-known *Conversations-Lexikon* produced by the Leipzig publisher Friedrich Arnold Brockhaus. It soon became a standard work and from 1928 has been called *Der Grosse Brockhaus*.

Karl Duncker and Peter Humblot founded at Berlin the publishing firm bearing their names.

Publication of *Philosophie zoologique*, by J. B. P. A. de M. de Lamarck. Paris: 'chez Dentu et chez l'Auteur'. (Two volumes.) This book contains the classical account of Lamarck's theory of evolution.

Between 1809 and 1811 the publisher Rudolph Ackermann (1764–1834) ran his 'Poetical Magazine' which included a series of plates by Thomas Rowlandson depicting the adventures of a touring schoolmaster, for which William Combe was asked to supply the text. The *Schoolmaster's Tour* was such a success that it was reprinted by Ackermann in 1812 as the *Tour of Dr. Syntax in search of the Picturesque*. Combe also wrote the text for Ackermann's histories of *Westminster Abbey* (1812), the *University of Oxford* (1814), and the *University of Cambridge* (1815). This period also saw the publication of the *Microcosm of London*, one of the most famous of Ackermann's publications, and which necessitated the hand-colouring of 104,000 aquatint plates.

Charles Brightley, printer and publisher of Bungay, Suffolk, issued *An account of the method of casting stereotype, as practised by the author*.

William Miller, formerly of the Glasgow Foundry, established his own business, which in 1838 became Miller and Richard. Richard became a partner in the firm in 1832.

First edition of the *Fables* by Ivan Andrevitch Krylov (1768–1844), the appearance of which immediately made the author famous.

Archibald Binny and James Ronaldson issued *A Specimen of Metal Ornaments cast at the Letter Foundrey of Binny and Ronaldson*. This was probably the first American type-founders' specimen book (*see also* 1812). Single sheets had previously been issued by Mein and Fleeming (*c.* 1767) and by Abel Buell in 1769.

Foundation of the New York Typographical Society under the style of the Franklin Typographical Society.

1810

Charles-Jacques Brunet (1780–1867) brought out the first edition of his *Manuel du libraire et de l'amateur de livres*, on which he continued to work for a further fifty years, continually perfecting it until its fifth edition in 1860. The *Manuel* was augmented by two supplementary volumes in 1878–80, the work of Pierre-Gustave Brunet (no relation of Charles-Jacques) and Pierre Deschamps.

In December first appeared in Paris the *Journal général de l'Imprimerie et de la Librairie*. From November 1811 until December 1814 it took the title of *Bibliographie de l'Empire français*, and thereafter appeared as *Bibliographie de la France*.

Léger Didot (1767–1829) established at Sorel, the first paper-making machine in France.

Promulgation in France of the decree of 5 February, 1810, which set up a Direction Générale de l'Imprimerie et de la Librairie, by which the number of printers in each town was rigorously limited, and all had to be officially appointed and sworn in.

A decree of Napoleon, dated 3 August, ordered that each Département of France should have one newspaper only.

Richard Porson, the famous Hellenist (1759–1808) designed a Greek fount which was cut by Richard Austin and cast by Caslon and Catherwood for use by the Cambridge University Press. It was used in Æschylus, *Prometheus Vinctus*, edited by C. J. Blomfield, and published by the Press in 1810 with the note 'Typis Academicis'.

The first English patent for a power-driven printing machine taken out by Friedrich König, a native of Thuringia.

Charles Whittingham the Elder (1767–1840) leased the High House in Chiswick Mall and fitted it up as a printing office (*see* 1811). His London business was left in charge of his foreman Robert Rowland under the style of Whittingham & Rowland.

Death of Thomas Kirkgate, for many years printer to Horace Walpole at Strawberry Hill.

Isaiah Thomas, one of the most scholarly of early American printers, published his *History of Printing in America*. A second, revised edition appeared in 1874 in two volumes (a reprint of the 1810 edition appears in *Archaeologia Americana*, Vols. 5 and 6).

The Bibliotheca Nacional at Rio de Janeiro founded, the nucleus of the collection being the library of the Prince Regent, John VI.

Printing began at Jamestown, St. Helena, with the *St. Helena Monthly Register*, printed and published by J. Coupland.

1811

At Madrid, Juan Josef Sigüenza y Vera published his *Mecanismo del arte de la Imprenta* (etc.).

The imprint of the Chiswick Press first used by

its founder, Charles Whittingham the Elder. (*See* 1810.)

On 5 April, died Robert Raikes, proprietor of the *Gloucester Journal*, philanthropist and founder of the Sunday school.

Archibald Binny of Philadelphia devised a great improvement in the hand casting of type by attaching a spring lever to the mould, giving it a quick return movement which enabled the caster to double his output.

1812

König built his first cylinder printing machine, which was displayed at König and Bauer's workshop in White Cross Street, London. John Walter II printed *The Times* on the new machine on 29 November, 1814.

Formation by Thomas Dibdin and other prominent bibliophiles of the Roxburghe Club, for the printing of rare works for the benefit of its members. It was named after the famous book collector John Ker, 3rd Duke of Roxburghe (1740–1804), whose library was sold by auction, 1812.

Death of John Walter I, principal proprietor of *The Times*.

Binny and Ronaldson, type-founders of Philadelphia (*see* 1809), brought out their second type specimen book, *Specimen of Printing Types*. The firm began in 1796, and in the following year acquired all the printing material which Adam Gerard Mappa had brought from Holland. In 1806 they bought from the executors of B. F. Bache the type-founding apparatus brought to Philadelphia from Paris in 1785 by Benjamin Franklin. For some time after 1806 they were the only type-founders in the U.S. (Facsimiles of both specimen books were published by the Columbiad Club, Connecticut, 1936.)

The first press was established at Santiago, Chile, by Camilo Henriquez, who issued, on 13 February, the first number of the *Aurora de Chile*.

1813

Richard Bacon of Norwich and Bryan Donkin of Bermondsey brought out the Bacon and Donkin press based on the rotary principle. The type was arranged on the four sides of a rotating horizontal prism and the impression was obtained from another 'cylinder' of a shape suitable for coming into contact with the formes of type.

First edition of *Pride and Prejudice* by Jane Austen (1775–1817). It was published anonymously. Three volumes. London: T. Egerton.

Sir Samuel Egerton Brydges founded the Lee Priory Press, one of the most famous private presses of the first half of the nineteenth century, at Ickham, near Canterbury. He died 8 September, 1837 at Grosjean, near Geneva, aged 75.

John Ruthven, Edinburgh printer, patented a hand press which was soon afterwards manufactured by Adam Ramage in Philadelphia. Ramage was a Scotsman who went to America in 1795.

John Watts, brother of Richard Watts (Printer to the University of Cambridge 1802–09), emigrated to America and printed there, first at Philadelphia and later at New York, where he printed the first stereotype book produced in America, an edition of *The Larger Catechism*, 1813. (*See* 1816.)

1814

Death of Jean-Michel Moreau le Jeune (b. 1741), celebrated draughtsman and engraver, brother of the landscape painter, and nephew of the printer Prault. He succeeded Cochin as draughtsman of the Cabinet du Roi. Some of his most delightful illustrations are contained in the first volume of songs by Benjamin de la Borde (1773).

First edition of Sir Walter Scott's *Waverley*, the first volume of which appeared on 7 July and successfully established its author as one of the outstanding writers of the historical novel. Edinburgh: J. Ballantyne for A. Constable. Three volumes.

Between 1814 and 1815 T. F. Dibdin published the four volumes of the *Bibliotheca Spenceriana*, one of the handsomest and most elaborate catalogues ever produced of a private library. George John, 2nd Earl Spencer (1758–1834), was one of the world's most famous book collectors.

On the night of 28–29 November, *The Times* was printed for the first time by machinery, making use of König's new machine, which increased the rate of production to 1,100 impressions an hour, as compared with the maximum 250 on the Stanhope hand press.

Matthew Duncan, the first printer in Illinois, set up a press at Kaskaskia, then the capital of Illinois, and there printed the *Illinois Herald*.

First vernacular printing press in Bombay established by Fardunji Marzaban (1787–1847).

1815

Foundation of the Vereeniging ter bevordering van de belangen des Boekhandels, the Dutch Booksellers' and Publishers' Association. Its main purpose at the time was to suppress pirated reprints.

Edward Cowper patented an invention for curving stereotype plates in order to fasten them to a cylinder.

Vincent Figgins cut a type-face which he named 'Antique' and showed it in his specimen of this year. With its thick slab serifs, it was the first all-bold type.

On 22 November, died James Lackington (b. 1746) the celebrated bookseller of Finsbury Square (*see* 1791). His shop was known as the 'Temple of the Muses'. He published his *Memoirs* in 1791, and his *Confessions* in 1804.

The Stamp Duty on newspapers was raised to fourpence.

The ruler of Egypt, Mohammad Ali, sent Nikola Masabki to Italy to study the art of printing. After about four years, he returned to Cairo, where, at Bulaq, he organised the Government Press, furnishing it with presses as well as Arabic, Persian and European types. Today it is probably the biggest printing establishment in the Near East and has its own foundry. Since the Arabic alphabet has no capitals, in 1929 King Fuad I set up a committee for designing them. They are known as ET-TAJJ ('Crown Letters') and their use is restricted to the Government Press.

1816

Bodoni's friend, Giuseppe de Lama, published in two volumes at Parma, *Vita del Cavaliere Giambattista Bodoni, tipografo italiano e catalogo cronologico delle sue edizioni*.

Publication at Haarlem of Jacobus Koning's *Verhandeling over den oorsprong, de uitvinding, verbetering en volmaking der boedrukkunst*.

At Paris, Gottfried Engelmann established the first lithographic workshop in France.

John Watts (*see* 1813) returned to Europe and entered into a contract with the Haarlem firm of Enschedé to teach them the process of making stereos.

First edition of *Adolphe* by Henri-Benjamin Constant de Rebecque. London: Colburn—Paris: Tröttel & Wurtz. The London printing preceded the Paris edition.

The first sans serif type appeared as a single line specimen under the heading 'Two lines English Egyptian', in William Caslon IV's specimen book of 1816.

On 23 May, died Caleb Stower, printer, of Hackney—the author of the *Printer's Grammar* (1808).

Samuel Bagster removed to 15 Paternoster Row, London.

American Mission Press established in Bombay.

On 15 October the Baptist missionary the Rev. George Henry Hough arrived at Rangoon to work the first printing press. This and a fount of Burmese type, were the gift of the Serampore missionaries, and thus was established the American Baptist Mission Press.

Printing press established at Amboyna by the London Missionary Society.

At Teheran, the first press was established in Persia.

1817

Having left London, Friedrich König bought the disused convent of Oberzell, near Würzburg, and there established the firm of König & Bauer.

Between 1817 and 1824 was published *Les Roses* by Pierre-Joseph Redouté (1759–1840). Redouté was flower-painter by appointment first to Marie-Antoinette and later to the Empress Josephine. The volume contains 170 plates in stipple engraving, printed in colour and finished by hand. (*See also* 1802.)

Charles Thompson, a pupil of Bewick, settled in Paris, where he created a school of engravers on wood, among them Porret and Best. This school was in the main an 'atelier de clicherie' (polytypage) for engraving vignettes from the drawings of well-known artists. In 1828 Pinard published *Recueil de vignettes gravées sur bois et polytypée par Thompson*.

At London, Bensley & Son printed Johann Friedrich Blumenbach, *Institutions of Physiology*, in the English translation by John Elliotson. The volume is stated by the translator to have been 'the first book ever printed by machinery'.

At London, Richard Watts printed for Samuel Bagster *The New Testament of the English Version of the Polyglot Bible*. This Bible contained a selection of over 60,000 parallel references mainly selected and all verified by Bagster himself. Although the production of Bibles in the United Kingdom was a monopoly, it had been decided that the patent did not apply to Bibles printed with notes. (*See also* 1794 and 1831.)

Publication of *The Bibliographical Decameron* by the Rev. Thomas Frognall Dibdin. In three volumes, it was printed by William Bulmer at the Shakespeare Press.

Blackwood's Magazine begun by William Blackwood, Edinburgh.

The *Literary Gazette* began publication.

The American publishing firm of Harper & Brothers founded as J. & J. Harper by James and John Harper.

In S. Africa, the earliest place to have a secular press was Graaff Reinet, Cape Colony, where the printer, about whom nothing is known, was P. C. Wahlstrand, who ran the Districts Drukkery.

1818

Alois Senefelder published his *Vollständiges Lehrbuch der Steindruckerey* at Munich. An English edition, *A Complete Course of Lithography*, was published in London the following year.

The second and final edition of the *Manuale Tipografico* of Giambattista Bodoni was published (two volumes) by the widow Paola Margherita Dall'Aglio. (A facsimile edition was published at Parma in 1965 by Franco Ricci, together with a number of hitherto unpublished documents and specimens.)

Jacquemin engraved nine body sizes of a new type for the Imprimerie Royale, Paris. Marius Audin writes that it is 'one of the handsomest models in our State printing-house', and qualifies it as 'un beau didot gras'.

In this year Senefelder went to Paris where he obtained a 'brevet' as lithographic printer, and placed on sale a portable lithographic press, enclosed in a box with accessories and instructions for the price of 300 francs. There was no stone, but paper treated with a calcareous substance.

René-Pierre Lorilleaux (1788-1865), previously a pressman at the Imprimerie Royale, Paris, set up his own firm specialising in the manufacture of printers' ink, at a time when most printers made their own ink. He also supplied printers' material, from presses to type. His son Charles was the founder of the printing firm of Charles Lorilleaux & Cie.

The Chiswick Press (*see* 1811) moved from the High House to College House, Chiswick Mall.

The first American printers' manual issued: *The Printers' Guide* by C. S. Van Winkle. The book contains 27 leaves of type specimens from the foundries of E. White and D. & G. Bruce of New York.

The first printer at Free Town, Sierra Leone, was M. Tilley, who began to print *The Royal Gazette & Sierra Leone Advertiser* probably about June 1818.

At Serampore, India, the Mission Press issued a *Dictionary of the Bengali language*, in two volumes. This was the last and greatest achievement of the missionary William Carey (1761–1834), and ran to 1,544 pages, covering 85,000 words.

The first books printed in Tasmania at Hobart Town by Bent.

Printing introduced into the Society Islands at Tahiti, where a press was set up at Afareaitu.

1819

On 24 June, the punch-cutter Johann Andreas Gottfried Schelter (b. 1775) and the type-founder Christian Friedrich Giesecke (b. 1785) established the type-foundry of Schelter & Giesecke at Leipzig.

At Leipzig, publication of Arthur Schopenhauer, *Die Welt als Wille und Vorstellung*.

Christiaan Andersen Spin settled in Amsterdam and became one of the best printers in Holland for the next quarter of a century.

Publication of *Spécimen des nouveaux Caractères de la Fonderie et de l'Imprimerie de P. Didot l'aîné*.

Sir William Congreve (1772–1828) invented a machine for printing the background of banknotes, etc., in several colours to prevent forgery. The printing surfaces consisted of composite or split metal plates, constructed so that each portion can be raised for inking in a selected colour and then lowered flush with the rest of the plate for printing.

Publication of the second edition of *Biographical Memoirs of William Ged; including a particular account of his progress in the art of Block Printing.* Newcastle: Printed by S. Hodgson and sold by E. Charnley. This was a straight reprint of Nichols' edition of 1781 (*q.v.*) save for some notes on the books printed by Ged inserted by the editor, T.H.

Charles Joseph Hullmandel (b. 1789) set up a lithographic establishment in Great Marlborough Street, London, probably about 1819. *His Twenty-four views of Italy* had been published in 1818 from an address in Somers Town. Hullmandel was one of the most important figures connected with the early days of lithography in England. He translated De Charleville Raucourt's *Manual of Lithography*, and in 1824, in association with Rudolph Ackermann, he published *The Art of Drawing on Stone.*

Richard Austin issued a type specimen from the Imperial Letter Foundry which he had recently established in Worship Street, London.

The firm of Blake, Garnett & Co., typefounders, came into being with the purchase of the foundry of William Caslon IV. About 1830 the style of the firm became Blake & Stephenson, and in 1841 it became Stephenson, Blake & Co.

The publishing firm of W. & R. Chambers, Edinburgh, founded by William Chambers (1800–83). A printing office was later added and in 1832 William was joined by his brother Robert, in which year they launched the very successful *Chambers's Journal*, which continued for more than a century.

William Collins (1789–1853) founded at Glasgow the firm of publishers which still bears his name. His son William II became Queen's Printer in Scotland and was knighted, 1881. Under his management, the business rapidly expanded to become one of the largest publishing and stationery businesses in the world, with its own paper mills.

First daily paper in Norway, published at Christiania (Oslo)—*Morgenbladet*, founded by N. Wolfsburg.

1820

Publication in Berlin of J. F. Flick: *Handbuch der Buchdruckerkunst.*

Charles Nodier and Baron Taylor began publication of *Voyages pittoresques et romantiques de l'Ancienne France*, with illustrations by Horace Vernet, Isabey, Fragonard fils, Bonington, and

Célestin Nanteuil. The work was not completed until 1878 (twenty-five volumes).

William Blake (1757–1827) published his *Jerusalem*, one of his finest works. Blake was his own printer, and composed his own text, designed the illustrations, and coloured them by hand, making use of the etching technique.

First issue of *The New Observer*; after a few months its name was changed to *The Independent Observer*. In 1822 it became the *Sunday Times*.

Death of Robert Thorne, type-founder. In June of this year, his foundry was bought by William Thorowgood, who issued his first specimen at the end of 1820. It represented the stock of Thorne's foundry at the time of his death; a second specimen followed on 1 January, 1821.

The American, Daniel Treadwell, took out a patent for applying power to the bed movement of a printing press by means of a treadle, or lever worked by the foot.

The first American missionaries to the Hawaiian Islands arrived on 14 April at Honolulu from Boston, bringing with them a press and a printer, Elisha Loomis. The first book in the Hawaiian language, a spelling book, came from their press in 1822.

1821

The only polyglot edition of the Prayer Book— the *Book of Common Prayer . . . in eight languages* —was published by Samuel Bagster. The languages employed were English, French, Italian, German, Spanish, Latin and ancient and modern Greek.

William Pickering started his Diamond Classics, set in $4\frac{1}{2}$ point Greek and Roman type. Mostly printed by Charles Whittingham, they were bound in calico with a printed label on the spine. This seems to have been the first use of publishers' cloth bindings in England.

On 16 June, died John Ballantyne, printer and bookseller of Edinburgh. He and his elder brother James printed Sir Walter Scott's *Minstrelsy of the Scottish Border* (1802–03).

On 11 May, died George Howe, proprietor of the *Sydney Gazette*. (*See* 1803.)

The first printing at Surat, Bombay Presidency, was the New Testament in Gujarati, printed by Baptist missionaries working for the Bombay Auxiliary of the British and Foreign Bible Society.

Ambroise Firmin-Didot established on the island of Chios the first press in what is now the kingdom of Greece.

1822

Publication of the first volume of Joseph Basile Bernard van Praet, *Catalogue des livres imprimés sur vélin de la Bibliothèque du Roi*. Paris: De Bure Frères. The six volumes were completed in 1828.

The printer William Savage (1770–1843) published *Practical Hints on Decorative Printing, with illustrations engraved on Wood and printed in Colours at the Type Press*. (*See also* 1841.)

Edward Cowper completed two steam-driven printing presses for *The Morning Herald*.

The Albion hand press was invented by R. W. Cope about 1822, and may have been so named as a counterblast to the American Columbian press, introduced into England in 1817. Both presses were used commercially well into the twentieth century. Several private presses in the United Kingdom, among them the Kelmscott, Doves, and Ashendene presses, employed the Albion.

British patent granted to William Church of Vermont, U.S.A., for what was the earliest patented composing machine—part of an invention of Church which embodied an improved printing press, casting machine and composing machine.

First printing at Honolulu by missionaries who landed there in 1820. On 7 January, 1822, King Liholiho pulled the first sheet printed in the islands.

1823

At Bonn, August Wilhelm Schlegel set up the first press in Germany for printing Indian books, and issued the *Bhagavad Gita*.

First issue of the *Messager des Sciences et des Arts*, published at Ghent by the Société des Beaux Arts et des Lettres, etc. By 1880, fifty-four volumes had been issued containing many very interesting articles on the history of printing. It ceased publication in 1896.

The French printer Henri Didot invented a type-casting machine called the 'Polymatype', which he brought out around 1819. In 1823 Louis John Pouché acquired the patent rights for the United Kingdom, but could not market the machine in England owing to the opposition of the type-founders. 'English trades-unionism,' wrote J. R.

Johnson (*Journal of the Society of Arts*, 21 March, 1873), 'deemed the introduction of machinery hostile to its interests.'

First issue of the first edition of Charles Lamb, *Essays of Elia*. London: Taylor and Hessey. In the first issue the publishers' address is given as 'Fleet Street' only.

The first number of the well-known medical periodical *The Lancet* appeared under the date Sunday, 5 October. It was published by George Churchill at 423 Strand, London.

Presentation to the British Museum by George IV of the Royal Library, much of which had been assembled by George III.

The Bannatyne Club founded by David Laing and others for printing early Scottish writings.

1824

At Paris, Jean-François Champollion le Jeune (1790–1832) published his *Précis du système hiéroglyphique des anciens égyptiens* (two volumes, Vol. II plates).

John Johnson, master printer, published his treatise *Typographia; or the Printers' Instructor*, in two volumes. It was printed in four sizes: 32mo, 16mo, 8vo and royal 8vo—the last, known as 'Roxburghe copies', had an additional engraved title-page to each volume.

David Napier (1785–1873) built his 'Nay Peer' perfecting press, a drawing of which, together with a detailed description, is to be found in Hansard's *Typographia* (1825). The first was installed in the printing office of T. C. Hansard. Napier constructed various presses, one of which, a cylinder machine resembling that of Applegath and Cowper, was bought by an American publisher and became the first cylinder press employed in the U.S.

Printing began in Bolivia after General Santa Cruz had endowed the University of Chuquisaca with a printing press.

The Australian, the second newspaper printed at Sydney, N.S.W., was begun under the editorship of Ralph Wardell.

The *Singapore Chronicle* founded by F. J. Bernard.

1825

Karl Christoph Traugott Tauchnitz, publisher, printer, and type-founder (1761–1836), who started the firm of that name at Leipzig in 1797, issued the only specimen of types from his foundry. His nephew Baron Christian Bernhard, was responsible for the celebrated 'Collection of English Authors' published under his imprint. (*See* 1841.)

Founding, at Leipzig, of the Börsenverein der deutschen Buchhändler, which soon became an extremely efficient organisation embracing publishers, wholesalers and retailers of books throughout the German-speaking world.

In Paris, Henri Brun, a former foreman of the printing firm of Jules Didot, published his *Manuel pratique et abrégé de la typographie française* which was entirely composed by himself and his two sons. A pirated edition was published at Brussels in 1826.

Henri Fournier published at Paris the first edition of his *Traité de la Typographie*, reprinted at Brussels the following year. A second, revised, edition was published at Tours in 1854, and a third edition printed by Mame at Tours in 1870. Comparison of the three editions shows the changing typographical fashions in France during half a century.

First edition of *Typographia* by Thomas Curson Hansard. A second edition was published 1869. His son, who bore the same Christian names, wrote the article on printing and type-founding in the 7th edition of the *Encyclopædia Britannica*, 1841. Thomas Curson Hansard the Elder was the son of Luke Hansard, for many years printer to the House of Commons.

First edition, Oxford, of *A Typographical Gazetteer Attempted*, by the Rev. Henry Cotton. A second, augmented, edition appeared in 1831, and a third edition in 1852. The book speedily became a standard work of reference.

The first book cloth, specifically so called, was marketed by Archibald Leighton, and was made from white calico suitably glazed and dyed. In 1821 Pickering had used red cloth for some of his publications, but this was probably made especially for him.

John and Christopher Phipps granted an English patent for what is thought to be the first 'dandy-roll' for watermarking paper.

The *Diary of Samuel Pepys* was printed for the first time under the editorship of Lord Braybrooke. The manuscript diary, bequeathed by Pepys to Magdalene College, Cambridge, was deciphered from the author's shorthand by Mr. John Smith. The original printed edition consisted of two volumes only, but later editions contain much additional material.

The first regular newspaper in Russia—*Severnaya Pchela*, founded at St. Petersburg by Gretsch and Bulgarin.

At Smyrna, the *Spectateur de l'Orient* was founded by Alexander Blocque, the real founder of journalism in Turkey. Later, as the *Courrier de Smirne* it had a considerable influence during the Greek insurrection of 1825–28. In 1831, Blocque founded at Constantinople the *Moniteur Ottoman*, official journal of the Sublime Porte, which in 1832 appeared in a Turkish edition, *Taguimi Vagai*.

1826

Publication began of Ludwig Hain's *Repertorium Bibliographicum ad annum 1500*. It was completed, in four volumes in 1838, and published at Stuttgart and Tübingen. In this work, 16,299 incunabula are arranged alphabetically by authors. A supplement in three volumes by Walter Copinger was published 1895–1902, correcting 7,000 items and describing 6,619 additional incunabula. The final volume, Konrad Burger's *Printers and Publishers of the 15th century*, forms an index to the supplement.

First edition of the *Gedichte* of Friedrich Hölderlin (1770–1843). Stuttgart and Tübingen: Cotta. His collected works were first published by Cotta in two volumes, 1846.

The Paris newspaper *Le Figaro* founded. It ran until 1833 and was revived by Villemessant in 1854.

The famous French novelist, Honoré de Balzac, set up as a printer in association with A. Barbier on 12 April, at 17 rue des Marais-Saint-Germain (now rue Visconti), Paris. He abandoned the venture in 1828.

Louis Christophe Hachette (1800–64), a printer at Algiers, came to Paris and took over the Librairie Brédif.

Charles Knight and his associates founded the Society for the Diffusion of Useful Knowledge.

On 26 November, died John Nichols, F.S.A., printer and editor for many years of the *Gentleman's Magazine*, as well as the compiler of *Literary Anecdotes of the Eighteenth Century*.

Thomas MacKellar (b. New York, 12 August, 1812) entered the printing office of Harper Bros. as an apprentice. In 1833, he moved to Philadelphia and became foreman in the stereotyping department of L. Johnson & Co's type-foundry. In 1845 he was made a partner in the firm.

Publication of *The Malacca Observer and Chinese Chronicle*, the first English newspaper printed at Malacca. It ceased in 1829.

1827

Foundation of the Frankfurt foundry of Dresler & Rost-Fingerlin.

First edition of Manzoni's classic *I Promessi Sposi*. Milan, three volumes. Although bearing dates 1825, 1826, the work was actually published in 1827. Another edition appeared the same year at Leghorn.

At Paris Joseph-Marie Quérard (1796–1865) published the first volume of his *La France littéraire*, completed in 1839 in twelve volumes. In Vol. XI, under the pseudonym of Jozon d'Erquar, an anagram of his real name, Quérard wrote his autobiography under the title of *Un martyr de la bibliographie*.

In October, the Printers' Pension Society of London established.
The Times installed a new four-cylinder press constructed by their engineers Cowper and Applegath, which gave 4,000 to 5,000 impressions per hour on one side of the paper only. This type of press continued in use at *The Times* until 1848.

Publication of the first volume of Audubon's *Birds of America*, completed in four volumes, elephant folio, in 1838 (with 435 colour plates).

In December, James Cameron of the London Missionary Society printed a sheet containing part of *Genesis* in the Malagasy language at Antananarivo, capital of Madagascar.

1828

At Leipzig, Anton Philipp Reclam inaugurated the 'Literarische Museum' from which resulted the foundation of the publishing firm of Philipp Reclam junior.

Balzac printed a specimen book of the Laurent & De Berny foundry, one of his last efforts as a printer. It is historically interesting in that it shows examples of the typographical material used by the general run of printers at that time. It is noticeably rich in ornamental borders and vignettes. Jean François Laurent's partnership with Lucien Charles Alexandre De Berny (1809–

81) lasted for twenty years. In 1840, De Berny, who now spelt his name Deberny, became sole proprietor. In 1877, he went into partnership with Charles Tuleu, who, on Deberny's death carried on the business as Deberny et Cie., a trade name which lasted until 1914.

At Paris, a French edition of Goethe's *Faust* was published with lithographs by Eugène Delacroix, a landmark in the history of Romantic book-illustration.

David Napier invented 'tumbler grippers'—an improvement on the Cowper and Applegath perfectors. The grippers seized the sheet at the feedboard, held it during the first impression, and opened to release it when the grippers in the second cylinder came into action. After the second impression the grippers released the sheet, which was conveyed by tapes to the 'taker-off'.

On 28 November, died Miller Ritchie, sometimes called 'the father of English fine printing'. His skill in printing was not equalled by business ability; his business failed and he was succeeded by Thomas Bulmer.

On 29 October, died Luke Hansard (b. 1752), since 1774 Printer to the House of Commons.

On 8 November, died Thomas Bewick, the wood engraver. He was born 12 August, 1753 at Cherry Burn, in the parish of Ovingham, Northumberland. (*See* 1790, 1797.)

First publication, in New York, of Noah Webster's *An American Dictionary of the English Language*, which became the standard American dictionary. Printed by Hezekiah Howe in New Haven.

The first Bulgarian press was established at Samokov by Nikola Karastojanow. He set it up secretly in a cellar, since the Turkish government had forbidden the printing of books under penalty of death.

1829

In France, Louis Braille (1809–52), himself blind, had been experimenting with the raised dot system for printing for the blind from about 1825. In this year he published in Paris his *Procédé pour écrire au moyen des points*, the first successful system for enabling the blind to read. The only known copy of the original is in the library of the Association Valentin Hauy in Paris. Hauy (*see* 1784) was the founder in 1785 of the first school for the blind. Braille, first used at the Institution for the Young Blind in Paris, superseded his method. It became the standard system for the blind in England in 1868.

Jean-Baptiste Genoux (d. 1835) took out a patent dated 26 June, 1829, for his process of stereotyping with clay, paper and plaster of Paris, a method which became known as 'stéréotypie genouxienne'.

The use of papier-mâché instead of plaster of Paris for moulding stereotype plates introduced in Lyons. A British patent was taken out in 1839.

Despite the opposition of the pressmen to the introduction of mechanical presses, five Cowper machines were installed at the Imprimerie Royale in Paris.

On 29 December, Ambroise Firmin Didot was appointed 'Imprimeur du Roi', the last time this title was granted in France.

At Paris the newspaper *Le Temps* was founded.

Honoré Daumier (1808–79) issued his first lithographs.

James Conner, a foreman at the Boston Type Founders Co., entered the type-making industry with a series of light-face romans and italics designed and cut by David Bruce junior who subsequently invented a type-casting machine (1838). The Conner type-foundry continued, managed by sons and grandsons, until 1892, when it was sold to the American Type Founders Co.

1830

A University printing house was founded at Würzburg by Friedrich Ernst Thein. Taken over by Ludwig Stürtz in 1869, it developed into the great printing firm of Stürtz A.G.

At Paris, appeared Charles Nodier, *Histoire du roi de Bohême et de ses sept Châteaux*, a milestone in the history of French book production during the nineteenth century; for the first time the vignette was incorporated in the text in an intimate fashion. But this 'romantic folly' is said to have ruined the publishers, the brothers Delangle.

The first comic periodical in France—*La Caricature*—was published by Charles Philipon, who, in 1832, began the famous *Charivari*, which formed the model upon which was based *Punch, or the London Charivari*, begun in 1841.

E. Duverger became director of the Imprimerie Royale, Paris, on 29 July.

In Sweden, Lars Johan Hierta founded the Stockholm newspaper *Aftonbladet*.

1831

The Imprenta de Cabrerizo, Valencia, issued a type specimen book.

Thomas De La Rue (1793–1866) printed a New Testament in gold on porcelain paper for presentation to William IV.

Samuel Bagster issued his *Biblia Sacra Polyglotta*, edited by Samuel Lee (1783–1852), Regius Professor of Hebrew at Cambridge. The Old and New Testaments were given in eight languages, and this was the most inclusive Polyglot Bible since the London Polyglot of 1655–57 (*q.v.*). Bagster had printed a Polyglot Bible in 1822, but the sheets were destroyed by fire.

Firm of Henry G. Bohn established at 4 York Street, Covent Garden, London.

On 26 February, died John Bell, founder of *Bell's Weekly Messenger* and other periodicals. (*See also* 1796.)

On 15 March, died Thomas Payne the younger (b. 1752) of the firm of Payne and Foss, known as the 'father of the booksellers'.

On 25 August, died Andrew Strahan, printer to the King, and son of William Strahan. (*See* 1739.)

1832

The first 'Baedeker' was published at Coblenz. It was a guide to the Rhineland.

Gustave Doré, one of the greatest book illustrators of the nineteenth century born at Strassburg. Among the many works which he illustrated were the Bible, Balzac's *Contes drôlatiques*, *Don Quixote*, Dante's *Divine Comedy*, and La Fontaine's *Fables*. He died in Paris 1883.

Felice Le Monnier founded the Florence firm of that name. Le Monnier left Paris, where he had been a compositor at *Le Temps*, in 1831 to try his fortune abroad. He obtained employment with the Borghi printing firm at Florence and, in 1832, took over the business himself. In 1865 Le Monnier retired and ceded his business to a society, the Casa Editrice Successori Le Monnier. He died at Florence 1884.

Antoine-Isaac Silvestre de Sacy (1758–1838) appointed Inspector of Oriental Types at the Imprimerie Royale, Paris.

The first stamping press for gold blocking on binder's cloth was introduced by Thomas De La Rue.

In his specimen of 1832, the English typefounder Vincent Figgins first used the word 'sans serif' to describe a type-face which William Caslon IV had already shown in 1816 under the label 'Egyptian'.

William Savage (1770–1843) published his *Preparation of Printing Ink*, the first practical treatise on the subject.

On 1 April, appeared, under the auspices of the Society for the Diffusion of Useful Knowledge, the first number of the *Penny Magazine*, founded by Charles Knight and one of the many excellent educational ventures of that enterprising publisher. It was printed by William Clowes on Applegath & Cowper presses, and was one of the first British periodicals to make use of woodcuts on a large scale.

Between 1832 and 1837 were published the five volumes of John Gould's *The Birds of Europe*, containing 449 coloured plates. His *Birds of Great Britain* came out between 1862 and 1873. Gould's splendid paintings were transferred to the lithographic stone by W. Hart and H. Richter.

William and Robert Chambers published the first number of *Chambers's Edinburgh Journal*.

The first stitching machine was built by Philip Watt.

On 7 April, died of the cholera in Paris (aged 64) John M'Creery, a noted printer of Tooks Court, London, who while still in business in Liverpool, had printed a poem called *The Press* in 1803. He published the second part in London in 1827.

1833

Johann August Genzsch (b. 1800) founded at Hamburg a Schrift-Schneiderei, Schrift- und Stereotypen-Giesserei, which grew into the famous firm of Genzsch & Heyse, printers and type-founders.

Publication of the first number of the German *Pfennigmagazin* by Bossange and later (until 1855) by Brockhaus.

At Paris this year, appeared the highly successful *Magasin Pittoresque*, founded and published by La Chevardière. Its chief engravers after its second year were the Englishmen Andrew and Best, and the French artist Leloir, a trio of artists who worked both on boxwood and on copper in the style of wood engraving. It was the French counterpart of Charles Knight's *Penny Magazine*, both being concerned with the spread of education among the working classes.

Death of James Ballantyne (b. Kelso 1772). He opened a printing office at Kelso in 1796 and

from there he published the *Kelso Mail*. He later moved to Edinburgh and established The Border Press. His first book was Scott's *Minstrelsy of the Scottish Border*; from that time he printed all Scott's work. (*See* 1821.)

On 11 September, died the eminent London printer, Thomas Bensley.

George Palmer Putnam (b. Brunswick, Maine, 1814), founder of the American publishing firm of that name, entered the firm of Wiley and Long as a partner, the firm then becoming Wiley & Putnam. The house of G. P. Putnam's Sons remained in the hands of the founder's family until the 1930s.

Death of Robert Hoe. He was succeeded as head of the firm by his son Richard March Hoe.

1834

At Brunswick, J. H. Meyer founded the *Journal für Buchdruckerkunst, Schriftgiesserei und die verwandten Fächer*, which, well edited and printed, met with deserved success and ran until 1919. After 1880 it was published at Hamburg.

Appearance of the first regular weekly periodicals for the book trade. The *Börsenblatt für den deutschen Buchhandel* first appeared on 3 January, and the Dutch *Nieuwsblad voor de boekhandel* on 8 January.

Louis Braille, a pupil and later professor of the Institution Nationale des Jeunes Aveugles, Paris, perfected his system for enabling the blind to read by means of varying combinations of six embossed dots within a rectangle. There are sixty-three possible combinations of these dots, and those not used to form the letters of the alphabet are used for punctuation and contractions. This system is the one now universally used. (*See* 1829.)

From the lithographic works of Émile Simon Fils at Strassburg came the *Spécimens des Ecritures Modernes et Anciennes* (three parts, 1834–35) by the French artist, lithographer and calligrapher Jean Midolle. There are 120 finely executed plates.

On 16 September, died William Blackwood (b. 1776), the eminent bookseller and publisher of Edinburgh.

John Martin brought out a *Bibliographical Catalogue of Books privately printed*.

Publication of Part I (four volumes) of *The Bibliographer's Manual* by William Thomas Lowndes.

Opening, on 30 April, of the Pitt Press, Cambridge, by the Marquess of Camden.

Death of Rudolf Ackermann (b. 1764 at Stolberg in Saxony). Fine-art publisher and bookseller, he founded in 1809 the very successful 'Repository of the Arts . . .' which appeared regularly until 1828 (forty volumes). With his death, aquatint, which he used extensively for his publications, began to decay as a process of book illustration and was succeeded by an era of etching. (*See also* 1809.)

Died in London, George Clymer, born in Pennsylvania, descendant of a Swiss family, in 1750. About 1813 he invented the hand press known as the Columbian, which was introduced into England in 1817, manufactured by Messrs. Clymer & Dixon at 10 Finsbury Street, Finsbury Square, London. In this press the pressure was obtained not by a screw, but by a set of levers connected with a counterweight in the form of a cast iron American eagle.

The first regular press was set up at Monterey, California, by Agustín Vicente Zamorano.

Ramón Abreu established a press managed by Jesús María Baca, in Santa Fé, New Mexico.

1835

The French firm of Paulin published Le Sage, *Gil Blas*, with 600 wood engravings by Jean Gigoux, in which for the first time in the history of the 'Romantic' book the illustrations were set within the text, whereas previously they had appeared either as full page plates or as chapter headings and tail pieces.

On 23 October, George Baxter was granted a patent for reproducing paintings in colour by means of printing in letterpress from a number of relief blocks on a key printed from a metal plate or lithographic stone. The first Baxter prints had appeared the previous year as title-page vignettes in Vols. 1 and 2 of Mudie's *Feathered Tribes of the British Islands* and as a frontispiece to Mudie's *The Natural History of Birds*.

In this year appeared for the first time the *Railway Magazine*, later entitled the *Railway Journal*. It contained engraved plates and detailed maps of a very high standard of craftsmanship.

On 17 February, printing began of the first book printed in New Zealand. This was a translation into Maori of the *Epistle of St. Paul to the Philippians and the Ephesians*. The printer was the missionary William Colenso (1811–99), who had previously been with the printing firm of Richard Watts & Son, printers to the British and Foreign Bible Society and to the Church Missionary Society. In 1830, the Rev. William Yate had printed a 6-page catechism, of which only two copies are now known, but it was a very poor and amateurish piece of work, and Colenso can fairly be described as the first printer in New Zealand. (*See* 1836.)

1836

Establishment at Paris of the Fonderie Générale, which incorporated Firmin Didot frères, Jules Didot, Laboulaye frères and other foundries. Later it was amalgamated with Peignot et Fils and in 1923 the style of the firm was altered to Deberny & Peignot.

At Paris, Emile de Girardin founded *La Presse*.

On 24 April, at Le Mesnil sur Estrée died Firmin Didot, greatest of this celebrated family of French printers. In 1827 he handed over his business to his sons and devoted his time to public affairs as Deputy for Nogent-le-Rotrou.

George Routledge (1812–88), founder of the famous publishing firm of that name, began business as a retail bookseller at 11 Ryder's Court, Leicester Square, London, and began publishing the same year, his first book being *Beauties of Gilsland* by William Steele (1836).

In April, appeared the first part of Charles Dickens's *Pickwick Papers*. It was completed in twenty shilling parts before being issued in bound form in 1837.

John Adamson published his *Bibliotheca Lusitana* which contains notices on early Portuguese printers. Newcastle-on-Tyne: T. & J. Hodgson (privately printed).

In the United States, Isaac Adams brought out an improved version of the power-driven bed-and-platen press invented by him in 1830. During the next twenty years or so some 90 per cent of good American book printing was done on Adams presses.

Joel Munsell (1808–80), American printer, publisher and bookseller, started in business at Albany, New York. He later specialised in scholarly works and printed for historical and bibliographical societies. In 1870 he published *Bibliotheca Munselliana*, listing and describing more than 2,000 books which he had printed.

The first press in Iowa established at Dubuque.

On 11 May, appeared the first issue of the *Dubuque Visitor*.

The American publishing firm of J. B. Lippincott Company founded by Joshua Ballinger Lippincott.

The first piece of printing in English done in New Zealand was the 8-page *Report of the Formation and Establishment of the New Zealand Temperance Society*, printed by William Colenso. (*See* 1835.)

1837

Johann Christian Bauer (1802–67) founded his type-foundry at Frankfurt-am-Main, which was opened on 25 July. In 1859 he brought out a type-casting machine.

Founding, at Stuttgart, of the Ferdinand Enke Verlagsbuchhandlung.

Unveiling at Mainz of Thorwaldsen's monument to the memory of Gutenberg.

At Paris was published *Nouveau manuel complet de l'imprimeur en taille-douce* by MM. Berthiaud & Boitard. This very explicit manual on the art of copperplate engraving is of considerable interest by reason of its drawings of presses and equipment.

George Crapelet (1789–1842) published the first volume of his *Etudes pratiques et littéraires sur la typographie*. He died before the contemplated second volume was finished. His daughter married Charles-Auguste Lahure (1809–69), who decided to follow the career of his father-in-law and became a printer. The firm still exists.

Eugène Renduel established his business at 6 rue Christine, Paris, and became the publisher of Victor Hugo, Saint-Beuve, Théophile Gautier, Alfred de Vigny, and Charles Nodier among others.

Chapman & Hall published the *Pictorial Album or Cabinet of Paintings* with illustrations by Baxter (title vignette and 10 full-page plates). Burch describes it as 'the first book of a popular character illustrated by pictures printed in colours that was published in England'. Baxter's process employed the colouring of an impression from an outline or key block (copper, steel, zinc or even litho stone) by successive impressions from colour blocks of wood or metal, one for each tint used.

In September the firm of Sampson Low published the first number of *The Publishers' Circular*. In 1959 the title was changed to *British Books*.

Publication in Philadelphia of Thomas F. Adams,

Typographia; or, the Printer's Instructor, which contains some interesting illustrations of early iron presses. It was reprinted, 1845. The text is mostly taken, without acknowledgment, from Johnson and from Hansard.

In Liberia, a Mission Press (American) began to print at Fair Hope, Cape Palmas.

1838

Issued in thirty parts, L. Curmer's Paris edition of *Paul et Virginie & La Chaumière Indienne*, by J. H. Bernardin de Saint Pierre, is considered one of the finest illustrated books of the Romantic period. It contains 450 vignettes in the text engraved on wood after Johannot, Meissonnier, Isabey, Steinheil, Paul Huet, and others, as well as 29 plates engraved on wood and seven portraits engraved on steel. The work in 10,000 copies is said to have cost the publisher over 233,000 francs. The first printing of *Paul et Virginie* was in 1787, in *Études de la Nature*. This work first appeared in 1784, in three volumes. Later editions were in five and eight volumes, of which Vol. 4 contained *Paul et Virginie*.

First number issued of *Annales de la Typographie française et étrangère, par M. Alkan aîné et plusieurs autres anciens typographes de Paris*.

Eugène Burnouf (1801–52) appointed Inspector of Oriental Types at the Imprimerie Royale, Paris, on the death of Silvestre de Sacy. (*See* 1832.)

Charles Knight (1791–1873) patented a colour-printing process which he called 'Patent Illuminated Printing'. The process was used in two of Knight's educational publications—*Old England*, published in ninety-six parts 1844–45, and *Old England's Worthies*, 1847.

Publication of Charles H. Timperley's *The Printer's Manual*.

On 29 June, an edition of the *Sun* newspaper was printed in gold by William Clowes and Sons in honour of Queen Victoria's coronation.

Founding of the Camden Society for the printing of unpublished material and the reprinting of rare works on the 'civil, ecclesiastical or literary history of the United Kingdom'. In 1897 it was affiliated to the Royal Historical Society.

Excise duty on paper reduced from 3d to 1½d per lb. It was not abolished until 1861.

The first successful mechanical type-casting machine was patented 17 March by David Bruce junior of New York. He sold the patent to his uncle who had the machine built by a locksmith named Brandt, who later went to Europe and marketed the design as the Brandt Typecasting Machine.

On 27 October, George Arden and Thomas Strode printed at Melbourne the *Port Phillip Gazette* on an old press with type bought at 2d. a lb.

1839

First edition of *La Chartreuse de Parme* by Marie-Henri Beyle, called Stendhal (1783–1842). Paris: Ambroise Dupont.

First edition of Charles H. Timperley's *Encyclopædia of Literary and Typographical Anecdote*, published by Henry G. Bohn. A second edition came out in 1842.

Publication of Robert Hunt, *The Art of Photography*; the first manual on the subject in English.

In October, George Bradshaw of Manchester issued his first series of railway time-tables.

At Edinburgh, Peter Lecount, *A Practical Treatise on Railways*. The first railway treatise, by a civil engineer on the staff of the London & Birmingham Railway.

Edwin O. Hall, a missionary printer, visited Idaho to aid in the conversion of the Indians of the Pacific North-West, and in particular the Nez-Percé tribe. He had been sent from Honolulu by the native Christian women of Hawaii, and brought with him a press on which he printed in May 1839 an 8-page book called *Nez-Percés First Book*, with the imprint 'Clear Water: Mission Press'.

The American publishing firm of Dodd, Mead & Co. Inc., founded in New York by Moses Woodruff Dodd and John S. Taylor.

In this year a Protestant Missionary Press was established at Bangkok, Siam. The Catholics set up a press there in 1849.

The process of electrotyping was invented, independently of one another, by H. von Jacobi of St. Petersburg, Thomas Spencer of Liverpool and C. J. Jordan of London (*see Athenæum*, 1839, p. 334).

1840

To celebrate 400 years of printing, no fewer than 143 memorial volumes were published. Among the outstanding works called into being by this

KCP

quatercentenary were Karl Falkenstein, *Geschichte der Buchdruckerkunst* (Leipzig: Teubner) and Heinrich Meyer, *Gutenberg Album* (Brunswick: H. Meyer) as well as the book by Duverger mentioned below.

The Saxon weaver, Friedrich Gottlob Keller, took out a German patent for a wood-grinding machine. It was acquired in 1846 by the papermaker Heinrich Völter, and marked the beginning of wood pulp production for paper-making on a commercial scale.

L. E. Mayer published at Augsburg *Die Buchdruckerskunst in Augsburg bei ihrem Entstehen*. It contains a chronological list of Augsburg printers from 1468 to 1840.

Two firms established by nephews of Frederic König, inventor of the mechanical press. These were (*a*) the firm of Frederic Helbig (who was partnered by Leo Muller), founded at Mödling, near Vienna; (*b*) that of Louis Sander, founded at Augsburg. The latter was taken over, four years later, by Charles Reichenbach and Charles Buz, and eventually became the present M.A.N. (Maschinenfabrik Augsburg–Nürnberg).

Publication of the first volume of Carl Joseph Meyer *Grosse Konversation Lexicon*, completed in forty-four volumes in 1852.

In the second edition of Manzoni, *I Promessi Sposi*, published by Raedelli at Milan, the anonymous lithographs of the first edition (1825–26) were replaced by 400 beautiful wood engravings by Francesco Gonin. In 1951 the Officina Bodoni at Verona reprinted an English translation of this work for the Limited Editions Club, illustrated with Gonin's wood engravings recut by Bruno Bramanti.

Gustav Silbermann (1801–76), printer at Strassburg, published his *Album Typographique*, showing specimens of the founts provided by all the principal French foundries.

Publication in Paris of *Histoire de l'Invention de l'Imprimerie par les Monuments*, by E. Duverger. 150 copies were printed in folio and a second edition, quarto, was limited to 850 copies. It contains an illustration of the Stanhope press as modified by Didot as well as representations of early type-founding apparatus. 'De l'imprimerie, rue de Verneuil'.

Etienne Robert Gaubert patented in England a type-distributing machine called the Gérotype.

Patent granted on 13 March, to James Young and Adrian Delcambre for their composing machine. This is the first composing machine known to have been used in a printing office, since there is no evidence that William Church's machine (*see* 1822) was ever built. (*See* 1842.)

In September, appeared *The Compositors' Chronicle*, the first printing-trade periodical published in Britain. The price was 2d.

On 1 May, William Blades (1824–1890) was apprenticed to his father, Joseph Blades, of the firm of Blades & East, printers, at 11 Abchurch Lane, London. After his seven years' apprenticeship he was admitted as partner in the firm, the name of which was changed to Blades, East and Blades. (*See also* 1861, 1877, 1895.)

The Swede, C. A. Holm, took out an English patent for his platen press known as the Scandinavia Press.

Samuel Nelson Dickinson, a Boston printer, started the Dickinson Type Foundry and issued his first specimen book in 1842. At his death in 1848 the business was bought by Phelps & Dalton, and in 1892 it was merged with the American Type Founders Co.

New Zealand's first newspaper, the *New Zealand Gazette and Britannia Spectator* was printed at Wellington by Samuel Revans, the first issue appearing on 18 April, 1840. It preceded by two months *The New Zealand Advertiser and Bay of Islands Gazette*, the first number of which appeared at Kororareka on 15 June, 1840.

Printing first introduced into the Seychelles in the island of Mahé by a French settler from Mauritius named Thomy Mamin. The first product of his press was a weekly newspaper, *Le Feuilleton des Séchelles*, the first issue of which appeared on 10 January, 1840. No copy has apparently survived.

1841

The Tauchnitz 'Collection of British and American Authors' begun at Leipzig by Christian Bernhard Tauchnitz, son of the founder of the firm. (*See* 1792.)

First edition of William Savage, *A Dictionary of the Art of Printing*. Although the work is alphabetically arranged, it is really more of an encyclopaedia than a dictionary, some of the articles being very extensive. (A reprint was published in 1966 by the Gregg Press.)

Samuel Bagster published the *English Hexapla*, containing six English versions of the New Testament; namely those of Wyclif (1380), Tyndale

(1534), Cranmer (1539), the Geneva version (1557), the Anglo-Rhemish (1582), and the Authorised Version (1611). (*See also* 1817, 1821 and 1831.)

A. Parkes granted a patent for a process for electro-depositing of matrices.

The first number of *Punch* appeared.

Joseph Cundall (1818–95) acquired a publishing business in Old Bond Street, London, where he issued a number of very charming illustrated children's books, as well as general picture books and gift books. The illustrations were mainly executed by chromolithography or by coloured wood blocks.

A press was established at Pietermaritzburg, Natal, by the American Board of Commissioners for Foreign Missions.

1842

Between 1842 and 1852, the Imprimerie Nationale, Paris, assembled a collection of punches for Egyptian hieroglyphics. They were cut by Delafond (from designs by J.-J. Dubois) and Ramé fils (from designs by Eugène Devéria).

First issue of the *Illustrated London News*, the most outstanding of all the illustrated periodicals of its day, and still in existence. It was founded by Herbert Ingram.

A composing machine made by Henry Bessemer for Young and Delcambre was used for the London weeklies *The Family Herald* and *London Phalanx*. (*See* 1840.)

Joseph Zaehnsdorf from Budapest set up his own bindery in London.

The first 'Mudie's Lending Library' opened in London. Its founder was Charles Edward Mudie (1810–90) who set himself up not so much as an arbiter, but rather as a dictator of literary taste. The business closed down in 1937.

1843

H. Ternaux-Compans published in Paris *Notices sur les Imprimeries qui existent ou ont existé en Europe*. A supplement was issued in 1849, and *Nouvelles Additions* in 1860.

On 4 March, the French weekly, *L'Illustration*, was founded by V. Paulin, A. Joanne, E. Charton and M. Dubochet at 33 rue de Seine, Paris. In June 1933 its new and up-to-date printing works were opened at Bobigny, near Paris.

The London publishing firm of Macmillan founded by Daniel and Alexander Macmillan.

The American branch was founded in New York in 1869. (*See also* 1896.)

A small jobbing printer and stationer named George Watson bought a printing office in the Hatton Garden area of London. This was the origin of the present-day firm of Hazell, Watson & Viney Ltd.

Bradley Thomas Batsford opened a small second-hand bookshop from which grew the modern firm of B. T. Batsford Ltd., the first publications of which date from 1874.

1844

At Munich the painter Caspar Braun and the bookseller Friedrich Schneider founded the *Fliegende Blätter*.

Aloys Auer (1813–69), later Auer von Welsbach, director of the Imperial Printing-house at Vienna, issued a *Pater Noster (Das Vater Unser)* printed in 256 languages and dialects, with translation below, to enable missionaries to teach this prayer to the natives of whatever country they might visit. In 1849, the Imperial Printing-house issued another edition, this time in 608 tongues. It was about this time that Auer von Welsbach became interested in nature-printing and in 1854 he published *Die Entdeckung des Naturselbstdruckes*, the text of which was printed in German, English, French and Italian.

Death of Charles-Emmanuel Nodier (b. 1780) the erudite curator of the Bibliothèque de l'Arsenal, Paris, and the author of the charming *Contes de la Veillée* and *Contes fantastiques*. With the help of the bookseller Joseph Techener (1802–73) he founded the *Bulletin du Bibliophile*, which first appeared in 1834. (*See also* 1830.)

1844–45. Publication of Charles Knight's *Old England*, issued in ninety-six parts and containing 24 colour plates and no fewer than 2,488 numbered wood engravings. Knight was the first English publisher to offer printed colour plates to the popular market. The work was reissued twenty years later by James Sangster, with the colour plates printed by Leighton Brothers. (*See also* 1838.)

Charles Whittingham the Younger printed for Longman *The Diary of Lady Willoughby* set in Caslon's Old Face, which had been cast for an edition of Juvenal for Eton College which did not appear until 1845. This paved the way for the gradual reintroduction of old faces into English printing.

Formation in the United Kingdom of the National Typographical Association. It was dissolved a year or two later, and in 1848 the London branch reconstituted itself as an independent group, called the London Society of Compositors.

1845

The *Kreisblatt* of Frankenberg in Saxony was the first newspaper to use a mixture of rag and wood pulp.

The Imprimerie Royale, Paris, issued a magnificent folio specimen book under the auspices of King Louis Philippe, in which are to be found examples of all the founts contained in the royal printing office at the date of publication.

Napoléon Chaix (1807–65), who began his career as a compositor at Châteauroux, France, founded the firm which, from 1846 onwards, specialised in railway time-tables, and to which was successively added by his son and grandson all the elements of a successful firm of printers. The first Livret-Chaix appeared in September 1846.

The foundry of Thorowgood and Besley registered a type-face called Clarendon, an Egyptian with bracketed serifs drawn by Robert Besley and cut by Benjamin Fox. 'There had been types of similar design before Besley's,' writes T. B. Reed, 'which went under the name of Ionic.'

Completion, with the fifty-ninth part (twenty-eight volumes quarto), of the *Encyclopædia Metropolitana* begun in 1817. Of this work the *Quarterly Review* (CXIII) wrote: 'The plan was the proposal of the poet Coleridge, and it had at least enough of a poetical character to be eminently unpractical.' But if the plan was defective, many of the articles were excellent.

The Rev. C. H. O. Daniel, then a student at Oxford, and later Provost of Worcester College, set up a private press, the Daniel Press. He had begun printing as a boy, at Frome. (*See also* 1874 *and* 1877.)

1846

In 1846 Alphonse de Boissieu began to publish his *Inscriptions Antiques de Lyon* (completed in 1854), for which the Lyons printer Louis Benoit Perrin designed a fount of capitals, cut by Fugère and cast by Francisque Rey, and to which he gave the name of 'caractères augustaux'. They are shown to advantage on the title-page of the book, which bears the imprint 'Louis Perrin, Imprimeur à Lyon, M.D.CCCXLVI-M.D.CCCLIV.' To these capitals he later added (about 1855) a lower case, and issued an undated specimen sheet showing eleven sizes of capitals and five sizes of lower case (roman and italic), with the inscription 'Caractères augustaux Louis Perrin, imprimeur à Lyon, rue d'Amboise 6—Francisque Rey, graveur et fondeur à Lyon, Place Saint-Jean 4'. The lower case gave the signal for the revival of Elzévir types used with effect by Lemerre from 1869 onwards.

First edition of *Carmen*, by Prosper Mérimée (1803–70). Paris: Michel Lévy frères.

An Italian named Vanoni introduced into England a method of making moulds in papier-mâché which had been patented in 1844 by J. M. Kronheim. (For the method invented by Jean Baptiste Genoux of Lyons, *see* 1829.)

Death of the Rt. Hon. Thomas Grenville (b. 1755), a politician who, after retiring from office as First Lord of the Admiralty in 1807, devoted the rest of his life to building up his collection of books, amounting to more than 20,000 volumes, most of them in impeccable condition. The entire library was bequeathed to the British Museum.

On 21 January, appeared the first number of the *Daily News*, printed and published by Bradbury & Evans and at first under the editorship of Charles Dickens.

The Hoe four-cylinder rotary type revolving press, patented 1845, was erected for the first time in the printing house of the Philadelphia *Ledger*. This was the first true rotary newspaper printing press, invented by Richard Hoe (b. New York, 1812–d. Florence, 1886). In this machine the formes of type were securely affixed to a horizontal central cylinder by means of tapering column rules.

The American publishing house of Charles Scribner's Sons founded in New York by Charles Scribner and Isaac D. Baker as Baker and Scribner.

The Smithsonian Institution opened at Washington D.C., by Act of Congress for 'the increase and diffusion of knowledge among men'.

The first Californian newspaper, *The Californian*, in English and Spanish, was started at Monterey by means of the old Zamorano press. (*See* 1834.)

1847

On 31 March, Franz Otto Spamer (1829–86) founded a publishing house at Leipzig. Thirty years later, in 1877, he founded the well-known Spamersche Buchdruckerei.

The Paris newspaper *La Presse* installed a four cylinder Marinoni rotary press.

First edition of *Wuthering Heights*, by Emily Brontë. London: T. C. Newby.

Bernard Quaritch (1819–99) left the firm of Henry Bohn and with two or three of his colleagues set up a book agency in Great Russell Street. In the autumn of that year the agency came to an end owing to a dispute with Mr. Bohn, and Bernard Quaritch thereupon set up for himself at No. 16 Castle Street, Leicester Square.

James Lenox of New York bought the first 'Gutenberg Bible' to cross the Atlantic for the 'crazy price' of £500!

The first trade photographic periodical *The Daguerrotype* appeared at Boston.

1848

Publication of G. Melzi, *Dizionario di opere anonime e pseudonime di scittori italiani* (three volumes, 1848–69)—the Italian equivalent of the British 'Halkett and Laing'. Supplementary volumes were published by G. Passano in 1887 and by E. Rocco in 1888.

In London was published the *Manifest der Kommunistichen Partei*, with the imprint, 'Gedruckt in der Office der "Bildungs-Gesellschaft für Arbeiter" von J. E. Burghard. 46 Liverpool St., Bishopsgate'.

The Applegath vertical cylinder eight-feeder press used by *The Times*, which had taken out patents for the machine in 1846. Unlike the Hoe machine of the same period it had a vertical type cylinder instead of a horizontal one.

On 1 July, appeared the first number of a weekly periodical *The Standard of Freedom*, published by John Cassell. From this publication dates the foundation of the publishing business now known as Cassell & Company Ltd. (*See also* 1858.)

On 1 November, W. H. Smith's first railway bookstall was opened at Euston Station, London.

1849

The Swiss book trade formed the Schweizerischer Buchhändlerverein.

The first two volumes of Macaulay, *History of England*, were published, and the work became an immediate best-seller. London: Longman & Co. Five volumes, 1849–61.

Following the opening in the previous year of the first railway bookstall in England, George Routledge (1812–88) published the first number of Routledge's 'Railway Library' at one shilling per volume in 'fancy boards' and 1s 6d in cloth. The first title was Cooper, *The Pilot*, and the venture was so successful that by 1898 the firm had issued 1,300 titles in this series.

On 3 November appeared the first number of *Notes and Queries*, 'for an interchange of knowledge amongst literary men'. It was published by George Bell at 186 Fleet Street, London.

James M. Goodhue set up the first press in Minnesota at St. Paul and printed the *Minnesota Pioneer*, the first issue being dated 28 April, 1849.

Death of the great Japanese illustrator Hokusai.

1850

In France, Firmin Gillot (1820–72) took out patents for a process of line engraving on zinc, which he called *paniconographie*. Later the method became known, in France, as *gillotage*, after its inventor.

The publisher Plon of Paris published miniature editions of the *Fables* of La Fontaine and the works of Gresset, set in a 2⅔-point roman from the Laurent and Deberny foundry.

T. Nelson, founder of the firm of Nelson & Sons of Edinburgh, constructed a model stereo rotary which was exhibited at the Great Exhibition of 1851 and is now in the Science Museum at South Kensington.

1851

Foundation of the Prussian Staatsdruckerei, merged into the German Reichsdruckerei in 1879.

The Berlin punch-cutter Ferdinand Theinhardt cut for Richard Lepsius, the Egyptologist, a hieroglyphic script.

The wet collodion process of photography was introduced by Thomas Scott Archer, and for some time, until the introduction of the dry plate in 1871, it was the only medium for the making of line and half-tone negatives for reproduction purposes.

The first great international exhibition held in Hyde Park, London—the Exhibition of the Works of Industry of All Nations, the great success of which was due to the untiring enthusiasm of Prince Albert. Many new inventions in the printing industry were on show, including the Livesey folder, invented by James Livesey, son of the proprietor of the *Preston Guardian*. It proved an immediate success, being employed in a great number of newspaper offices.

Vassili Timms founded the *Russkii Khudozhestvennyi Listok* (Russian Artistic Gazette), the first illustrated news-periodical in Russia. It ran until 1862.

The American *Publishers' Circular* founded as *Norton's Literary Advertiser*. After several changes of name it became known in 1872 as *The Publishers' Weekly* after it had been merged with Frederick Leypoldt's *Weekly Trade Circular*.

In the United States, F. Otto Degener patented his successful Liberty Job Press.

On 11 January, was issued the first number of *The Lyttelton Times*, the first newspaper in Canterbury, N. Z. It bore the imprint of Ingram Shrimpton, Crown Yard Printing Office, Oxford, England, through whose enterprise it was published.

1852

Completion of the first edition, in thirty-seven volumes, of Meyer, *Neues Konversations-Lexicon*, begun in 1839.

Rose-Joseph Lemercier (1802–87) lithographer, together with the optician Noël Lerebours, published *Lithophotographie*, the first successful example of photolithographic printing.

In France, Philippe-Henri Plon (1806–72) appointed printer to the Emperor Napoleon III. The family Plon is of Danish origin, and in 1583 Jehan Ploën left Denmark and joined the first printing house established at Mons by his father-in-law Rutger Velpen.

Pierre Larousse (1817–75), lexicographer, founded his bookshop in Paris in association with Pierre Augustin Boyer (1821–96).

Death of the French book illustrator Tony Johannot (b. 1803), the famous vignettist of the Romantics. His output was prodigious. He was the brother of Alfred Johannot (1800–37), likewise a book illustrator.

First edition of Harriet Beecher Stowe, *Uncle Tom's Cabin*. Two volumes. Boston and Cleveland. This famous anti-slavery novel first appeared in serial form in the *National Era*, a Washington abolitionist newspaper.

The publishing firm of E. P. Dutton & Co. Inc. founded in Boston by Lemuel Ide and Edward P. Dutton under the name of Ide & Dutton.

The American firm of Houghton Mifflin Co. founded by Henry Oscar Houghton as the printing firm of H. O. Houghton & Company, the press being known as the Riverside Press.

1853

The Berlin foundry of C. G. Schoppe brought out their 'Centralschrift' which combined a roman upper half with a Fraktur lower half. Steinberg calls it, 'The most remarkable specimen of typographical folly ever thought of'.

First issue of the German magazine *Gartenlaube*, which combined popular instruction with light entertainment. By the early 1870s it had 400,000 subscribers, and the periodical lasted until 1916; and until 1938 as the *Neue Gartenlaube*.

Publication of Auguste Joseph Bernard, *De l'Origine et des Débuts de l'Imprimerie en Europe*. Two volumes. Paris. Printed by permission of the Emperor (Napoleon III) at the Imprimerie Impériale.

Two Frenchmen, MM. Coupier and Mellier invented the first successful process for making paper from straw.

In France, Renard published *Paris photographié*, illustrated with actual photographic prints. It constitutes, says Robert Brun (*Le Livre Francais*), a 'véritable incunable photographique'.

Death of Antoine-Augustin Renouard (b. 1765), a one-time manufacturer of gauze fabrics who became bookseller, printer, bibliophile, and bibliographer. He was the author of the *Annales de l'imprimerie des Alde* and *Annales de l'imprimerie des Estienne*.

The London publisher William Pickering issued *The Book of Common Prayer* based on John Day's *A Book of Christian Prayers* (*see* 1569), often called 'Queen Elizabeth's Prayer Book'. It was printed at the Chiswick Press by Charles Whittingham with illustrations from over a hundred wood blocks cut by Mary Byfield, mostly based on designs of Holbein, Dürer, Tory and other artists of that time. The type used was Caslon's Old Face.

Charles Watt and H. Burgess obtained a U.K.

patent for the manufacture and use of wood pulp for paper-making. They took out an American patent in 1854.

October saw the publication of the first issue of *The A.B.C. or Alphabetical Railway Guide* showing train services to and from London.

A type-setting machine was patented on 30 August by William H. Mitchell of New York, and an improvement on the patent was granted 16 May, 1854. Several of Mitchell's machines were used in printing the 1861 edition of *Appleton's Cyclopaedia*, but the machine was eventually abandoned for lack of a suitable mechanical type distributor. A description of the machine is given in Mitchell's *Type-setting by Machinery*, London, 1863.

1854

Publication of Heinrich Meyer, *Adressbuch der Buchdruckereien von Mittel-Europa*, etc., Braunschweig. This was the first printing-trades directory published in German.

Publication of Giacinto Amati, *Manuale di Bibliografia del Secolo XV . . . .* Milan.

Inauguration at Turin of UTET (Unione Tipografico-Editrice Torinese) with the financial and material help of the printing firm of Giuseppe Pomba and others.

The type known as 'Basle roman' first used in the Rev. William Calvert's volume of religious verse, *The Wife's Manual*, printed by the Chiswick Press. This face was cut for the Press by William Howard, who had a small foundry off Great Queen Street from 1838 to 1859. The type received its name because it was based on the type familiar in Basel-printed books of the first half of the sixteenth century.

Paul Pretsch of Vienna (1803–73) took out a British patent for the production of 'copper and other printing plates' for the first half-tone process. The first commercial use of half-tone was a print by Pretsch and de la Rue of 'Scene in Gaeta after the explosion'. Pretsch formed the Photo-Galvanographic Company to commercialise his method of producing intaglio printing surfaces, but the enterprise failed, and Pretsch returned to Vienna in 1863.

The publishing firm of Ward & Lock established at 158 Fleet Street, London by Ebenezer Ward and George Lock.

Printing began in Nebraska with the issue at Bellevue on 15 November, 1854, of the *Nebraska*

Palladium newspaper (originally printed from July to beginning of November, 1854 in Iowa).

1855

Richard Lepsius published his *Das allgemeine linguistische Alphabet*, in which he propounded a phonetic alphabet for scientific purposes, a fount of which was cut at Berlin by Theinhardt. The book had a wide circulation, and an English edition was printed at Berlin for London the same year.

Alfred Firmin-Didot (1828–1913) took over the firm and managed it for thirty-seven years (1855–92). He published, *inter alia*, *L'Ornement polychrome* and *Le Costume Historique* for which he set up a special press room for chromolithographs. He gave a great impetus to the celebrated commercial directory, the *Didot-Bottin*. His sons René and Maurice were taken into partnership.

The repeal of the Newspaper Stamp Act caused an immediate increase in the number of new daily papers. In June the *Manchester Guardian*, previously a weekly, became a daily paper. This year also saw the appearance of the *Liverpool Post*, *Sheffield Telegraph*, *Edinburgh Scotsman* and the *Birmingham Telegraph*, as well as the *Daily Telegraph* (29 June), originally called the *Daily Telegraph & Courier*. With No. 45 the word 'Courier' was dropped.

The Frenchman Louis Adolphe Poitevin (1819–82) granted a British patent for the process now known as collotype. He called it 'phototypie'.

The American type-founders MacKellar, Smiths & Jordan of Philadelphia issued the first U.S. printing journal—a quarterly called *The Typographic Advertiser*. Thomas MacKellar founded it to circulate type specimens, but it later developed into a general technical magazine.

At Brooklyn appeared the first edition of Walt Whitman, *Leaves of Grass*. Of this original edition, a slim quarto containing only twelve poems, about 800 copies were printed, at the author's expense, by Rome Brothers of Brooklyn, N.Y.

The Davis Oscillating Press, invented by Merwin Davis, a New York printer, and built by C. Potter Junior, was first demonstrated at the New York Exhibition of 1855. It was very successful and sold in large numbers up to the time of the outbreak of the Civil War.

The first type-foundry in Chicago—the Chicago Type Foundry—was established as a branch of C. T. White & Co., New York. In 1869 it became Marder, Luse & Co., and was for many years the leading type-foundry west of the Ohio. (*See* 1881.)

1856

First edition in book form of *Madame Bovary* by Gustave Flaubert (1821–80). It was serialised in the *Revue de Paris* between October and December 1856.

First edition of Owen Jones's Chromolithographed masterpiece, the *Grammar of Ornament*, with 100 folio plates drawn on stone by Francis Bedford. It embodied his research into the decorative styles of many countries and many eras.

The *Illustrated London News* became the first periodical in the world to include regular colour plates, which were printed by George Cargill Leighton, who had been apprenticed to George Baxter. (*See* 1842.)

About 1856, the present-day publishing firm of Chatto & Windus was founded by Andrew Chatto, who bought the business which had once belonged to John Camden Hotten from his widow, and took as partner W. E. Windus.

The American George P. Gordon brought out a treadle platen which was the forerunner of the modern platen machine. It was introduced into Britain as the Franklin by Messrs. Cropper and proved so popular that nearly all treadle platens became known to jobbing printers as 'Croppers' irrespective of the maker.

David McConnell Smyth of Hartford, Connecticut, invented the first thread sewing machine for bookbinding, at first manufactured solely for the publishers D. Appleton & Co.

Cyrus Chambers of Philadelphia took out a patent for a folding machine. Most of those developed later were based on this invention.

In the U.S. Timothy Alden brought out the composing and distributing machine on which he had spent some twenty years of his life and a small fortune. A company was formed in 1862, after the inventor's death, by his cousin, Henry W. Alden, to exploit the machine which, however, was eventually abandoned as a failure.

At Bloemfontein, Orange Free State, a press was set up by the Church Mission. The earliest book from this press was a spelling and reading book—*Orange Vrystaat A.B.C.*

1857

First edition of *Les Fleurs du Mal* by Charles Baudelaire (1821–67). Paris: Poulet-Malassis et de Broise.

At Paris, the Librairie Roret published *Nouveau manuel de bibliographie universelle* by Ferdinand Denis, P. Pinçon and De Martonne.

The first Monegasque journal, *Eden*, founded, which altered its title with the third number to *Journal de Monaco*.

Robert Hattersley of Manchester invented a composing machine which was used in a number of provincial newspaper offices. Some of these machines were still in use in 1914.

At London, Bland & Long published J. Pouncy, *Dorsetshire Photographically Illustrated*, the first book issued in England in which photographs were transferred to lithographic stones.

Lloyd's Weekly Newspaper installed a Hoe six-cylinder press at their premises in Salisbury Square, off Fleet Street. Other newspaper proprietors at once saw its value and between 1857 and 1858 *The Times* replaced their Applegath 'nine-feeder' by two Hoe 'ten-feeders'.

First number of *The Scottish Typographical Circular*, the oldest surviving journal of the printing trade. Later its name was changed to the *Scottish Typographical Journal*.

The first regular printing press in Greenland was established in the colony of Godthaab by the Dane, Hinrich Rink, Crown Inspector for South Greenland. (*See also* 1793.)

1858

Foundation of the firm of H. Berthold A.G., type-founders, Berlin.

The idea of printing a newspaper from a continuous roll of paper first patented in Vienna by Alois Auer. It was developed in the U.S.A. by William Bullock (1813–67). (*See* 1865.)

Samuel Leigh Sotheby published his *Principia Typographica* in three folio volumes, limited to 250 copies. The British Museum possesses, bound up in one volume, the whole of the author's revises for this work. Only 245 complete copies with all the plates could be assembled. Collation and binding were executed at the British Museum by Charles Tuckett Jnr. 215 copies were sold by auction on 5 May.

Introduction of the first Wharfedale stop-cylinder machine, invented by David Payne.

Developed in detail, though basically unchanged, at the end of the century the Wharfedale was still the favourite machine of British book-printers and printers of small circulation periodicals.

Death of Thomas Bonsor Crompton (b. 1792), proprietor of the Farnworth paper mills and at one time proprietor of the *Morning Post*. He invented in 1821 a continuous drying apparatus for the Fourdrinier which was introduced into France in 1826 at Firmin Didot's mill at Mesnil. In 1828 Crompton and Enoch Miller obtained a patent for cutting the endless web of paper lengthwise by revolving circular blades.

Joseph Whitaker founded the book-trade periodical *The Bookseller*.

The publishing firm of John Cassell reconstituted as Cassell, Petter & Galpin.

In May appeared the first issue of *The Printer*, a monthly periodical published at New York by Henry & Huntington.

Frederick Marriott printed the first issue of his weekly newspaper the *Vancouver Island Gazette*. It was printed on an iron hand press brought from France to British Columbia about 1856 by Bishop Modeste Demers.

1859

Heinrich Friedrich Gottlob Flinsch acquired in 1859 the Schleussnersche foundry which had been founded by the punch-cutter F. W. Schröter in 1757 and which in 1827 was carried on under the title of Firma F. Dresler & Rost-Fingerlin. The firm grew into one of the largest type-foundries in Europe under the direction of Ferdinand Flinsch (b. 1839). Edgar Flinsch became a partner in 1899. In 1916 the business was bought by the Bauer foundry at Frankfurt-am-Main and was combined with it.

Theodore Graesse (1814–85), Librarian to the King of Saxony from 1848, began publication of his *Trésor de livres rares et précieux*, published in eight quarto volumes.

First edition of Charles Darwin, *On the Origin of Species*. London: John Murray.

Thomas Moore published *The nature-printed British ferns*. London: Nature printed by H. Bradbury. Two volumes. 114 nature-printed plates.

The first machine to cast ready-dressed types was patented by Johnson and Atkinson.

R. Hoe & Co. of New York purchased from Isaac Adams of Boston his entire interest in the patents peculiar to the 'Adams Printing Press' (taken out between 1830 and 1836), together with the entire printing establishment of Messrs. Adams.

1860

Henri Voirin invented and patented his lithographic printing press.

The type-founding firm of Miller and Richard, the first house successfully to introduce machinery for the casting of type in Britain, issued an octavo booklet, *Specimens of Old Style*, showing eight sizes of their modernised Old Face cut by their employee in Edinburgh, Alexander C. Phemister. In 1861 Phemister went to America, where he cut another version, known as Franklin Old Style for the Dickinson Foundry at Boston. After a lengthy career as a type designer Phemister died in the United States in 1894.

Bernard Quaritch (*see* 1847) published his first complete catalogue with about 7,000 entries.

John Marder (b. 1835) established an American system of point bodies. At 16 he began work in a printing office at Akron. In 1860 he went to Chicago and became book-keeper at the Chicago Type Foundry. In 1862 the business was acquired by D. Scofield & Co. in which Marder was a partner. One of the most notable of American type-founders, he became manager of the Chicago branch of the American Type Founders Co.

On 23 June, Congress instituted the United States Government Printing Office in Washington.

According to *The Paper Trade Journal* the number of paper mills in the United States in this year was 555.

1861

First publication of the *Osservatore Romano*, the daily newspaper of the Vatican. From 4 November, 1929 it was printed inside the Vatican City.

Louis Piette (1803–62), son of a paper mill owner at Dilling, near Saarlouis, published his chief work, *Die Fabrication des Papieres aus Stroh, Heu, etc.* Two volumes. Paris, Cologne and Dresden. The materials he investigated, in addition to straw and hay, included jute, yucca, pisang, aloe and palmetto. He published several other treatises on paper-making, and in 1854 began a remarkable technical periodical, the *Journal des Fabricants de Papier*.

Second (and best) edition of Fr. Francisco Mendez, *Tipografía Española*, revised and augmented by Dionisio Hidalgo. Madrid: Imprenta de las escuelas pias.

J. Dellagana patented his 'mangle' press for moulding flong on formes to make stereotype matrices.

The firm of Waterlow made use of the first really successful two-colour machine, made and patented by the engineer W. Conisbee.

Between 1861 and 1863 appeared the first edition, in two volumes, of *The Life and Typography of William Caxton*, by W. Blades. In 1877 the work was corrected and published in one volume as *The Biography and Typography of William Caxton*.

Hoe and Company adapted their rotaries to take stereo plates instead of type. This was of great advantage to newspaper owners since they could now run as many machines as they wished by casting plates from the type instead of having to print direct from it.

1862

At Vienna, Karl Faulmann had cut for him a series of shorthand signs.

A *Spécimen Album* (188 pp. folio) was issued by the Gravure et Fonderie de C. Derriey. Derriey was the inventor of the mitreing machine for the joining of brass and type metal, and also of a typographic numbering apparatus. He was a master at the art of type-casting. His successor, Jules Derriey, issued a specimen in 1878. Jacques Charles Derriey (1808–77) was known in his day as the 'Raphael of the engravers', and was one of the most famous 'graveurs-fondeurs' in France. He began his career as an apprentice printer at Besançon, and later worked for Jules Didot as an engraver. His brother Jean-Joseph Derriey (1818–84) became a constructor of printing machines.

Pierre-Jules Hetzel (1814–86) founded the publishing firm of that name in Paris. He himself wrote a number of works under the pseudonym of P.-J. Stahl. In 1914 the business was taken over by the firm of Hachette.

First appearance of *J. & R. M. Wood's Typographic Advertiser*, the first house organ of a type-foundry published in England. The Wood foundry was established in 1815 by Richard Austin. On the death of his son, who had succeeded to the business, it was managed by R. M.

Wood in partnership with S. and T. Sharwood, under the style of the Austin Type Foundry. In 1856 the foundry was sold at auction and bought in by the sons of Wood, who continued it until about 1894.

The treadle platen press invented in 1861 by the American George Phineas Gordon (1810–78) was shown at the 1862 Exhibition in London. It was manufactured in England under the name of the Minerva. Gordon invented his first platen, the Gordon Jobber, in 1854, combining his own ideas with those of Daniel Treatwell (1827) and Stephen Ruggles (1831).

1863

In Germany, Ernst Werner Siemens built a composing- and casting-machine worked by spools of perforated paper.

John Curwen established a press at Plaistow for printing music. It continued as a small press devoted to music printing until 1917, when Harold Curwen (1885–1949), a grandson of the founder, took over control and began miscellaneous printing, adding book-printing in 1921.

The *Printer's Register* started, first published by James Caton, Salisbury Square, Fleet Street.

William Bullock of Pittsburg (1813–67) patented (14 April) his rotary self-feeding and self-perfecting press, for use with curved stereos cast from flong.

The American inventor Merritt Gally (1838–1910) patented a new style of platen press known as the Universal in the United States and as the Phoenix in Europe. The makers were Colt's Armory, Hertford, Connecticut, and when a new and improved model was put on the market around 1885, it was known as the Colt's Armory Press.

On 7 October, died Dr. William Church of Vershire, Vermont, at the age of 85. He came to England about 1822 and worked in Birmingham as a mechanical engineer until 1859, when he returned to Vermont, where he died. His patents and inventions were very numerous. (*See* 1822.)

1864

At Leipzig, Alexander Waldow founded *Archiv für Buchdruckerkunst*, later *Archiv für Buchgewerbe*, which was the first technical periodical to carry inserts of type specimens, and soon acquired a considerable reputation.

The Stuttgart Bible Co. issued a sixty-four volume Bible in relief capitals for the use of blind people. It took seven years to complete.

At Prague, Josef Mikuláš began *Veleslavin*, the first technical periodical for the printing industry in the Czech language.

Publication begun of the *Grand Dictionnaire Universel du XIXe Siècle* by the Librairie Larousse, Paris (*see* 1852), in seventeen volumes including two supplements, 1878, 1888. In 1869 Pierre Larousse became a printer, at 17 rue du Montparnasse, in order to maintain this publication. Although the first volume bears the date 1866, it was actually issued in 1864.

Charles Delagrave started his bookselling and publishing business in Paris. He later made a success with his publication of the *Souvenirs entomologiques* of J.-H. Fabre.

First publications issued by the Early English Text Society (in progress). The Society was founded by F. J. Furnivall.

First periodical published in Bulgaria, at Rustchuk, was *Dounav* printed in Turkish and Bulgarian. A Bulgarian magazine *Liouboslovie* was published at Smyrna in 1844.

1865

Jules Chéret (1836–1932), one of the most celebrated French poster artists, first drew attention to his work in this year by his poster for a play *Biche au Bois* at the Porte Saint-Martin theatre, in which Sarah Bernhardt appeared. In 1866 he set up a lithographic workshop in Paris and specialised in artistic posters in colour lithography. (*See* E. Maindron, *Les affiches illustrées*. 1886.)

In the Passage Choiseul, Paris, Alphonse Lemerre started his publishing business. Strangely enough the fortunes of the firm, during the remainder of the nineteenth century, were based on poetry. After a beginning with non-copyright works, such as the poets of the Pléiade, Lemerre became the publisher of Villiers de l'Isle Adam, Sully Prud'homme, François Coppée, Leconte de Lisle, J.-M. Hérédia, and for a time of Verlaine.

First edition of *Alice's Adventures in Wonderland* by Lewis Carroll [Charles Lutwidge Dodgson]. London: Macmillan & Co. (printed by the Clarendon Press, Oxford). This edition was suppressed, only about a score of the original 2,000 copies surviving. The first authorised edition was 1866. *Through the Looking-Glass* appeared for Christmas 1871, although dated 1872.

The *Printer's Journal and Typographical Magazine* started. It ran until 22 March, 1869.

Foundation of the London publishing firm of Frederick Warne & Co. Ltd., after Warne had dissolved his partnership with the Routledges.

William Bullock successfully completed (from plans patented in 1863) his web perfecting cylinder press which printed from a continuous roll of paper on both sides. A folding mechanism was added in 1868. The firm of William Bullock was later taken over by the Hoe Company.

1866

At Venice was founded the publishing firm of Ongania (Ferdinando Ongania Editore). Ongania was at the time employed by the Libreria Münster, and he acquired the business because the Austrian proprietor had to leave it when the Veneto was united to Italy.

The *Eastern Morning News*, Hull, installed two of Robert Hattersley's composing machines.

Thomas MacKellar, of the firm of MacKellar, Smiths & Jordan, type-founders of Philadelphia, published his book *The American Printer: a manual of typography*. Philadelphia.

At Moscow was published *The Year 1805* by L. N. Tolstoi. This was the first edition of a work later republished as Vol. I of *War and Peace*, of which Vols. 1–4 were published in 1868, and Vols. 5 and 6 in 1869.

H. W. Alden and W. Mackay, of New York, patented (23 January) a type-setting machine.

J. Kelly started the *American Catalogue of Books*.

Foundation of the American publishing firm of Henry Holt & Co. Inc.

The first book printed at Zanzibar—*Specimens of the Swaheli language*, produced at the press of the Universities Mission to Central Africa.

1867

Death, at Frankfurt-am-Main, of Johann Christian Bauer (*see* 1837). He left some 10,000 personally engraved punches, and it was from his workshop and materials that the Bauersche Giesserei developed.

The first title issued of the famous 'Reclams Universal-Bibliothek' issued. It was an edition of Goethe's *Faust*, and sold at 20 pfennigs (then equivalent to $2\frac{1}{2}$d), a price which was maintained until 1917.

The Plantin Press at Antwerp ceased work after 312 years of printing.

At Brussels was published the first edition of Charles de Coster, *La Légende d'Ulenspiegel*, with illustrations by Félicien Rops and other famous artists.

Alexander Mackie invented a type-composing machine which was used in the printing office of the *Warrington Guardian*. He anticipated Lanston in being the first to use a perforated ribbon to actuate his composing machine.

Henry Bradshaw (1831–86), eminent bibliographer, became chief Librarian at Cambridge University, a post which he held until 1886.

Foundation of the University of Illinois Library at Urbana.

1868

At Feltre, his birthplace, a memorial was erected to the printer Pamfilo Castaldi, who worked in Milan around 1472, on the mistaken idea that he was the inventor of printing.

Publication of *Monuments typographiques des Pays-Bas au XVe siècle* by J. W. Holtrop, Chief Librarian of the Royal Library at The Hague. It contains 130 plates. These *Monuments* (generally called HMT) marked the beginning of a new study of incunabula and Holtrop's effort was indeed, as Bradshaw called it, 'a remarkable work'.

On 8 September, died in Paris the eminent French bibliographer Auguste Bernard (b. 1811 at Montbrison). Son of a master printer at Montbrison, he wrote many books on the history of printing, and in 1862 was appointed Inspecteur-Général de l'Imprimerie et de la Librairie.

Publication in Paris of the first series of *Lettres d'un Bibliographe* by J. P. A. Madden. A second series followed in 1873, a third in 1874, a fourth in 1875, a fifth in 1878, and a sixth in 1886. The letters were later continued in a trade journal, *La Typologie Tucker*, house organ of the Paris branch of the Caslon type-foundry, edited by Henry J. Tucker.

The Marinoni rotary introduced at *Le Petit Journal*. It was the most rapid of all the sheet-fed presses of its time, since the sheet was perfected at one operation.

In Paris, the contract for printing the *Moniteur Universel* and *Moniteur du Soir* given to Wittersheim & Co., who ordered five of Marinoni's new rotary perfecting presses.

Armand Colin, formerly an employee of Charles Delagrave, took a partner, M. Le Corbellier, and started his own successful publishing business.

The famous Walter press, the first complete rotary newspaper press as known today, was used to print *The Times*. The speed is said to have been 12,000 perfected copies per hour.

In Moscow appeared the first edition of L. N. Tolstoi, *War and Peace* (Vols. I–IV). Vols. V–VI followed in 1869. (*See also* 1866.)

1869

At Mainz, on the spot where once stood the birthplace of Gutenberg, was founded the Deutsche Buchdrucker-Verein.

Damase Jouaust (1835–93), Paris printer and publisher, founded the Librairie des Bibliophiles. He had succeeded his father in 1863 and greatly increased the firm's prestige with his elegantly printed collections of ancient and modern French literature, such as the 'Bibliothèque Elzévirienne'.

A keyboard type-setting machine was invented by Karl Kastenbein. An improved version was later used in printing *The Times*, making it the first mechanical composing machine to be used by a London newspaper. (*See* 1872.)

In Great Britain, the Newspapers, Printers, and Reading Rooms Repeal Act required every person printing any paper or book for publication or disposal by other means to print his name and address on the first or last leaf of the work.

London Society of Lithographic Printers founded.

Cornell became the first American university to establish a university press. The original press closed in 1883 owing to financial difficulties, and was succeeded by the present one in 1930.

William Golding of Boston marketed his Golding Jobber platen press. This and his Pearl Jobber were used extensively all over the United States, and a few were to be found in England.

The American, Merritt Gally (1838–1916), invented and built his Universal platen press,

patented the same year. It was first shown in Europe at the Paris Exposition Universelle in 1878, and was quickly imitated.

1870

The Leipzig printing and publishing firm of Poeschel & Trepte founded by Heinrich Ernst Poeschel, Justus Naumann and Emil Trepte. Heinrich Poeschel's son Carl Ernst (b. 1874) joined the firm in 1906.

Ulrico Hoepli (1847–1935), a native of Tuttwil (Turgovia) settled in Milan in 1870, and with the help of a brother in Manchester bought the bookshop of Theodore Laegner in the Galleria de Christoforis. This was the beginning of the famous publishing firm of Ulrico Hoepli. After his death the business was carried on by his descendants.

In France, an ordinance of 10 December did away with the 'brevet' system instituted in 1810, and allowed anyone to set up in business as printer or bookseller without having to take out a patent.

The proclamation in France of the liberty of the Press led to the immediate augmentation in the number of small printing offices, their growth facilitated by the opportune appearance of the treadle platen.

THE CHANGES IN STYLE OF THE IMPRIMERIE NATIONALE, PARIS

Imprimerie Royale	1620–1789
Du Louvre	1790–1791
Nationale Exécutive du Louvre	1792
Nationale du Louvre	1793
Nationale	1794
de la République	1795–1804
Impériale	1804–14
Royale	1814
Impériale	1815
Royale	1815–30
du Gouvernement	1830
Royale	1830–48
du Gouvernement	1848
Nationale	1848–52
Impériale	1852–70
Nationale	1870 onwards

The 'folder' came into use for the newspaper press. Until 1870 presses delivered the copies flat, and a practical folder was first devised by the Englishman George Ashley Wilson, inventor of the Victory printing and folding machine, first used in 1870 for the production of the *North British Daily Mail* and the *Glasgow Weekly Mail*.

A Russian compositor, Peter Paul Kniagininski exhibited a composing machine at the St. Petersburg Industry and Crafts Exhibition. It was an ingenious piece of mechanism, but, unable to find financial backing for the machine, the inventor took to drink and died insane.

1871

John Southward published a *Dictionary of typography and its accessory arts* which was presented to subscribers to the *Printers' Register*.

John Ruskin, the art critic, in order to publish his own writings, started a publishing venture with his friend and pupil George Allen, under the style of George Allen & Son. Their first publication was Ruskin's *Fors Clavigera*.

J. Luther Ringwalt published at Philadelphia his *American Encyclopaedia of Printing*.

1872

Hippolyte Marinoni (1823–1904), an apprentice of the engineer Gaveaux, installed his first web-fed rotary in the premises of the Paris newspaper *La Liberté*. It printed 10,000 copies of the paper per hour.

Théophile Beaudoire (1838–1909), French type-founder and designer, became manager of the Fonderie Générale. An excellent draughtsman, he designed a number of type-faces of a style now rather outmoded. About 1858, he resurrected some of the early sixteenth-century faces which he baptised 'Elzevirs'. The Peignot foundry took over the Fonderie Générale in 1912.

The 'Prestonian' reel-fed rotary first used for printing the *Preston Guardian*. It differed from the Walter and Hoe machines in that movable types could be used as an alternative to stereotype plates.

The Kastenbein composing machine installed at *The Times*, at first on an experimental basis.

In December appeared the first number of *The Paper and Printing Trades Journal*, published at 50 Leadenhall Street, London, by Field and Tuer, who ran it for nearly twenty years, after which it was continued by John Southward.

Merritt Gally, inventor of the Universal press (*see* 1869), was granted U.S. patents (16 and 23 July, 1872) for a machine for assembling matrices and automatically spacing them by means of

wedges. His patents were sold in 1884 to the parties interested in the Mergenthaler Linotype. Incidentally, Gally was the inventor of several self-playing musical instruments, including the 'Pianola' and 'Æolian Organ'. Many of his musical patents were acquired by the Æolian Company.

First issue of the American *Publishers' Weekly*.

1873

First issue of *Il Tipografo*, founded by the Journeymen Compositors Society of Rome.

1873–94 saw the publication of *Bibliographische Adversaria*—1st series five volumes, 2nd series one volume. The Hague. It contains important articles on Dutch printers and bibliography.

First edition of Jules Verne, *Le Tour du Monde en 80 Jours*. Paris: J. Hetzel. (*See* 1862.)

At Paris, the Tourlot type-foundry came into being when Alfred Turlot (1847–1902) bought the foundry of the Virey brothers in the rue de Rennes. It acquired several other firms, but in 1921 was merged in the Fonderie Typographique Française.

Publication of Quaritch's *Bibliotheca Xylographia, Typographica, et Paleographica*; a catalogue of block-books and of early productions of the printing-press in all countries.

J. R. Johnson's paper 'On certain improvements in the manufacture of printing types' published in the *Journal of the Society of Arts*, 21 March.

William Moon published his *Light for the Blind*, in the first practical type for blind people. Moon simplified the outlines of the ordinary alphabet which was printed in relief. The Moon system is still used since some blind people find it easier to learn than Braille.

On 9 March, died Charles Knight, printer and publisher, born at Windsor 1791.

First issue of *Typografisk Tidende*, Copenhagen. Published by the Danish Typographic Union.

1874

At Paris the publishing and antiquarian bookselling firm of Champion was founded by Honoré Champion (1846–1913).

First edition of the *Reference Catalogue of Current Literature*. This consisted of 135 publishers' catalogues of uniform size bound in two volumes, with a separate index.

First appearance of *Willing's Press Guide*, under that title. It began in 1871 as *Frederick May's London Press Directory*.

The Rev. Charles Henry Oliver Daniel, who had started to print as a boy at Frome, continued his private press as Provost of Worcester College, Oxford. The Daniel Press revived the use of the Fell types and printed some fifty-eight books up to 1903, mostly for private distribution among friends of the printer.

1875

At Leipzig, the firm of Duncker & Humblot published the first volume of R. von Liliencron and F. X. Wegele, *Allgemeine Deutsche Biographie*.

Friedrich Johannes Frommann (1797–1886) head of the family business of booksellers, Firma Friedrich Frommann, wrote the first history of the 'Börsenverein'. In his father's house he became acquainted with Goethe, who there met Minna Herzlieb, the foster-daughter of Freidrich's father.

Died, in Berlin, Theodor Hosemann (b. 1807), a prolific book illustrator. He began as a lithographer and learned his craft with the firm of Arnz and Winckelmann in Düsseldorf. Later he specialised in woodcuts.

At Paris, Paul François Dupont issued his *Premier spécimen*. A successful printer and typefounder, he was also the author of a *Histoire de l'Imprimerie* (two volumes, 1854).

About 1875, the Ingram rotary press, designed by William Ingram, son of the founder of the *Illustrated London News*, on the plans of the engineer James Brister, was built by Middleton & Co. It had enormous cylinders.

Stephen Tucker patented a device called a rotating folder cylinder which folded newspapers as fast as they were printed.

The India Paper Bible, the paper for which was made at Wolvercote paper mill, which the Clarendon Press had bought in 1870, sold a quarter of a million copies in the space of a few weeks. The monopoly for the paper, termed 'Oxford India', was shared by the Oxford University Press and the firm of Brittains, makers of thin copying and other papers.

Between 1875 and 1877 was published Edward Arber, *Transcript of the Registers of the Company of Stationers of London, 1554–1640*. Four volumes. The *Index* was published in 1894.

Oscar H. Harpel published at Cincinnati his *Poets and Poetry of Printerdom*.

1876

The famous printing office of the Plantin Press at Antwerp was bought from the proprietor, Edouard Joannes Hyacinth Moretus-Plantin, by the City of Antwerp, and on 19 August, 1877, was opened to the public as the Plantin-Moretus Museum. Its first curator was Max Rooses, author of the first great biography of Christopher Plantin.

Jean-Claude Motteroz printed the first volume of the *Librairie du Victor Hugo Illustré*. This was *Les Travailleurs de la Mer*, illustrated by Victor Hugo and Daniel Vierge. After a varied career as compositor, pressman, lithographer and machine-minder, Motteroz started his own printing firm in rue Visconti, Paris. In 1897 he became managing director of the Librairies-Imprimeries Réunies. F. Thibaudeau, the printer and author (*see* 1921), was a pupil of Motteroz.

Publication of *The Invention of Printing*, by Theodore Low De Vinne. New York. A second edition, published in New York and in London, came out in the following year.

The American Library Association founded in Philadelphia by about a hundred librarians, including Melvil Dewey, originator of the decimal system of library classification named after him. In the same year appeared the first number of *The Library Journal*. In 1909 the headquarters of the association was established in Chicago.

The American publishing firm of Funk & Wagnalls founded by Isaac Kaufman Funk (soon to be joined by Adam Willis Wagnalls) under the style of I. K. Funk & Company.

1877

Albert Quantin (1850–1933), printer and publisher at Paris, published his own book *Les Origines de l'Imprimerie et son introduction en Angleterre*. In 1876 he acquired the Imprimerie Claye, in which he had worked as foreman. In 1882 he sold the business to Imprimeries-Libraires Réunies. He was publisher of the magazine *Monde Moderne*.

The quatercentenary of the introduction of printing into England by William Caxton was celebrated by an exhibition of 'antiquities and curiosities connected with the art of printing'. It was opened, 30 June, in the western galleries of the former International Exhibition Buildings, behind the Albert Hall. A guide to the exhibition was written by William Blades and printed at the Elzevir Press for N. Trübner & Co. In connection with the opening of the Exhibition the Oxford University Press published 100 copies of a Caxton Memorial Bible, which was printed and bound within the twelve hours which preceded Mr. Gladstone's opening speech. Ten copies bound in turkey morocco reached the Exhibition by two o'clock in the afternoon.

The Rev. C. H. O. Daniel (*see* 1845 and 1874) revived the use of the Fell types in a reprint of a seventeenth-century sermon issued by the Daniel Press.

1878

Publication of Albert Fidelis Butsch, *Die Bücher-Ornamentik der Renaissance*. Leipzig: Georg Hirth. Two parts, 1878, 1881.

Henri Voirin invented and patented in France a machine for printing on tin and metal plate by transfer on to a cylinder with a rubber overlay —the precursor of the present-day 'offset' machine.

The first international meeting of printers was held at the Grand Hotel, Paris, on 20 August, 1878. It was attended by representatives from France, Austria, Belgium, England, Germany, Italy, Portugal, Russia, Spain, Switzerland, Turkey, and U.S.A.

Bernard Quaritch founded the society known as 'Ye Sette of Odd Volumes', of which he was three times President. The first publication of the society was *Opuscula I*, 1880.

Publication of Charles Hindley, *The Life and Times of James Catnach*. He was also the author of *The History of the Catnach Press* (1886).

Foundation of the Index Society.

Death of the famous book illustrator and caricaturist George Cruikshank (b. 1792).

First edition, at Moscow, of L. N. Tolstoi, *Anna Karenina*. Three volumes.

The Chicago type-founders Marder, Luse & Co., began to sell type with bodies based on a point system.

First periodical in Cyprus, *Kypros*, was started at Larnica.

1879

Karl Klić of Arnau invented the photo-mechanical intaglio process known as photogravure.

G. Duncan and G. A. Wilson patented their 'Auxiliary printing mechanism for Late News'— the first patent in Britain for a stop-press printing mechanism or 'fudge-box'. In the course of the next twenty years many improvements were made in this device.

The first rotary bill machine (for printing newspaper contents bills) was constructed by R. Hoe & Co. for use by the *Daily Telegraph* of London. This printed from wood type.

The Printing Review, a monthly periodical of the printing trade first issued on 7 January. It was discontinued after twelve numbers. The title was revived in 1931.

1880

First edition of Konrad Duden, *Orthographische Wörterbuch der deutschen Sprache*, published by the Bibliographical Institute at Leipzig. In 1903, he issued *Rechtschreibung der Buchdruckereien deutscher Sprache* ('Buchdruckerduden').

Publication of Alphonse Willems, *Les Elzevier*. Brussels: G. A. van Trigt. A source book for the history of this famous firm.

Foundation in France of the Société des Amis des Livres. The first president was M. Eugène Paillet, who remained in office until 1901.

Publication of Vol. 1 of *A Bibliography of Printing*, compiled by E. C. Bigmore and C. W. H. Wyman. London: Bernard Quaritch. Vol. 2 appeared in 1884, and Vol. 3 in 1886. (A reprint was published in New York, 1945.)

The first number appeared of the *Printers' International Specimen Exchange*, edited by Andrew Tuer, which ran until 1898. It contained work by the Americans William J. Kelly, John Earhart and Andreas Haight which greatly influenced British jobbing printing.

The London *Standard* was printed this year on six 'Prestonian' rotaries. (*See* 1872.)

On 4 March, Stephen Henry Horgan printed the now famous illustration of 'Shantytown' in the New York *Daily Graphic*—the first half-tone block printed in a newspaper. The plate was made through a screen, but was printed on a lithographic press.

William Addison Dwiggins (*pseudonym* Hermann Püterschein), American typographer, book decorator, and calligrapher, born at Martinsville, Ohio. Awarded the gold medal by the American Institute of Graphic Arts in 1929. The first book in which his name appears is Robert Browning's *In a Balcony*, Chicago: Blue Sky Press, 1902.

The first printing press in Alberta, Canada, was established at Edmonton by Hon. Frank Oliver. Its first publication was *The Bulletin*, which appeared on 6 December, 1880. It was a diminutive newspaper with a page size of $5\frac{1}{4}$ by $6\frac{1}{2}$ in. There were two columns per page, and four pages to each issue.

1881

The Bauer foundry at Frankfurt-am-Main built in conjunction with the English engineer John Mair Hepburn a new and efficient type-casting and finishing machine, based on a machine built by Johnson and Atkinson in 1862.

First edition of the 'Revised Version' of the New Testament printed in Oxford at the University Press.

Frederick Wicks (1840–1910) patented his rotary type-casting machine, first invented about 1878. This machine was said to have been capable of casting 60,000 finished sorts each day, and was used at *The Times* office in conjunction with the Kastenbein type-setter.

The American firm of Marder, Luse & Co. became the first founders to cast point on type in English-speaking countries.

Robert Wiebking arrived in America, bringing with him from Germany a matrix engraving machine. He became a notable punch-cutter and type designer.

Foundation of the publishing firm of The Century Company at New York. In 1933 the company was merged with Appleton and Co.

At Sofia a State Printing House was founded.

1882

Publication of Karl Faulmann, *Illustrerte Geschichte der Buchdruckerkunst*. Published in 25 fascicules by A. Hartleben Verlag, Vienna, Pest and Leipzig (*see* 1803). It was printed by the Hof- und Staatsdruckerei, Vienna.

The first practicable photographic half-tone process for letterpress printing was patented at Munich by George Meisenbach. Two years later the process was introduced into England by the Meisenbach Company.

Max Rooses, first curator of the Plantin-Moretus Museum at Antwerp, published the first edition of his *Christophe Plantin, imprimeur Anversois*. It was the first extensive, documented biography of the great printer.

The brothers Henri and Jules Desclée founded a press at Tournai, Belgium, under the style of 'Société de Saint Jean l'Évangéliste', for the printing of liturgical works.

Publication of the first volume of *A Dictionary of the Anonymous and Pseudonymous Literature of Great Britain*, compiled by Samuel Halkett and John Laing. The final volume appeared in 1888. Between 1926 and 1932 a new and enlarged edition in six volumes was issued, edited by J. Kennedy, W. A. Smith and A. F. Johnson. Supplementary volumes 7, 8 and 9, were added in 1934, 1956, and 1962, the last two being edited by D. E. Rhodes and Anna E. C. Simoni.

R. Hoe & Co. introduced 'turning-bars' for their presses, although the invention was not patented until 1885.

The first Hoe 'double-supplement' press installed in the premises of the *New York Herald*.

1883

Publication of Anton Mayer, *Wiener Buchdruckergeschichte*, a comprehensive and well documented work.

The Society of Authors was founded by Sir Walter Besant and incorporated in the following year under the presidency of Lord Tennyson.

Horace Hart was appointed Printer to the University of Oxford. He at once began to modernise the printing house, installing new printing machines and renovating the type-foundry, and throughout his printing career showed himself to be a remarkable combination of scholar and business man.

The point systems of Didot (*see* 1775) and Marder (*see* 1881) related only to type bodies. In 1883 Linn Boyd Benton, of the North-western Type Foundry, Milwaukee, was granted a patent for type that was also 'point system both ways', *i.e.* type set. Benton was born at Little Falls, N.Y., in 1844.

The brothers Max and Louis Levy of Philadelphia perfected the first commercial half-tone screen.

1884

Died at Dresden, the German book illustrator Ludwig Richter (b. 1803).

On 1 February, publication began with the fascicule A–Ant of *A New English Dictionary on Historical Principles*. More generally known by the shorter title of the *Oxford English Dictionary* (and so called in the 'corrected re-issue'), it was edited by James Murray (d. 1915), Henry Bradley, W. A. Craigie and C. T. Onions. Publication in twelve volumes was completed by the Oxford University Press in 1933.

The first newspaper to be printed by electricity in England was the *Somerset County Gazette*, In June. It was printed on a Wharfedale flat-bed press driven by electric power from the Corporation mains. The experiment was not wholly successful, and the printers reverted to steam power.

Publication in London of Mark Twain, *The Adventures of Huckleberry Finn*. The first edition of this work was printed in London; the second appeared in the United States the same year.

Death of Nicholas Trübner (b. Heidelberg, 1818), founder of the publishing house of Nicholas Trübner & Co., Ludgate Hill. He came to England in 1847 and joined the firm of Longmans.

The Grolier Club, New York, founded for 'the literary study and promotion of the arts pertaining to the production of books'. The same year saw the society's first publication—*A Decree of Star Chamber concerning printing*, reprinted from the first edition by Robert Barker, 1637. This reprint, limited to 148 copies, was printed by the De Vinne Press, founded in 1883.

Robert Miehle of Chicago (b. 1860) patented his first two-revolution machine, constructed with the help of his brother John (1885–87). The prototype was used to print the *Swedish Weekly Newspaper*, Chicago.

1885

First issue of the heraldic annual, the *Münchener Kalender*, which made generally known the talent of the designer Otto Hupp (1859–1949). He designed the following type-faces: Hupp-Liturgisch (1906), Hupp-Antiqua and Hupp-Unziale (1909), and Hupp-Fraktur (1910) for the Klingspor foundry. Hupp's special field was heraldry.

LCP

The first edition of the 'Revised Version' of the Bible printed at Oxford at the University Press.

Publication began of the *Dictionary of National Biography*, the first editor of which was Sir Leslie Stephen.

Frederick Ives of Philadelphia was the first to make a cross-line screen for half-tone photography, making possible the fine photo-engraving plates of the present day. In the following year he perfected this process, upon which he had been experimenting since 1877 and introduced it at the printing firm with which he was connected.

Ottmar Mergenthaler patented his typesetting and type-casting machine known as the Linotype, casting whole lines of type in the form of slugs. (*See* 1886.)

Linn Boyd Benton patented his original punch-cutting machine. (British patent 11894; American patent 327855). This was an automatic borer attached to a pantograph which replaced traditional punch-cutting by hand.

The Goss Printing Press Company established in Chicago by the brothers Fred and Sam Goss specialising in the construction of presses for small-sized newspapers.

Construction in America of the Huber-Hodgman two-colour press.

1886

The firm of Cassell started their National Library under the editorship of Henry Morley, and at a price of 3d per volume paper-bound and 6d in cloth. It was highly successful and sold for many years.

G. Routledge and Sons began to publish the World Library edited by H. R. Haweis, of which forty volumes were issued.

The Swede, Alexander Lagerman, designed an automatic composing stick which he called the 'Typotheter'.

Waldemar Zachrisson (1861–1924) established at Göteborg, Sweden, the printing firm bearing his name.

After many trials and discards the first commercially successful Linotype machine was marketed by Ottmar Mergenthaler (1854–99). In 1886 the *New York Tribune* issued the first newspaper in the world to be set by Linotype.

On 17 September, the twenty-four member companies in the American Type Founders Company formally adopted the point system as standard, basing it on the pica of the MacKellar, Smiths and Jordan foundry of Philadelphia. The result was a typographic point measuring 0·0138 in.

The first Goss newspaper printing press erected at Grand Rapids, Michigan, giving a production of 4,000 copies an hour.

Richard March Hoe died at Florence on 13 September.

1887

First edition of *A History of the Old English Letter Foundries* by Talbot Baines Reed (1852–93), son of Sir Charles Reed, proprietor of the Fann Street Foundry. This book was the best and most complete book on the history of type-foundries that had ever been written. (A new edition, revised and enlarged by A. F. Johnson of the British Museum was published in 1952.)

Tolbert Lanston demonstrated the prototype of his 'Monotype' composing machine.

Introduction of the Miehle two-revolution machine, the invention of Robert Miehle of Chicago (1860–1932), who perfected the idea of the lift-up cylinder first suggested in 1831 by the French engineer Gaveaux (1801–85).

The first book composed on a Linotype—*The Tribune Book of Open Air Sports*—was published in New York. It bore the notice: 'This book is printed without type, being the first product in book form of the Mergenthaler machine which wholly supersedes the use of movable type.'

Hannibal Goodwin, a New Jersey minister, was granted a patent for a celluloid film for photography.

1888

The London publisher J. M. Dent began to issue his Temple Library, the first serious attempt in England to combine quality with cheapness. It was followed in 1894 by the Temple Shakespeare.

The periodical *The British Printer* was started, first published by the firm of Raithby, Lawrence & Co. of Leicester.

First appearance of *Book Prices Current*.

On 15 November, a lantern lecture given by Emery Walker to the Arts & Crafts Exhibition Society determined William Morris to take a practical interest in printing.

In Denmark, the typographer Frederik Hendriksen (1847–1938) started the Forening for Boghaandvaerk (Society for Bookcraft) which is still extant.

A new rotary press, known as the 'three page wide press', by R. Hoe & Co. made its appearance.

Henry Barth (b. Leipzig, 1823) perfected and introduced an automatic type-casting machine which delivered type in lines ready for examination and paging. It was used by the American Type Founders Company. Barth arrived in America in 1849, and was employed by the Cincinnati Type Foundry, of which he became President in 1861.

1889

At Paris, Henri Omont published his *Spécimens de Caractères Hébreux, Grecs, Latins, et de Musique gravés à Venise par Guillaume Le Bé.*

On 25 December, appeared the first number of the *Mercure de France,* founded by Alfred Vallette.

Vol. 1 of *The Library* appeared as the organ of the Library Association of the United Kingdom, published by Elliot Stock. In 1900 Vol. 1 of a New Series was published as a quarterly review of Bibliography and Library Lore (edited by J. Mac Alister) by Kegan Paul, Trench, Trübner & Co. Ltd.

John Cunningham Petch and Thomas Mussel, both of Middlesbrough-on-Tees, were granted a patent for a means of rapidly inserting extra matter in stereotype plates by means of a special spring-acting frame.

The Typefounders' Society, London, founded.

Edinburgh Bibliographical Society founded.

The first Goss newspaper presses were installed in Britain. (*See* 1885.)

1890

On 14 June, appeared the first number of *The Clique*, the trade journal of the British antiquarian book trade.

In 1890, Bernard Newdigate (1869–1944) entered his father's printing business, The Art and Book Company, at Leamington Spa. There he was joined in 1903 by Joseph Thorp, who later set up in London as a freelance typographer. In 1904, Newdigate's firm became the Arden Press, for which he acted as printer, designer, publisher and editor. (*See* 1908.)

Edward Prince cut the Golden Type based by William Morris on incunabula types of Nicholas Jenson and Jacques Le Rouge.

The Kynoch Press opened at Birmingham, directed at first by Herbert Simon.

Death of William Blades.

1891

In September the *Birmingham Daily Gazette* used electric power for the first time to drive a Victory and a Foster single roll press. A 24 h.p. Crompton motor provided the power. This was the first British newspaper produced on a rotary press driven by electric power.

Printing began at the Kelmscott Press, established at Hammersmith, London, by William Morris and Emery Walker. The first book from the press, completed in April, 1891, was Morris's own *The Story of the Glittering Plain*.

First issue of *Printing World*.

The Saint Bride Typographic Library established.

Edward Prince cut the Troy Type for William Morris.

1892

Karl Klingspor senior took over the Rudhard type-foundry at Offenbach-am-Main. (*See* 1895.)

Founding of the Bibliographical Society following a paper by W. A. Copinger 'On the necessity for the formation of a Bibliographical Society of the United Kingdom', read at the Annual Meeting of the Library Association held at Nottingham, September 1891. Copinger was supported in his proposal by Sir John MacAlister.

First edition of the famous medical textbook of Sir William Osler (1849–1919)—*Principles and practice of Medicine*. Edinburgh: Young J. Pentland.

The widow of the Lancashire merchant and philanthropist John Rylands (1801–88) purchased the famous Althorp Library, assembled by George John, 2nd Earl of Spencer, and presented it to the city of Manchester as a memorial to her late husband. (*See* 1899.)

The Globe became the first London newspaper to adopt the Linotype machine. The *Financial News* soon followed suit.

1893

Simone Lattes left the Libreria Casanova to found the Turin firm of S. Lattes Editori.

Sarah Treverbian Prideaux, the eminent woman bookbinder, and pupil of Cobden-Sanderson, published her *Historical Sketch of Bookbinding*. London: Lawrence & Bullen. In 1903 she wrote *Bookbinders and their Craft*. London: Zaehnsdorf.

Arts and Crafts Essays, by members of the Arts and Crafts Exhibition Society, was published by Rivington, London. It contained the celebrated essay 'Printing' by William Morris and Emery Walker. The society was founded to promote a revival in the decorative arts.

Horace Hart issued, in a 24-page 16mo booklet, his *Rules for Compositors and Readers at the University Press, Oxford*. Originally intended solely for internal use at the Press, in 1904 an enlarged 15th edition was put on sale to the public. In 1967, the 37th edition was published, completely revised and reset, having grown to 141 pages.

Wilbur Stephen Scudder constructed a typesetting machine called the Monoline, working on principles similar to those employed by the Linotype. It failed to attract purchasers and manufacture ceased in 1910.

Cobden-Sanderson established his Doves Bindery at Hammersmith, London. Apprenticed to him was Douglas Cockerell.

Barnhart Bros. and Spindler, American typefounders, first produced type point-set, making their product completely point-set, point-line, and point-body.

Daniel Berkeley Updike left the Riverside Press at Cambridge, Mass. and set up as a typographic adviser. In 1893 he established in Boston, Mass., a press known from 1896 as the Merrymount Press.

Columbia University Press founded.

1894

At Paris, was held an International Exhibition of the Book and Paper Industries.

John Lane and Elkin Matthews founded their publishing business at the sign of the Bodley Head in Vigo Street, London, and in April published the first issue of *The Yellow Book*, an illustrated quarterly edited by Henry Harland. It ran for thirteen issues, and was published in the U.S.A. by Copeland and Day of Boston. It gained a certain notoriety from the rather exotic drawings of Aubrey Beardsley, who provided the cover designs and many of the illustrations for the first four numbers.

The Eragny Press, called after the village of that name in Normandy, was founded at Hammersmith, London, by Lucien Pissarro. The first book issued, *The Queen of the Fishes* (1894), consisted of wood engravings with hand-written text reproduced by photographic line process.

The Ashendene Press was founded by C. H. St.

John Hornby. In 1900 Emery Walker and Sydney Cockerell designed for him the Subiaco Type based on that used by Sweynheym and Pannartz at Subiaco in 1465. The punches were cut by Edward Prince.

J. W. Paige of Rochester, N.Y., who invented and patented a type-setting machine called the Paige Compositor, tested it in September 1894 in the printing house of the *Chicago Herald*. It was described as a commercial failure but an intellectual miracle.

The present University of Chicago Press founded.

The first printing at Bulawayo, Rhodesia, was *The Bulawayo Chronicle*, the first issue of which was dated 12 October, 1894.

1895

Founding of the D. Stempel foundry at Frankfurt-am-Main by David Stempel (1869–1927). In 1897 he bought the Juxberg-Rust foundry at Offenbach, founded in 1858, and established a printing office and bookbindery.

In 1895 appeared the first issue of the German art and literary magazine *Pan*, which heralded a renaissance in German printing. Very 'Jugendstil' or 'Art Nouveau' in general appearance, it contained articles by leading German writers, accompanied by many excellent lithographs, etchings, wood engravings, etc. Published at Berlin, it was edited by W. Bode and continued until 1899.

Karl and Wilhelm Klingspor joined their father, Karl Klingspor senior, in the management of the Rudhard foundry (*see* 1892). The latter died in 1903, and in 1906 the name of the foundry was changed to Gebrüder Klingspor. With Karl Klingspor the younger (1868–1950), were associated many of the finest German designers of the first half of the twentieth century, such as Rudolf Koch, Otto Eckman, E. R. Weiss and Ernst Schneidler.

Foundation at Brussels of the Institut International de Bibliographie, due to the initiative of two Belgian lawyers, Paul Otlet (1868–1944) and Henri La Fontaine (1853–1943).

At Lyons, the Librairie Auguste Brun in association with Picard of Paris published the First Series of the *Bibliographie Lyonnaise*. This had been prepared by Julien Baudrier from the notes and collections of his father, Henri Louis, the Président Baudrier (1815–84). Julien Baudrier died in 1915 and the work was completed by his brother-in-law, H. de Terrebasse in 1921 with the publication of the Twelfth Series. The volumes were printed by A. Rey at Lyons. An index and tables were added in 1950 and 1952 with a supplement in 1963.

On 2 April, Arthur Christian (1838–1906) was appointed director of the Imprimerie Nationale, Paris. In 1900 he published the *Origines* and in 1905 the *Débuts de l'Imprimerie en France*.

About 1895 Karl Klič (1841–1926), inventor of the intaglio process known as photogravure, made his first successful prints by this method. He was assisted in developing the process by Samuel Fawcett.

First issue of the *Process Work Year Book* of A. W. Penrose & Co., printed by Percy Lund and Co., The Country Press, Bradford. This was the forerunner of the present-day *Penrose's Annual*, and originally it was a monthly circular and house organ dealing with the specialities of the firm of A. W. Penrose & Co., The Photo Process Stores, 8a Upper Baker Street, Clerkenwell, London, as well as with photo-mechanical processes in general.

Falconer Madan published in *Bibliographica* an article on 'Early Representations of the Printing Press'.

On 20 November, the St. Bride Foundation Printing Library was opened by Sir Walter Besant. It was the library of William Blades, J. Southward and Tabot B. Reed which formed the nucleus of what was rapidly to become one of the world's finest technical libraries for both printers and historians.

In October at New York, the American Type Founders Co. issued a *Collective Specimen Book*. This was the first specimen book issued by the A.T.F.C., which had originated in 1892 from an amalgamation of the principal type-foundries of the U.S. It contains specimens of all the type-faces most used in the U.S. in 1895, and all the type-faces added after the merger of 1892.

Publication began of *American Book Prices Current*.

Frederic Goudy (1865–1947) started the Camelot Press in Chicago.

Will Bradley (1868–1961) started his Wayside Press at Springfield, Mass., after having worked since 1887 as designer with the Chicago printing firm of Knight & Leonard. After serving as art editor with many of America's leading magazines, in 1920 Bradley became art and typographic supervisor for the Hearst organisation.

1896

In Munich, were founded the periodicals *Simplicissimus* (by Albert Langen and Th. Heine) and *Jugend* (by Georg Hirth), which gave its name to the art movement known as 'Jugendstil'.

One of the earliest patents for a method of composing alphabetic characters by photographic means was granted to E. Porzholt.

Foundation at Florence of the publishing firm of Eugen Diederichs.

At Antwerp, the Museum Plantin-Moretus published *Specimen Characterum Architypographiae Plantinianae*, which displayed post-Plantinian types together with Plantin's own, accompanied by notes written by Max Rooses, the Curator of the Museum. It was reprinted with an index in 1905. The Plantin types were identified by Harry Carter in *The Library*, September 1956.

In Paris, Edouard Pelletan established a publishing firm and issued his first book, *Les Nuits & Souvenir* by Alfred De Musset, with wood engravings by Florian from designs by A. Gérardin. The book was printed on hand presses by the Maison Lahure in two separate editions, 4to and 8vo, with different typography for each.

Death of Baron Jérôme-Frédéric Pichon (b. 1812), an enthusiastic and erudite bibliophile and collector of books. From 1844–94 he was President of the Société des Bibliophiles Français. The catalogue of his library was published in Paris in three parts, with an introduction by G. Vicaire, 1897–98.

Edouard Lambert (1859–1933), together with his friend J. Bidermann, founded the Paris firm of Edouard Lambert & Cie., constructors of printing presses.

Publication of William Morris's masterpiece, *The Works of Geoffrey Chaucer*, printed at the Kelmscott Press, Hammersmith, London. It contained 87 woodcuts designed by Sir Edward Burne-Jones. 425 copies were printed on hand-made paper and 13 on vellum.

On 4 May, appeared the first number of Alfred Harmsworth's newspaper the *Daily Mail*, the first daily newspaper to reach a circulation of a million copies.

In January, appeared the first number of *The Savoy*, an illustrated quarterly, with Aubrey Beardsley (who designed the cover) as art editor and Arthur Symons as literary editor. Published by Leonard Smithers, and printed by the Chiswick Press it only ran for eight issues.

Foundation of the Publishers' Association of Great Britain and Ireland, with Charles J. Longman as its first president.

The Vale Press founded by Charles Ricketts at the Sign of the Dial, Warwick Street, London, moving to Craven Street, Strand, in 1899. The press closed down in 1904, having produced eighty-three books.

At Philadelphia was published *One Hundred Years*, the history of the MacKellar, Smiths & Jordan Foundry. A special fount was cut for this book, 15 point Ronaldson Old Style Roman, which is said to be the only fount on 15-point body ever cast.

The American branch of the London publishing firm of Macmillan (*see* 1843) separated from the English house and became an independent corporation under the name of the Macmillan Company of New York.

1897

Zeitschrift für Bücherfreunde founded by Fedor von Zobeltitz (1859–1934) at Leipzig. From 1909, it was the organ of the Gesellschaft der Bibliophilen. It was replaced in 1937, by the *Wandelhalle der Bücherfreunde* published at Weimar by the Gesellschaft der Bibliophilen.

The Electrotypograph composing and casting machine patented by C. Méray-Horvath of Budapest.

Émile Leclerc (1857–1932) published in Paris his *Nouveau Manuel complet de Typographie*. Leclerc was the editor-in-chief of the magazine *Fonderie Typographique* from its inception in September 1899 until its disappearance in 1910.

1898

The Reichsdruckerei Berlin, issued a folio edition of *Die Nibelungen* printed in a type-face designed by Joseph Sattler based on manuscript hands of the early Middle Ages. The text was that of Karl Lachmann.

The 'Caractères de l'Université' revived by the director of the Imprimerie Nationale, Paris, Arthur Christian. The fount was completed in time for the Paris Exhibition of 1900.

Eugène Grasset designed, after a roman of Sebastian Gryphius, a type-face which he called 'elzévirien gras' which was cast by the Deberny-Peignot foundry 1898–99.

Publication begun of Robert Proctor, *Index to the Early Printed Books in the British Museum.* London: Kegan Paul, Trench, Trübner & Co.

C. R. Ashbee founded the Essex House Press at Essex House, Mile End Road, London. In 1902 the press removed to Chipping Campden, Gloucestershire. It ceased in 1909.

The Crocker-Wheeler Company of Ampere, New Jersey, brought out a single-motor press drive. Mechanical trouble led to only a few being made.

1899

In Germany, the *Gesellschaft der Bibliophilen* was founded at Weimar.

The periodical *Die Insel* founded by Rudolf Alexander Schröder, Alfred Walter Heymel, and Otto Julius Bierbaum.

Founding of the German publishing firm of Insel-Verlag at Leipzig.

Printing completed at Oxford of the *Yattendon Hymnal* (edited by Robert Bridges and H. Ellis Wooldridge) set in Fell types together with the music types engraved by Peter Walpergen, unused since the end of the seventeenth century.

The John Rylands Library, Manchester, was formally dedicated to the public. The building had begun in 1890, and was given to the city by the widow of John Rylands as a memorial to her late husband. In 1901 she added to the collection the 6,000 illuminated manuscripts which had been purchased from Lord Crawford in 1900 for £200,000.

The Pear Tree Press was started in Essex by James Guthrie.

On 17 December, died in London the famous antiquarian bookseller Bernard Quaritch. He was born at Worbis im Eichsfeld, Erfurt, on 23 April, 1819. (*See* 1847.)

Death of Myles Birket Foster (b. 1825), one of the most popular English book illustrators of the mid-nineteenth century. His best work was probably his *Pictures of English Landscape*, with verses by Tom Taylor, 1862.

Between 1899 and 1908 appeared Hjalmar Pettersen's *Nordisk Boglexicon 1643–1813*, published at Christiania (Oslo).

The Blue Sky Press founded in Chicago by Alfred G. Langworthy and Thomas Wood Stevens. It ceased to function in 1906.

In S. Africa, the *Mafeking Mail* was established on 20 May as a weekly. During the siege it appeared, shells permitting, on all kinds and colours of paper. It became a daily in September, 1900.

1900

In the *Festschrift der Stadt Mainz*, issued in connection with the commemoration of the 500th anniversary of the birth of Gutenberg, Dr. Karl Schorbach published a series of twenty-seven documents concerning the inventor of printing—*Die urkundlichen Nachrichten über Johann Gutenberg, mit Nachbildungen und Erläuterungen.*

A special 'Festschrift' was issued for the 500th anniversary of the birth of Gutenberg, edited by Heinrich Wallau. 584 pp. with 34 plates.

Heinz König's 'Walthari' fount brought out by the type-foundry of the Klingspor Brothers—the first German foundry deliberately to employ well-known artists for designing their type. The 'König Antiqua' came out in 1905. Otto Eckmann's 'Eckmann Schrift' also came from the Klingspor foundry in 1900.

The first book printed in Heinz König's Walthari type—Friedrich Schneider, *D. Johann Dietenbergers Bibeldruck, Mainz, 1534.* This was one of the numerous 'Hausdrucke' printed at the private press of the Brothers Klingspor, all of which are of considerable interest to students of typography.

The first book printed in Otto Eckmann's Eckmann Schrift—Max Martersteig, *Der Schauspieler.* Leipzig: Breitkopf and Härtel for Eugen Diederichs.

Publication in Leipzig and Vienna of Sigmund Freud, *Die Traumdeutung*, perhaps Freud's greatest work, and one which opened up a whole new field of study.

First appearance of the book which introduced the Quantum Theory—Max Planck, *Zur Theorie des Gesetzes der Energieverteilung in Normalspectrum.* Leipzig.

Publication of *Festschrift zur Gutenbergfeier herausgegeben von der Königlichen Bibliothek zu Berlin. Am 24 Juni, 1900.* It contained a thorough investigation of the 42- and 36-line Bibles.

First appearance of *Klimsch' Jahrbuch.* Published up to 1940 (thirty-three volumes). Frankfurt-am-Main.

The Steglitzer Werkstatt for fine typography was established by Georg Belwe, artist and type-designer, F. H. Ehmcke, and F. W. Kleukens (later artistic director of the Ernst Ludwig Presse at Darmstadt). (*See* 1907.)

Foundation of the Gutenberg-Gesellschaft and Museum, at Mainz.

Genzsch & Heyse produced the Grasset Antiqua designed by Eugène Grasset (1841–1917), French artist, book illustrator and type designer.

Publication of W. J. Van Eys, *Bibliographie des Bibles et des Nouveaux Testaments en langue française des XV et XVI siècles*. Two volumes, 1900–01. Geneva: Henry Kündig.

For the Great Exhibition at Paris, the Imprimerie Nationale issued the first volume of *Histoire de l'Imprimerie en France au XVe et au XVI siècle* by Anatole Claudin (1833–1906). His death occurred before the work was completed, and it was finished by Arthur Christian, Director of the Imprimerie Nationale. A fourth volume was published under the direction of Léopold Delisle by Paul Lacombe (four volumes, 1900–14).

The Paris art dealer and publisher Ambroise Vollard issued his first book—a de luxe version of Verlaine's *Parallèlement*, for which Pierre Bonnard lithographed more than a hundred illustrations. Vollard followed this with many other books illustrated by leading French artists. (*See also* 1938.)

From the Oxford University Press came the important folio *Notes on a Century of Typography at the University Press, Oxford, 1693–1794*. It contains reproductions of all the type specimens issued by the Press between those dates, with an introduction, annotations and appendixes by Horace Hart, Printer to the University.

Publication of Henry R. Plomer, *A Short History of English Printing 1476–1898*. London: Kegan Paul, Trench, Trübner & Co. Ltd.

The Doves Press founded by T. J. Cobden-Sanderson and Emery Walker. The first published work of this private press was the *Agricola* of Tacitus (1901). The type was cut by Edward Prince of Islington.

Douglas Cockerell appointed instructor in art binding at the London Central School for Arts and Crafts.

Theodore Low De Vinne's *Practice of Typography* (Century Co. 1900–04) began with the volume called *Plain Printing Types*, a treatise on the processes of type-making, etc. The series was completed in 1904, and the four volumes were reissued between 1914 and 1925 by the Oswald Publishing Co., New York. De Vinne (1828–1914) was one of America's outstanding printers of the end of the nineteenth century.

1901

The firm of Hoepli, Milan, began publication of Adolfo Venturi, *Storia dell'Arte Italiana*, completed in 1939 (in eleven volumes), and a landmark in the history of art.

Douglas Cockerell published his classic and influential *Bookbinding and the Care of Books*. London: John Hogg.

The first two-colour bill machine built by R. Hoe & Co. for *Lloyd's Weekly News*.

The 'World's Classics' series of popular reprints inaugurated by Grant Richards. In 1905 the series was taken over by the Oxford University Press.

First official meeting on 28 May, of the newly formed Federation of Master Printers and Allied Trades of the United Kingdom of Great Britain and Ireland. In 1931 it was restyled the British Federation of Master Printers.

1902

The first book designed by Carl Ernst Poeschel: Rudolf Kautzsch, *Die Neue Buchkunst*. Published by the Weimar Gesellschaft der Bibliophilen and set in a new type by Peter Behrens.

G. Y. Zedler, librarian at the Nassauische Landesbibliothek, Wiesbaden, announced his discovery of a Calendar printed with the 36-line Bible type. It was reproduced in the first volume of the publications of the Gutenberg Gesellschaft. The finding established 1448 or earlier as a date when printing was practised. (*See* 1448.)

Death of Otto Eckmann (b. 1865) the master of the so-called 'Jugendstil' decoration (*see* 1896). Painter, metalworker, and industrial designer, he designed type-faces for Karl Klingspor.

Robert Proctor designed a Greek fount which Victor Scholderer described as 'the finest Greek face ever cut'. It was based on the Greek of the Complutensian *Polyglot*.

The Victory Kidder Printing Machine Co. erected a two-page wide press for the *Wiltshire Times*. Known as the 'Victory arched-frame tandem', it was a step towards the unit type of press, having a gangway between the press and the delivery mechanism, so that access to cylinders and rollers was made possible without reaching over the machine.

The Dun Emer Press founded by Elizabeth

Corbet Yeats at Dundrum, near Dublin in association with Dun Emer Industries. In 1908, the printing side of the business was separated from the rest of the concern and reorganised as the Cuala Press, which continued its activities until 1948. It specialised in works by Irish authors, in particular William Butler Yeats.

Publication began of *The Times Literary Supplement*.

First issue of *The Monotype Recorder* was published.

The Hoe Company introduced the first double octuple press. It had eight rolls, four pages wide, and on its appearance the proprietors of *Lloyd's Weekly News* ordered seven of these mammoth presses, at that time the largest and most powerful printing press in the world. It was the first of the 'decker' type of press.

Robert Hoe III (1839–1909) published *A Short History of the Printing Press*. New York: R. Hoe.

Bertram G. Goodhue designed the popular type-face known as Cheltenham for the Cheltenham Press of Ingalls Kimball at New York.

1903

Ernst Voullième published, through the Gesellschaft für Rheinische Geschichtskunde, *Der Buchdruck Kölns bis zum Ende des fünfzehnten Jahrhunderts*, a bibliographical description of the incunabula printed at Cologne.

Walter Tiemann (1876–1951) began to teach at the Staatliche Akademie der Graphischen Künste, Leipzig, of which he became the head for more than twenty years. Painter, illustrator, book and type designer, he was, after Rudolf Koch (*see* 1934), the most important type designer at the Klingspor foundry.

First appearance of the bibliographical periodical *Tijdschrift voor Boek- en Bibliotheekwezen*. Antwerp, & Ghent: De Nederlandsche Boekhandel. It lasted under that style until 1911. In 1912 a second series was begun under the title *Het Boek* (The Hague: M. Nijhoff). It ceased publication with Vol. 37, 1967.

The Dutch type designer, S. H. de Roos, designed his first book, a translation of lectures by William Morris published under the title *Kunst en Maatschappij*. De Roos was also an industrial designer with much the same ideals as Morris himself.

Publication begun at the Doves Press (*see* 1900)

of the five-volume edition (completed in 1905) of the Bible, the masterpiece of the Press and in its magnificent simplicity one of the noblest printed books ever produced in this country. It was hand set, and all five volumes were produced on one hand press, the sole compositor being J. H. Mason, who later became head of the London School of Printing.

On 16 February, the *Globe* newspaper announced: 'Today for the first time the *Globe* is entirely printed by electricity.'

On 2 November, the *Daily Mirror* was published for the first time. It was the first daily newspaper anywhere to be illustrated throughout with half-tone blocks.

Hugo and Carl Lagerström founded at Stockholm the publishing firm of Lagerström Brothers which produced during the early part of the century some of the finest books in Sweden, devoted largely to old Scandinavian literature.

Frederic W. Goudy and Will Ransom established the Village Press at Park Ridge, Illinois. Ransom soon withdrew from the business, which was carried on by Mr. and Mrs. Goudy. It later moved, first to Hingham Mass., and then to New York City.

1904

At Frankfurt-am-Main, Klimsch & Co. published the first edition of Friedrich Bauer, *Handbuch für Schriftsetzer* (Compositor's Handbook).

To celebrate the centenary of the founding of the Vienna Stadtsdruckerei, a memorial volume was issued for which a new fount was designed by Rudolf von Larisch. The illustrations were by C. O. Czeschka and ornaments by Koloman Moser.

The Shakespeare Head Press was founded by A. H. Bullen at Stratford-on-Avon for the printing of the works of the poet in his native town. In 1920 the press was taken over at Bullen's death by a group of people interested in the fine printing of works of scholarship, with the active participation of the printer Bernard Newdigate and the publisher Basil Blackwell. The Press was moved to Oxford in 1929.

Ira W. Rubel, a New York lithographer, commercially developed offset printing on paper. He designed a special press for the purpose which was built by the Potter Printing Press Co. of New York. The first similar British machine was patented in 1906 and built by George Mann, incorporating various improvements.

The Bibliographical Society of America founded at St. Louis, Missouri.

1905

Konrad Häbler published his famous study of incunabula types entitled *Typenrepertorium der Wiegendrucke*. Six parts in five volumes. Halle & Leipzig, 1905–24. Haebler made an exhaustive study of early type, and the work forms an invaluable aid to bibliographical research.

Anton Kippenberg (1874–1950) took over the direction of Insel Verlag. For its series of German classics called the 'Grossherzog Wilhelm Ernst Ausgabe' the format was designed by Emery Walker, and title-pages and half-titles were drawn by Edward Johnston and Eric Gill.

Melchior Lechter (1865–1937) founded the Einhorn Presse. He was devoted to the principles of the aesthetic movement in Germany known as 'Jugendstil' which flourished around 1900 and was the equivalent of the 'Art Nouveau' of France and other countries.

In Florence, Leo S. Olschki published G. Fumagalli, *Lexicon typographicum Italiae*. Text in French. Printed by L. Franceschini & Co., Florence.

Vojtěch Preissig (1873–1944), Czech typographer and artist, founded a graphic workshop at Prague.

At Paris, Hachette et Cie published P. Mellottée, *Les transformations économiques de l'imprimerie sous l'ancien régime*, a work of considerable importance on the economic history of the book trade in France prior to the Revolution. Printed at Châteauroux by P. Mellottée.

Publication by the Imprimerie Nationale, Paris, of A. Christian, *Débuts de l'imprimerie en France*, etc. The book, by a director of the Imprimerie Nationale, consists of twenty-one chapters each printed from a different fount. Among the faces employed are those of Garamond and Grandjean, the 'millimetric' type of Firmin Didot, the Jaugeon, and others. In all seventy different type-faces were used.

The *Iconografia de las ediciones del Quijote de Miguel de Cervantes Saavedra* published at Barcelona. It reproduces facsimile title-pages of no fewer than 611 editions of *Don Quixote* published between 1605 and 1905.

The *Morning Post* made use of a battery of Wicks composing machines supplied daily with new type from the Wicks foundry in Blackfriars Road, London. They were replaced by Linotype machines in 1910.

Caspar Hermann, a lithographer from Germany, built his first offset press at Niles, Ohio, about the same time that W. Rubel constructed one in Jersey City.

1906

Friedrich Bauer designed the book face Nordische Antiqua, issued by the foundry of Genzsch & Heyse. It was later renamed Genzsch Antiqua.

Rudolf Koch appointed designer to the Klingspor foundry at the age of 30. (*See also* 1934.)

Lloyd's Weekly News was the first newspaper in England to produce a double-page spread of pictures all printed from half-tone blocks.

Edward Johnston published his classic work *Writing & Illuminating & Lettering*. London: John Hogg. The work and teaching of Johnston created a calligraphic movement which influenced type design, particularly in Germany.

The first volume of Dent's 'Everyman's Library' made its appearance—Vol. 1 of Boswell's *Life of Samuel Johnson*. This series of popular reprints of the best in English literature was edited from its inception until his death in 1946 by Ernest Rhys. The first fifty titles were published *en bloc* in February 1906. The covers, end papers and title-pages were designed by the architect Reginald L. Knowles, and their swirling floral decoration shows a distinct 'Art Nouveau' influence.

Death of Michael Patrick McCoy (b. Dublin 1850), editor and publisher of the *Modern Printer*.

The Ludlow, a type-casting machine casting large size type for display purposes was invented by Washington I. Ludlow and marketed by the Ludlow Typograph Company of Chicago. It was introduced into England about 1911.

In 1906 was published the first issue (Vol. 1, Part 1, 1904–5) of the *Proceedings and Papers of the Bibliographical Society of America* (founded 1904). It contains the articles of constitution of the B.S.A., and list of members at 31 December, 1905. The first President of the Society was William Coolidge Lane, Librarian of Harvard

University. Printed at The Cheltenham Press, New York.

1907

At Leipzig, publication of the first of the *Veröffentlichungen der Gesellschaft für Typenkunde des XV Jahrhunderts*. This monumental undertaking resulted in a vast number of reproductions of title-pages, analytical tables of type-forms, etc.

In October, was founded at Munich the Deutsche Werkbund, among the founders of which were F. H. Ehmcke, calligrapher and designer, the publisher Eugen Diederichs, and the architect Hermann Muthesius. Although primarily concerned with industrial design and architecture, the Werkbund exerted an influence on the art of the book in Germany, rejecting the decoration of the 'Jugendstil' and relying on appropriateness of material and design.

Carl Ernst Poeschel (1874–1944) founded the Janus Presse—a private press—in Leipzig, which printed a few books of fine quality with types and initials designed by Walter Tiemann (1876–1951).

First issue of the *Jahrbuch der Bücherpreise*.

At Darmstadt, F. W. Kleukens (1878–1956), in charge from 1907 to 1914, and his brother Ch. H. Kleukens (1880–1955), in charge from 1918 until 1937, founded, in conjunction with Grand Duke Ernst Ludwig of Hesse, the Ernst Ludwig Presse, a private press endowed by the Grand Duke.

Emil Rudolf Weiss (1875–1942) appointed professor at the Staatsschule für freie und angewandte Kunst, Berlin. Weiss became an outstanding book illustrator and type designer.

Painter and architect Paul Renner (1878–1956) appointed designer and production manager for the Munich publishing firm of Georg Müller (founded 1903)—a post Renner held until 1917, when Müller died.

In a small printing office at Ostiglia the 17-year-old Arnoldo Mondadori printed on an old hand press a political sheet called *Luce!* This was the humble origin of the great printing-publishing firm of Arnoldo Mondadori Editore, today probably the largest graphic-editorial complex in Europe, with its headquarters and editorial offices at Milan and its enormous works just outside Verona.

Publication of Charles Moïse Briquet, *Les Filigranes. Dictionnaire historique des marques du papier dès leur apparition vers 1282 jusqu'en 1600*. Geneva: A. Jullien, 1907. (A reprint was published at Leipzig in 1923. In 1968 appeared a new edition, edited by Allan Stevenson and J. S. G. Simmons, with an introduction, addenda and corrigenda, and an extensive bibliography.)

The Cambridge University Press published the first volume of the *Cambridge History of English Literature*, edited by A. W. Ward and A. R. Waller. Fourteen volumes. (*See also* 1941.)

1908

Hans von Weber (1872–1924) launched at Munich his bi-monthly *Hyperion*. He had started a publishing firm in 1906, and from 1912–14 issued the Hyperion-Drucke with texts of European classics, finely printed by Poeschel and by Enschedé. He also acquired a reputation with his hand-printed 'Drucke für die Hundert' (thirty-nine volumes, 1909–23), largely made up of old Germanic texts, Norse sagas and early German poetry. In 1914 he began the collection called 'Reihe der Hundertfünfzig'.

The Hamburg firm of Genzsch & Heyse, typefounders, brought out a comprehensive specimen book, *Typen Revue*, of 138 double-column pages.

Death of Wilhelm Busch (b. 1832), one of the best-known German book illustrators of the nineteenth century. In addition to his book work he was a regular contributor to *Fliegende Blätter* (Munich) between 1858 and 1871.

Karel Dyrynk (1896–1949) published his *Pravidla typografiké sazby* (Rules for typographic composition).

Publication at Haarlem of Ch. Enschedé, *Fonderies de caractères et leur matériel dans les Pays-Bas du XVe au XIXe siècle*. One of the classics of the history of printing types. It contains about 500 illustrations, many of them printed from ancient types in the possession of the Enschedé foundry at Haarlem.

The Arden Press (*see* 1890) was bought by W. H. Smith & Son, and the business transferred to Letchworth. Bernard Newdigate remained with the firm as typographical adviser until he joined the army in 1914. (*See also* 1920.)

One of the richest collections of printing literature, both historical and technical, the Typographical Library at Jersey City, was established by the American Type Founders Co. It later passed into the care of Columbia University. One of the prime movers in gathering together this collection was Henry Lewis Bullen.

1909

The Tempel Verlag founded at Leipzig. It issued the famous series of Tempel-Klassiker under the artistic direction of Emil Rudolf Weiss, who also designed the type.

Publication begun in Paris of G. Lepreux, *Gallia typographica*, the seven volumes of which were completed by 1913. They are divided as follows:

Série Départementale: I. Flandre, Artois, Picardie (1909)
II. Champagne et Barrois (1911)
III. Normandie. 2 vols. (1912)
IV. Bretagne (1913)
Série Parisienne: Tome I. Livre d'Or des Imprimeurs du Roi (2 vols., 1910, 1911)
Paris: Honoré Champion. Printed by Imp. Darantière, Dijon.

The Riccardi Press founded by Herbert P. Horne for the publications of the Medici Society. Horne also designed the Riccardi type, for which E. P. Prince cut the punches; the printing was done by the Chiswick Press. Horne also designed, for the firm of Chatto and Windus, his Florence type.

1910

As a result of the researches carried on by Dr. Mertens of Freiburg, the *Freiburger Zeitung* became the first newspaper to be illustrated throughout in photogravure printed on the normal newsprint of the paper. This achievement was carried out on a rotary press built by the Mulhouse firm Société Alsacienne de Constructions Mécaniques. In England one weekly newspaper, the *Southend Standard*, adopted the process.

The Stamperia Vaticana and the Typographia Polyglotta were merged under the style of Tipografia Poliglotta Vaticana.

Jan Greshoff and Jacques Bloem, later joined by P. N. van Eyck, founded the Dutch private press known as De Zilverdistel (The Silver Thistle). The first publication, in 1910, was P. N. van Eyck, *Worstelingen*, printed at Haarlem by Joh.

Enschedé en Zonen in an eighteenth-century type of J. M. Fleischman. In 1913 the press was run by P. N. van Eyck and J. F. van Royen, and in 1915 came under the direction of J. F. van Royen alone. His first publication (1913) was *Lanseloet van Denemerken*, of which 100 copies were hand-printed. In 1923 the Zilverdistel was renamed the Kunera-Pers. Its first publication was *Oostersch*, verses after Persian and Arabic poets by J. H. Leopold, printed by J. F. van Royen and set in Lucien Pissarro's Disteltype.

On 1 September, died at Seville the printer D. Enrique Rasco, whose active career dated from 1883, in which year he printed his first book, Juan de Robles, *El culto sevillano*, for the Sociedad de Bibliófilos Andaluces.

J. C. Grant and L. A. Legros designed and patented their improved punch-cutting machine, described and illustrated in their book, *Typographical Printing Surfaces*—London: Longmans, Green & Co. 1916. In this machine the micrometer reading could be seen by the operator while seated.

Between 1910 and 1913 was published the *Bibliotheca Lindesiana*—a catalogue of the remarkable private collection formed at Haigh Hall, Wigan, by successive Earls of Crawford.

1911

Eduard Wilhelm Tieffenbach (1883–1948) founded the Officina Serpentis at Berlin-Steglitz. After 1918 he specialised in printing for bibliophile societies, and in 1930 printed for the Berlin Bibliophiles his own book, *Über den Satz im schönen Buch*.

At Bremen, Willi Wiegand (1886–1961) and others founded the Bremer Presse, which lasted until 1934. Until its closure it was one of the finest of the private presses in Germany. Many of the initials and title-page lettering used by this press were drawn by Anna Simons, a pupil of Edward Johnston, and cut on wood by Joseph Lehnacker. All its books were printed in roman types designed by Wiegand.

A new Copyright Act was passed in Great Britain which repealed either wholly or in part some twenty-one previous Acts concerning copyright, and provided that duration of copyright should be for the author's lifetime and fifty years afterwards. The Stationers' Company ceased to exercise a function it had carried out for more than three centuries when Registration was abolished in this year. Books no longer bore the words 'Entered at Stationers' Hall'.

The Cambridge University Press published the famous eleventh edition of the *Encyclopædia Britannica*.

King George V deposited on permanent loan in the British Museum the royal collection known as the King's Music Library.

Died William Griggs (b. 1832) the inventor of photo-chromolithography. His first notable work was the plates illustrating Dr. Forbes Watson, *Textile Manufactures and Customs of the People of India* (1866), followed in 1868 by plates for James Fergusson, *Tree and Serpent Worship in India*. Griggs was appointed chromolithographer to Queen Victoria, and later to King Edward VII. He was employed at the India Office until 1885, after which he devoted his time to his own business.

1912

Anton Kippenberg (*see* 1905) founded the Insel-Bücherei, which in fifty years had produced some 800 titles.

Insel-Verlag published at Leipzig, edited by Paul Schwenke, a facsimile of the 42-line Bible.

The eminent Dutch book and type designer S. H. de Roos (1877–1962), completed his first type-face, Hollandsche Mediaeval, followed by his Silvertype for the use of J. F. van Royen's private press (*see* 1910). There followed Erasmus-Mediaeval (1923), Grotius (1925), Meidoorntype for his own private press (1927), Egmont (1932–34), Libra (1938), and De Roos roman (1948).

First issue of the Dutch periodical for bibliophiles, *De Witte Mier* edited by the poet J. Greshoff, one of the founders of De Zilverdistel (*see* 1910). The first series, which closed down in 1913 contains some of the earliest lettering of Jan Van Krimpen.

In 1912, Georges Peignot, with the financial help of the *Gazette du Bon Ton*, launched his Cochin series of type-faces, and at the same time recast the Fournier ornaments. As one of the country's leading type-founders, Georges Peignot greatly influenced book printing in France from 1900 until the outbreak of the First World War. Among other faces for which he was responsible were those designed by Eugène Grasset, Georges Auriol and Bernard Naudin.

The first intaglio rotary (German built) in Britain was installed by the *Illustrated London News*.

The Times brought out, to celebrate its 40,000th number, a supplement devoted to the history of printing and the newspaper press.

1913

Emil Rudolf Weiss designed one of his finest founts, the Weiss-Fraktur, used extensively in the standard editions of the 'Tempel-Klassiker' (*see* 1909). The fount is shown in the *Probe der Weiss-Fraktur* issued by the Bauersche Giesserei, Frankfurt-am-Main in 1913.

Count Harry Kessler (1868–1937) founded a private press, the Cranach Presse at Weimar (once the home of the famous artist Lucas Cranach). Among the illustrators employed by the press were Eric Gill, Aristide Maillol, E. Gordon Craig, and Marcus Behmer. The rise of the Nazis in Germany forced Kessler to leave the country and his work was disrupted. Among the outstanding books from the Cranach Presse were Shakespeare's *Hamlet* with woodcuts by Edward Gordon Craig, the *Song of Solomon* illustrated by Eric Gill, and Virgil's *Eclogues*, with woodcuts by Maillol. This last work was printed in a Jenson-style roman cut by Edward Prince and an italic designed by Edward Johnston. It was published at Leipzig in 1926 by Insel-Verlag. *Hamlet* appeared, translated into German by Gerhart Hauptmann, in 1928; in 1930 it was issued in an English edition, edited by J. Dover Wilson.

At Berlin, Julius Bard published Emil Schaeffer, *Von Bildern und Mensch der Renaissance*, the first book printed in Peter Behrens's Behrens Mediaeval.

Ernst Rowohlt and Julius Schröder acquired the rights in the Hyperion-Drucke from Hans von Weber (*see* 1908) and they were continued until 1923 as 'Dreiangeldrucke'.

At Munich the Rupprecht-Presse was founded by F. H. Ehmcke. It functioned until 1934, and in the course of its existence issued fifty-seven hand-printed works set in Ehmcke's own type-faces. Ehmcke was for many years a professor at the Kunstgewerbeschule (now the Akademie) at Munich.

The first number appeared of *The Imprint*, started by Gerard Meynell of the Westminster Press as a journal devoted to 'improving and spreading technical knowledge in printing'. It appeared only for nine monthly issues—January to November 1913. Among the staff was Stanley Morison, then aged 24. A type-face cut for the periodical in 1912 was called Imprint Old Face.

The title and border were pen-drawn by Edward Johnston for reproduction by line block.

The first British-built Unit-type press, constructed at R. Hoe & Company's London works, was installed by the Paris newspaper *Le Matin*.

The present Harvard University Press was founded—the descendant of a printing office established about 1871 for the execution of minor printing jobs for the university.

First conceived by Herman Ridder in 1911, the first factory-made Intertype composing machine was installed in the printing house of the American *Journal of Commerce*.

1914

The first 'Heidelberg' machine was built by the Schnellpressenfabrik A.G. of Heidelberg. This was a platen machine. The cylinder 'Heidelberg' —a single revolution machine—was first marketed in 1936.

In February BUGRA, an Exhibition of Graphic Arts, was held at Leipzig.

Intertype, a new line composing and casting machine, appeared on the market, manufactured by the International Typesetting Machine Company, New York. The prototype was first demonstrated in November 1912, and in March 1913 one of the machines was in use by the New York *Journal of Commerce*.

Foundation of the American Institute of Graphic Arts.

On 16 February, died Theodore Low De Vinne (*see* 1900), American printer, author and type designer. Born at Stamford, Connecticut, on 25 December, 1828, he was one of the founders of the Grolier Club and printed many of its publications.

1915

Imre Kner (1890–1944), son of the founder of the publishing firm of Kner at Gyoma (Hungary), took charge of the business in 1915 after having served his apprenticeship in his father's printing office. An exceptionally gifted typographer and book designer, he began to publish the Kner Classics in 1921, and in 1925 published his own views on the work of a typographer. He died in a concentration camp in 1944.

The Montague Press, Massachusetts, published a translation of Maurice de Guérin, *The Centaur*, using a fount of type designed by Bruce Rogers which was named Centaur after the book in which it first appeared. The fount was cut by Robert Wiebking of Chicago, and in 1929 Centaur was again cut for machine composition by the Monotype Corporation of London.

In 1915 Hoe and Company introduced a number of new features to their presses, the most important of which were the Hoe ink pumps, which did away with the unpleasant work of filling ink ducts by hand.

1916

The 'Drucke der Marées-Gesellschaft' inaugurated by Julius Meier-Graefe and published by R. Piper. The formats varied and the contents ranged widely over a variety of subjects with considerable technical skill. The productions included the annual *Ganymed*, of which five numbers appeared up to 1925.

J. F. van Royen and P. N. van Eyck published *Over boekkunst en de Zilverdistel* (*see also* 1910). The Hague: De Zilverdistel. It was printed in black and red, in S. H. de Roos's Zilvertype.

The St. Dominic's Press was founded at Ditchling, Sussex, by Hilary Pepler. Until its closure in 1937, it was a centre of experiment in printing craftsmanship. One of its most notable productions was a *Book of Hours* (1923) illustrated by Eric Gill.

With the aid of the Victoria House Publishing Company, the Pelican Press was founded by Francis (later Sir Francis) Meynell. Its aim was to provide fine mechanical printing for jobbing as well as bookwork.

Closure of the Doves Press (*see* 1900), upon which occasion the punches, matrices and types were thrown from Hammersmith Bridge into the Thames by T. J. Cobden-Sanderson.

Akke Kumlien (1884–1949), distinguished Swedish calligrapher and book designer, was appointed art director of the printing and publishing firm of Norstedt, at Stockholm, a post he held until his death in 1949. He designed a roman type-face, Kumlien Mediaeval, which was cut and cast by the Klingspor foundry in Germany. In 1945 P. A. Norstedt & Sons published a 'Festschrift', *Akke Kumlien som bokkonstnär*.

1917

From Klingspor Bros. at Offenbach came Hans Bethge, *Lieder des Orients*, *Nachdichtungen*. Dedicated to C. E. Poeschel as a tribute to his twenty-five years as a printer, it was the first book set in Rudolf Koch's Frühlings Schrift.

Charles Nypels, the Dutch typographer and publisher (1895–1952) began his career as an apprentice with S. H. De Roos. (*See also* 1920.)

At Paris, from 11–17 March, was held the Congrès National du Livre.

The Hogarth Press was established at 52 Tavistock Square, London, by Leonard and Virginia Woolf and associates. The first book from this press was *Two Stories*, by Leonard and Virginia Woolf (1917).

Her Majesty's Stationery Office, founded in 1786, acquired for the first time its own printing works, as a result of the vast increase in Government printing brought about by the war.

Publication of E. Gordon Duff, *Fifteenth Century English Books* (Bibliographical Society Monograph No. 18). A folio which shows all English types of the fifteenth century.

The first number of the Russian newspaper *Izvestia* appeared on the Julian calendar date 28 February, 1917 (13 March by the Gregorian calendar). When it first appeared it had a circulation of 35,000. It now claims the largest circulation of any daily newspaper in the world—8,670,000.

Edwin and Robert Grabhorn published their first book in Indianapolis under the imprint of the Studio Press. It was an edition of T. L. De Vinne, *Typographical Effect*. In 1919 the Grabhorns moved to San Francisco. (*See* 1919.)

At New York, the Grolier Club published a translation of that section of Dürer's *Unterweyssung der Messung* which treats of letters, under the title: 'Of the Just Shaping of Letters'. (*See* 1525.)

1918

First publication of the Marées-Gesellschaft, Munich—Goethe, *Clavigo*, illustrated by G. von Seckendorff, with type ornaments by E. R. Weiss. The society had been founded in 1916 by Julius Meier-Graefe in memory of Hans von Marées (1837–1887).

Birth of Hermann Zapf, calligrapher and typographer, who became one of the most successful book designers in Germany. He published *inter alia*, *Feder und Stichel* (1952) and *Manuale typographicum* (1955).

Carl P. Rollins (1880–1962) joined the Yale University Press, and in 1920 became Printer to the University, where he remained for thirty years. He had previously managed the Montague Press at Montague, Massachusetts.

1919

The Ratio-Presse was founded at Darmstadt by Friedrich Wilhelm Kleukens (*see* 1907). Its first publication was *Vogel–ABC*, with 52 illustrations lithographed by Kleukens and hand-coloured.

The Bauhaus was founded by Walter Gropius at Weimar, and later continued after 1925 at Dessau as Hochschule für Bau und Gestaltung. It was the focal point of post-war revolutionary ideas concerning art and design.

The Czechoslovakian Státní Tiskarna (Government Printing Works) founded under the direction of Karel Dyrynk.

Formation of the Joint Industrial Council of the Printing and Kindred Trades.

Founding of the Gosizdat, the Russian State Publishing House. It was reorganised, 1931, as O.G.I.Z.

The Grabhorn Press was founded at 510 Pine Street, San Francisco, California, by Edwin and Robert Grabhorn. It became one of the best known of American private presses.

Bruce Rogers was appointed adviser to the Harvard University Press.

1920

Charles Nypels (1893–1952) designed his first book, F. J. H. Lousbergh, *Verzen en fragmenten*, set in Hollandsche Mediaeval with woodcuts by Henri Jonas. (*See* 1917 *and* 1939.)

On the initiative of some 150 publishers and 800 booksellers in France, was founded the distributive organisation called the Maison du Livre Français, or M.L.F.

The Goss Company introduced into Britain the first of what is known as the Line type of newspaper press—a multiple low construction press and folder units in one line on floor level, as opposed to the Deck system, with one press above the other.

In England, the Society of Wood Engravers was formed. Among its original members were Lucien Pissarro, Gordon Craig, Eric Gill, Robert Gibbings and John Nash. Commercial publishers in England being unwilling to make use of this medium for illustrating their books, it was left to the private presses to exploit the work of a talented group of wood engravers.

The Golden Cockerel Press founded at Waltham St. Lawrence by Harold Midgely Taylor. It was taken over in 1924 by Robert Gibbings, who remained its director until 1933. It was then reorganised by Christopher Sandford and Owen Rutter, and its publications were printed by the Chiswick Press.

The Cloister Press founded at Heaton Mersey, near Manchester, by C. W. Hobson, who entrusted its management to the printer Walter Lewis (*see* 1923). Stanley Morison was the typographical adviser.

After his army service, the printer Bernard Newdigate began a fruitful association with the Oxford bookseller and publisher Basil Blackwell who, together with others, bought the Shakespeare Head Press on the death of A. H. Bullen in 1920. (*See* 1904.)

The Favil Press, a private press, was founded in London by P. Sainsbury, whose partner, C. A. Birnstingl took it over in 1922. It closed down about 1948.

Henry E. Huntington (1850–1927) turned over to the public his magnificent library at San Marino, California.

1921

At Stuttgart, the Felix Krais Verlag published Hans Loubier, *Die Neue Deutsche Buchkunst*, with 157 reproductions of title- and text-pages from works of the leading German publishers and designers of the beginning of the twentieth century, and of specimens of type designs by Behrens, Koch, Tiemann, Ehmcke, Kleukens and others.

The first book published by the Staatlichen Akademie für graphischen Künste und Buchgewerbe, Leipzig: Shakespeare, *Troilus and Cressida*, illustrated with 12 coloured lithographs by Kurth Werth.

Rudolf Koch (*see* 1934) published a short autobiography in *Plakat* (Jahrg. 12, Heft 9).

At Stuttgart the illustrator and book designer Ernst Schneidler (1882–1956) founded the Juniperus-Presse. He was the designer of several type-faces, including Schneidler-Mediaeval, Zentenar-Fraktur, and the script face, Legende; he was also a professor at the State School for Arts and Crafts at Stuttgart.

Aloys Ruppel became director of the Gutenberg Museum at Mainz.

At Milan, appeared *Pagine di antichi maestri della tipografia Italiana* by Raffaello Bertieri, the text of which was a paper read by Bertieri at the opening of the 1920–21 session of the Scuola del Libro, Milan. The book was printed 'coi tipi della Scuola'.

At Paris, from 13–18 June, was held the Deuxième Congrès National du Livre. (*See* 1917.)

Publication, at Paris, of *La lettre de l'imprimerie*, set in types designed by George Auriol. In 1924, the author, Francis Thibaudeau issued his *Manuel français de la typographie moderne*.

1922

Der Sammler by Alfred Lichtwark, issued as a 'Hausdruck' by the Klingspor foundry at Offenbach-am-Main, was the first book to be set in Koch Antiqua, designed by Rudolf Koch.

In Prague was founded the Prùmyslová Tiskárna (Industrial Printing Establishment) under the direction of Method Kaláb (b. 1885), an influential Czech typographer who with Karel Dyrynk and Vojtěch Preissig laid the foundations of modern Czech typography.

Alexandre Stols (b. Maastricht, 1900), the son of a printer, began his career as a publisher in his native town, soon acquiring a reputation for his stylishly printed books. His first work was Vondel, *Aenleidinge ter Nederduitsche Dichtkunste* (January 1922), a booklet printed in De Roos's Hollandsche Mediaeval.

In February appeared the first edition of James Joyce, *Ulysses*, in an edition of 1,000 numbered copies. Paris: Shakespeare & Company (Sylvia Beach). It was printed by Maurice Darantière at Dijon.

Mr. Stanley Morison was appointed typographical adviser to the Monotype Corporation, Ltd.

The St. Bride Foundation Printing School moved to Stamford Street and was renamed the London School of Printing & Kindred Trades. (*See* 1949.)

State Publishing Houses were founded at Moscow and Leningrad.

First edition of Daniel Berkeley Updike, *Printing Types; their History, Forms, and Use*. Cambridge,

Mass.: Harvard University Press. Two Volumes. One of the classics of printing history, this work was based on lectures he had given at Harvard University between 1911 and 1916, and was printed at Updike's own Merrymount Press. (*See* 1893.)

1923

Insel-Verlag of Leipzig published Rainer Maria Rilke, *Duineser Elegien*. Printed by the Klingspor Brothers, this was the first book set in Walter Tiemann's Tiemann-Antiqua.

The Bauhausverlag was established and issued its first book: *Staatliches Bauhaus in Weimar 1919–1923*, edited by Moholy-Nagy and Walter Gropius.

Dr. Oscar Jolles published *Die deutsche Schriftgiesserei*, a trade bibliography with contributions by Friedrich Bauer, Gustav Mori, and Heinrich Schwarz. Berlin: Schriftgiesserei H. Berthold A.G.

In April, appeared the first publication of the Officina Bodoni, founded by Giovanni Mardersteig at Montagnola di Lugano, Switzerland. The work was A. A. Poliziano, *Orphei Tragedia*. In 1927, the press was moved to Verona. Many of the books printed by this press have made use of Bodoni type recast from matrices preserved at the Biblioteca Palatina in Parma. Mardersteig has himself designed three founts of type: Griffo (1930), Zeno (1936) and Dante (1954) for his own private press, and also Fontana for Collins. (*See* 1936.)

Publication of the first volume of the new series of *De Gulden Passer/Le Compas d'Or*, the organ of the Society of Antwerp Bibliophiles. Antwerp & The Hague.

At The Hague, publication of Part I of Wouter Nijhoff and M. E. Kronenberg, *Nederlandsche Bibliographie van 1500 tot 1540*. Part II by M. E. Kronenberg was published 1940, and supplementary volumes forming Part III were published 1951, 1958 and 1961.

In London, 'At the Office of the *Fleuron*', was published *A Brief Survey of Printing History and Practice* by Stanley Morison and Holbrook Jackson, printed at the Kynoch Press. A small portion had previously appeared in a printing supplement issued with the *Manchester Guardian*, 23 May, 1922. Two years later, a re-writing of the subject by Stanley Morison alone appeared in a double number of the *Monotype Recorder*, under

the title *Type Designs of the Past and Present*. In 1926 this reappeared with some slight alterations as an octavo volume under the imprint of *The Fleuron*. In 1962 a slightly enlarged and revised edition was published by Ernest Benn Ltd.

Publication of the first number of *The Fleuron*, a handsomely produced and inspired magazine devoted to the history and practice of typography. Seven numbers appeared between 1923 and 1930. The first four were edited by Oliver Simon and printed by the Curwen Press; the last three were edited by Stanley Morison and printed by the Cambridge University Press.

Walter Lewis was appointed Printer to the Cambridge University Press in succession to J. B. Peace. Lewis had previously been manager of the Cloister Press at Heaton Mersey. (*See* 1920.)

Publication of William Gamble, *Music Engraving and Printing. Historical and Technical Treatise*. London: Sir Isaac Pitman & Sons, Ltd.

The Gregynog Press, a private press founded at Newtown, Montgomeryshire, by Gwendolyn and Margaret Davies, issued its first book, the *Poems* of George Herbert, set in Frederic Goudy's Kennerly type. The press was established with a view to reviving Welsh craftsmanship by printing Welsh and English literature. It closed in 1940 with a tally of forty-two books.

The Nonesuch Press was founded by Francis Meynell and Vera Mendel. Most of the books issued by this press were designed by Francis (later Sir Francis) Meynell and the edition printing was undertaken by various printing firms subject to those exacting standards of setting and presswork upon which Meynell insisted.

Porter Garnett (1871–1951), a native of San Francisco, founded the Laboratory Press at the Carnegie Institute of Technology, Pittsburgh, which trained printers in hand composition and presswork. It closed down in 1935.

1924

In Germany, was founded the Soncino-Gesellschaft der Freunde des jüdischen Buches. One of its finest publications was the Hebrew Bible, of which unfortunately only the five books of Moses (Thora) appeared, printed in the Hebrew script and initials designed by Marcus Behmer.

Founding of the Büchergilde Gutenberg at Mainz.

The type-foundry of Girard & Cie, founded by Alexandre Deberny (1809–81) was amalgamated with the Peignot foundry, established by Gustave Peignot (1839–99).

Publication of *Catalogue raisonné of books printed at the Curwen Press, 1920–1923*. This catalogue, with an introduction by Holbrook Jackson, is illustrated by reproductions of title-pages, text pages, and designs in colour by Albert Rutherston and Claude Lovat Fraser.

Stanley Morison, *Four Centuries of Fine Printing*, was first published in a limited folio edition by Ernest Benn. The text was printed by the Cambridge University Press, and the 600 or more collotype plates were executed by Albert Frisch, at Berlin.

The Double Crown Club was founded in London by Oliver Simon and Hubert Foss. Associated with them were G. Wren Howard, Gerard Meynell, and S. C. Roberts. Holbrook Jackson became the first President of the club, which was formed for 'the purpose of exchanging ideas on good printing'.

R. Hoe and Co. introduced into Britain the 'flying paster' used for joining up magazine reels without stopping the press. It had been in use in America for some time.

The library collected by John Pierpont Morgan (1837–1913) was placed in the hands of trustees and opened to the public.

1925

At Munich, appeared Adolf Hitler, *Mein Kampf*, the Bible of National Socialism. It was written in prison after the abortive Munich 'putsch' of 1923.

At Leipzig, was published the first volume of the *Gesamtkatalog der Wiegendrucke*, a complete catalogue of incunabula prepared in accordance with the recommendations of a Commission set up under the presidency of the bibliographer Dr. Konrad Häbler in 1904 by the Prussian Board of Education. By 1938, seven complete volumes had been published. One further part—Vol. 8, Part 1, was published but most of the stock of it was destroyed in Germany during the Second World War.

Julius Rodenberg published his *Deutsche Pressen*, a bibliographical catalogue accompanied by notes and type specimens. Zürich, Vienna, and Leipzig: Amalthea Verlag. A supplementary volume appeared in 1931.

Giuseppe Fumagalli (1863–1939), author of *Lexicon Typographicum Italiae* (1905) founded the Instituto Italiano del Libro.

McP

Robert Haas founded his private press, the Officina Vindobonensis at Vienna.

A prototype of the machine for photo-composition known as the Uhertype, was introduced by the Hungarian engineer Edmund Uher.

An Exhibition of the books designed by Raffaello Bertieri (1875–1945) was held at the Plantin-Moretus Museum, Antwerp. In 1926 this Florentine book and type designer created the Paganini alphabet, cast by the Nebiolo foundry at Turin, of which he was the artistic adviser. It was first used in A. Calabi, *L'Arte Tipografica in Italia al 1928* (Milan, 1928).

The Lutetia type of Jan van Krimpen (1892–1958), commissioned in 1924 by Dr. J. Enschedé, was brought out in time for the Exposition des Arts Décoratifs at Paris in 1925. It was called Lutetia from the old Roman name for Paris.

The Tapestry, poems by Robert Bridges, privately printed by F.W. (Frederick Warde) and S.M. (Stanley Morison) in a type based upon the hand of the calligrapher-printer Ludovico degli Arrighi, for which the punches were cut by hand. In 1929 this Arrighi script was cut for 'Monotype' machine composition to match with Centaur. (*See* 1915.)

Publication of *Specimens of Books printed at Oxford with the types given to the University by John Fell*. Oxford: Clarendon Press. A folio memorial volume in honour of John Fell on the 300th anniversary of his birth (1625). The specimens shown are from ancient and modern works set in the types which bear Fell's name.

Formation of the National Book Council.

Stanley Morison became typographical adviser to the Cambridge University Press.

John Johnson (1882–1956) appointed Printer to the Oxford University Press.

In Norway, the Oslo daily *Aftenposten* began to run two-colour advertisements. In 1952 the same paper began producing four-colour R.O.P. (Run of the press).

1926

Publication of Rudolf Koch, *Das Zeichenbuch*, printed by Offenbacher Werkstätten, Offenbach-am-Main, and published by Verlag Wilhelm Gerstung. It contains 493 symbols used from ancient times up until the Middle Ages, redrawn and explained by Rudolf Koch and cut on wood by Fritz Kredel. An English translation by

Vyvyan Holland was published in 1930 by the First Edition Club, London, set in Koch's Magere Deutsche.

At Mainz, the first issue appeared of the *Gutenberg Jahrbuch*, an international review of the art and history of the book, published by the Gutenberg Gesellschaft and edited by Dr. Aloys Ruppel.

At Leipzig, Insel Verlag published a 'Fest-Schrift', edited by Herbert Reicher, in honour of the 50th birthday of E. R. Weiss.

Jan Tschichold engaged by Paul Renner (*see* 1907) to teach typography and calligraphy at the Munich Meisterschule für Deutschlands Buchdrucker, of which Renner had, in that year, become head of the Meisterschule für Deutschlands Buchdrucker at Munich; a post he held until 1933. Previously he had worked for ten years with the publisher Georg Müller (1877–1917), and the experience so gained led him to write a manual called *Typographie als Kunst* (1922), renamed *Die Kunst der Typographie* in subsequent editions. As a type designer he is well known for his Futura (1925).

A sans serif type which achieved wide popularity, especially as a news headline type in America, is Erbar, designed between 1926 and 1930 by Professor J. Erbar for the firm of Ludwig & Mayer, Frankfurt-am-Main. A range of Erbar is provided in Britain by the Linotype Company.

S. H. de Roos founded at Hilversum, Holland, his Heuvelpers. The first product of this press, the *Tractatus Politicus* of Spinoza, appeared in June 1928, set in de Roos's own Meidoorn type.

Publication of Ph. Renouard, *Les marques typographiques parisiennes des XVe et XVIe siècles.* Paris: Champion. It reproduces 1,150 printers' marks in their actual sizes, and short notices on each printer and bookseller.

At Paris, appeared *Le Papier: Recherches et Notes pour servir à l'histoire du papier,* by Louis Le Clert. It was published 'A l'Enseigne du Pégase' under the patronage of the Société des Bibliophiles Français.

The Bibliographical Society, London, issued the *Short-Title Catalogue of English Books, 1475–1640.* Edited by A. W. Pollard and G. R. Redgrave.

Publication of T. E. Shaw (T. E. Lawrence), *Seven Pillars of Wisdom.* The work was printed for distribution among friends, a few more being sold by subscription to cover printing costs. A revised abridgement was later published under the title *Revolt in the Desert.*

The process known as Aniline Printing was introduced. In this process very fluid inks coloured by aniline dyes are transferred from flexible rubber plates to a fast-moving web on a rotary press. It is used mainly for colour printing on plastics, foils and fabrics, hard-calendered papers and similar hard-surfaced materials. Although originally the inks for this process were made of aniline dyes dissolved in alcohol, which had practically no opacity, today the inks may be highly pigmented and fully opaque. (*See also* 1952.)

Dr. Otto F. H. Vollbehr in Berlin bought a Gutenberg Bible on vellum from the Abbey of St. Paul, Lavantthal, Carinthia, for approximately 305,000 dollars. In 1930 it was bought by the Library of Congress, Washington, as part of the Vollbehr collection, which comprised some 3,000 incunabula. The U.S. Government spent about a million and a half dollars on it.

1927

The annual *Buch und Schrift* first published by Verlag des deutschen Vereins für Buchwesen und Schrifttum zu Leipzig.

Christian Heinrich Kleukens (1880–1955) founded the Mainzer-Presse in that city. The press was forced to close by the Second World War, after having produced more than fifty books, set mainly in Kleukens's own types.

The Russian Colonel Avenir Tchemerzine, who settled in Paris after the 1917 Revolution, published the first volume of his *Bibliographie d'Editions Originales et Rares d'Auteurs Français des XVe, XVIe, XVIIe et XVIIIe Siècles.* Paris: Marcel Plée. The tenth and final volume was published in 1933, and the whole was illustrated with 6,000 facsimiles of title-pages and engravings.

The first number of the periodical *Arts et Métiers Graphiques*, started by Charles Peignot. Paris: Imprimerie de Vaugirard.

A Greek type known as New Hellenic was designed by Victor Scholderer on behalf of a committee of the Society for the Promotion of Hellenic Studies and cut by the Monotype Corporation. It is shown in *Greek Printing Types 1465–1927*—a collection of facsimiles from an exhibition of books illustrating the development of Greek printing shown at the British Museum.

London: Printed by the Oxford University Press for the Trustees of the British Museum. According to Dr. Scholderer the design was based on *Macrobius* [Joannes Rubeus?] Venice, 1492.

Barnett Freedman, a young artist, was invited by the publishers Faber and Gwyer to submit two drawings for Walter de la Mare's poem *The Wonder Night*. This was his first attempt at working for graphic reproduction, a sphere in which he soon made a name for himself. In 1931 he lithographed illustrations for Siegfried Sassoon, *Memoirs of an Infantry Officer*, and set off on a noteworthy career as illustrator and graphic designer, not only for books, but also for book jackets, stationery, packaging and labels. He designed George V Jubilee stamp, and from 1939 to 1945 was an official war artist.

The Clarendon Press issued Ronald B. McKerrow, *An Introduction to Bibliography for Literary Students*.

Victor Gollancz, who had previously worked for the firm of Ernest Benn, set up his own publishing house.

A. A. M. Stols founded the Halcyon Press, the first publication from which was the *Odes* of John Keats (1–27).

Formation in Chicago of the Society of Typographic Arts, founded, 'to promote high standards in the typographic arts by all possible means; to foster and encourage education in these arts; to elevate public taste in matters typographic; and to co-operate with all other organisations and institutions having similar aims.'

1928

Jan Tschichold published *Die neue Typographie*. Berlin: Verlag des Bildungsverbandes der deutschen Buchdrucker.

Founding at Lausanne of the firm of Albert Skira.

Publication of *A Specimen of the several sorts of Letter given to the University by Dr. John Fell*, a reproduction in collotype facsimile of the first English type specimen book, taken from the most perfect copy known (in the possession of the publishers), the only one containing the twenty-eighth leaf headed Anno Domini MDCXCIV. London: James Tregaskis & Son. The text printed by the Oxford University Press and collotypes by Donald Macbeth.

The sans serif type known as Gill Sans (in the first of its many variants), designed by Eric Gill

(1882–1940) was cut by the Monotype Corporation. It was followed in 1929 by his Perpetua. (See *also* 1940.)

The Curwen Press published their *Specimen Book of Types and Ornaments*. Charles Prentice, a director of Chatto & Windus described it as 'a perfect model of what a specimen book should be'. It was published for the Curwen Press by The Fleuron Ltd. in an edition of 135 copies.

The firm of Birrell & Garnett issued their now famous catalogue of (I) Typefounders' Specimens; (II) Books printed in types of historic importance; (III) Works on Typefounding, Printing and Bibliography.

In February, Mr. S. C. Ratcliffe discovered at the Public Record Office, London, an Indulgence of Pope Sixtus IV printed by Caxton, and dated by hand 13 December, 1476.

Formation of the British Typographers' Guild, with Vincent Steer as the first president.

Foundation stone laid of the library built by Henry Clay Folger (1857–1930) to house his priceless collection, particularly rich in Shakespeariana. After his death the building and collection were presented to the Trustees of Amherst College (where Folger was educated) to be administered for the American people.

Turkey adopted the Latin script and prohibited the publication of books printed in Arabic characters.

1929

At Milan the Casa Editrice Valentino Bompiani was founded by V. Bompiani, at one time general secretary of Mondadori and later director of Casa Ed. Unitas.

Dr. Giovanni (Hans) Mardersteig's Officina Bodoni (*see* 1923) obtained the exclusive right to use Bodoni's punches.

World Congress of Libraries held at Rome.

On 29 October, *The Times* published a review of technical progress called *Printing in the Twentieth Century*.

Publication of Vol. 1 (1489–1539) of *Early Portuguese Books 1489–1600 in the Library of H.M. the King of Portugal*, printed at the University Press, Cambridge, for Maggs Bros. London. The third and final volume (which included a supplement) appeared in 1935. The edition was limited to 45 copies, with text in English and Portuguese.

In April an International Typographic Conference was held in London.

Death of R. W. Crabtree (b. 1841), metallurgist and constructor of rotary printing presses.

William Addison Dwiggins (1880–1956) designed his first type, Metro, for the Mergenthaler Linotype Company. In all he designed eleven faces for them, though some were never put into production. Electra (1935) and Caledonia (1938) were the most successful. Another type, Falcon, was introduced in 1962, after Dwiggins's death.

The Limited Editions Club was founded in New York by George Macy (1900–56) for the purpose of providing its members with books planned by leading designers and typographers and illustrated by the finest artists. The first publication, October 1929, was *The Travels of Lemuel Gulliver*, edited by Harold Williams with illustrations by Alexander King.

In America a photo-setting machine was introduced called the Luminotype, which, it was claimed, could set photographically 7,000 letters an hour.

Will Ransom (1878–1955) published his *Private Presses and their Books*. New York: R. R. Bowker Co.

1930

Stanley Morison rescued from near oblivion the handsome types of John Bell with the publication of his *John Bell, 1745–1831*. London: Cambridge University Press. In the following year Bell's type was cut for machine composition by the Monotype Corporation from the original punches which had passed into the possession of the Stephenson, Blake foundry.

Publication of Michael Sadleir, *The Evolution of Publishers' Binding Styles 1770–1900*. London: Constable & Co. Ltd. and New York: Richard R. Smith Inc. This book, the first to shed light on an obscure and little studied subject, had its origin in a paper read by the author before the Double Crown Club.

The Cambridge University Press published Seymour de Ricci, *English Collectors of Books and Manuscripts (1530–1930)*.

Formation of The Printing Industries Research Association, now one of the world's leading research organisations for the printing and packaging industries. In 1947 its style was changed to Printing, Packaging, and Allied Trades Research Association, (Patra), and in 1948 a new laboratory,

workshops, and library were opened at Leatherhead, Surrey.

Publication began of *The Book-Collector's Quarterly*, founded by A. J. A. Symons and Desmond Flower. It was printed by the Curwen Press for Cassell & Co. Ltd., and the First Edition Club, and ran for seventeen numbers, until 1935.

Emery Walker was knighted for his services to printing.

The Colophon, A Book Collector's Quarterly, made its first appearance from the offices of Pynson Printers, New York. This bibliographical magazine closed down in 1940, but was resumed in 1948 as *The New Colophon* (New York: Duschnes).

Dard Hunter, the historian of paper-making, published his *Papermaking through eighteen centuries*. New York: W. E. Rudge.

1931

Publication of Fritz Milkau, *Handbuch der Bibliothekswissenschaft*. Leipzig: Harrassowitz. A second revised edition was published 1952–59.

The firm of Albert Skira, Lausanne, published *Les Metamorphoses* of Ovid with 30 etchings by Picasso—the first of a series of books illustrated by famous modern artists which established the fame of this Swiss publisher.

The Hungarian type designer and illustrator Imre Reiner (b. 1900) settled in Switzerland, where he greatly influenced book design both through his writings and by his work with Swiss publishers. In 1948 he published *Modern and Historical Typography*. St. Gallen: Zollikofer.

Eric Gill, with his son-in-law René Hague, founded his own press at Pigotts (Bucks.). The first publication was Gill's *An Essay on Typography*, printed in the Joanna type designed by him for this press.

First issue of *Printing Review*, edited by Bertram Evans. (*See* 1879.)

In March, the Swedish archaeologist Folke Bergman discovered, while exploring near Kharakhoto, what may be the oldest example of paper now extant, probably manufactured about the time of Ts'ai Lun. (*See* 105.)

First edition of Lawrence C. Wroth, *The Colonial Printer*, issued by the Grolier Club, New York. A second edition, revised and enlarged, came from the Southworth-Anthoensen Press in 1938. The work is a study of every aspect of the printer's trade in North America from 1639 to the end of the Colonial period.

1932

The Verein Deutscher Buchkünstler held an exhibition at Leipzig on the occasion of the Goethe celebrations. It was called 'Goethe in der Buchkunst der Welt'.

S. H. de Roos, Dutch book and type designer, first brought out his Magere-Egmont, followed by its italic in 1933. Then came his Egmont, 1933, with its italic Bold, and open Capitals in 1934. De Roos worked for many years for the type-foundry 'Amsterdam', and also ran a private press at Hilversum called the Heuvelpers (Hill Press). (*See* 1912 and 1926.)

On 3 October, *The Times* first used the type-face known as Times New Roman, prepared under the supervision of Stanley Morison. At first cut only in $5\frac{1}{2}$-point, 7-point, and 9-point, for the needs of *The Times*, it proved so popular and so versatile that it now exists in sizes ranging from $4\frac{3}{4}$-point to 14-point for line composition, together with a display range up to 72-point in roman and italic and also Bold and Bold italic.

A monumental letter, with thickened terminals replacing serifs, known as Albertus Titling was cut by the Monotype Corporation. It is the work of Berthold Wolpe, the calligrapher, well-known as the creator of some excellent devices.

1933

At Milan, appeared a specimen book of types designed by the Italian designer Raffaello Bertieri: *20 Alfabeti brevemente illustrati da Raffaello Bertieri*. The founts displayed were Sinibaldi, Ruano, Inkunabula, Romano Moderno, Bodoniano, Normanno, Paganini, Belwe, Behrens, Parcival, Egiziano, Iliade, Grasset (after drawings by Eugène Grasset), Semplicità, Landi, and Jost. The book bears the date 'Anno Undecimo' (of the Fascist era).

The Swiss publisher Albert Skira founded the review *Minotaure*.

First edition of Marius Audin, *Les Livrets Typographiques des Fonderies Françaises créés avant 1800*. Paris: A l'Enseigne de Pégase; printed by the Cambridge University Press. (It was reprinted 1964 by Gérard Th. van Heusden at Amsterdam.)

The famous *Codex Sinaiticus* purchased by the British Museum from the Soviet government for £100,000 with the help of the British Government and the general public.

Sir Emery Walker died, 22 July. The last book to bear his name as printer was an edition of the *Odyssey* translated by T. E. Lawrence. It was printed in 1932 by Emery Walker, Wilfred Merton and Bruce Rogers, and set in the Monotype version of Bruce Rogers's Centaur.

No. 1 of *The Dolphin*, a 'Journal of the Making of Books' was published in New York by the Limited Editions Club. Four numbers were issued between 1933 and 1941. No. 3 (1938) is *A History of the Printed Book*.

1934

The Bremer-Press at Munich printed *Icones Anatomicae* of Vesalius with illustrations made from the original blocks of the 1543 edition (*q.v.*). The printing was carried out for the Academy of Medicine, New York, and the University Library of Munich.

On 9 April, died Rudolf Koch (b. 1876), eminent German calligrapher and one of the most remarkable type designers and punch-cutters of modern times. From 1906 until his death, he was employed by the Klingspor type foundry at Offenbach-am-Main. One of his pupils was Berthold Wolpe, who worked in Britain from 1935 onwards. Among the type-faces designed by Koch were Maximilian and Maximilian Antiqua (1914), Koch Antiqua (1922), Neuland (1923), Jessen (1924–30), Claudius (1931–37) and Prisma (1928–31).

The Teletypesetter (TTS) first introduced into Britain by *The Scotsman*, to link their London and Edinburgh offices. This system of remote operation of a Linotype or similar machine was afterwards adopted by *The Times* for setting Parliamentary reports, transmitted by keyboard from the Houses of Parliament direct to the composing room at Printing House Square. For TTS operation specially fast slug machines are used.

John Carter and Graham Pollard published *An Enquiry into the Nature of Certain Nineteenth Century Pamphlets*, exposing the forgeries of Thomas J. Wise. At the time of writing a revised edition is in preparation.

First edition of *Type Designs: their History and Development*, by A. F. Johnson. London: Grafton and Co. A revised edition appeared in 1960.

The Linotype Company revived the roman of Anton Janson (1620–87). (*See* 1659.)

On 22 October, King George V opened the new Library of Cambridge University, designed by Sir Giles Scott.

1935

Publication of *Lexikon des Gesamten Buchwesens*, compiled and edited by Karl Löffler, Joachim Kirchner, and Wilhelm Olbrich. Leipzig. Three volumes, 1935–37: Verlag Karl W. Hiersemann.

At Frankfurt-am-Main died the punch-cutter Louis Hoell, who had worked for the Bauer and Flinsch foundries and for the Bremer-Presse.

Publication of Jan Tschichold, *Typographische Gestaltung*. Basel: Schwabe. Tschichold was for some years art director of Schwabe and Birk-häuser and the Holbein-Verlag at Basel.

Jan Tschichold created for the Schelter & Giesecke foundry a sans serif italic called Saskia (after the wife of Rembrandt).

Publication of the monumental edition of *The History of The Times from 1785* in an edition limited to 125 copies. It was printed at the Cambridge University Press with collotype plates by the Oxford University Press. The text is largely the work of Stanley Morison, who was responsible also both for the Times New Roman type in which it was set, and for the layout of the work.

First appearance of Penguin Books, the brain-child of Allen Lane, and issued at 6d each. The Pelican series first appeared in May 1937.

In November appeared the first number of *Signature*, a 'quadrimestrial of Typography and the Graphic Arts'. Edited by Oliver Simon, it continued until December, 1940 (15 numbers), when the war brought it to an untimely end. In July 1946, a new series was begun, still under the editorship of Oliver Simon, and lasted until January 1954 (18 numbers).

Publication of the Oxford Lectern Bible designed by Bruce Rogers, one of America's foremost type and book designers. It was printed in the Monotype Corporation's version of Bruce Rogers's own Centaur type, and is a masterpiece of modern book production.

The Oxford University Press published W. Turner Berry and A. F. Johnson, *Catalogue of Specimens of Printing Types by English and Scottish Printers and Founders*. With an introduction by Stanley Morison. (*See* 1953.)

The New York club known as the Typophiles produced its first book, *Spinach from many gardens*, to celebrate the 70th birthday of the type designer Frederic Goudy. The title-page was by Bruce Rogers. The Typophiles is an organisation of book and type designers, graphic arts executives and book collectors.

1936

Cambridge University Press published Stanley Morison's masterly essay on *First Principles of Typography*. It had previously appeared in a slightly different version in the *Encyclopædia Britannica* (12th edn., 1929) and in Vol. 7 of *The Fleuron* (1930).

Giovanni Mardersteig designed a type-face called Fontana for the publishing firm of Collins, for whom he was then acting as typographical consultant. Fontana was based on a type originally cut by Alexander Wilson at Glasgow around 1760.

In the autumn, the first number was issued of the quarterly periodical *Typography*, edited by Robert Harling and published by the Shenval Press, London. It ran until the summer of 1939. (For continuation, see *Alphabet and Image*, 1946.)

On 15 July King George VI formally opened the National Library of Wales in its new building overlooking Aberystwyth and Cardigan Bay. The library came into existence officially on 1 January, 1909, when it was opened in provisional premises in the Old Assembly Rooms at Aberystwyth.

Publication of George A. Kubler, *Historical Treatises, Abstracts, and Papers on Stereotyping*. New York: Printed for the author by J. J. Little and Ives Company, N.Y.

1937

F. H. Ernst Schneidler (1882–1956) the pupil of Peter Behrens, designed his Zentenar-Fraktur, cut and cast by the Bauer foundry. Schneidler was one of the artists employed by the Bauersche Giesserei, for whom he designed several interesting faces. He was the originator of the so-called 'Stuttgarter Schule'.

Death of Melchior Lechter (b. 1865), German book designer, who was closely connected with the poet Stefan George and his disciples. (*See also* 1905.)

1938

At Paris, Ambroise Vollard published one of the most impressive private press books of the first half of the twentieth century. This was *Cirque de l'Etoile Filante*, illustrated with a number of coloured etchings and no fewer than 82 wood engravings to the designs of George Rouault engraved by Georges Aubert. The etchings were printed by Roger Lacourière and the text and wood engravings by Henri Jourde.

At Lyons, Audin & Cie printed Alfred Cartier, *Bibliographie des éditions des De Tournes, Imprimeurs Lyonnais*. Paris: Editions des Bibliothèques Nationales de France. (Two volumes, 1937–8.)

The Bell Telephone System of America brought out their Bell Gothic space-saver for the setting of such things as directories, market prices, etc. Originally cut by the Mergenthaler Linotype Company, this sans serif face is issued in Britain by Intertype and has been adopted for the British telephone directory.

Anatol Girs and Boleslaw Barcz started the Warsaw printing house Oficyna Warszawska. The press was destroyed and Barcz was killed in the Warsaw uprising in 1944. Girs was imprisoned at Auschwitz and Dachau, and after the liberation he went to Munich where he published a number of beautiful Polish books.

In September, Faber & Faber published Nicolette Gray, *Nineteenth Century Ornamented Types and Title Pages*. A second impression was issued in 1951.

British Photo-Litho Reproducers' Association founded.

As the third number of *The Dolphin* (*see* 1933), the Limited Editions Club of New York published *A History of the Printed Book*, edited by Lawrence C. Wroth.

The Typophiles of New York (*see* 1935) published *Left to their own Devices* in which no fewer than 113 individual artists contributed 156 suggested devices and printers' marks for the organisation. Among the contributors were Reynolds Stone, Alfred Fairbank, Method Kalab, Oldrich Menhart, and Karel Svolinsky. The book was printed at twenty-one different presses.

1939

Charles Nypels (*see* 1917 and 1920) was attached to the Uitgeverij Het Spectrum, Utrecht, as typographic adviser.

First edition of Theodore Besterman, *A World Bibliography of Bibliographies*. Printed by the Oxford University Press for the author and published by him at 98 Heath Street, London.

The aim of this publication was to bring up to date Julius Petzholdt, *Bibliotheca Bibliographica* (Leipzig, 1866). A fourth edition of Besterman's work, revised and greatly enlarged, was published in five volumes at Lausanne by Societas Bibliographica, 1965–66.

Publication of Vol. I of the *Bibliography of English Printed Drama to the Restoration*, by W. W. Greg (Sir Walter Greg). Printed by the Oxford University Press for the Bibliographical Society. Four volumes. The fourth and final volume appeared in 1960.

A machine for photo-composition was introduced by William C. Huebner, on which the characters were arranged around a circular plate, and an optical projection unit was provided for each character, which was photographically recorded by the operation of a keyboard.

An issue which ran into 45 million printed copies—the National Registration Identity Card.

Death of Frederic Warde (b. 1894), book designer and typographer. Between the two world wars he was for a few years printing director of the Princeton University Press. (*See also* 1925.)

First American edition of *The Book in America*, by Hellmut Lehmann-Haupt in collaboration with Lawrence C. Wroth and Ruth Shepard Grannis. A revised and enlarged edition appeared in 1951, this time with the collaboration of Lawrence C. Wroth and Rollo G. Silver.

Pocket Books started a major revolution in American publishing.

1940

Publication of Konrad F. Bauer, *Aventur und Kunst*—a chronicle of the printing craft from the invention of movable type to the present time. Frankfurt: Bauersche Giesserei.

Death of Eric Gill (b. 1882), artist, sculptor, calligrapher, book illustrator and engraver of letter forms. Between 1925 and 1937 he designed eleven type faces: Perpetua, Gill Sans Serif, Golden Cockerel, Solus, Perpetua Greek, Joanna, Aries, Jubilee, Bunyan, Hebrew and Arabic. In 1953, Linotype and Machinery Ltd. issued their Linotype Pilgrim, a recutting of Gill's Bunyan together with an italic to accompany it, under the direction of Walter Tracy. Both Joanna and Bunyan were designed especially for the firm of Hague and Gill, run by his son-in-law René Hague; Joanna, in the Monotype version, proved a very successful bookletter.

Publication of George Parker Winship, *Printing in the Fifteenth Century*. Philadelphia: University of Pennsylvania Press.

At San Francisco appeared Jackson Burke, *Prelum to Albion: a history of the development of the hand press from Gutenberg to Morris.*

1941

Publication of *Die Erfindung Gutenbergs*, Basel: Gewerbemuseum. Based on an exhibition held jointly at Basel by the Gewerbemuseum and the University Library, 15 December, 1940–16 February, 1941.

The Cambridge University Press published George Sampson, *The Concise Cambridge History of English Literature*, which, though based on the fourteen volumes of the *Cambridge History of English Literature*, was a critical assessment of the subject by the author, and far more than a mere summary of the original. (*See* 1907.)

Publication of D. B. Updike, *Some aspects of printing old and new.* New Haven: William Edwin Rudge.

Claudius F. Mayer began publication of his *Bio-Bibliography of Medical Authors* with Fasciculus I (Abarbanel–Alberti). Washington: U.S. Government Printing Office.

1942

A. A. M. Stols published in Amsterdam *Het Werk van S. H. de Roos*, a tribute to the Dutch artist and type designer Sjoerd Hendrik de Roos on the occasion of his 65th birthday. It was set in De Roos's Hollandsche Mediaeval. (*See also* 1912, 1932.)

On 10 June, died in a concentration camp at Amersfoort, Jean François van Royen, born at Arnhem 27 June, 1878 (*see* 1910). From 1913 onwards, he was the major force in the productions of De Zilverdistel. Towards the end of 1914, his friends the Pissarros sent him from England an Albion press with which he printed many books himself for De Zilverdistel and his private Kuneta-pers. *De acht lyedekens van suster Bertken*, first printed at Leyden in 1518 by Jan Seversen was reprinted in April 1918 by Van Royen with the Disteltype specially designed for the Zilverdistel (Silver Thistle) by Lucien Pissarro.

1943

The type designer Max Caflisch (b. 1916) appointed art director of the publishing firm of Benteli at Bern-Bümplitz, for whom he designed Columna, a full series of open capitals. He later became head of the graphic department at the Kunstgewerbeschule, Zürich. Caflich received his technical training at Zürich and subsequently worked for several Swiss publishing firms.

Publication of René Billoux, *Encyclopédie Chronologique des Arts Typographiques*. Paris: Printed for the author by Les Orphelins-Apprentis d'Auteuil, and published under the patronage of the firm of Charles Lorilleux & Cie.

At Paris, publication of *Les premiers caractères de l'Imprimerie Royale*, by Jeanne Veyrin-Forrer and André Jammes. A type specimen in the possession of the Imprimerie Royale, Paris, in 1643, of which the only known copy seems to be the one recently discovered at the Bibliothèque Nationale, and here described.

1944

On 19 May, died Carl Ernst Poeschel, the Leipzig printer and publisher (b. 1874), head of the Offizin Poeschel & Trepte, Leipzig (*see* 1870; 1902). Poeschel was one of Germany's finest printers; his premises and archives were destroyed in November 1943.

Death of Vojtěch Preissig (b. 1873), an outstanding Czech graphic artist who devoted much of his life to the theory and practice of type design, though his types were more original than useful.

Foundation of the National Book League, a development of the National Book Council of 1924, the aim of which is to encourage the wider use of books by the general public and act as a link between the public and the book trade in general. From time to time it holds book exhibitions at its premises in Albemarle Street, London.

The Times began to print part of its edition on india paper for overseas circulation by air mail.

Death of the scholar-printer Bernard Newdigate. For seventeen years he contributed monthly 'Book-production Notes' to *The London Mercury*, and edited three special numbers of *The Studio* on 'The Art of the Book'. (*See also* 1904.)

1945

Death of Raffaello Bertieri (b. 1875), a Milanese printer whose influence was widely felt in Italy during the first three decades of the twentieth century. In 1925 an exhibition of books designed and printed by Bertieri was held in the Plantin-Moretus Museum at Antwerp (*see* 1921, 1923,

1933). Founder and for many years editor of the periodical *Il Risorgimento Grafico*.

Jan Tschichold published his *Schatzkammer der Schreibkunst*, comprising 200 plates illustrating the masterpieces of calligraphy during 400 years. Basel: Verlag Birkhäuser.

Publication of Oliver Simon, *Introduction to Typography*. Simon, who died in 1956, was a very fine designer of both books and periodicals. In 1935, he founded the typographical journal *Signature*. He was also editor of the first four numbers of *The Fleuron* (*see* 1923), and published his autobiography, *Printer and Playground* in 1956. (London: Faber & Faber.)

Lord Kemsley founded the Dropmore Press, a private press for experimental work in book production. Among the works published were *The Royal Philatelic Collection* by Sir John Wilson (1952) and *The Holkham Bible Picture Book* (1954).

Sir Francis Meynell was appointed honorary typographical adviser to H.M. Stationery Office.

The basic principles of Xerography and Xeroprinting first set out in the U.S. patents of Chester F. Carlson. Research on this new method of reproduction was carried out by the Battelle Memorial Institute of Columbus, Ohio.

Publication began of the *Short-Title Catalogue of books printed in England, Scotland, Ireland, Wales, and British America, and of English books printed in other countries, 1641–1700*. Printed for the Index Society in three volumes, 1945–51, by the Columbia University Press, New York. This continuation of the S.T.C. of Pollard and Redgrave (*see* 1926) was compiled by Donald Wing of the Yale University Library.

1946

The city of Mainz instituted for the new Johannes Gutenberg University a Chair for Calligraphy, Printing and the Arts of the Book.

King George VI formally opened the New Bodleian Library, Oxford, the foundation stone of which had been laid by Queen Mary in 1937. The architect was Sir Giles Gilbert Scott, and three-fifths of the cost of the new building was generously borne by the Rockefeller Foundation.

The Shenval Press published the first number of the magazine *Alphabet and Image*, which ran until No. 8, in December, 1948. It was edited by Robert Harling. (For continuation see *Image*, 1949.)

What proved to be the first really effective photo-composing machine, the Intertype Fotosetter, was installed at the Government Printing Office, Washington. A small pamphlet of 16 pages, *The National Gallery of Art, Washington*, was composed on this machine in 1946; the first complete filmset book, *Handbook of Basic Microtechnique* (1952) was also composed on the Fotosetter.

The Typophiles, New York, published *A Half-Century of Type Design and Typography, 1895–1945*, by Frederic W. Goudy. Two volumes. (*See also* 1947.)

The magnificent library of Lessing J. Rosenwald was presented to the American nation by a deed of gift executed 30 January, 1946, and placed in the custody of the Library of Congress.

1947

The Folio Society, London, a general book club formed by Christopher Sandford, Charles Ede, and A. J. Bott, to 'publish editions of well-produced, illustrated reprints of the great literary classics . . . at relatively low prices.'

Ellic Howe's study of *The London Compositor 1785–1900* was published by the Bibliographical Society, London.

Charles Batey became Printer to the University of Oxford on the retirement of Dr. John Johnson.

Typography of Penguin Books reorganised by Jan Tschichold in conjunction with Hans Schmoller.

The Fairchild Scan-a-Graver placed on the market by the Fairchild Camera and Instrument Corporation of New York. It is an electronic photo-engraving machine producing half-tone blocks by means of a photo-electric scanner which follows the picture as it revolves on a cylinder, transmitting impulses, which vary according to the tonal densities of the original, to the engraving tool which, by means of a heated stylus, burns out parts of the plastic foil block placed upon a second cylinder revolving on a common shaft with the first.

First issue (Vol. 1, No. 1, Winter) of the *Harvard Library Bulletin*. Cambridge, Mass.

On 11 May, died Frederic W. Goudy (b. Bloomington, Illinois, 1865), creative type designer, writer on printing, and consultant to the Lanston Monotype Company. His Village Press at Marlborough on the Hudson, founded 1903, has been preserved as a shrine for printers. Goudy designed and cut well over a hundred type-faces, including Pabst Old Style roman

(1902), italic (1903), designed originally as lettering for the Pabst Brewing Co., and later redrawn for type cutting; Forum roman caps (1911) based on traditional Roman lettering; Kennerley Old Style (1911, Italic, 1918) designed for the publisher Mitchell Kennerley and cut by R. Wiebking; and also the Goudy family—Antique, Old Style and Modern.

1948

The Dutch-built Hadego Photocompositor first introduced. It was designed primarily for display work, but has also been used for the printing of children's books.

Introduction of the first British filmsetting machine to be placed on the market, invented by George Westover and manufactured by the Coventry Gauge & Tool Co. Ltd. The machine, called the Rotofoto, worked in conjunction with a standard Monotype keyboard, and was used from 1949 onwards at the London School of Printing and Graphic Arts.

Publication of Vol. 1 of the *Papers of the Bibliographical Society of the University of Virginia*, edited by Fredson Bowers. Charlottesville, Virginia.

1949

Walter Brudi (b. 1907), calligrapher, book designer, and illustrator, became teacher of book design at the Stuttgart Akademie. As type designer, he has been responsible for the book faces Brudi-Mediaeval (1958) and Pan (1954).

Death of the German calligrapher and type designer Otto Hupp (b. 1859). (*See* 1885.)

The London School of Printing and Kindred Trades was united by the London County Council with the L.C.C. School of Photo-Engraving & Lithography (formerly the Bolt Court Technical School) and given the title of London School of Printing and Graphic Arts. In 1963 the School, which had been operating at Stamford Street and at Back Hill, Clerkenwell, moved into its present premises at the Elephant and Castle as the London College of Printing.

Brooke Crutchley appointed Printer to the Cambridge University Press.

Publication of *Image*, a quarterly of the visual arts. Eight numbers appeared, from Summer 1949 to Summer 1952.

The periodical *Typographica* started under the editorship of Herbert Spencer.

Karl-Erik Forsberg (b. 1914) succeeded A. Kumlien (*see* 1916) as art director of the Swedish firm of P. A. Norstedt & Sons. He designed the roman faces Carolus and Berling Antikva, cut and cast at the Berling type-foundry at Lund, Sweden.

In the U.S.A. was introduced the Photon-Lumitype, a development of the Photon, invented by the French engineers René Higonnet and Louis Moyroud, and developed by the Graphic Arts Research Foundation Inc. of Cambridge, Massachusetts. This machine has a keyboard resembling that of an electric typewriter, and depressing the keys operates electronic memory devices which convey to a computer in the photographic unit the character selected and its width, and at the same time the spacing is recorded for automatic justification. The codified information is passed in the form of electrical impulses to the photographic unit where the selected character is photographed by a powerful light source as it passes before the lens.

The World Publishing Company of Cleveland, Ohio, produced their large folio World Bible designed by Bruce Rogers. It was printed under the direction of A. Colish in Goudy's Newstyle face, slightly modified by Bruce Rogers with Goudy's permission, and later renamed Goudy Bible. Rogers also used other Goudy faces—Deepdene Italic, Forum and Goudy Old Style.

1950

On 1 January, died Dr. Karl Klingspor (b. 1868), one of the outstanding figures in the German type-founding industry, in his 82nd year, and shortly after the publication of his book *Über Schönheit von Schrift und Druck, Erfahrungen aus fünfzigjähriger Arbeit*. Frankfurt-am-Main: Georg Kurt Schauer. 1949. The Klingspor Museum, founded to his memory, preserves his work and that of his craftsmen (R. Koch, O. Hupp and W. Tiemann) and is a centre of modern typography.

Death of Gustav Mori (b. 1872), author of numerous scholarly works on the history of type-founding.

Publication at Hilversum by the Paper Publications Society (ed. E. J. Labarre) of E. Heawood, *Watermarks mainly in the 17th and 18th centuries*. This was the first volume in the series *Monumenta papyraceae historiam illustrantia*. Up to 1965 eleven volumes had been published in this series.

In January, was published the first issue of the *British National Bibliography*, listing every new work published in Great Britain and based on the deposits at the Copyright Office at the British Museum.

1951

Gotthard de Beauclair (b. 1907), for many years on the production side of Insel-Verlag, and chief designer for that firm from 1951 until 1962, founded the Trajanus-Presse, which acted as the house press of the Stempel foundry at Frankfurt-am-Main.

G. W. Ovink published his *Honderd jaren letter-gieterij in Amsterdam*.

Lucien Neipp, master printer and former director of the Imprimeries Réunies de Lausanne, published his *Les Machines à Imprimer depuis Gutenberg*. Paris: Club Bibliophile de France.

On 18 June, *The Times* introduced a $4\frac{3}{4}$-point size of Times New Roman (named Claritas) for the printing of Stock Exchange prices, sports results, etc. Because it is economical of space without sacrifice of legibility, it was soon adopted by the *Manchester Guardian* and the London *Evening News*.

Faber and Faber published David Bland, *The Illustration of Books*. A second revised edition was published in 1953, and in 1958 a third and greatly augmented edition, called *A History of Book Illustration*, appeared with nearly three times as many illustrations as in the original edition.

1952

Universal Copyright Convention held at Geneva under the auspices of U.N.E.S.C.O.

Aniline printing (*see* 1926) became known, by general consent of the printing industry, as flexography.

Publication of Jan Tschichold, *Meisterbuch der Schrift*. Ravensburg: Otto Maier. It contains 175 annotated plates in addition to 60 pages of text with illustrations. It was later published in New York by Reinhold under the title *Treasury of Alphabets and Lettering*.

At London, Faber and Faber issued a new edition of Talbot Baines Reed, *A History of the Old English Letter Foundries*, revised and enlarged by A. F. Johnson.

1953

The Blandford Press published the first edition of *The Encyclopaedia of Type Faces* by W. Turner Berry and A. F. Johnson. A third revised edition was published in 1962. It contains around 1,400 type specimens, each with date of origin, founder and designer's name, together with a brief history. (*See* 1935.)

First issue of *Printing & Graphic Arts*, published by the Stinehour Press, Lunenberg, Vermont.

1954

Konrad F. Bauer, in collaboration with Walter Baum (b. 1921) issued from the Bauer foundry at Frankfurt-am-Main a new series of book faces known in Germany as Imprimatur, but exported under the name of Horizon. Baum, a pupil of the Offenbach School of Arts and Crafts, joined the Bauer foundry as house artist in 1948. For the jobbing printer he designed Alpha, a lower-case brush script, and Beta, a brush script version of an italic Ionic.

Publication of Charles Rosner, *Die Kunst des Buchumschlages* (The Art of the Book Jacket). Stuttgart: Gerd Hatje.

Death of Jan Kalf (b. 1873), Dutch typographer and lecturer on printing.

Introduction of the Monotype Corporation's 'Monophoto' filmsetter. This machine retains the normal keyboard as used in the Monotype as well as the perforated ribbon control of the positioning of the matrix-case, the main difference between the two machines being that the 'Monophoto' substitutes for the caster a photographic unit. Output is comparable with the hot-metal caster.

Linotype and Machinery Ltd., London, introduced Jubilee, the first original news text face since Times Roman in 1932. It was designed especially to meet the needs of high-speed rotary letterpress printing of newspapers and periodicals. Both the *Daily Telegraph* and *Sunday Times* adopted Jubilee in place of Ionic for their text.

Publication of Elizabeth Armstrong, *Robert Estienne, Royal Printer*. Cambridge: University Press.

Dow Chemicals International of America marketed a machine to operate the Dow process of high-speed powderless etching on which they had been working for some years. Apart from electronic engraving (*see* 'Scan-a-Graver', 1947), one of the major block-making developments of the post-war years was the perfecting of the rapid powderless etching process which did away with the four successive and tedious treatments of the plates with acid-resist which had previously been necessary to avoid the undercutting of the plate by the etching acid. Blocks that hitherto had taken well over half an hour to complete could now be finished in five minutes.

A new American Copyright Act extended copyright protection to non-American authors whose countries were signatories to the Universal Copyright Convention of 1952.

1955

The Stempel type-foundry at Frankfurt-am-Main issued Gustav Mori, *Frankfurter Schrift-proben aus dem 16 bis 18 Jahrhundert*. It contains facsimiles of type specimens of the Frankfurt type founders from the time of the Konrad Berner foundry in 1592 to that of the Johann Becker foundry in 1770. These were assembled by the late Gustav Mori with an introduction by Robert Diehl.

Publication at Barcelona of *Documentos para la historia de la imprenta y librería en Barcelona 1474–1553*, containing more than 500 documents from the archives of Barcelona selected by José Maria Madurell Marimón and annotated by Jorge Rubió y Balaguer. The work contains a vast amount of information on contracts, prices, material, etc., invaluable to the student of printing history.

First edition of S. H. Steinberg, *Five Hundred Years of Printing*. London: Penguin Books (Pelican series). A revised edition appeared in 1961. It appeared also in hard covers, published by Faber & Faber, and has been translated into German and Italian.

Publication of the *Bibliotheca Walleriana* by Hans Sallander. The books collected by Erik Waller and given to the library of the Royal University of Uppsala illustrate the history of medicine and science. Stockholm: Almquist & Wiksell. Two volumes.

1956

Death of the Parisian punch-cutter Charles Malin (b. 1883). In 1926, he cut the punches for Eric Gill's Perpetua, the matrices for which were struck and type cast by Ribadeau Dumas of Paris. Malin later cut the Dante type for G.

Mardersteig, first used by him at the Officina Bodoni, Verona, in 1954. Malin also recut, at the instigation of Frederick Warde, the italic of Arrighi's *La Operina* (*see* 1522), first made available for hand setting in 1926. In 1929 it was issued as the Arrighi fount for machine composition by the Monotype Corporation. One of Malin's last type-faces was the elegant Tallone.

The Oxford University Press published Hugh Williamson, *Methods of Book Design*, set in Monotype Ehrhardt roman, named after the eighteenth-century Leipzig foundry of that name.

Passing of the Copyright Act of 1956 which embodied all the existing English laws of copyright. The new British Copyright Act decreed that 'copyright subsisting in a work shall continue to subsist for a full fifty years from the end of the calendar year in which the author dies, and shall then expire'. One section of the Act grants the publisher the copyright of the typographical arrangement of a published edition of a work for a period of twenty-five years.

Death of William Addison Dwiggins (b. 1880), one of America's foremost calligraphers, book designers and typographers. He designed two roman faces for the Linotype Company—Electra (1935) and Caledonia (1938). He also wrote an important textbook, *Layout in Advertising* (1928).

1957

Start of the German bibliophile and bibliographic journal *Philobiblon*, Hamburg, Hauswedell.

Death of Arthur Novák (b. 1876), Czech writer and editor of the Prague bibliographical periodical *Vitrinka*.

The Paris firm of Berger-Levrault published Beaumarchais, *Le Mariage de Figaro*, printed at their Nancy printing works. This was the first book in Europe to be filmset by the Lumitype photo-composing machine. The text is set in A. Frutiger's Méridien.

Publication, at Paris, of Stanley Morison, *L'Inventaire de la fonderie Le Bé, selon la transcription de Jean-Pierre Fournier*. The preface is in English.

Publication of Andra Delen, *Boktrycket I Finland*. Helsingfors: Grafiska Klubb.

1958

The Mergenthaler Linotype Company first demonstrated in Europe their 'Linofilm' at

DRUPA, the international printing exhibition held at Düsseldorf in 1958. This is an adaptation of their hot-metal Linotype for filmsetting.

Death of Jan Van Krimpen (b. 1892), the eminent Dutch designer of type and lettering, who from 1925 onwards acted as artistic adviser to the Haarlem printers and publishers Messrs Enschedé en Zonen. Among the best-known faces designed by Jan Van Krimpen are Lutetia, Romanée, Romulus, Spectrum and Sheldon. He will be remembered as one of the finest book designers of the second quarter of this century. His influence on design, especially in America, has been considerable. He designed many books for the Nonesuch Press, the Limited Editions Club, the Heritage Press, and the Typophiles, as well as his editions for the Halcyon Press of A. A. M. Stols, the many Enschedé publications, and the clandestine Balkema publications during the war (*see* 1925). A critical assessment of his work by S. L. Hartz appeared in *Penrose's Annual*, Vol. 54, 1960.

Adrian Frutiger (b. 1928) appointed art director at the foundry of Deberny & Peignot. Beginning his career as a printer's apprentice in Switzerland, he learned the fundamentals of letter design at the Kunstgewerbeschule at Zürich. In 1952, he was invited to Paris by Charles Peignot, who had been struck by his work in Switzerland. Perhaps the best known of his type designs, which include Phoebus, Méridien, and Ondine, is the sans serif type known as Univers, which he began in Switzerland and perfected in France. Univers is a complete sans serif series, conceived as a type which should have an universal appeal—hence its name. Some twenty-one varieties of Univers are available. Frutiger also teaches the history and practice of letter design at the École Estienne in Paris.

Vivian Ridler appointed Printer to the Oxford University Press in succession to Charles Batey (1946–58).

1959

On 8 June, the *Irish Times* published a special supplement commemorating the founding of the paper 100 years previously.

At New York was published *Quarto-Millenary. The first 250 publications and the first 25 years (1929–1954) of the Limited Editions Club (see*

1929). The book contains critical contributions from Paul Beaujon (Mrs. Beatrice Warde), Paul A. Bennett, James Laver and others; a bibliography of the Club's publications; and a great number of specimen text and title-pages, illustrations and reproductions of bindings.

1960

Inauguration, 20 May, of the Bibliothèque Albert I at Brussels.

Publication of *A Glossary of the Book* by Geoffrey Glaister. London: George Allen & Unwin.

1961

At Paris, the Librairie Paul Jammes published André Jammes, *La Réforme de la Typographie Royale sous Louis XIV. Le Grandjean*. This important study is accompanied by 110 of the original copperplate engravings, preserved at the Imprimerie Nationale.

In a limited edition of Sir Herbert Read, *Design Oration 1961*, printed and published by the Vine Press, appeared for the first time the type-face known as Octavian, designed by the printer Will Carter and the sculptor and letter carver David Kindersley.

On 6 January, Stanley Morison was presented with the Diploma of Royal Designer for Industry by the Royal Society of Arts, London.

Victor Scholderer, one of the world's leading incunabulists, was made a Companion of the British Empire. President of the Bibliographical Society from 1946 to 1948, he became a Gold Medallist of the Society in 1951.

1962

Publication of the first volume of *Polygraph Jahrbuch*, the German equivalent of *The Penrose Annual*.

After a century and a half of notable work the Chiswick Press ceased to exist. The archives of the Press have been deposited in the British Museum.

1963

At Milan, was published Jeanne Veyrin-Forrer, *Campionari di Caratteri nella Tipografia del Settecento* with 48 plates. It is an anthology of the major type specimens published in Europe by the eighteenth-century founders, and the types are discussed in the introductory essay. The book forms the second volume of the series *Documenti sulle Arti del Libro*.

The new Bodonian Museum was inaugurated at Parma in November.

Publication of Stanley Morison and Kenneth Day, *The typographic book 1450–1935: a study of fine typography through five centuries*. London: Ernest Benn Ltd. It contains 377 plates representing pages from interesting and important books from the 42-line Bible to the Oxford Lectern Bible of 1935. Accompanying the illustrations, is a 66-page essay by Stanley Morison, which is in effect a revision of the preface to the original edition of his *Four Centuries of Fine Printing* (1924).

From 16–27 July was held the eleventh International Printing Machinery and Allied Trades Exhibition (IPEX) in connection with which exhibitions called 'Printing and the Mind of Man' were held at the British Museum and Earls Court, London.

Opening of the National Paper Museum at St. Mary Cray, Kent. More than 120 companies and organisations contributed to the formation of the museum which has as its main object the preservation of old paper-making techniques.

Publication of *Copy and Print in the Netherlands*, a bibliographic atlas by W. G. Hellinga and others.

1964

Publication, at Siegburg, of Otto Treptow, *Johann Lair von Siegburg, 'John Siberch': Der Erstdrucker von Cambridge und seine Welt*. In this book, owing to the diligent researches of Herr Otto Treptow, we know at last not only what happened to the printer after he had left Cambridge and England in 1523, but also something of his life before his arrival in this country.

The *Bibliotheca Belgica* of Ferdinand van der Haegen was republished in book form at Brussels (five volumes), edited by Marie-Thérèse Lenger.

On 18 December, at Lyons, took place the opening ceremony of the Musée de l'Imprimerie.

Founding, at London, of the Printing Historical Society, under the chairmanship of James Moran.

1965

The city of Leipzig awarded its Gutenberg Prize, the highest European award for typography, to Jan Tschichold. In June, the Royal Society of

Arts, London, conferred on him the distinction of Honorary Royal Designer for Industry, 'for outstanding contributions as a typographer and book designer'.

The Wolvercote paper mill of the Oxford University Press installed the first computer to give direct physical control over the process of paper-making.

Publication of the first number of the *Journal of the Printing Historical Society*, edited by James Mosley.

The University of Newcastle was given a research contract by the Ministry of Technology to develop the industrial applications of electronic digital computers in printing and type-setting.

Publication of Howard Mayer Brown, *Instrumental Music printed before 1600. A bibliography*. Cambridge: Harvard University Press, London: Oxford University Press. Some 520 books are listed, of which over 180 exist in unique copies.

1966

At Amsterdam, the firm of Menno Hertzberger published Wytze and Lotte Hellinga, *The fifteenth-century printing types of the Low Countries*. Two volumes, with 291 plates. This monumental reference work contains a chronological survey of each individual press and its publications and a detailed analysis of the types shown in the vast collection of plates which form the greater part of the second volume.

At London, Ernest Benn Ltd. published *Book Typography 1815–1965 in Europe and the United States of America*, edited by Kenneth Day. A symposium by nine contributors: Fernand Baudin, Gérard Blanchard, Maximilien Vox, Miss P. M. Handover, Franco Riva, G. W. Ovink, Willy Rotzler, and James M. Wells.

Publication of D. F. MacKenzie, *The Cambridge University Press 1696–1712. A bibliographical study*. Cambridge: The University Press. Two volumes. This thorough study of the reorganisation of the University Press under the impetus of the then Chancellor, the Duke of Somerset, and the great classical scholar, Richard Bentley, contains also a valuable bibliography of the books produced during the period under review.

1967

At Paris, was published (as Vol. 3 of *Documents Typographiques Français*), *Sixteenth Century French Typefounders: The Le Bé Memorandum* edited by Harry Carter with a foreword by Stanley Morison.

On 11 October, died Stanley Morison, typographer, scholar, and historian of printing (b. 1889). He only just saw the publication of his book (in which he was assisted by Harry Carter) *John Fell: The University Press and the 'Fell' Types*, a work on which he had been engaged since 1925. Oxford: Clarendon Press.

INDEX

2¢ per day fine for overdue book